Women's Entrepreneurship in the 21st Century

Women's Entrepreneurship in the 21st Century

An International Multi-Level Research Analysis

Edited by

Kate V. Lewis

Massey University, New Zealand

Colette Henry

Dundalk Institute of Technology, Ireland and Tromsø University Business School, Norway

Elizabeth J. Gatewood

Wake Forest University, USA

John Watson

The University of Western Australia

Edward Elgar
Cheltenham, UK • Northampton, MA, USA

© Kate V. Lewis, Colette Henry, Elizabeth J. Gatewood and John Watson 2014

All rights reserved. No part of this publication may be reproduced, stored in a retrieval system or transmitted in any form or by any means, electronic, mechanical or photocopying, recording, or otherwise without the prior permission of the publisher.

Published by
Edward Elgar Publishing Limited
The Lypiatts
15 Lansdown Road
Cheltenham
Glos GL50 2JA
UK

Edward Elgar Publishing, Inc.
William Pratt House
9 Dewey Court
Northampton
Massachusetts 01060
USA

A catalogue record for this book
is available from the British Library

Library of Congress Control Number: 2014943897

This book is available electronically in the ElgarOnline.com
Business Subject Collection, E-ISBN 978 1 78254 461 6

ISBN 978 1 78254 460 9

Typeset by Servis Filmsetting Ltd, Stockport, Cheshire
Printed and bound in Great Britain by T.J. International Ltd, Padstow

Contents

List of contributors	vii
Foreword	xiv
Candida G. Brush, Nancy M. Carter, Elizabeth J. Gatewood, Patricia G. Greene and Myra M. Hart	
Introduction: an international multi-level research analysis	1
Kate V. Lewis, Colette Henry, Elizabeth J. Gatewood and John Watson	

PART I   MACRO: THE ENTREPRENEURSHIP ECOSYSTEM

1 Advancing theory development in venture creation: signposts for understanding gender   11
   Candida G. Brush, Anne de Bruin and Friederike Welter

2 Academic entrepreneurship: multi-level factors associated with female-led incubator projects   32
   Diamanto Politis, Jonas Gabrielsson and Åsa Lindholm Dahlstrand

3 Gender congruency theory, experience of discrimination and access to finance   50
   Natalie Sappleton

4 Female entrepreneurship in rural Vietnam: an exploratory study   74
   Cuc Nguyen, Howard Frederick and Huong Nguyen

5 Women entrepreneurs in Asia: culture and the state in China and Japan   95
   Kathryn Ibata-Arens

PART II   MESO: FIRM-LEVEL ANALYSIS

6 Gender differences in innovation among US entrepreneurs   117
   Alicia Robb and Susan Coleman

7   A gender perspective on family business succession: case
    studies from France   138
    Janice Byrne and Salma Fattoum

8   Gender-based differences in the performance of Slovenian
    high-growth companies   165
    Karin Širec and Dijana Močnik

9   Growth process of small and medium-sized manufacturing in
    developing countries: a study of women-owned firms in
    Bangladesh   186
    Mosfeka Jomaraty and Jerry Courvisanos

PART III   MICRO: INDIVIDUALS AND DYNAMICS

10 Women entrepreneurs' networking behaviors: perspectives
    from entrepreneurs and network managers   215
    Claire M. Leitch and Richard T. Harrison

11 Heterogeneity of spousal support for French women
    entrepreneurs   236
    Stephanie Chasserio, Typhaine Lebègue and Corinne Poroli

12 The divisions of labour and responsibilities in business and
    home among women and men copreneurs in the Czech
    Republic   258
    Alena Křížková, Nancy Jurik and Marie Dlouhá

13 Centering Caribbean women's gendered experiences and
    identities: a comparative analysis of female entrepreneurs in
    St Lucia and Trinidad and Tobago   278
    Talia Esnard

14 Self-employment and motherhood: the case of Poland   297
    Ewa Lisowska

Index   311

Contributors

Candida G. Brush holds the Franklin W. Olin Chair in Entrepreneurship, and is Division Chair for Entrepreneurship at Babson College, Boston, USA. A Research Director of the Arthur M. Blank Center for Entrepreneurship, Professor Brush holds an honorary doctorate in business and economics from Jonkoping University, Sweden, and is a visiting adjunct at the Nordlands University Graduate School of Business in Bodø, Norway. She is co-founder of the Diana Project, and recipient of the International Entrepreneurship Research Award for her pioneering work on women's entrepreneurship. She has published more than 120 scholarly articles and serves on several editorial review boards.

Janice Byrne is Assistant Professor at IÉSEG School of Management, Paris, France. Her research interests include entrepreneurship, gender, training and development. Her PhD comprised four papers looking at entrepreneurship education and training for women, corporate managers and engineers. Dr Byrne has published her research in the *Academy of Management Learning and Education*, and *Industry and Higher Education*, as well as in numerous book chapters.

Stephanie Chasserio is Associate Professor at the Department of Management, Leadership and Organization, SKEMA Business School, Lille, France. She holds a PhD from University of Québec at Montréal, Canada. Her dissertation was on work–family practices and policies in new economy firms. Currently, she works on topics such as women entrepreneurship, well-being at work, psychosocial risk and fairness in management.

Susan Coleman is a Professor of Finance at the University of Hartford, in West Hartford, Connecticut, USA. She teaches courses in entrepreneurial and corporate finance at both the undergraduate and graduate levels. Dr Coleman's research interests include entrepreneurial and small business finance. She has published extensively on the topic of financing women-owned firms, and is frequently quoted in the business press. Dr Coleman recently completed a book (with Alicia Robb) entitled *A Rising Tide: Financing Strategies for Women-Owned Firms* (published 2012).

Jerry Courvisanos is Associate Professor of Innovation and Entrepreneurship in the Federation Business School, Mt Helen Campus at the Federation University Australia (formerly University of Ballarat). He has had his work published in two major books, in several book chapters and in peer-reviewed journals. Jerry's basic research is centred on the processes of innovation and their impact on investment, business cycles, sustainable development and the evolution of businesses. This work informs applied research into innovation and entrepreneurial activity for regional development.

Anne de Bruin is Professor of Economics in the School of Economics and Finance, and founding Director of the New Zealand Social Innovation and Entrepreneurship Research Centre, at Massey University, New Zealand. Her current research interests focus on women's entrepreneurship, social entrepreneurship and social innovation, creative entrepreneurship, and labour market dynamics. Professor de Bruin has received a Fulbright New Zealand Senior Scholar Award to research entrepreneurship.

Marie Dlouhá is a Research Assistant at the Czech social science data archive at the Institute of Sociology, and a doctoral student of sociology at the Faculty of Social Sciences at Charles University in Prague, Czech Republic. She is interested mainly in qualitative research, gender and entrepreneurship issues, virtual communication and interaction. She participated in research on 'Institutions in Life Stories' and she is co-author of the article 'Interpretative cooperation with biographical texts: a semiotic approach to analysing collective memory' (with Martin Hájek, in *Memory Studies*, 7 (2), 2014).

Talia Esnard is an Assistant Professor of Sociology at the Centre for Education Programmes at the University of Trinidad and Tobago. Her main research interests include gender and entrepreneurship, poverty and entrepreneurship, mothering and entrepreneurship, entrepreneurial education and educational leadership as it relates to Caribbean societies. She has published in several areas including gender, mothering and entrepreneurship, poverty and new venture creation, educational leadership of early career school principals, and entrepreneurship education.

Salma Fattoum is an Assistant Professor at INSEEC Business School at the Department of Management in Lyon, France. Her research areas are family business, succession and gender. Her PhD deals with the attitudes of successors joining the family firm and the role the predecessor plays in the integration phase. Dr Fattoum has contributed to various international conferences such as the Academy of Management (AOM), Research in Entrepreneurship and Small Business (RENT) and the Family Enterprise

Research Conference (FERC). She has previously published in the *Journal of Enterprising Culture* and *Journal of Applied Business Research*.

Howard Frederick is a serial entrepreneur with three information technology (IT) companies and a chocolate factory to his credit. Howard carries the title Honorary Professor of Entrepreneurship Education at Deakin University, Australia. He has developed award-winning entrepreneurship curricula and has taught entrepreneurship in the USA, New Zealand and Australia. Many of his students have founded their own successful enterprises.

Jonas Gabrielsson is an Associate Professor of Entrepreneurship at the Centre for Innovation, Research and Competence in the Learning Economy (CIRCLE), Lund University, Sweden. He is also an Associate Professor of Business Administration at the School of Business and Engineering, Halmstad University, Sweden. His current research interests include the commercialization and diffusion of new technology, boards and governance in new and small firms, and entrepreneurship among academics. He also has a general interest in the creation and evolution of markets and industries.

Elizabeth J. Gatewood is Associate Director of the Center for Enterprise Research and Education at Wake Forest University, USA, and has directed the University's Kauffman Campus Initiative, a programme focused on multidisciplinary entrepreneurship education. In addition to directing academic entrepreneurship units at Wake Forest University and Indiana University, USA, she directed the Small Business Development Center (SBDC) Network for southeast Texas. She is a co-founder of the Diana Project, which won the International Award for Entrepreneurship and Small Business Research, which recognizes scholars who produce scientific work of outstanding quality and importance.

Richard T. Harrison is Professor of Entrepreneurship and Innovation at Edinburgh University, UK, where he is associated with the Strategic Leadership Centre and the Centre for Entrepreneurship Research. He was previously Dean of Queen's University Management School, Belfast, UK, has held chairs at Edinburgh, Aberdeen and Ulster, and visiting positions in China, Australia and the USA. His research focuses on the dynamics and impact of the entrepreneurial process, and he has published eight books and over 150 scholarly articles. He is founding co-editor of *Venture Capital: An International Journal of Entrepreneurial Finance*, and sits on several editorial review boards.

Colette Henry is Head of Department of Business Studies at Dundalk Institute of Technology, Ireland and Adjunct Professor of Entrepreneurship at Tromsø University Business School, Norway. Prior to this, Colette held the Norbrook Chair in Business and Enterprise at the Royal Veterinary College (RVC), University of London, UK, and was President of the Institute for Small Business and Entrepreneurship (ISBE), UK. Colette is also founding editor of the *International Journal of Gender and Entrepreneurship*, and has published widely on entrepreneurship education and training, programme evaluation, gender, the creative industries, and women and veterinary business.

Kathryn Ibata-Arens is Director of Global Asian Studies and Associate Professor of Political Economy at DePaul University, USA. She specializes in high technology policy and the Japanese political economy. Her current work is on biomedical entrepreneurship and 'networked technonationalism' in Asia. Her book *Innovation and Entrepreneurship in Japan: Politics, Organizations and High Technology Firms* (2005) analysed strategic networks of high-technology firms and regional economies in Kyoto, Osaka and Tokyo. Dr Ibata-Arens has held fellowships from the Fulbright Commission, the Japan Foundation Center for Global Partnership, the Mansfield Foundation and the Social Science Research Council.

Mosfeka Jomaraty is currently undertaking doctoral research studies in the Federation Business School, Mt Helen Campus at the Federation University Australia (formerly University of Ballarat). She is also Assistant Professor in the Department of Management Studies, University of Dhaka (Bangladesh) and holds a BBA and an MBA (University of Dhaka). Her research interests are in international business policies and their implications for domestic economies, small business enterprises and female entrepreneurship.

Nancy Jurik is Professor of Justice and Social Inquiry in the School of Social Transformation at Arizona State University (ASU), USA. Her research and teaching interests focus on gender, occupations, work organizations, entrepreneurship, and media constructions of gender and work. Her books include *Doing Justice, Doing Gender: Women in Legal and Criminal Justice Occupations* (2007, 1996), and *Provocateur for Justice: Jane Tennison and Policing in 'Prime Suspect'* (2012). She is a past President of the Society for the Study of Social Problems and a distinguished faculty in the College of Liberal Arts and Sciences at ASU.

Alena Křížková is a Senior Researcher and Head of the Gender and Sociology Department at the Institute of Sociology of the Czech Academy of Sciences, Czech Republic. Her research focuses on the economic independence of women, gender wage gap, gender in organizations, management and entrepreneurship, women and citizenship, gender and social inclusion, gender in care and family policies. She has authored or co-authored several books, including: *Management of Gender Relations, Position of Women and Men in Organization* (2004), *Working Paths of Women in the Czech Republic* (2011) and *Sexualized Reality of the Working Relations* (2006).

Typhaine Lebègue is Associate Professor of Entrepreneurship and HRM at France Business School, Tours, France. She holds a PhD in women's entrepreneurship in France. Currently, she is working on research relating to women's entrepreneurship and the support of women entrepreneurs.

Claire M. Leitch is Professor of Management Learning and Leadership at Lancaster University Management School, UK, where she is both Director of Research and Doctoral Programmes. Previously she was a Senior Lecturer in Management and Director of Education at Queen's University Management School, UK. She has held visiting positions at universities in Denmark and the UK. Her research interests focus on the development, enhancement and growth of the individual and the organization in an entrepreneurial context. She is particularly interested in the application of alternative research methodologies, such as critical incident technique and action research.

Kate V. Lewis is a Senior Lecturer in Massey University's School of Management, New Zealand. She is a Research Associate at the New Zealand Social Innovation and Entrepreneurship Research Centre, and the New Zealand Work Research Institute at Auckland University of Technology. Dr Lewis is also a past Vice-President of the Small Enterprise Association of Australia and New Zealand, an associate editor of the *Journal of Small Business Management*, and editor of the journal *Small Enterprise Research*. Her research interests include youth entrepreneurship, gender and identity in the entrepreneurial context, social enterprise and sustainability for small and medium-sized enterprises (SMEs).

Åsa Lindholm Dahlstrand is a Professor of Entrepreneurship and Innovation at the Centre for Innovation, Research and Competence in the Learning Economy (CIRCLE), Lund University, Sweden. The overriding theme in her research is technology-based entrepreneurship and the linking of entrepreneurship and innovation. Her specific research interests include studying new and small technology-based firms and the role of entrepreneurs in the development of companies and economies.

Ewa Lisowska, PhD is a Lecturer in the Warsaw School of Economics, Poland. She conducts research on women in the labour market, their financial independence and their motivation to start businesses. Her teaching interests focus on gender equality and the economy. Between 2004 and 2008 she led a team of experts on the Gender Index project, a measure of equal treatment between men and women in the workplace. Between 2011 and 2012 she headed the European Union (EU) project entitled 'Equal treatment standard or good governance', which aimed to create a Diversity Index in state institutions.

Dijana Močnik is an Associate Professor at the University of Maribor, Faculty of Electrical Engineering and Computer Science, Slovenia. She teaches and researches in the fields of economics, media economics, business policy and strategic management, services management and entrepreneurship. Prior to commencing her academic career at the University of Maribor, she worked for eight years as a researcher and appraiser of companies at a manufacturing firm, research institution and consultancy firm.

Cuc Nguyen is currently completing her PhD at Deakin University, Australia. She has almost ten years of teaching experience in management at Hanoi University, Vietnam (2005–2011) and Deakin University (2011–2014). She ran her own business in the education sector for six years (2005–2011) in Hanoi, before starting her PhD. Her research interests include micro-entrepreneurship, female entrepreneurship and family businesses.

Huong Nguyen was a student at the Faculty of Management and Tourism, Hanoi University, Vietnam. She graduated in 2012, and currently works in a telecommunication corporation in Hanoi.

Diamanto Politis is an Associate Professor of Entrepreneurship at the Sten K. Johnson Centre for Entrepreneurship (SKJCE), Lund University, Sweden. She is also affiliated with the Centre for Innovation, Research and Competence in the Learning Economy (CIRCLE), Lund University. Her current research interests include academic entrepreneurship, early-stage technology commercialization and learning in entrepreneurial contexts. She is also currently involved in research on the role and importance of external (or surrogate) entrepreneurs for promoting the commercialization of public research and development (R&D).

Corinne Poroli is Associate Professor of Strategic Management and Entrepreneurship at SKEMA Business School, Paris, France. She holds a PhD in Management from ESSEC Business School (École Supérieure des Sciences Économiques et Commerciales), Cergy-Pontoise, France. Her current research is dedicated to gender and entrepreneurship. She is also interested in organizational resilience and impacts of social digital networks on management.

Alicia Robb is a Senior Fellow with the Kauffman Foundation, a Research Associate with the University of California at Santa Cruz, USA, and a Visiting Scholar with the Federal Reserve Bank of Atlanta, USA. Her research interests include entrepreneurship, entrepreneurial finance, and entrepreneurship by women and minorities. Dr Robb has previously worked as an economist for the US Small Business Administration and US Federal Reserve Board of Governors. In addition to numerous journal articles and book chapters, she is the co-author of two books on entrepreneurship.

Natalie Sappleton is a Senior Lecturer at Manchester Metropolitan University, UK. Her research interests include the intersections between social networks, gender segregation and gender stereotyping in the context of entrepreneurship. She has been involved in several initiatives such as Women Audio Visual Engineers (WAVE), and numerous investigations into sex discrimination at the Equality and Human Rights Commission. Her PhD thesis investigates the role of gender role (in)congruency on the ability to acquire resources among New York City entrepreneurs.

Karin Širec is an Associate Professor of Business Economics and Entrepreneurship in the Department for Entrepreneurship and Business Economics at the Faculty of Economics and Business, University of Maribor, Slovenia. Her research interests include general entrepreneurship, growth, women's entrepreneurship and entrepreneurship policy.

John Watson is a Professor in the Department of Accounting and Finance at the University of Western Australia. His research interests lie in the area of small and medium-sized enterprise (SME) performance evaluation and measurement, including the comparison of male- and female-controlled SMEs. He has published in a number of leading international journals, such as the *Journal of Business Venturing, Entrepreneurship Theory and Practice*, the *Journal of Small Business Management, Small Business Economics* and the *International Small Business Journal*.

Friederike Welter is President of the IfM Bonn (Institut für Mittelstandsforschung) and Professor for SME Management and Entrepreneurship, at the University of Siegen, Germany. She holds Visiting Professorships at Jönköping International Business School in Sweden and the Small Business Research Centre at Kingston University, UK. Her research interests include entrepreneurial behaviour and policies in different contexts and women's entrepreneurship. Friederike is on the review board of several leading entrepreneurship journals, and is also an associate editor of *Entrepreneurship Theory and Practice*. She is a Fellow of the European Council of Small Business and Entrepreneurship (ECSB).

Foreword

Candida G. Brush, Nancy M. Carter, Elizabeth J. Gatewood, Patricia G. Greene and Myra M. Hart

The Diana Project was launched in 1999 by Candida Brush, Nancy Carter, Elizabeth Gatewood, Patricia Greene and Myra Hart as a multi-university research consortium to provoke social change and alter attitudes, opinions and practices about women's entrepreneurship research. At the time, businesses owned by women in the United States were on average smaller than those of their male counterparts, whether measured by size of revenues generated or by the number of people employed. Using a research-based focus, the Diana Project sought to identify the factors that determined the size disparity between men- and women-owned businesses, and specifically draw attention to the inequity women face in securing financial capital and other resources needed to grow their businesses. The aim was to raise awareness and expectations of women business owners for the growth of their firms, and educate equity capital providers and policymakers about opportunities for enhancing portfolio diversification and returns by including more women-owned ventures.

With funding from the Entrepreneurship and Small Business Research Institute (ESBRI), the Kauffman Center for Entrepreneurial Leadership, the US Small Business Administration and the National Women's Business Council, the founders established a four-phase research project, including: (1) charting the landscape of knowledge on women's entrepreneurship through an exhaustive annotated literature review; (2) developing findings from primary research on the demand side of the equation – women's experiences seeking growth financing; (3) developing findings from primary research on the supply side – the characteristics and practices of the venture capital industry; and (4) scaling the project by establishing Diana International to engage researchers from around the world.

The first phase of the project established that there was a lack of research on women entrepreneurs and their businesses in comparison to men (Gatewood et al., 2003). Notably absent from the general entrepreneurship literature was an understanding of factors affecting the growth of women-owned businesses, even though the success of women-owned businesses was deemed vital for wealth creation, innovation and economic advancement throughout the world. The review showed that women entrepreneurs seldom acquire sufficient funds to grow their businesses aggressively, raising the question 'Do women face unique challenges in acquiring growth capital?' (Brush et al., 2006a). This led to a focus on growth strategies, funding expectations, experiences and characteristics of women entrepreneurs and their teams seeking high growth.

For the second phase of the project, Diana assembled and analysed data on the population of women business owners seeking high growth for their business, including those attempting to secure venture capital. With support and funding from the Kauffman Center for Entrepreneurial Leadership, Diana was able to follow more than 100 high-tech women's ventures involved in a path-breaking initiative linking women's businesses with the equity capital community during the Springboard 2000 Venture Forums (Brush et al., 2002).

Research in the third phase of the project showed that although there was considerable demand by women entrepreneurs for equity capital, there was a mismatch between the women, their ventures and sources of growth funding. By examining employment strategies and characteristics of venture capital firms and the career paths of women employed in these firms, Diana showed that women in the industry were severely under-represented and without sufficient power to influence funding decisions that would bring more women's ventures into funding portfolios (Brush et al., 2004a). The findings prompted great interest among policymakers, practitioners and educators interested in ways to increase women entrepreneurs' receipt of growth capital through better infrastructure of programmes and curricula for women who wished to grow larger businesses.

Findings from the first three phases of the project showed convincingly that women-led growth ventures in the United States faced unique challenges, received significantly little venture capital, and that women were under-represented in decision-making positions in the venture capital industry. This raised an interesting question as to whether the Diana results were unique to the United States or generalized to other parts of the world. Diana International was established to answer this question.

In 2003 the Diana Project team, in partnership with ESBRI (Entrepreneurship and Small Business Research Institute), Sweden, convened two international gatherings of scholars to develop a shared research agenda. The goal of this research collaboration was twofold:

1. To provide a platform from which to develop, conduct and share a global research agenda.

2. To create an international community of scholars dedicated to answering questions about women entrepreneurs and growth oriented businesses.

A summary of the presentations about the state of women's entrepreneurship by country was released in the spring of 2005.

In 2004, the second Diana International conference was held in Sweden and produced an edited volume, *Growth Oriented Women Entrepreneurs and Their Businesses: A Global Research Perspective* (Brush et al., 2006b). The book focused on the nature of women's participation in entrepreneurship, growth orientation and access to resources for growth in various countries. It also delved more deeply into the relationship between social and human capital, financing, risk, motivations and skills of women entrepreneurs as growth factors. One major outcome of this effort was a two-volume special issue on women's entrepreneurship in *Entrepreneurship Theory and Practice* (2006 and 2007), which showcased the work of Diana researchers worldwide, and called for new themes and methodologies in research about women entrepreneurs. In addition, in 2004, the Diana co-founders published *Clearing the Hurdles: Women Building High-Growth Businesses* (Brush et al., 2004b).

In 2005 the Diana founding team led a symposium at the Academy of Management entitled Research on Women's Entrepreneurship: Global Questions – National Approaches. The symposium was designed to further explore the breadth and depth of questions related to women's entrepreneurship, and the sophistication and variety of the research tools available.

In 2007 a third Diana International conference was held in Madrid, Spain at Instituto de Empresa, sponsored by Babson College, Wake Forest University and the University of St Thomas, USA. This conference held a special workshop, the Diana International Emerging Scholars Workshop, to provide a forum and mentorship for emerging scholars studying women's entrepreneurship and to connect senior and junior scholars around topics of research interest.

The fourth Diana International conference was held in 2008 in Belfast, UK, with the University of Ulster and Dundalk Institute of Technology. Candida Brush, Anne de Bruin, Elizabeth Gatewood and Colette Henry co-edited a second volume, *Women's Entrepreneurship and Growth Influences: An International Perspective* (Brush et al., 2010) from the papers presented at the conference. This volume examined women's entrepreneurship across a variety of developed and less-developed countries using a multi-level framework (individual, venture and environment). This conference was also marked by the launch of a new journal to advance research in this area: the *International Journal of Gender and Entrepreneurship*.

By the fifth conference in Banff, Canada, Diana International had grown more than fourfold, with more than 80 scholars presenting scholarly work. The focus moved from documenting the state of women's entrepreneurship in various countries to capturing the diversity of women's entrepreneurship. Understanding the heterogeneity of women's entrepreneurship is crucial not only to developing theory, identifying policies, practices and educational initiatives for women, but also to our understanding of entrepreneurship in general. Karen Hughes and Jennifer Jennings co-edited the volume from the 2010 conference, *Global Women's Entrepreneurship Research: Diverse Settings, Questions and Approaches* (Hughes and Jennings, 2012).

The sixth Diana conference was held in Perth, Australia, in conjunction with the annual ACERE (Australian Centre for Entrepreneurship Research Exchange) conference. While this conference provided a venue for continued work with doctoral students, it also attracted new scholars. This current text – the fourth in the series of Diana conference books, *Women's Entrepreneurship in the 21st Century: An International Multi-Level Research Analysis*, edited by Kate Lewis, Colette Henry, Elizabeth Gatewood and John Watson – has been compiled as a result of the Australian conference.

The seventh Diana conference was held in Stockholm, Sweden, in June 2014, bringing the global group full circle from their origin. The Stockholm event focused on the impact of women's entrepreneurship and innovation, and brought together policymakers, educators, academics and practitioners. The conference, co-chaired by Colette Henry and Friederike Welter, was sponsored by ESBRI and directed by Magnus Aronsson.

Today more than 100 researchers from 35 countries are involved in the Diana International Project. These global scholars generate research used for policy creation and implementation to advance the cause of women entrepreneurs around the world. In addition to the formal conferences, they have produced special issues in academic journals, written academic papers and made countless conference presentations.

The global importance of the Diana Project was recognized in 2007 when the founders were presented with the International Award for Entrepreneurship and Small Business Research by the Swedish Development Agency and the Swedish Foundation for Small Business Research. The award, the foremost global award for entrepreneurship research, recognizes scholars who produce scientific work of outstanding quality and importance, and contribute to theory-building about entrepreneurship and small business development.

The Diana Project represents a new model of collaborative research with the goal of supporting researchers around the world in working together to seek answers to important questions about women's entrepreneurship. The founders are grateful to all those who have contributed to Diana through research and conference support. We congratulate the editors and chapter contributors in this volume; their work will help to extend extant scholarship on women's entrepreneurship globally.

REFERENCES

Brush, C.G., Carter, N.M., Gatewood, E.J., Greene, P.G. and Hart, M.M. (2002), 'The Diana Project: Women business owners and equity capital – the myths dispelled', *Venture Capital Review*, 10 (Summer), 30–40.
Brush, C.G., Carter, N.M., Gatewood, E.J., Greene, P.G. and Hart, M.M. (2004a), *Gatekeepers of Venture Growth: The Role of Women in the Venture Capital Industry*, Kansas City, MO: Kauffman Foundation.
Brush, C.G., Carter, N.M., Gatewood, E.J., Greene, P.G. and Hart, M.M. (2004b), *Clearing the Hurdles: Women Building High-Growth Businesses*, Upper Saddle River, NJ: Financial Times-Prentice Hall.
Brush, C.G., Carter, N.M., Gatewood, E.J., Greene, P.G. and Hart, M.M. (2006a), 'Women's entrepreneurship in the United States', in Brush, C.G., Carter, N.M., Gatewood, E.J., Greene, P.G. and Hart, M.M. (eds), *Growth Oriented Women Entrepreneurs and Their Businesses: A Global Research Perspective*, Cheltenham, UK and Northampton, MA, USA: Edward Elgar, pp. 184–204.
Brush, C.G., Carter, N.M., Gatewood, E.J., Greene, P.G. and Hart, M.M. (eds) (2006b), *Growth Oriented Women Entrepreneurs and their Businesses: A Global Research Perspective*, Cheltenham, UK and Northampton, MA, USA: Edward Elgar.
Brush, C.G., de Bruin, A., Gatewood, E.J. and Henry, C. (eds) (2010), *Women Entrepreneurs and Growth Influences: An International Perspective*, Cheltenham, UK and Northampton, MA, USA: Edward Elgar.
Entrepreneurship Theory and Practice (2006), 30 (5), 585–718.
Entrepreneurship Theory and Practice (2007), 31 (3), 323–492.
Gatewood, E.J., Carter, N.M., Brush, C.G., Greene, P.G. and Hart, M.M. (2003), *Women Entrepreneurs, Their Ventures, and the Venture Capital Industry: An Annotated Bibliography*, Stockholm: ESBRI.
Hughes, K.D. and Jennings, J.E. (eds) (2012), *Global Women's Entrepreneurship Research: Diverse Settings, Questions and Approaches*, Cheltenham, UK and Northampton, MA, USA: Edward Elgar.

Introduction: an international multi-level research analysis
Kate V. Lewis, Colette Henry, Elizabeth J. Gatewood and John Watson

One of the many rich opportunities presented via an endeavour such as the Diana Project is to aggregate a cohort of researchers around a bounded topic of interest, and observe the way in which their discoveries both coalesce around key dimensions and break out to push forward the boundaries of understanding. An associated privilege of such a network is to seek from its members, and interested observers, written contributions to books that capture the vibrancy and value of those research activities. The international nature of the Diana network, and its associated activities such as conferences, is fertile ground for attaining the type of scope and scale that is often difficult to achieve in terms of linked individual research projects. We are fortunate to build on a fine tradition of Diana volumes (Brush et al., 2006; Brush et al., 2010; Hughes and Jennings, 2012) and it is our view that this current book has been no less successful in achieving its international ambitions. The 14 chapters in this volume span a wide geographic spread, and derive data from a diverse range of countries: the Czech Republic, the United States of America, China, Japan, Bangladesh, Vietnam, Poland, Northern Ireland, Sweden, France, Slovenia and the Caribbean.

Rather than gender merely being a variable of inquiry, the range of topics for which gender is now used as a lens to understanding is as varied as it is impressive (Jennings and Brush, 2013). Taking a gendered perspective to exploring 'mainstream' constructs has now been legitimized, rather than gender remaining notable only in a discrete list of topics that are deemed particularly germane to women and/or gender researchers (Henry et al., 2013). This is in part a function of how far gender and entrepreneurship has come as a field, but also mirrors the rich myriad of ways in which women enact entrepreneurship in their daily lives (Garcia and Welter, 2013; Gatewood et al., 2003). As a reflection of this enrichment of the gendered entrepreneurship agenda, and as a tribute to the urgent calls from scholarly leaders in the field to further extend the ambit of focus to move beyond work that 'recreates the idea of women as being secondary to men and of women's businesses being of less significance' (Ahl, 2006, p. 595), we deliberately sought contributions to this book that traversed two axes of exploration: the first was the continuum of conceptualizations of entrepreneurship in and of itself (that is, as a policy, a process, an act and/or an outcome), and the second was a spectrum of chapters that extended across the macro, meso and micro architecture of analysis. We were fortunate to achieve that objective and, as a result, have chosen to organize the work according to that structure. Each of the three parts – macro, meso and micro – is previewed in the remainder of this Introduction, along with brief vignettes of the chapters contained therein.

PART I: MACRO: THE ENTREPRENEURSHIP ECOSYSTEM

The impact of the broader context (at the level of country, state and culture, and so on) on the entrepreneurial activity of firms and individuals is well established (Welter, 2011). Further, it is said to be particularly influential on women and, unfortunately, more often in a burdensome or disadvantageous fashion (Brush et al., 2009). Part I of the book contains five chapters that are oriented to this macro focus from a diverse range of vantage points, and spanning the theoretical–empirical spectrum. It opens with a chapter led by Diana founder Candida Brush, joined by colleagues Anne de Bruin and Friederike Welter. Their contribution is theoretical in nature and has, at its heart, the construct of embeddedness; something they describe as a 'basic building block' in understanding gender-driven differences in venture creation. They articulate the relevance of several forms of embeddedness (family, cultural and structural) to gendered considerations of entrepreneurship specifically, and they hypothesize in relation to the nexus of embeddedness (and variants of it) and gendered perceptions of desirability and feasibility in relation to start-up.

The second chapter of the book is an examination of gender and academic entrepreneurship in the context of Swedish incubator projects, and is authored by Diamanto Politis, Jonas Gabrielsson and Åsa Lindholm Dahlstrand. Echoing the terminology of the Part I title, it has a very strong ecosystem focus with its emphasis on unbundling the impact of institutionally based structures in, and around, university incubators. The multi-level research model that forms the core of the chapter reveals a number of findings, including the fact that the proportion of female-led incubator projects is impacted upon by both the proportion of female faculty in senior positions at the associated university, and the presence of women on incubator boards. This, in turn, evidences that university based ecosystems are not impervious to (and, rather, are embedded in) broader gender structures.

Natalie Sappleton, in the third chapter of the macro-oriented part of the book, takes as her subject matter the discrimination women face in obtaining external financing for their ventures. Utilizing a sample from the United States of America, and gender congruency theory to underpin a quantitative methodology, she explores whether women in male-dominated fields suffer more perceived discrimination than women who are not in such sectors. An overarching thrust of her concluding argument is against the pervasiveness of 'sex-as-a-variable' approaches to the investigation of such issues, as it can create a masking effect. Rather, she delineates and evidences the need for, and importance of, within-category differences in groups separated by gender (rather than the undifferentiated approach to sampling that can be a common occurrence).

The next chapter of the book shifts geographic focus to the developing countries generally, and rural Vietnam specifically. Cuc Nguyen, Howard Frederick and Huong Nguyen examine the potential for rural entrepreneurship to be an economic growth stimulant, as well as an emancipatory pathway for women in the region who are constrained by a number of factors (and typically pushed to engage in necessity-driven forms of entrepreneurship). Whilst the women may enter self-employment via a particular route that may be perceived as negative in motivation terms, it is the lack of support architecture that actually prevents them from moving forward with their endeavours. This juxtaposition of original intent with willingness and desire to upskill once engaged demonstrates how such scenarios can be oversimplified, and consequently opportunities to scaffold women into even better positions via self-employment may be being missed.

The final chapter of Part I retains an Asian focus but moves to the economies of China and Japan. Kathryn Ibata-Arens examines the influence of national culture and cultural norms (including the maintenance of women in traditional roles within broader 'masculine societies') in relation to female entrepreneurship. Using a case-study-driven methodology, she seeks to unpack the potential influence of state policies and cultural norms on incidences of opportunity-driven women engaging in entrepreneurial behaviours. In doing so, she contrasts cultural approaches with those that are statist in nature, and concludes (in these cases) that infrastructure-related interventions and institutional barriers are more of an impediment to engagement by women than the pervasive impact of cultural norms.

PART II: MESO: FIRM-LEVEL ANALYSIS

The second part of the book takes the firm as its dominant unit of analysis, or lens. Our understanding of women in the context of entrepreneurship has been energetically advanced via studies that seek to unbundle or nuance the relationship between women and venture creation, leadership and management (Moore et al., 2011; Patterson et al., 2012). Studies have sought to differentiate outcomes in management practice, enterprise performance and firm characteristics via gender comparative approaches. Whilst successful in many respects in revealing distinctions rooted in gender, firm-oriented approaches have also moved away from being dominated by those strategies primarily comparative in orientation, and now are also equally as likely to explore women-led firms in their own right and from the perspectives of excellence and gender-led behaviours (that is, not only in comparison with male counterparts) (Ahl and Marlow, 2012). The balance of the four chapters that comprise this meso part of the book are weighted towards both approaches, with two taking a gender-specific lens to understanding, and two a comparative perspective.

Chapter 6 (by Alicia Robb and Susan Coleman) uses a sample of 200 entrepreneurs from the United States of America to interrogate differences according to gender in respect of attitudes and behaviours in relation to innovation. They found that many differences identified in the first phase of analysis (for example, women being more likely to innovate in the domain of practice; to not pursue intellectual property protection; and be more reticent to implement innovative ideas due to a perceived lack of 'how to' knowledge) did not remain significant when certain variables (such as age and firm size) were controlled for. Their conclusions expand on the implications of such methodologically oriented observations and the need for the broadest possible conceptualization of what innovation is (and is not) in relation to female entrepreneurs.

The following chapter (Chapter 7) takes France as its geographic locale and considers the implications for French family businesses of the lack of daughters on the succession pathway. Janice Byrne and Salma Fattoum shift away from what they term an essentialist approach to gender inequality, and situate their contribution at the intersection of person, firm, gender and context. They argue that not to pursue such an approach denies the heterogeneity of participation of women in the family business context and stifles further understanding of that diversity. A key conclusion of their chapter is that to reduce the gender-driven differences in family business succession to the differences in socialization experienced by men and women is a gross simplification, and an attribution that disempowers notions of female agency. Further, they add that it is not the dominant reason for the absence of women; rather, they offer data that reveal the key roles that exclusion and separation play as deniers of experience for women in the family business context.

In Chapter 8, Karin Širec and Dijana Močnik report that, in the context of high-growth Slovenian firms, firm size mediated by gender is negatively related to firm growth. The authors also note that female entrepreneurs particularly resist the pursuit of high growth until a stable level of profitability is achieved. In identifying areas for further work, they note that there is a need for a better understanding of the firm growth related competencies required by female entrepreneurs (rather than just at the point of start-up).

In a similar vein, but contrasting global context, Mosfeka Jomaraty and Jerry Courvisanos in Chapter 9 also focus on gender in relation to high-growth firms, but in the context of the traditional Islamic society and developing-country context of Bangladesh. Their chapter, the last in this part of the book, takes cases of female-led, high-growth outliers. They conclude that in addition to the specific growth actions and practices implemented within the firm, the individual perceptions of self-efficacy and the growth aspirations of the women entrepreneurs themselves were critical to success.

PART III: MICRO: INDIVIDUALS AND DYNAMICS

The 'person behind the firm', embodied in sociological approaches that tend towards the privileging of the subjective and interpretive, are increasingly argued as being germane to understanding the enactment of female entrepreneurship (Hamilton, 2013; Lewis, 2013). This enriching of the body of knowledge relating to gender and entrepreneurship (frequently through narrative and life history) is one of the many advances of the modern turn of gendered understandings of entrepreneurship that has revealed not only why but how women engage. This part of the book includes five chapters that span a diverse range of foci, but all have stories of the female entrepreneur at their centre.

Part III opens with Chapter 10 in which Claire Leitch and Richard Harrison examine the networking behaviour of a group of Northern Irish women entrepreneurs. The novelty of their focus is that they emphasize the process of networking rather than the substance or structure of the networks that are formed by the women. One of the notable conclusions of their work is the importance for female entrepreneurs of 'indirect reciprocity' via generalized exchange (rather than close dyadic ties) in cementing the networking relationship and any potential ensuing benefits.

The subsequent chapter, authored by Stephanie Chasserio, Typhaine Lebègue, and Corinne Poroli, takes a gendered perspective on spousal support for French female entrepreneurs, in terms of both instrumental and emotional forms of support. Spousal support is often described as an asset for entrepreneurial women, and as a resource that can be harnessed to mitigate tensions that may emerge between the work and family domains. The authors of this chapter paint a contrasting picture in their elaboration, in that they describe how the spousal support offered can be tenuous and can alter in shape, form and efficacy according to the stage of the venture life-cycle.

Our focus shifts in Chapter 12 to the nature of the copreneurial dynamic in the Czech Republic. Here, authors Alena Křížková, Nancy Jurik and Marie Dlouhá note the invisible leadership of women in such dynamics (even if they were not technically owners or managers), and the tendency towards gender-oriented divisions of labour despite the supposedly copreneurial nature of the relationship. The authors observed some atypical splits (however, never in terms of labour in the home domain) but noted that the prevailing organization was towards culturally driven, gender-oriented norms. Utilizing a methodology that involved both partners being interviewed, the authors were also able to determine that the actual divisions of labour in the work domain were frequently incongruous with those described during the interview process.

The penultimate chapter of the volume is situated in the Caribbean, and through the use of the construct of entrepreneurial identity seeks to contribute understanding of how the reconciliation of work and family conflicts occurs in a cultural context with strongly traditional gender norms. Talia Esnard notes in her chapter the contradictory nature of the socio-cultural messages around expectations that women receive relative to the motivations and intentions of those same women who are determined to be enterprising.

The book closes with Chapter 14 by Ewa Lisowska who interrogates the impact of motherhood on women who are self-employed in the transition economy of Poland. She reports that self-employment is not the reported solution to the tensions such dual roles encapsulate, and that in some instances self-employment fuels the conflict by juxtaposing the role demands so acutely. At best, she describes self-employment as a potential easing mechanism, but notes that the inability of women to access institutional forms of childcare is an ongoing impediment to both active participation and fulfilment for those women engaging in self-employment in Poland.

REFERENCES

Ahl, H. (2006), 'Why research on women entrepreneurs needs new directions', *Entrepreneurship Theory and Practice*, 30 (5), 595–621.

Ahl, H. and Marlow, S. (2012), 'Exploring the dynamics of gender, feminism and entrepreneurship: advancing debate to escape a dead end?' *Organization*, 19 (5), 543–562.

Brush, C.G., Carter, N.M., Gatewood, E.J., Greene, P.G. and Hart, M.M. (eds) (2006), *Growth Oriented Women Entrepreneurs and their Businesses: A Global Research Perspective*, Cheltenham, UK and Northampton, MA, USA: Edward Elgar.

Brush, C.G., de Bruin, A., Gatewood, E.J. and Henry, C. (eds) (2010), *Women Entrepreneurs and Growth Influences: An International Perspective*, Cheltenham, UK and Northampton, MA, USA: Edward Elgar.

Brush, C.G., de Bruin, A. and Welter, F. (2009), 'A gender-aware framework for women's entrepreneurship', *International Journal of Gender and Entrepreneurship*, 1 (1), 8–24.

García, M-C.D. and Welter, F. (2013), 'Gender identities and practices: interpreting women entrepreneurs' narratives', *International Small Business Journal*, 31 (4), 384–404.

Gatewood, E., Carter, N.M., Brush, C.G., Greene, P.G. and Hart, M.M. (2003), *Women Entrepreneurs, their Ventures and the Venture Capital Industry: An Annotated Bibliography*, Diana Project, Stockholm: ESBRI.

Hamilton, E. (2013), 'The discourse of entrepreneurial masculinities (and femininities)', *Entrepreneurship and Regional Development*, 25 (1–2), 90–99.

Henry, C., Foss, L. and Ahl, H. (2013), 'Parallel lines? A thirty-year review of methodological approaches in gender and entrepreneurship research', paper presented at the 2013 ISBE Conference, Cardiff, UK.

Hughes, K.D. and Jennings, J.E. (eds) (2012), *Global Women's Entrepreneurship Research: Diverse Settings, Questions and Approaches*, Cheltenham, UK and Northampton, MA, USA: Edward Elgar.

Jennings, J.E. and Brush, C.G. (2013), 'Research on women entrepreneurs: challenges to (and from) the broader entrepreneurship literature', *Academy of Management Annals*, 7 (1), 663–715.

Lewis, P. (2013), 'The search for an authentic entrepreneurial identity: difference and professionalism among women business owners', *Gender, Work and Organization*, 20 (3), 252–266.

Moore, D.P., Moore, J.L. and Moore, J.W. (2011), 'How women entrepreneurs lead and why they manage that way', *Gender in Management: An International Journal*, 26 (3), 220–233.

Patterson, N., Mavin, S. and Turner, J. (2012), 'Envisioning female entrepreneur: leaders anew from a gender perspective', *Gender in Management: An International Journal*, 27 (6), 395–416.

Welter, F. (2011), 'Contextualizing entrepreneurship – conceptual challenges and ways forward', *Entrepreneurship Theory and Practice*, 35 (1), 165–184.

PART I

Macro: the entrepreneurship ecosystem

1. Advancing theory development in venture creation: signposts for understanding gender

Candida G. Brush, Anne de Bruin and Friederike Welter

INTRODUCTION

Women are one of the fastest-growing populations of entrepreneurs worldwide and make a significant contribution to employment, innovation and economic growth in all economies (Kelley et al., 2011). The Global Entrepreneurship Monitor (GEM) shows that 126 million women in 67 economies started and managed businesses in 2012, representing more than 52 per cent of the world's population and 84 per cent of the world's gross domestic product (GDP) (Kelley et al., 2013). Another 98 million women across these regions ran businesses they launched at least three years ago. Yet, in nearly all of the 67 economies the rate of men's venture creation is higher than that of women (Kelley et al., 2013). This raises questions as to why the rate of men's venture creation exceeds that of women, and what factors explain these differences.

Theory development exploring the role of gender in venture creation and sources of possible differences between men and women in this process is limited. Notwithstanding a growing body of literature and notable initiatives (namely the Diana Project, which since 1999 has worked to grow research in the field), there remains a comparative paucity of theoretically grounded research on the topic (Brush et al., 2010b; Hughes et al., 2012; Sullivan and Meek, 2012). Without theory development regarding gender in entrepreneurship, we lack strong conceptual foundations for exploring variation in venture creation and growth between male and female entrepreneurs, and among groups of women (Jennings and Brush, 2013). A brief review of the literature shows that most current frameworks of venture creation are approached from an objective economic perspective, less often considering the influence of social settings, such as family and household, culture and context (Aldrich and Cliff, 2003; Bird and Brush,

2002; Shapero and Sokol, 1982). Therefore, gender differences between men and women that might result from context can be masked in the venture creation process.

We address this shortcoming by building on a gender-aware framework that argued for explicit recognition of social embeddedness at the micro family level, and the meso and macro levels (Brush et al., 2009; Welter, 2011). Then, drawing from early work of Shapero and Sokol (1982) and their successors, we develop a framework and propose propositions that explore how perceptions of feasibility and desirability will differentially influence the venture creation process between men and women. We argue that variations in the degree of embeddedness will explain a greater or lesser likelihood of start-up for women entrepreneurs compared to their male counterparts. We highlight how the start-up process may be constrained or facilitated by the impact of family and household resources, and how social roles can facilitate and/or impede entrepreneurial action of women compared to their male counterparts.

Following this introduction, we explore the concept of embeddedness and elaborate how it has featured in entrepreneurship literature to lay a contextually rich perspective from which we build our conceptual framework; positing that perceptions of desirability and feasibility lead to venture creation. Thereafter, we argue gender moderates the relationship aspects of embeddedness, desirability and feasibility, and venture creation. We then present propositions, discuss implications and research directions.

EMBEDDEDNESS PERSPECTIVE

The embeddedness concept emphasizes that economic behaviour cannot be understood outside the context of its social structure and social relations (Granovetter, 1985, 1990). Economic action is embedded in interpersonal relations and structural embeddedness is the 'structure of the overall network of relations' (Granovetter, 1990, p. 99). Structural embeddedness has a rich history in organizational strategy studies. For example, Gnyawali and Madhavan (2001) explore the structural embeddedness of competitive dynamics. Instead of identifying different forms of embeddedness, however, some studies broadly refer to 'social embeddedness' (e.g. Hayton et al., 2012).

Zukin and DiMaggio (1990, p. 18), similarly to Granovetter (1990), define structural embeddedness as 'the contextualization of economic exchange in patterns of ongoing interpersonal relations', but extend the typology further to include cognitive, cultural and political embeddedness.

Cognitive embeddedness refers to how structured rigidities and regularities of mental processes limit economic reasoning. Thus, entrepreneurs are socially situated and immediate and interactive conversations, relationships and interpersonal aspects influence entrepreneurial action (Mitchell et al., 2011). The environment could limit an individual's cognitive ability to envision and create opportunities for new ventures. Although analytically separate, cognitive and cultural embeddedness are closely intertwined. Cognitive structures are also culturally acquired, resulting from social interactions as well as predominant norms and values governing individual behavior (Dequech, 2003). In the remainder of the chapter, we therefore subsume cognitive embeddedness under cultural embeddedness.

Cultural, political (e.g. Zukin and DiMaggio, 1990) and institutional embeddedness (e.g. Baum and Oliver, 1992) are representative of social context pertaining to the overarching environment. Institutional embeddedness denotes interconnections with the institutional environment. In general, these three concepts highlight how the wider institutions of society influence economic actors. They align broadly with cognisance of 'institutions' both formal (constitutions, laws, rules, regulations, property rights) and informal (norms, values, traditions, taboos, customs, codes of conduct), that structure, constrain or promote forms of social, economic and political interaction and behaviour (North, 1990).

Subtle differences in the social, economic and politico-institutional concepts are sometimes highlighted. Zukin and DiMaggio (1990, p. 20) use power influences to differentiate political embeddedness, arguing that 'economic institutions and decisions are shaped by a struggle for power that involves economic actors and nonmarket institutions'. Cultural embeddedness includes norms, values and conventions as well as everyday practices that shape behaviours. Zukin and DiMaggio (1990, p. 17) elaborate on cultural embeddedness, emphasizing, '[C]ulture, in the form of beliefs and ideologies, taken for granted assumptions, or formal rule systems, also prescribes strategies of self-interested actors.' Hence, their exposition of cultural embeddedness encompasses the impact of institutions.

EMBEDDEDNESS IN ENTREPRENEURSHIP RESEARCH

The entrepreneurship literature considers structural, cultural and political, and institutional embeddedness, and more recently, family embeddedness. At the structural level, embeddedness is frequently presented in terms of the identification, formation and exploitation of networks and network ties in relation to resources and other benefits that they yield (Allen, 2000; Anderson et al., 2010; Lechner et al., 2006). Johannisson et al. (2002) examine individual exchange relationships of small business owners within networks, considering first-, second- and third-order ties. Hite (2005) explores how network ties within social relationships represent a strategic form of organizing for the practices of emerging entrepreneurial firms. Literature that captures social capital implications for entrepreneurship also fits under the structural embeddedness umbrella. While limited studies mention structural embeddedness, it is safe to assume that this form of embeddedness applies when the discussion centres on networks, alliances and ties. Research also shows that the relational context within which prospective entrepreneurs are situated influences their social networks and opportunity recognition (Anderson et al., 2012; De Carolis et al., 2009; Korsgaard and Anderson, 2011), mentorship (Ozgen and Baron, 2007) and perceptions of feasibility or desirability of opportunities that affect intentions.

Institutional embeddedness is studied relative to the influence of the formal and regulatory framework on the nature and extent of entrepreneurship (Acs et al., 2008; Henrekson and Sanandaji, 2011; Stenholm et al., 2013). Minniti (2008) citing North (1990) refers to the institutional environment, which determines the formal and informal rules of the game, and places constraints on human action. These institutions (and policies) are crucial in shaping entrepreneurial behaviour, and several studies demonstrate how institutional elements such as legal systems impact on entrepreneurial cognition and the new venture creation decision (Lim et al., 2010).

Research also examines how entrepreneurship is embedded in national and local traditions, rules and values (Hechavarria and Reynolds, 2009). Kloosterman et al. (1999) study the multi-embeddedness of ethnic entrepreneurs and suggest the concept of 'mixed embeddedness' which embraces the interplay between social, economic and politico-institutional contexts, as well as structure and agency. Following this line, Jack and Anderson (2002) examine entrepreneurship as an embedded socio-economic process and explore the links between agent and structure. The notion of cultural embeddedness is implicit in research that examines the impact of the welfare state on women's entrepreneurship. For instance, Neergaard and Thrane (2011) argue that while the Nordic welfare model might facilitate women's wage employment, it does not favour women selecting an entrepreneurial career. Cultural embeddedness can also explain why Middle Eastern and North African economies contain the lowest proportion of women entrepreneurs (Kelley et al., 2011). Customs and traditions of Islamic and Arab society reserve the place of women to the home and private domain, and they do not have similar opportunities to men (Ahmad, 2011). When women are embedded in conservative patriarchal families, such as home-based embroiderers in Jordan (Al-Dajani and Marlow, 2010), their perceptions of entrepreneurial opportunities could be constrained. Relatedly, cultural norms and family division of labour could restrict the time availability of women, limiting the desirability of ventures outside the home. This has been shown for women entrepreneurs in post-Soviet countries (Welter and Smallbone, 2008).

Hence, we argue that women's entrepreneurship is highly dependent on the specific contexts in which it occurs (Welter, 2011). This includes the overall political and cultural context, as well as family and household contexts. While family embeddedness considerations are relevant in other areas of study such as family conflict (e.g. Carr et al., 2008), in entrepreneurship the family and private domain factors have only recently gained importance (Aldrich and Cliff, 2003; Jennings and McDougald, 2007). Family embeddedness is participation in family roles, household resources and social network relationships (Aldrich and Cliff, 2003; Ruef et al., 2003). This captures the characteristics of the entrepreneurs' family systems (transitions, resources, norms, attitudes and values) that influence the processes involved in venture creation (Aldrich and Cliff, 2003). Ahl (2006, p. 604) notes that women's entrepreneurship studies fail to address interconnections between work and family satisfactorily because they commonly 'assume a division between work and family and between a public and a private sphere of life'.

Family is at the core of family business literature but its relationship to the venture is viewed in different ways. For instance, Carter and Schwab (2008) consider the embeddedness of family relationships and their impact upon business performance, but not the impact of the business upon family relationships. This unidirectional impact of family on firm is variously replicated in several other articles. In contrast, Hall and Nordqvist (2008) and Litz (2008) view interactions between family and business as more recursive and interactive. The interesting exposition by Litz (2008) uses the Mobius Strip metaphor to examine the interconnectedness of family and business over time, but equally, the image is useful in describing ways in which business and family can appear as distinct entities yet seamlessly morph into one another.

In sum, we propose 'embeddedness' as the basic building block, and theoretical rationale, for explaining the venture creation process and accounting for gender differences, and to obtain a holistic understanding of entrepreneurial activity. We distinguish three types of embeddedness: family, cultural and structural. For analytical separateness, our conceptual framework differentiates structural embeddedness as pertaining to all characteristics of social exchange relations, networks and alliances.

BUILDING THE CONCEPTUAL FRAMEWORK

Entrepreneurial activity is likely to occur when an individual makes a shift from one life path to another, and there are positive pushes and pulls, as well as negative displacements, that can form an entrepreneurial event and motivate entrepreneurial behaviour (Shapero and Sokol, 1982). The concern is about what brought about the action that led to a change in the entrepreneur's former life path, and why this path generates an entrepreneurial event and not another available possible action (Shapero and Sokol, 1982, p.78). Extreme negative displacements may be political and religious refugees; but there are also job-related displacements; or job dissatisfaction may also push someone to entrepreneurship. Shapero and Sokol (1982) suggest that positive pulls can be the perception of an opportunity, and that desirability precedes feasibility.

More recently, Krueger et al. (2000) expand on these arguments, pointing out that before a new venture event can take place, perceptions and other cognitive aspects influence the viability or feasibility of the opportunity. Explaining organizational opportunity emergence and creation, they argue that perceptions of opportunities can be catalysed by either positive or negative factors. Further, they posit that desirability and feasibility are linked to intentional behaviour, which can have a venture creation outcome. The antecedents to desirability include perceived social norms and personal desirability, while perceived feasibility is influenced by perceived self-efficacy and perceived collective efficacy.

Perceived Desirability

According to Shapero and Sokol (1982), these are the social and cultural factors that enter into the formation of entrepreneurial events, and are most felt through the formation of individual value systems. If a social system places high value on the formation of new ventures, then more individuals will choose that path in times of transition. Krueger et al. (2000) follow Ajzen's 'theory of planned behavior' and define this as personal attitude, which depends on the consequences of outcomes from performing the target behaviour; their likelihood, as well as the magnitude of positive or negative consequences. This is an expectancy-based perception, whereby an individual will act in a certain way based on expectations that the act will be followed by a certain outcome (expectancy), and depending on the attractiveness of that outcome to the individual (value or valence) (Vroom, 1964). Preferences for certain outcomes are established by employing criteria for desirability, which is a form of value (Steel and König, 2006).

Further, social norms that are the perceived normative beliefs of family, friends, co-workers or others influence perceptions of the individual as well (Kolvereid, 1996). Household and family norms and values influence work behaviours, time spent working on the venture, and the social support received by the entrepreneur (Brush and Manolova, 2004; Welter and Smallbone, 2008). Family members and peers play a role in establishing desirability, together with the prevailing social attitude towards entrepreneurship. For example, in both Russia and China it has been shown that entrepreneurs have many more entrepreneurs among their relatives (parents, aunts, uncles, siblings, cousins) and also among their childhood friends (Djankov et al., 2006a, 2006b).

Perceived Feasibility

This concerns perceptions as to whether or not creation of a business is feasible, and is related to the perception of having the capability to act on an opportunity and start a business. Feasibility and desirability interact, so if a venture is perceived as undesirable, the person may never consider its feasibility (Fitzsimmons and Douglas, 2011). Similarly, if a new venture is perceived as not feasible, it might be viewed as undesirable. Krueger et al. (2000) use self-efficacy as a predictor of perceptions of feasibility, arguing that action takes into account not only expectancy of outcomes but also perceived self-efficacy about an individual's ability to execute some behaviour. Self-efficacy perception involves the internalization of competencies and the belief in mastery of skills, and is influenced by the psychological and emotional support of peers (Boyd and Vozikis, 1994). Similarly, self-efficacy perceptions play a powerful role in managerial and employee behaviour, whereby gender and ethnicity differences in work interest and performance can often be traced to differences in self-confidence (Krueger et al., 2000). This in turn might also partly, and indirectly, reflect social roles and norms within a society.

Entrepreneurs perceive feasibility as their ability to support the venture financially, including the ability to secure capital from external sources (Erikson, 2002). Perceptions of feasibility in relation to finance can be linked to the entrepreneur's view on capital as a commodity rather than a scarce resource. When entrepreneurs perceive informal venture capital as a commodity then capital acquisition is about finding 'competent capital' where investors have requisite expertise and contacts (Saetre, 2003).

Our proposed framework is dynamic, where feasibility and desirability might be considered simultaneously instead of sequentially. It also captures how structural, cultural and family embeddedness influences

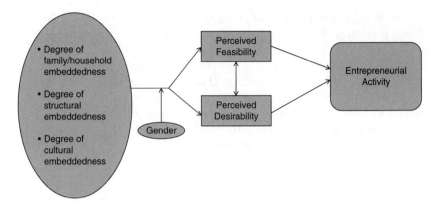

Figure 1.1   Conceptual framework

perceived feasibility and desirability differently for men and women (see Figure 1.1).

THE INFLUENCE OF GENDER IN VENTURE CREATION

Several studies have investigated factors explaining disparities between male- and female-owned businesses in the start-up process. For instance, research examining start-up decisions found that men tend to start businesses in manufacturing, construction and high-technology industries, and women within the service industry or in retail due to human capital and experience (Hisrich and Brush, 1983; Neider, 1987). Furthermore, women are especially motivated to start their own businesses in the hopes of attaining a better balance between work and family (Hughes, 2005). While both men and women are motivated by opportunity and necessity, and these motivations vary widely by level of country development (Kelley et al., 2011), there is evidence that, on balance, women are more often motivated by economic necessity in the USA (Buttner, 1993; Hisrich and Brush, 1983; Hughes, 2005; Orhan and Scott, 2001). There is growing evidence that women entrepreneurs in transition and less-developed economies, as well as ethnic minority women entrepreneurs, are more likely to be motivated by economic necessity (Welter et al., 2006; Smith-Hunter, 2004).

Research examining socio-cognitive influences on entrepreneurial behaviour suggests that a better understanding of the intentions of nascent entrepreneurs in the early phase of new venture development might help to explain the start-up process, as well as why women-led firms ultimately end up smaller, and grow more slowly (Krueger et al., 2000; Orser and Hogarth-Scott, 2005). Intentions have proved the best predictor of planned behaviour, particularly in the context of new businesses which emerge over time and involve considerable planning (Krueger et al., 2000). Expectancies also have an impact on aspirations for growth in nascent entrepreneurs, and women are more likely to have more complex expectancies, economic and social, whereas men are more likely focused on economic expectancies (Manolova et al., 2012).

There is a strong theoretical rationale as to why we might expect differences in the entrepreneurial start-up behaviour of men and women. Social learning theory argues that as a result of women's different socialization experiences they may lack strong expectations for personal efficacy with regard to career-related behaviours and, therefore, may not fully attain their potential (Hackett and Betz, 1981). A variety of factors influence gender development (for example, peers, media, educational practices, occupational systems) and explain differences in female and male socialization (Bussey and Bandura, 1999). In the entrepreneurial context, performance accomplishments and vicarious learning are two major sources of difference (Hackett and Betz, 1981). Successful performance on a task provides information increasing the expectations of efficacy, while vicarious learning via role models, sex roles and occupational stereotypes can increase efficacy expectations from vicariously observing others succeed.

APPLICATION OF THE FRAMEWORK

In this section we present generalized propositions framed in line with three types of embeddedness: structural, cultural and family (with cognitive embeddedness, as mentioned earlier, subsumed under both cultural and family embeddedness). Separation of desirability and feasibility is often not possible because they are interconnected and interact. The portrayal of our conceptual framework shows this interaction. Fitzsimmons and Douglas (2011, p.433) also stress that entrepreneurial intentions are likely to be 'in the general case, not only a function of the main effects of perceived feasibility and perceived desirability but also a function of the interaction between these factors'. Given this interaction, and to shed light on the gender gap in venture creation, we wished to highlight the importance of distinguishing the differential impacts of forms of embeddedness on a holistic entrepreneurial motivation where both perceived feasibility and desirability intermingle. Therefore, our propositions specify both perceptions.

Structural Embeddedness

Networks with more structural holes produce better information (Burt, 1992). Personal and professional networks define the types of people one interacts with, and can be an asset or a liability in entrepreneurship. Improved or diminished access to information will affect the ability of an entrepreneur to access funding or other key resources. Further, social power in formal networks can exclude some entrepreneurs and welcome others. Social power in a network is a function of position and access to unique informational resources (Burt, 1992). It is advantageous for aspiring entrepreneurs to be embedded in interpersonal networks where they can access resources pertinent to venture creation (for example, financiers, business service providers). There is increasing recognition that both networking activity and social capital play an important role in women business owners' access to finance (Carter et al., 2007; Shaw, 2006). Hence, women spending more time and having more ties in networks where resource exchanges can occur would have a greater degree of structural embeddedness and be more likely to have success at venture creation.

Some women entrepreneurs and ethnic minorities are embedded in networks that have different characteristics and which may produce different constraints (Ibarra, 1993). For instance, the network structure for a woman entrepreneur with caring responsibilities for young children might be more likely to have a network of other mothers and care-givers. This homophily of personal contacts (Ruef et al., 2003) might be disadvantageous because this network may not have the information, or access to financial resources, needed for a particular venture. For women deeply embedded in a network of other women with primary care-giving responsibilities, the effects of their family roles in managing non-standard work (part-time, home-based), as well as career interruptions, affects their ability to maintain, diversify and intensify business networks.

Entrepreneurial networks tend to comprise more males than females in nearly every country, partly because men are more likely to be entrepreneurs. Further, it is well known that the venture capital industry and angel networks are heavily male-dominated (Becker-Blease and Sohl, 2007). Empirical evidence suggests that gender differences in network composition disadvantage women (Ibarra and Smith-Lovin, 1997). Allen (2000) refers to women's networks including fewer entrepreneurs than male networks, which might restrict their outreach and usefulness to a female entrepreneur. Other studies report more homogeneous and less outreach-ing networks for women entrepreneurs, compared with men, as well as less frequent network activities (Schutjens and Stam, 2003). Women tend to rely more on homogeneous networks with a larger share of relatives; on family (that is, strong ties) advice and less on professionals, such as their accountants, than their male counterparts (Renzulli and Aldrich, 2005). This has an impact on their perception of opportunity (Brush et al., 2010a). While these tendencies might be changing, when aspiring women entrepreneurs are deeply embedded in predominantly female networks they may miss opportunities to interact and develop relationships with male entrepreneurs, service providers, or financiers to support their ventures.

Therefore, we posit:

Proposition 1: The degree of structural embeddedness differentially influences men and women entrepreneurs' perceptions of feasibility and desirability which influences the likelihood of venture creation.

Cultural Embeddedness

Cultural embeddedness comprises political (Zukin and DiMaggio, 1990) and institutional embeddedness (Baum and Oliver, 1992), reflecting the social context pertaining to the overarching environment. These institutions influence the ways entrepreneurs behave due to rules, values and societal norms. Early social learning experiences are related to career decisions, with males having a higher preference for entrepreneurship (Matthews and Moser, 1996). A national study of entrepreneurial tendencies among youths finds females less interested in starting a business and less confident in their abilities (Kourilsky and Walstad, 1998). Other studies show female students had lower self-efficacy than male students, and during start-up men were more likely to stress economic expectancies (risk and profitability) while women more often stress personal expectancies (autonomy and challenge) (Chen et al., 1998; Ljunggren and Kolvereid, 1996). However, social learning varies when women are raised in family firms, and/or have mothers or husbands as entrepreneurial or business role models (Coleman, 2007). When women are educated in business and entrepreneurial training, they can develop more confidence in their entrepreneurial skills (Wilson et al., 2007). Hence, women who may not have role models or may not have business education can be less culturally embedded in the entrepreneurship community.

Women's intentions for launching and managing new businesses may differ from men's (Langowitz and Minniti, 2007; Verheul et al., 2012). A study of new venture strategies suggests that male and female entrepreneurs have different socialization experiences, which shape different expectancies, effort and beliefs explaining performance differences (Carter et al., 1997). GEM data shows that perceptions of the feasibility of the opportunity vary dramatically based on the country level of economic development (Kelley et al., 2013). Similarly, women's confidence in their capabilities and perceptions of risk in starting a business vary depending on country development and perceptions of the value of entrepreneurship in their economy. Cultural norms and expectations for women's roles are influenced by the degree to which cultural expectations are stronger or weaker for women to be entrepreneurs. Gender and culture do matter in relation to perceptions of barriers to entrepreneurship and entrepreneurial intentions (Shinnar et al., 2012).

Fuwa (2004) documents how housework is embedded in complex and social factors relating to gender norms, and reproduction of society and other macro-level variables such as welfare regimes. He confirms that women in less egalitarian countries benefit less from their individual-level assets (relative resources, time availability and gender ideology) and suggests that cultural settings directly affect the family and household, entrepreneurs' motivation and perceptions of entrepreneurial activities. Family policies and labour market institutions (for example, gender wage inequality and public expenditure on childcare) impact indirectly on the decision to start a business through their effect on societal perceptions (Elam and Terjesen, 2010). In areas where property rights and other laws disadvantage women, these institutional factors may culturally embed women into more female roles, making it less likely that they would be interested in perceiving entrepreneurial opportunities, or able to.

Many societies mainly define women through roles connected to family and household responsibilities; societal values implicitly interpret women's entrepreneurship as less desirable and, as a result, provide lower normative support (Baughn et al., 2006; Welter and Smallbone, 2008, 2010; Welter et al., 2006). Further, culturally produced and socially learned gender stereotyping leads both men and women to self-impose occupational segregation in entrepreneurship (Gupta et al., 2009). For ethnic minority entrepreneurs or women entrepreneurs, there is no denying that institutional factors and cultural embeddedness can impact at the micro level. For example, women can subconsciously internalize certain behaviours from an early age (Babcock et al., 2003), which can influence their personal ambitions and willingness to choose among different opportunities in order to identify or create and pursue an idea. Also, entry may be self-restricted to feminized professions, sectors and business fields such as personal services or care professions (Marlow, 2002) because of early socialization. In societies or areas where the stereotype of the entrepreneur is more often associated with men, women are less likely to identify as entrepreneurs, and have more challenges in overcoming these perceptions. Social roles consistent with gender stereotypes may anchor women in a gendered social view, making it harder for them to become entrepreneurial.

Therefore, we posit:

Proposition 2: The degree of cultural embeddedness differentially influences men and women entrepreneurs' perceptions of feasibility and desirability, which influences the likelihood of venture creation.

Family Embeddedness

As entrepreneurs are embedded in family relationships, family member perceptions of desirability and credibility may encourage or discourage an entrepreneur's intentions in the venture creation process (Shapero and Sokol, 1982; Fitzsimmons and Douglas, 2011). Family dynamics can affect social learning and attitudes towards independence and achievement which are also associated with entrepreneurial behaviour (Vesper, 1980). The '5M framework' deliberately positioned the construct of 'motherhood' as the centrepiece of a framework, signalling that standard models of entrepreneurship, which tend to focus solely upon 'market/opportunity', 'money' and 'management', could not adequately account for the experiences of female entrepreneurs (Brush et al., 2009). In other words, the nature and effects of family on women's entrepreneurial activity are likely to vary across different institutional, societal, and cultural contexts. Society manifests itself through cultural norms, traditions and religion that influence roles ascribed to men and women (Welter et al., 2006).

Women in traditional businesses (for example, services, retail) have stronger career expectations of security and a balance between the demands of work and home than women in non-traditional businesses (for example, manufacturing) (Anna et al., 2000). Also, role models, self-assurance and marriage were positively related to the supply of female entrepreneurs; while education and experience were negatively correlated with entrepreneurship (Shiller and Crewson, 1997). Alternatively, social encouragement leads to the likelihood of a successful venture start-up, and resources available to the entrepreneur are influenced by household size, head and health of members of the household (Brush and Manolova, 2004). Research on portfolio entrepreneurship in the context of farm households supports this notion (Carter and Ram, 2003). Hence, family support is another dimension of embeddedness, in that women receiving less social support from their families are more likely to have less confidence in their entrepreneurial activities, and would be more deeply embedded in their family and, therefore, have less propensity to launch a venture.

Intra-family role expectations, and the extent to which there is an equal or unequal distribution of power and assets at the family level, are influenced by the degree of family embeddedness. Role expectations may mean that there is an unequal distribution of power and assets at the family level, so the degree of family embeddedness might be much stronger for women than for men. The extent of family embeddedness will also influence the time spent in creating and maintaining networks, as well as the formal and informal interactions among the entrepreneur and network members. If women are more involved in caring duties, and have less time for building and consolidating business and professional networks, the feasibility of venture creation is reduced.

Therefore, we posit:

Proposition 3: The degree of family embeddedness differentially influences male and female entrepreneurs' perceptions of feasibility and desirability, which influences the likelihood of venture creation.

CONCLUSIONS AND IMPLICATIONS

We have argued that differences in women's rates of entrepreneurship, and subsequent aspirations for growth, can be explained by applying an embeddedness perspective to our understanding of perceived feasibility and desirability. Following early work by Shapero and Sokol (1982) that argues venture creation is subsequent to perceptions of feasibility (capability and confidence to act) and desirability (beliefs in socio-cultural support, and expectancy for performance and outcomes), we suggest that these are influenced by the degree of embeddedness. Embeddedness is a methodological principle, advocating a holistic approach that incorporates institutions and social relations as an integral part of individual action and organizational operation (Gemici, 2008). Studies from entrepreneurship show that embeddedness influences venture creation, and we propose that existing differences in men's and women's actions can be explained by the degree of structural, cultural and family embeddedness. We argued that the degree of embeddedness differentially influences men and women in terms of their perceived feasibility and desirability for entrepreneurial activity. We allow for a dynamic perspective, in that embeddedness factors can operate collectively, and feasibility and desirability also interact.

The notion of embeddedness need not be static. Emirbayer (1997) highlights the socially negotiated, dynamic nature of social action and moves the idea of embeddedness forward by bringing in a spatial and temporal dimension to supplement relational aspects. We recognize spatial and temporal dimensions as relevant to our framework. For example, at the individual level of the entrepreneur, dynamic life-stage elements could impact on the degree of family embeddedness. This is of particular relevance to women since child-bearing and caring activity have life-stage implications. Spatial embeddedness is useful for encapsulating the importance of 'place' as a fostering or constraining element for entrepreneurship (Berg, 1997). Place is socially and culturally bounded (Thornton and Flynn, 2003), with cultural rules and shared meanings defining not only societies, but also local communities. Therefore, we suggest that the spatial element can be encapsulated in the broader embeddedness perspective brought forward in this chapter.

A better understanding of the ways different types of embeddedness influence entrepreneurs has the potential to explain why some groups of entrepreneurs are more likely to be funded than others. In the case of market access, ethnic or racial norms in communities may make it unacceptable for some entrepreneurs to break out of their community to sell products or services to those of other ethnic groups as they pursue growth. To the extent that embeddedness explains differential approaches to venture creation, there may be implications for policymakers to explore why certain cultural norms, institutions or political processes may inhibit women (and not their male counterparts), and how the extent of these differences depends on the level of economic development.

Embeddedness is 'a puzzle that, once understood, can furnish tools for explicating not only organizational puzzles but market processes' (Uzzi, 1997, p. 22). Endorsing this, we add that solving the embeddedness puzzle helps understanding beyond superficial market processes, enables comprehension of underlying forces that impinge on market and non-market outcomes and, therefore, can be a powerful tool for finding explanations for the venture creation gender gap. Research shows that male and female business owners enact very different strategies for managing the work–family interface, and that gender differences can be masked when examined at the aggregate (Jennings et al., 2010; Jennings and McDougald, 2007). Yet no significant gender difference emerged at the aggregate level, but when Jennings et al. (2010) tested for gender differences at the industry sector level, across-context differences were revealed: gender differences were more pronounced in some contexts despite being limited in others. Hence, we contend that fine-grained examination of context can unveil why venture creation by women consistently lags behind that of males. Disaggregating the contextual embeddedness of women in relation to how family, structural and cultural embeddedness impacts on the desirability, and feasibility, of venture creation by women can give more nuanced insights into reasons why the rate of women's venture creation remains persistently, and significantly, lower than that of men.

REFERENCES

Acs, Z.J., Desai, S. and Hessels, J. (2008), 'Entrepreneurship, economic development and institutions', *Small Business Economics*, 31 (3), 219–234.

Ahl, H. (2006), 'Why research on women entrepreneurs needs new directions', *Entrepreneurship Theory and Practice*, 30, 595–621.

Ahmad, S.Z. (2011), 'Evidence of the characteristics of women entrepreneurs in the Kingdom of Saudi Arabia: an empirical investigation', *International Journal of Gender and Entrepreneurship*, 3 (2), 123–143.

Al-Dajani, H. and Marlow, S. (2010), 'The impact of women's home-based enterprise on marriage dynamics: evidence from Jordan', *International Small Business Journal*, 28, 470–486.

Aldrich, H.E. and Cliff, J.E. (2003), 'The pervasive effects of family on entrepreneurship: toward a family embeddedness perspective', *Journal of Business Venturing*, 18, 573–596.

Allen, W.D. (2000), 'Social networks and self-employment', *Journal of Socio-Economics*, 29, 487–501.

Anderson, A.R., Dodd, S.D. and Jack, S. (2010), 'Network practices and entrepreneurial growth', *Scandinavian Journal of Management*, 26 (2), 121–133.

Anderson, A.R., Dodd, S.D. and Jack, S. (2012), 'Entrepreneurship as connecting: some implications for theorising and practice', *Management Decision*, 50, 958–971.

Anna, A., Chandler, G., Jansen, E. and Mero, N. (2000), 'Women business owners in traditional and non-traditional industries', *Journal of Business Venturing*, 15, 279–303.

Babcock, L., Laschever, S., Gelfand, M. and Small, D. (2003), 'Nice girls don't ask', *Harvard Business Review*, 81, 14–17.

Baughn, C.C., Chua, B.-L. and Neupert, K.E. (2006), 'The normative context for women's participation in entrepreneurship: a multicountry study', *Entrepreneurship Theory and Practice*, 30, 687–708.

Baum, J.A. and Oliver, C. (1992), 'Institutional embeddedness and the dynamics of organizational populations', *American Sociological Review*, 57, 540–559.

Becker-Blease, J. and Sohl, J. (2007), 'Do women-owned businesses have equal access to angel capital?' *Journal of Business Venturing*, 22, 503–521.

Berg, N.G. (1997), 'Gender, place and entrepreneurship', *Entrepreneurship and Regional Development*, 9 (3), 259–268.

Bird, B. and Brush, C. (2002), 'A gendered perspective on organizational creation', *Entrepreneurship Theory and Practice*, 26, 41–65.

Boyd, N.G. and Vozikis, G.S. (1994), 'The influence of self-efficacy on the development of entrepreneurial intentions and actions', *Entrepreneurship Theory and Practice*, 18, 64–77.

Brush, C., Allen, E., de Bruin, A. and Welter, F. (2010a), 'Gender embeddedness of women entrepreneurs: an empirical test of the "5m" framework', 2010 Babson College Entrepreneurship Research Conference, Lausanne, Switzerland, June.

Brush, C., de Bruin, A., Gatewood, E.J. and Henry, C. (2010b), 'Introduction: women entrepreneurs and growth', in Brush, C., de Bruin, A., Gatewood, E.J. and Henry, C. (eds), *Women Entrepreneurs and the Global Environment for Growth: A Research Perspective*, Cheltenham, UK and Northampton, MA, USA: Edward Elgar, pp. 1–16.

Brush, C.G., de Bruin, A. and Welter, F. (2009), 'A gender-aware framework for women's entrepreneurship', *International Journal of Gender and Entrepreneurship*, 1 (1), 8–24.

Brush, C. and Manolova, T. (2004), 'The household structure variables in the PSED questionnaire', in Gartner, W., Shaver, K., Carter, N. and Reynolds, P. (eds), *The Handbook of Entrepreneurial Dynamics: The Process of Organization Creation*, Newbury Park, CA: Sage, pp. 78–93.

Burt, R.S. (1992), *Structural Holes*, Cambridge, MA: Harvard University Press.

Bussey, K. and Bandura, A. (1999), 'Social cognitive theory of gender development and differentiation', *Psychological Review*, 106, 676–713.

Buttner, E.H. (1993), 'Female entrepreneurs: how far have they come?' *Business Horizons*, 36 (2), 59–65.

Carr, J.C., Boyar, S.L. and Gregory, B.T. (2008), 'The moderating effect of work–family centrality on work–family conflict, organizational attitudes, and turnover behavior', *Journal of Management*, 34, 244–262.

Carter, J. and Schwab, A. (2008), 'Turnaround strategies in established small firms', *Family Business Review*, 21, 31–50.

Carter, N., Williams, M. and Reynolds, P.D. (1997), 'Discontinuance among new firms in retail: the influence of initial resources, strategy, and gender', *Journal of Business Venturing*, 12, 125–145.

Carter, S. and Ram, M. (2003), 'Reassessing portfolio entrepreneurship', *Small Business Economics*, 21, 371–380.

Carter, S., Shaw, E., Wilson, F. and Lam, W. (2007), 'Gender, entrepreneurship and bank lending: the criteria and processes used by bank loan officers in assessing applications', *Entrepreneurship Theory and Practice*, 31, 427–444.

Chen, C., Greene, P. and Crick, A. (1998), 'Does entrepreneurial self-efficacy distinguish entrepreneurs from managers?', *Journal of Business Venturing*, 13, 295–316.

Coleman, S. (2007), 'The role of human and financial capital in the profitability and growth of women-owned small firms', *Journal of Small Business Management*, 45, 303–319.

De Carolis, D.M., Litzky, B.E. and Eddleston, K.A. (2009), 'Why networks enhance the progress of new venture creation: the influence of social capital and cognition', *Entrepreneurship: Theory and Practice*, 33, 527–545.

Dequech, D. (2003), 'Cognitive and cultural embeddedness: combining institutional economics and economic sociology', *Journal of Economic Issues*, 3, 461–470

Djankov, S., Qian, Y., Roland, G. and Zhuravskaya, E. (2006a), 'Entrepreneurship in China and Russia compared', *Journal of the European Economic Association, Papers and Proceedings*, 4, 352–365.

Djankov, S., Qian, Y., Roland, G. and Zhuravskaya, E. (2006b), 'Who are China's entrepreneurs?' *American Economic Review*, 96, 348–52.

Elam, A. and Terjesen, S. (2010), 'Gendered institutions and cross-national patterns of business creation for men and women', *European Journal of Development Research*, 22, 331–348.

Emirbayer, M. (1997), 'Manifesto for a relational sociology', *American Journal of Sociology*, 103, 281–317.

Erikson, T. (2002), 'Entrepreneurial capital: the emerging venture's most important asset and competitive advantage', *Journal of Business Venturing*, 17, 275–290.

Fitzsimmons, J. and Douglas, E. (2011), 'Interaction between feasibility and desirability in the formation of entrepreneurial intentions', *Journal of Business Venturing*, 26, 431–440.

Fuwa, M. (2004), 'Macro-level gender inequality and the division of household labor in 22 countries', *American Sociological Review*, 69, 751–767.

Gemici, K. (2008), 'Karl Polanyi and the antinomies of embeddedness', *Socio-Economic Review*, 6, 5–33.

Gnyawali, D. and Madhavan, R. (2001), 'Cooperative networks and competitive dynamics: a structural embeddedness perspective', *Academy of Management Review*, 26, 431–445.

Granovetter, M. (1985), 'Economic action and social structure: the problem of embeddedness', *American Journal of Sociology*, 91, 481–510.

Granovetter, M. (1990), 'The old and new economic sociology: a history and an agenda', in Friedland, R. and Robertson, A.F. (eds), *Beyond the Marketplace: Rethinking Economy and Society*, New York: Aldine de Gruyter, pp. 89–112.

Gupta, V., Turban, D., Wasti, S.A. and Sikdar, A. (2009), 'The role of gender stereotypes in perceptions of entrepreneurs and intentions to become an entrepreneur', *Entrepreneurship Theory and Practice*, 33, 397–417.

Hackett, G. and Betz, N.E. (1981), 'A self-efficacy approach to the career development of women', *Journal of Applied Social Psychology*, 30, 2137–2157.

Hall, A. and Nordqvist, M. (2008), 'Professional management in family businesses: toward an extended understanding', *Family Business Review*, 21, 51–69.

Hayton, J., Carnabuci, G. and Eisenberger, R. (2012), 'With a little help from my colleagues: a social embeddedness approach to perceived organizational support', *Journal of Organizational Behavior*, 33, 235–249.

Hechavarria, D. and Reynolds, P. (2009), 'Cultural norms and business start-ups: the impact of national values on opportunity and necessity entrepreneurs', *International Entrepreneurship and Management Journal*, 5, 417–437.

Henrekson, M. and Sanandaji, T. (2011), 'The interaction of entrepreneurship and institutions', *Journal of Institutional Economics*, 7 (1), 47–75.

Hisrich, R.D. and Brush, C. (1983), 'The woman entrepreneur: implications of family, educational, and occupational experience', in Hornaday, J., Timmons, J. and Vesper, K. (eds), *Frontiers of Entrepreneurship Research*, Wellesley, MA: Babson College.

Hite, J. (2005), 'Evolutionary processes and paths of relationally embedded network ties in emerging entrepreneurial firms', *Entrepreneurship Theory and Practice*, 29, 113–144.

Hughes, K.D. (2005), *Female Enterprise in the New Economy*, Toronto: University of Toronto Press.

Hughes, K.D., Jennings, J.E., Brush, C.G., Carter, S. and Welter, F. (2012), 'Extending women's entrepreneurship research in new directions', *Entrepreneurship Theory and Practice*, 36, 429–442.

Ibarra, H. (1993), 'Personal networks of women and minorities in management: a conceptual framework', *Academy of Management Review*, 18, 56–87.
Ibarra, H. and Smith-Lovin, L. (1997), 'New directions in social network research in gender and organizational careers', in Jackson, S. and Cooper, C. (eds), *Creating Tomorrow's Organizations: A Handbook for Future Research in Organizational Behavior*, New York: Wiley, pp. 359–384.
Jack, S. and Anderson, A.R. (2002), 'The effects of embeddedness on the entrepreneurial process', *Journal of Business Venturing*, 17, 467–487.
Jennings, J.E. and Brush, C.G. (2013), 'Research on women entrepreneurs: challenges to (and from) the broader entrepreneurship literature?' *Academy of Management Annals*, 7 (1), 661–713.
Jennings, J., Hughes, K. and Jennings, P.D. (2010), 'The work–family interface strategies of male and female entrepreneurs: are there any differences?', in Brush, C., de Bruin, A., Gatewood, E.J. and Henry, C. (eds), *Women Entrepreneurs and the Global Environment for Growth: A Research Perspective*, Cheltenham, UK and Northampton, MA, USA: Edward Elgar, pp. 163–186.
Jennings, J.E. and McDougald, M.S. (2007), 'Work–family interface experiences and coping strategies: implications for entrepreneurship research and practice', *Academy of Management Review*, 32, 747–760.
Johannisson, B., Ramirez-Pasillas, M. and Karlsson, G. (2002), 'The institutional embeddedness of local inter-firm networks: a leverage for business creation', *Entrepreneurship and Regional Development*, 14 (4), 297–315.
Kelley, D., Bosma, N. and Amorós, J. (2011), *Global Entrepreneurship Monitor 2010 Global Report*, Global Entrepreneurship Research Association, Wellesley, MA: Babson College.
Kelley, D., Brush, C., Greene, P. and Litovsky, Y. (2013), *Global Entrepreneurship Monitor 2012 Women's Report*, Wellesley, MA: Babson College.
Kloosterman, R., Van der Leun, J. and Rath, J. (1999), 'Mixed embeddedness: (in)formal economic activities and immigrant businesses in the Netherlands', *International Journal of Urban and Regional Research*, 23, 252–277.
Kolvereid, L. (1996), 'Prediction of employment status choice intentions', *Entrepreneurship Theory and Practice*, 21, 47–57.
Korsgaard, S. and Anderson, A.R. (2011), 'Enacting entrepreneurship as social value creation', *International Small Business Journal*, 29, 135–151.
Kourilsky, M.L. and Walstad, W.B. (1998), 'Entrepreneurship and female youth: knowledge, attitudes, gender differences, and educational practices', *Journal of Business Venturing*, 13, 77–88.
Krueger, N.F., Reilly, M.D. and Carsrud, A.L. (2000), 'Competing models of entrepreneurial intentions', *Journal of Business Venturing*, 15, 411–432.
Langowitz, N. and Minniti, M. (2007), 'The entrepreneurial propensity of women', *Entrepreneurship Theory and Practice*, 31, 341–364.
Lechner, C., Dowling, M. and Welpe, I. (2006), 'Firm networks and firm development: the role of the relational mix', *Journal of Business Venturing*, 21, 514–40.
Lim, D.S., Morse, E.A., Mitchell, R.K. and Seawright, K.K. (2010), 'Institutional environment and entrepreneurial cognitions: a comparative business systems perspective', *Entrepreneurship Theory and Practice*, 34, 491–516.
Litz, R.A. (2008), 'Two sides of one phenomenon: conceptualizing the family business and business family as a Mobius strip', *Family Business Review*, 21, 217–236.

Ljunggren, E. and Kolvereid, L. (1996), 'New business formation: does gender make a difference?', *Women in Management Review*, 11, 3–12.
Manolova, T., Brush, C., Edelman, L. and Shaver, K. (2012), 'One size doesn't fit all: growth expectancies for men and women nascent entrepreneurs', *Entrepreneurship and Regional Development*, 24, 7–27.
Marlow, S. (2002), 'Women and self-employment: a part of or apart from theoretical construct?', *International Journal of Entrepreneurship and Innovation*, 3 (2), 83–91.
Matthews, C. and Moser, S. (1996), 'A longitudinal investigation of family background and gender on interest in small firm ownership', *Journal of Small Business Management*, 34, 29–43.
Minniti, M. (2008), 'The role of government policy on entrepreneurial activity: productive, unproductive, or destructive?', *Entrepreneurship Theory and Practice*, 32, 779–790.
Mitchell, R.K., Randolph-Seng, B. and Mitchell, J.R. (2011), 'Socially situated cognition: imagining new opportunities for entrepreneurship research', *Academy of Management Review*, 36, 774–776.
Neergaard, H. and Thrane, C. (2011), 'The Nordic welfare model', *International Journal of Gender and Entrepreneurship*, 3 (2), 88–104.
Neider, L. (1987), 'A preliminary investigation of female entrepreneurs in Florida', *Journal of Small Business Management*, 25 (3), 22–29.
North, D.C. (1990), *Institutions, Institutional Change, and Economic Performance*, Cambridge: Cambridge University Press.
Orhan, M. and Scott, D. (2001), 'Why women enter into entrepreneurship: an explanatory model', *Women in Management Review*, 16, 232–247.
Orser, B.J. and Hogarth-Scott, S. (2005), 'Opting for growth: gender dimensions of choosing enterprise development', *Canadian Journal of Administrative Sciences*, 19 (3), 284–300.
Ozgen, E. and Baron, R.A. (2007), 'Social sources of information in opportunity recognition: effects of mentors, industry networks and professional forums', *Journal of Business Venturing*, 22, 174–192.
Renzulli, L.A. and Aldrich, H. (2005), 'Who can you turn to? Tie activation within core business discussion networks', *Social Forces*, 84 (1), 323–341.
Ruef, M., Aldrich, H. and Carter, N. (2003), 'The structure of founding teams: homophily, strong ties, and isolation among U.S. entrepreneurs', *American Sociological Review*, 68, 195–222.
Saetre, A. (2003), 'Entrepreneurial perfectives on informal venture capital', *Venture Capital*, 5 (1), 71–94.
Schutjens, V. and Stam, E. (2003), 'The evolution and nature of young firm networks: a longitudinal perspective', *Small Business Economics*, 21 (2), 115–134.
Shapero, A. and Sokol, L. (1982), 'The social dimensions of entrepreneurship', in Kent, C.A., Sexton, D.L. and Vesper, K.H. (eds), *The Encyclopedia of Entrepreneurship*, Englewood Cliffs, NJ: Prentice Hall, pp. 72–98.
Shaw, E. (2006), 'Small firm networking', *International Small Business Journal*, 24, 5–29.
Shiller, B.R. and Crewson, P.E. (1997), 'Entrepreneurial origins: a longitudinal inquiry', *Economic Inquiry*, 35 (3), 523–31.
Shinnar, R.S., Giacomin, O. and Janssen, F. (2012), 'Entrepreneurial perceptions and intentions: the role of gender and culture', *Entrepreneurship Theory and Practice*, 36, 465–493.

Smith-Hunter, A. (2004), 'Women's entrepreneurship across racial lines: current status, critical issues and future implications', *Journal of Hispanic Higher Education*, 3 (4), 363–381.

Steel, P. and König, C.J. (2006), 'Integrating theories of motivation', *Academy of Management Review*, 31 (4), 889–913.

Stenholm, P., Acs, Z.H. and Wuebker, R. (2013), 'Exploring country-level institutional arrangements on the rate and type of entrepreneurial activity', *Journal of Business Venturing*, 28 (1), 176–193.

Sullivan, D. and Meek, W.R. (2012), 'Gender and entrepreneurship: a review and process model', *Journal of Managerial Psychology*, 27, 428–458.

Thornton, P.H. and Flynn, K.H. (2003), 'Entrepreneurship, networks, and geographies', in Acs, Z.J. and Audretsch, D.B. (eds), *Handbook of Entrepreneurship Research*, Vol. 1, New York: Springer US, pp. 401–433.

Uzzi, B. (1997), 'Social structure and competition in interfirm networks: the paradox of embeddedness', *Administrative Science Quarterly*, 42, 35–68.

Verheul, I., Thurik, R., Grilo, I. and van der Zwan, P. (2012), 'Explaining preferences and actual involvement in self-employment: gender and the entrepreneurial personality', *Journal of Economic Psychology*, 33 (2), 235–341.

Vesper, K. (1980), *New Venture Strategies*, Englewood Cliffs, NJ: Prentice-Hall.

Vroom, V.H. (1964), *Work and Motivation*, New York: Wiley.

Welter, F. (2011), 'Contextualizing entrepreneurship – conceptual challenges and ways forward', *Entrepreneurship Theory and Practice*, 35, 165–184.

Welter, F. and Smallbone, D. (2008), 'Women's entrepreneurship from an institutional perspective: the case of Uzbekistan', *International Entrepreneurship and Management Journal*, 4, 505–520.

Welter, F. and Smallbone, D. (2010), 'The embeddedness of women's entrepreneurship in a transition context', in Brush, C.G., de Bruin, A., Gatewood, E.J. and Henry, C. (eds), *Women Entrepreneurs and the Global Environment for Growth: A Research Perspective*, Cheltenham, UK and Northampton, MA, USA: Edward Elgar, pp. 96–117.

Welter, F., Smallbone, D. and Isakova, N.B. (2006), *Enterprising Women in Transition Economies*, Aldershot: Ashgate.

Wilson, F., Kickul, J. and Marlino, D. (2007), 'Gender, entrepreneurial self-efficacy and entrepreneurial career intentions: implications for entrepreneurship education', *Entrepreneurship Theory and Practice*, 31, 387–406.

Zukin, S. and DiMaggio, P. (1990), *Structures of Capital: The Social Organization of the Economy*, New York: Cambridge University Press.

2. Academic entrepreneurship: multi-level factors associated with female-led incubator projects

Diamanto Politis, Jonas Gabrielsson and Åsa Lindholm Dahlstrand

INTRODUCTION

During the past decade there has been a growing interest in developing a better understanding of the issues related to gender in academic entrepreneurship. This stream of research has contributed much to our awareness of the potential barriers facing female academic entrepreneurs. For example: the strong male-oriented entrepreneurship discourse; an under-representation of female academic scientists in senior positions at universities; and the exclusion of women from high-level industrial links and commercial networks (see, e.g., Noordenbos, 2002; Rosa and Dawson, 2006; Murray and Graham, 2007; Ding and Choi, 2008; Tan, 2008; Fältholm et al., 2010). However, much of this research is qualitative with an emphasis on the subjective experiences of female academic entrepreneurs and, further, many of these studies suffer from small samples and poor theoretical grounding. Thus, there is considerable potential for developing this field of research using more theory-driven approaches and larger data sets.

In this chapter we set out to study how institutional structures in and around university-based incubators impact women's entry into academic entrepreneurship. University incubators are entities that operate within larger entrepreneurial ecosystems and whose aim is to accelerate the successful development of start-up and early-stage companies through an array of business support resources and services (Lindholm Dahlstrand and Klofsten, 2002; Hackett and Dilts, 2004; Bergek and Norrman, 2008). They are often funded by tax money and are, therefore, embedded in the political system. Apart from their explicit mission to boost entrepreneurship and innovation university incubators are in this respect also expected to be consistent with the broader democratic and political goals of society. These goals typically include promoting equality between men and women, and increasing public awareness of gender issues in business support systems (Granat Thorslund and Danilda, 2011). However, although university incubators can be a mechanism for promoting the participation of women in academic entrepreneurship there is also a risk that the social structure surrounding these organizations can reinforce (rather than break down) gendered stereotypes and, by so doing, contribute to the consolidation of existing normative gender patterns in society (Gupta et al., 2009; Lindholm Dahlstrand and Politis, 2013).

Scholarly knowledge about how incubators and their surrounding entrepreneurial ecosystems work in relation to gender issues is still relatively scarce. In this chapter we address this gap in the literature by examining institutional factors associated with the likelihood that a female will engage in the commercialization of university science by championing an incubator project. In developing our hypotheses, we draw on the existing theory and research concerning both academic and female entrepreneurship. Our empirical data comes from a unique database consisting of over 1400 venture projects in 19 Swedish incubators that are part of a nationally financed incubator programme. As the data suggest a multi-level structure, we apply multi-level logistic regression analysis to examine 793 new venture projects that entered an incubator between 2006 and 2009. We find that both a higher proportion of female faculty in senior positions at the university associated with the incubator and the presence of a female on the incubator's board of directors is positively associated with the existence of female-led incubator projects. In addition, we find a significant gender bias in terms of the technological sector in which the projects are represented. The findings show that women are more likely to be represented in information and communication technology (ICT) projects and are less likely to be represented in clean-tech projects. Based on our findings, we discuss the implications for promoting the involvement of female academic entrepreneurs in business incubators.

THEORETICAL FOUNDATIONS

Academic Entrepreneurship and Gender

In recent years there has been an exponential increase in the number of studies of academic entrepreneurship (Rothaermel et al., 2007). Many of these studies have applied theoretical frameworks and models that focus on how individual faculty members recognize and exploit science-based business opportunities (Gabrielsson et al., 2012). However, a growing stream of studies has also started to acknowledge the need to go beyond individual-level explanations by examining the broader ecosystem in which entrepreneurial actions and outcomes are embedded (e.g., Fetters et al., 2010; Kumaraswamy et al., 2008). This implies a gradual, but also important, shift towards more systemic approaches that emphasize the fact that the creation of new firms within an academic context is, typically, the result of interactions between individuals and the institutional environment (Politis et al., 2012).

Incubators are an important component in the institutional environment surrounding university-based entrepreneurship ecosystems (Fetters et al., 2010). These organizations have been placed high on the innovation policy agenda and have become central building blocks in national and regional efforts to promote the commercialization of university science. Incubators differ from science parks in that they are primarily focused on business incubation in the early phase of a venture's life (Bergek and Norrman, 2008). In addition to a joint location, they typically supply their incubatees with services and business support, and opportunities for networking, knowledge transfer and experience sharing.

In this chapter we are particularly interested in how institutional factors in and around incubators work in relation to women's entry into academic entrepreneurship. We embed our arguments in the idea that individual action is significantly impacted by the institutional context (Meyer and Rowan, 1977; DiMaggio and Powell, 1983). That is, individuals adopt mindsets and behaviours that reflect the 'dominant template' in their environment (DiMaggio and Powell, 1991). Such 'templates' typically consist of normatively sanctioned ideas about appropriate academic behaviour. As such, instead of being led by their individual interests (or competencies) individuals will adapt their practices to comply with broader institutional demands; that is, they behave according to institutional norms to gain social legitimacy (Meyer and Rowan, 1977).

Focusing on factors within the institutional environment seems particularly relevant when studying gender-related issues associated with incubator projects. For example, there are strong gendered norms, values and ideologies in the practice of entrepreneurship (Gupta et al., 2009), which may influence the perceived desirability of an entrepreneurial career among female academics. The creation and development of a new incubator project is, therefore, likely to be influenced by various normative and cognitive pressures within the surrounding university-based entrepreneurship ecosystem. As such, the institutional environment surrounding university incubators is likely to represent an important component of deeper and more resilient aspects of a gendered social structure that, over time, will become established as authoritative guidelines for entrepreneurial behaviour.

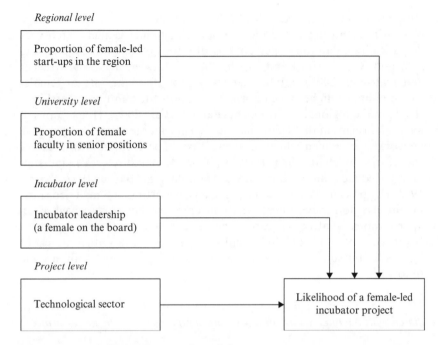

Figure 2.1   Multi-level research model

HYPOTHESES DEVELOPMENT

In the following subsections we develop hypotheses concerning four institutionally embedded factors that may influence prevailing gender norms and, thus, the perceived appropriateness of women becoming incubator entrepreneurs. As depicted in Figure 2.1, these factors relate to four interacting levels (or contexts) surrounding university-based entrepreneurship ecosystems: the regional context, the university context, the specific incubator and the new venture project.

Proportion of Female-led Start-ups in the Region

Entrepreneurship is a highly socio-economic phenomenon and environmental influences can play an important role in an individual's decision to set up a new firm (De Carolis and Saparito, 2006; Verheul et al., 2006). Similar rates of entrepreneurial activity are rarely found across regions within a country, as evidenced by studies in several European countries that have reported high regional variations in start-up rates (see, e.g., Audretsch and Fritsch, 1994; Keeble and Walker, 1994; Reynolds et al.,

1994, Armington and Acs, 2002). These variations are due to a range of factors operating at the regional level, including gender stereotypes and socially conditioned perceptions of appropriate behaviour among men and women (Bird and Brush, 2002; Gupta et. al., 2009; Mueller and Dato-On, 2008). Studies generally show that the rate of female-led start-ups is higher when normative support for entrepreneurship is strong in the regional environment (Baughn et al., 2006). Higher rates of female start-ups in the region may also create a larger pool of supportive networks for women which, in turn, may shape entrepreneurial career trajectories by channelling flows of information and referrals, and supplying feedback and political advice (Podolny and Baron, 1997; Ibarra, 1993; Higgins and Kram, 2001). A higher proportion of female-led start-ups in a region may indicate that entrepreneurship is perceived as an appropriate and attractive career choice for women in that environment (Bygrave, 1995; Gibson, 2004) and may, therefore, raise the interest of females in pursuing entrepreneurial activities. Thus, we hypothesize the following:

H1: A higher proportion of female-led start-ups in a region is positively associated with the likelihood that a woman champions a new incubator project.

Female Faculty in Senior Positions

The typical incubator entrepreneur is either a student or a faculty member coming from the university associated with the incubator, and both these groups are, to a large extent, influenced by the institutionalized gender structures that exist within their university context (Fältholm et al., 2010). For example, it is well known that women (on average) are underrepresented in senior university positions (Rosa and Dawson, 2006) and this is particularly evident in fields such as science, engineering and technology, which constitute the disciplinary background for a large bulk of all new incubator projects. For students, a relatively low proportion of female faculty is likely to mean that they are primarily exposed to male lecturers, mentors and role models. Among other things, this is likely to mean that the perceptions and attitudes of young women (and men) are distorted in a gender role stereotypic way (Eccles, 1994). Further, a low proportion of female faculty in senior positions means there are likely to be fewer women who have the position and seniority to develop industrial links and business networks (Rosa and Dawson, 2006) and, therefore, this is likely to reduce the level of interest among women in supporting and promoting the diffusion of academic knowledge to industry and the broader society. Conversely, a higher proportion of female faculty members in senior positions at a university can serve to increase the pool of women that are available to serve as role models and mentors within a university-based entrepreneurship ecosystem and, potentially, serve to reduce the gendered classification of certain disciplines or career trajectories as being typically masculine or feminine. Following these arguments, we expect that women are more likely to become incubator entrepreneurs if there is a high proportion of senior women serving as faculty members at the university associated with the incubator. Thus, we hypothesize the following:

H2: A higher proportion of female faculty in senior positions at the university associated with the incubator is positively associated with the likelihood that a woman champions a new incubator project.

Incubator Leadership

The strategic leadership of an incubator may play an important role in influencing the likelihood of female-led new incubator projects. While an incubator has a manager who is in charge of daily operations, the organization is also typically governed by a board of directors responsible for strategic affairs and for representing major stakeholders. Women enter professional and managerial ranks at about the same rate as men and they also make up half of the potential employee, customer and other stakeholder bases. Yet, women remain under-represented at more senior levels of most organizations, such as on boards of directors (Daily et al., 1999; Singh et al., 2008). One problem resulting from the lack of women on incubator boards is the risk that organization-wide decisions and actions are based on stereotypical gender roles (Ridgeway, 2001). When having a minority status, women are often pushed towards roles and tasks that are stereotypically feminine (Yoder, 1994). As a consequence, judgements and evaluations related to women entrepreneurs aspiring to become incubatees may suffer from such biases, which places potential female-led new incubator projects at a disadvantage compared to their male counterparts (Eagly and Carau, 2002). Having women on incubator boards may, therefore, send a positive signal to the surrounding community regarding gender equality. Female board members may also be more sensitive to gender stereotyping and call for the retention and advancement of women incubatees. Thus, incubators with female board members may be expected to more actively adopt initiatives that pay careful attention to the needs of women, and actively promote the incubator's existence and activities to potential women entrepreneurs. Thus, we hypothesize the following:

H3: Female representation on the board of directors of an incubator is positively associated with the likelihood that a woman champions a new incubator project.

Technological Sector of New Incubator Projects

Another factor that can be expected to influence the likelihood of incubator entrepreneurship among women is the prevailing gender norms related to the technological sector of the proposed new incubator project. Research has shown that different sectors have different gender role stereotypes that classify them as predominantly masculine or feminine (Miller and Budd, 1999). For example, the typical stereotype in the engineering field is masculine, while sectors that are more oriented to caring (such as nursing) tend to be seen as more feminine (Heilman, 1983). In the case of new incubator projects, the technological sector they represent can be classified in various ways. Typical sector classifications include: highly specialized technological sectors such as ICT, life sciences and clean-tech. Even if there is some cross-fertilization, each of these technological sectors is typically embedded in a specific set of underlying educational, disciplinary and professional structures that can frame its norms and cognitions. ICT work environments are, for example, seen as highly masculinized due to their association with technical expertise (Tapia and Kvasny, 2004) and women in the ICT industry are typically disfavoured and stereotyped into gendered roles (Crump et al., 2007). However, it has been argued that entrepreneurial firms in the life science industry are more favourably disposed to gender equality and, therefore, offer women richer opportunities for recognition and career advancement due to their flexible and highly networked structures (Smith-Doerr, 2004). Based on the available theoretical arguments and empirical findings, however, we believe it is too early to specify relationships beyond an expected gender bias in terms of the technological sector of the new incubator project. This leads us to the following hypothesis:

H4: There are technological sector biases that are likely to impact the likelihood that a woman champions a new incubator project.

DATA AND METHODS

Our Sample

The sample used in the study comes from a unique database administered by the Swedish government organization Innovationsbron. The database includes information on over 1400 venture projects operating in 19 Swedish incubators that are all part of a national incubator programme in Sweden. These incubators are, in turn, part of the larger Swedish business support system, which aims to accelerate the development of knowledge-intensive and growth-oriented companies. Data has been collected on the characteristics and performances of all venture projects in the incubators since 2005. For this study, we have analysed venture projects that made an entry into one of the incubators between 2006 and 2009. Our choice of time period was based on the availability of secondary data that could be used in the analysis. Our selection process resulted in a total of 793 venture projects that could be used in our analyses.

The Incubator Context and Business Support System in Sweden

Today there are about 50 incubators operating in Sweden. The first Swedish incubators were established in the 1970s and they followed the US incubator model of supporting university-employed academics to commercialize their research. The idea of having incubators as an integral part of the business support system in Sweden, however, was not developed until the mid- to late 1990s. This development resulted from an emerging view by political leaders that supporting entrepreneurship was important for societal development and economic growth.

The Swedish national incubator programme was started in 2003 by VINNOVA (the Swedish Agency for Innovation System) with the overall aim of generating high-technology and research-based start-ups with high growth potential. The main measures adopted to help achieve this goal were to co-finance the creation of incubators in close cooperation with universities and to increase the supply of early-stage finance for start-ups in the incubators. The responsibility for the programme was transferred from VINNOVA to Innovationsbron when this organization was founded in 2005. The number of incubators with financial support from the programme has increased from 13 in 2003 to 21 in 2010.

The Incubators in this Study

The database used in this study is restricted by confidentiality and two of the incubators in the programme do not allow researchers to access their data. Thus, the number of incubators that we were allowed to analyse was reduced from 21 to 19. Moreover, we are not allowed to reveal the names of the incubators. Given these restrictions, Table 2.1 provides an overall description of the 19 incubators included in this study.

As our sample consists of incubators, and venture projects within

Table 2.1 Descriptive overview of the incubators

Incubator	Starting year	Profile	Metropolitan area	Number of projects	Female-led projects (%)
A	2005	Technical	No	22	13.6
B	2005	Technical	No	26	15.4
C	1998	General	No	30	16.7
D	1999	Technical	Yes	26	0
E	1998	General	No	114	22.8
F	2001	Technical	Yes	52	17.3
G	1999	General	No	30	20.0
H	1995	General	Yes	16	18.8
I	2007	Medical	Yes	12	8.3
J	2004	Technical	Yes	24	12.5
K	2004	General	No	74	24.3
L	1996	Medical	Yes	30	26.7
M	2002	Technical	No	27	7.4
N	2004	Medical	Yes	36	22.2
O	2002	Technical	Yes	36	11.1
P	2006	General	Yes	40	20.0
Q	2005	General	No	63	20.6
R	2003	Medical	No	17	40.0
S	2003	General	No	118	17.8
Total				793	
Average					18.8

these incubators, our data has a multi-level structure. The 19 incubators included in this study started between 1995 and 2007, which results in a mean age of eight years at the time of this study. Seven of the incubators have a technical profile, four incubators have a medical profile, and the remaining eight incubators have a more general profile. About half the incubators are located close to a university in the major metropolitan areas of greater Stockholm, Gothenburg or Malmö/Lund, which each has a local labour market of about 1 million people or more. While the average number of venture projects in the incubators during the study period is 63, the dispersion in the sample is wide, ranging from a minimum of 12 to a maximum of 118 projects. The average share of female-led projects is 18.8 per cent and this ranges between 0 per cent and 40 per cent.

Variables

The criterion variable in this study is the gender of the person leading the new incubator project. The variable was measured on a binary scale based on information from the database. The variable was coded '1' if the project entering the incubator was led by a woman and '0' if it was led by a man. In addition, we have three variables related to our four hypotheses and four sets of predictor variables. The proportion of female-led start-ups in the region (hypothesis 1) was measured on a continuous scale using data from Statistics Sweden and the Swedish Agency for Economic and Regional Growth. A higher score on this scale indicates a higher proportion of female-led start-ups in the region. The proportion of female faculty in senior positions (hypothesis 2) was measured on a continuous scale. It was operationalized as the proportion of female faculty who had tenured positions, as lecturers or professors, at the university associated with the incubator at the time of the new entry into the incubator. Data for this variable was collected from yearly reports published by the Swedish National Agency for Higher Education. A higher score on this scale indicates a higher proportion of women in senior positions at the university. Female presence on the incubator board (hypothesis 3) was measured on a binary scale based on information collected from websites and through e-mails and telephone calls. The variable was coded '1' if the incubator had at least one female board member and '0' if it was governed only by men. Fourth, and finally, we measured the technological sector of the incubator project (hypothesis 4). This was based on whether the venture entering the incubator was primarily within the life sciences, ICT or clean-tech. Each dichotomous variable was coded '1' if the venture project matched the category and '0' if it did not. A fourth alternative with various miscellaneous industries served as the reference category.

While the criterion and predictor variables presented above represent the main theoretical focus of our study, we have also included some additional control variables due to their potential influence on the criterion variable. First, we control for the number of new start-ups per 1000 citizens in the region where the incubator is located. The rationale is that a local entrepreneurial culture (through examples and familiarity) may encourage individuals to start their own ventures. Second, we control for the size of the university where the incubator is located in terms of the total number of students. This variable influences the potential pool of both students and faculty members who may consider entrepreneurship as a viable career choice. This data was collected from the Swedish National Agency for Higher Education. The total number of students is highly correlated with the size of a university's research budget ($r = 65, p < 0.01$) and, thus, it also provides a reasonable proxy for the amount of academic research available for commercialization. Third, we control for the age of the incubator since organizations may institutionalize certain routines, practices and norms in response to their past experiences (Stinchombe,

1965), which may either promote or inhibit the rate of female academic entrepreneurs entering the incubator.

ANALYSIS

We used standard descriptive statistics to describe and summarize the data. A description of the variables used in the analysis is presented in Table 2.2. As our data include a multi-level structure together with a binary criterion variable we applied multi-level logistic regression. This statistical method has the advantage of allowing the variability attributable to each level to be determined and it includes random factors to account for the multiple structures. The data analysis was conducted using IBM SPSS Statistics Version 20.

Table 2.2   Characteristics of the sample at the project level

Variables	Range	n	%
Female-led project	Yes	149	18.8
(Criterion)	No	644	81.2
Proportion of female-led	Below 35%	77	9.7
start-ups in the region	35 to 40%	596	75.2
(Hypothesis 1)	Over 40%	120	15.1
No. of start-ups per 1000	Below 8 start-ups	388	48.9
inhabitants	8 to 10 start-ups	299	37.7
(Control)	Over 10 start-ups	106	13.4
Proportion of female faculty	Below 25%	153	19.3
(Hypothesis 2)	25 to 30%	400	50.4
	Over 30%	240	30.3
Size of university	Below 9 000 students	179	22.5
(Control)	9 000 to 15 000 students	324	40.9
	Over 15 000 students	290	36.6
Incubator leadership	Male-only board	119	15.0
(Hypothesis 3)	Female on board	674	85.0
Incubator age	Below 6 years	277	34.9
(Control)	6 to 10 years	384	48.4
	Over 10 years	132	16.7
Technological sector of project	ICT	214	27.0
(Hypothesis 4)	Life science	77	9.7
	Clean tech	223	28.1
	Other	279	35.2

Table 2.3 Multiple regression model for factors associated with female-led incubator projects

Variables	OR	95% CI	Prob
Female faculty (H2)	3.424	0.44–6.404	0.024
Female on board (H3)	0.618	0.029–1.207	0.040
Technological sector of project (H4)			
– ICT	0.524	0.054–0.994	0.029
– Clean Tech	−0.832	−1373–0.290	0.003

Note: OR = odds ratio; CI = confidence interval.

We started the analysis with a model that included all available explanatory variables. Thereafter, we selected variables based on the Akaike Corrected Information Criterion (ACIC) and in the final model a smaller number of predictive variables remained. The results are illustrated in Table 2.3. Only significant factors in the final model are presented, together with odds ratios (OR) and confidence intervals (CI).

As shown in Table 2.3, and as predicted in hypothesis 2, the final model found a positive and significant association between the proportion of female faculty in senior positions at the associated university and the likelihood that a female champions a new incubator project ($p < 0.05$). Consistent with hypothesis 3, we found that the presence of a female board member on the incubator increased the likelihood of a female-led new incubator project ($p < 0.05$). Finally, in support of hypothesis 4, we found a gender bias at play in terms of the technological sector of the new incubator project. Here we found that women are more likely to champion a new incubator project in ICT ($p < 0.01$) while they are less likely to champion a new incubator project in the life sciences ($p < 0.05$). In summary, three of our four initial hypotheses were supported. On the other hand, our findings suggest that neither the proportion of female-led start-ups in the region (hypothesis 1), nor any of our three control variables, are significantly associated with the likelihood of a new female-led incubator project.

DISCUSSION

Prior research on academic entrepreneurship has argued for the need to take a more systemic approach to better understand the creation of new firms within an academic context (Kumaraswamy et al., 2008). Moreover, studies of women's academic entrepreneurship have emphasized gender as a form of social structure that impacts the norm-setting masculinization of entrepreneurship in the higher educational system which, in turn, influences the entrepreneurial career choice of women. Following these insights, we created a multi-level research model to predict how institutional factors in the entrepreneurial system surrounding universities impact upon women's entry into academic entrepreneurship by championing an incubator project.

Our findings suggest that women's engagement in academic entrepreneurship can be related to a number of factors operating at multiple levels in and around incubators. In line with our hypotheses, we find systematic differences in the proportion of female-led incubator projects depending on characteristics related to: the proportion of female faculty in senior positions at the associated university; the presence of women on incubator boards; and the technological sector of the project itself. In summary, our findings largely support the notion that university-based entrepreneurship ecosystems can be seen as embedded in gendered structures where socially and culturally constructed roles and relationships between men and women create imbalances in their prospective career opportunities. Although previous studies have observed a peer effect from colleagues and friends in research commercialization (e.g., Louis et al., 1989), the explicit recognition of normative and cognitive influences related to gender stereotypes has not been highlighted with respect to female academic entrepreneurship.

IMPLICATIONS

The need to increase the proportion of female academic entrepreneurs is being increasingly emphasized in policy debates (Granat Thorslund and Danilda, 2011). Our findings suggest specific areas where policymakers can focus their efforts in order to reduce gender imbalances operating at multiple levels. We find that a higher proportion of female faculty in senior positions at the university associated with the incubator increased the likelihood that a woman will champion a new incubator project. Hence, there is a need to continue to support the development of gender equality in universities by increasing the number of women in tenured positions. Otherwise the relatively low proportion of female faculty members in senior positions at universities may continue to reproduce gendered processes and relations that can have a negative impact on the number of new female-led incubator projects.

Further, our results suggest that the presence of female members on incubator boards increases the likelihood of female-led incubator projects. This suggests a need to emphasize the recruitment of female board members to stimulate the subsequent entry of new female-led projects at the incubator level. Finally, we also find gendered norms at play in relation to the technological sectors in which male- and female-led new projects are situated. Even if the attention to gendered norms has been acknowledged in previous research on work settings (Heilmann, 1983; Miller and Budd, 1999), this reflection has not spilled over, to any large extent, to studies of academic entrepreneurship. Instead, technological sectors have been treated largely as a 'gender-neutral' concept used to classify the specific technology that the venture project under study belongs to. However, it can be argued that it is particularly important to emphasize the connection between technology and gender in the context of academic entrepreneurship.

It is our belief that attention to these issues has the potential to promote equality between men and women in business support systems that ultimately can increase the participation of women in academic entrepreneurship. However, we especially want to emphasize the need to initiate immediate action at the incubator level. Organizational development can largely be seen as an experiential process (Cyert and March, 1963) where adaption, through learning and experimentation, is made incrementally in response to feedback from the surrounding environment. Incubators that take systematic action to increase their share of female-led incubator projects can, in this respect, be expected to be more likely to develop and organize their organization in a way that attracts new women entrants. When only men are practising entrepreneurship in a certain localized context there is the risk that entrepreneurship is seen as a typically male practice (Lewis, 2006), which may marginalize and potentially exclude women. However, incubators will become better at avoiding stereotypical notions of entrepreneurship as a typically male practice when they gain experience in dealing with women incubatees. Such actions involve using gender-neutral expressions in policy documents and promotion material, engaging successful businesswomen as mentors and advisors, and inviting female entrepreneurs to present pep talks and seminars. It is only possible to break the institutionalization of gendered norms in the practices, systems and policies of incubators by direct action, and we therefore encourage policymakers and practitioners to recognize the various multiple levels on which these problems occur.

LIMITATIONS AND SUGGESTIONS FOR FUTURE RESEARCH

In designing this study we employed a highly systemic approach by examining various institutional (multi-level) factors associated with the likelihood that women will engage in the commercialization of university science by championing an incubator project. However, we are aware that we have de-emphasized the potential role of agency in the entrepreneurial process (Heugens and Lander, 2009). Therefore, future studies could overcome this limitation by integrating both institutional pressures and individual agency in their research designs. Another potential limitation of our study is that the majority of incubators in the national incubator programme have a particular focus on supporting high-technology and research-based start-ups with high growth potential. Although this context is highly relevant for studies of academic entrepreneurship among women, it also creates a potential bias, as it excludes incubators that focus on alternative industries such as art and design. Future studies should consider whether this potential bias might have any effect in explaining the likelihood of a woman engaging in the commercialization of university science by entering an incubator.

Finally, we would like to acknowledge that our study focused on a limited set of variables associated with the entrepreneurship ecosystem surrounding incubators. Future studies could, therefore, expand on the variables examined. For example, it seems reasonable to argue that there may be a link between the proportion of female students engaging in entrepreneurship courses at the associated university and the likelihood of a new female-led project entering the incubator. Similarly, it could be argued that the way an incubator is promoted (for example, on web pages and in other communication materials) could be associated with the number of women that are attracted to the incubator. We thus welcome approaches and research designs that include these issues in future efforts to examine and better understand gender issues in academic entrepreneurship.

ACKNOWLEDGEMENTS

The authors are grateful for the financial support provided by VINNOVA that made this study possible. The authors are also grateful to Innovationsbron for granting confidential access to the incubator database in our study. Finally we want to express our sincere thanks to Karl Wennberg for his valuable comments and feedback in the course of developing this work.

REFERENCES

Armington, C. and Acs, Z. (2002), The determinants of regional variation in new firm variation. *Regional Studies*, 36 (1), 33–45.

Audretsch, D.B. and Fritsch, M. (1994), The geography of firm births in Germany. *Regional Studies*, 28 (4), 359–365.
Baughn, C.C., Chua, B.L. and Neupert, K.E. (2006), The normative context for women's participation in entrepreneurship: a multicountry study. *Entrepreneurship Theory and Practice*, 30 (5), 687–708.
Bergek, A. and Norrman, C. (2008), Incubator best practice: a framework. *Technovation*, 28 (1), 20–28.
Bird, B. and Brush, C.G. (2002), A gendered perspective on organizational creation. *Entrepreneurship Theory and Practice*, 26 (3), 41–65.
Bygrave, D. (1995), Theory building in the entrepreneurship paradigm. In Bull, I., Thomas, H. and Willard, G. (eds), *Entrepreneurship Perspectives on Theory Building*, Oxford: Elsevier, pp. 129–158.
Crump, B.J., Logan, K.A. and McIlroy, A. (2007), Does gender still matter? A study of the views of women in ICT industry in New Zealand. *Gender, Work and Organization*, 14 (4), 349–370.
Cyert, R.M. and March, J.G. (1963), *A Behavioral Theory of the Firm*, Englewood Cliffs, NJ: Prentice-Hall.
Daily, C.M., Certo, S.T. and Dalton, D.R. (1999), A decade of corporate women: some progress in the boardroom, none in the executive suit. *Strategic Management Journal*, 20 (1), 93–99.
De Carolis, D.M. and Saparito, P. (2006), Social capital, cognition and entrepreneurial opportunities: a theoretical framework. *Entrepreneurship Theory and Practice*, 30 (1), 41–56.
DiMaggio, P. and Powell, W. (1983), The iron cage revisited: institutional isomorphism and collective rationality in organizational fields. *American Sociological Review*, 48 (2), 147–160.
DiMaggio, P. and Powell, W. (1991), *The New Institutionalism in Organizational Analysis*, Chicago, IL: University of Chicago Press.
Ding, W. and Choi, E. (2008), Divergent paths to commercial science: a comparison of scientists' founding and advising activities. *Research Policy*, 40 (1), 69–80.
Eagly, A. and Carau, S.J. (2002), Role congruity theory of prejudice towards female leaders. *Psychological Review*, 109 (3), 573–598.
Eccles, J.S. (1994), Understanding women's educational and occupational choices: applying the Eccles et al. model of achievement-related choices. *Psychology of Women Quarterly*, 18 (4), 585–609.
Fältholm, Y., Abrahamsson, L. and Källhammer, E. (2010), Academic entrepreneurship – gendered discourses and ghettos. *Journal of Technology Management and Innovation*, 5 (1), 51–63.
Fetters, M.L., Greene, P.G., Rice, M.P. and Butler, J.S. (2010), *The Development of University-Based Entrepreneurship Ecosystems: Global Practices*, Cheltenham, UK and Northampton, MA, USA: Edward Elgar.
Gabrielsson, J., Politis, D. and Tell, J. (2012), University professors and early stage research commercialization: an empirical test of the knowledge corridor theory. *International Journal of Technology Transfer and Commercialization*, 11 (2–4), 213–233.
Gibson, D. (2004), Role-models in career development: new directions for theory and research. *Journal of Vocational Behavior*, 65 (1), 134–156.
Granat Thorslund, J. and Danilda, I. (2011), Innovation and gender. Report from VINNOVA, Tillväxtverket and Innovation Norway.
Gupta, V.K, Turban, D.B., Wasti, S.A. and Sikdar, A. (2009), The role of gender

stereotypes in perceptions of entrepreneurs and intentions to become an entrepreneur. *Entrepreneurship Theory and Practice*, 27 (1), 397–417.

Hackett, S.M. and.Dilts, D.M. (2004), A systematic review of business incubation research. *Journal of Technology Transfer*, 29 (1), 55–82.

Heilman, M.E. (1983), Sex bias in work settings: the lack of fit model. In Staw, B. and Cummings, L. (eds), *Research in Organizational Behaviour, Volume 5*, Greenwich, CT: JAI, pp. 269–298.

Heugens, P. and Lander, M.W. (2009), Structure! Agency! (And other quarrels): meta-analyzing institutional theories of organization. *Academy of Management Journal*, 52 (1), 61–85.

Higgins, M.C. and Kram, K.E. (2001), Reconceptualizing mentoring at work: a developmental network perspective. *Academy of Management Review*, 26 (2), 264–288.

Ibarra, H. (1993), Personal networks of women and minorities in management: a conceptual framework. *Academy of Management Review*, 18 (1), 56–87.

Keeble, D. and Walker, S. (1994), New firms, small firms and dead firms: spatial patterns and determinants in the United Kingdom. *Regional Studies*, 28 (4), 411–427.

Kumaraswamy, A., Maggitti, P., Zimmerman, M. and Wadhams, T. (2008), A systems approach to entrepreneurship: determinants of successful technology transfer (summary). *Frontiers of Entrepreneurship Research*, 28 (16), available at http://digitalknowledge.babson.edu/fer/vol28/iss16/5.

Lewis, P. (2006), The quest for invisibility: female entrepreneurs and the masculine norm of entrepreneurship. *Gender, Work and Organization*, 13 (5), 453–469.

Lindholm Dahlstrand, Å. and Klofsten, M. (2002), Growth and innovation support in Swedish science parks and incubators. In Oakey, R., During, W. and Kauser, S. (eds), *New Technology-Based Firms in the New Millennium*, Oxford: Pergamon, Elsevier Science, pp. 31–46.

Lindholm Dahlstrand, Å. and Politis, D. (2013), Women business ventures in Swedish university incubators. *International Journal of Gender and Entrepreneurship*, 5 (1), 78–96.

Louis, K.S., Blumenthal, B., Gluck, M.E. and Soto, M.A. (1989), Entrepreneurs in academe: an exploration of behaviors among life scientists. *Administrative Science Quarterly*, 34 (1), 110–132.

Meyer, J.W. and Rowan, B. (1977), Institutionalized organizations: formal structure as myth and ceremony. *American Journal of Sociology*, 83 (2), 340–363.

Miller, L. and Budd, J. (1999), The development of occupational sex-role stereotypes, occupational preferences and academic subject preferences in children at ages 8, 12 and 16. *Educational Psychology*, 19 (1), 17–35.

Mueller, S.L. and Dato-On, M.C. (2008), Gender-role orientation as a determinant of entrepreneurial self-efficacy. *Journal of Developmental Entrepreneurship*, 13 (1), 3–20.

Murray, F. and Graham, L. (2007), Buying science and selling science: gender differences in the market for commercial science. *Industrial and Corporate Change*, 16 (4), 657–689.

Noordenbos, G. (2002), Women in academics of sciences: from exclusion to exception. *Women's Studies International Forum*, 25 (1), 127–137.

Podolny, J.M. and Baron, J.N. (1997), Resources and relationships: social networks and mobility in the workplace. *American Sociological Review*, 62 (5), 673–693.

Politis, D., Winborg, J. and Lindholm Dahlstrand, Å. (2012), Exploring the resource logic of student entrepreneurs. *International Small Business Journal*, 30 (6), 659–683.

Reynolds, P.D., Storey, D.J. and Westhead, P. (1994), Cross-national comparisons of the variation in new firm formation rates. *Regional Studies*, 28 (4), 443–456.

Ridgeway, C. (2001), Gender, status and leadership. *Journal of Social Issues*, 57 (4), 637–655.

Rosa, P. and Dawson, A. (2006), Gender and the commercialization of university science: academic founders of spinout companies. *Entrepreneurship and Regional Development*, 18 (4), 341–366.

Rothaermel, F.T., Agung, S.D. and Jiang, L. (2007), University entrepreneurship: a taxonomy of the literature. *Industrial and Corporate Change*, 16 (4), 691–791.

Singh, V., Terjesen, S. and Vinnicombe, S. (2008), Newly appointed directors in the boardroom: how do women and men differ? *European Management Journal*, 26 (1), 48–58.

Smith-Doerr, L. (2004), *Women's Work. Gender Equality vs. Hierarchy in the Life Sciences*, Boulder, CO: Lynne Rienner Publishers.

Stinchombe, A. (1965), Social structure and organizations. In March, J.G. (ed.), *Handbook of Organizations*, Chicago, IL: Rand McNally, pp. 142–193.

Tan, J. (2008), Breaking the 'Bamboo Curtain' and the 'Glass Ceiling': the experience of women entrepreneurs in high-tech industries in an emerging market. *Journal of Business Ethics*, 80 (3), 547–564.

Tapia, A. and Kvasny, L. (2004), Recruitment is never enough: retention of women and minorities in the workplace. Proceedings of the 2004 SIGMIS Conference on Computer Personnel Research: Careers, Culture, and Ethics in a Networked Environment, pp. 84–91.

Verheul, I., van Stel, A. and Thurik, R. (2006), Explaining female and male entrepreneurship at the country level. *Entrepreneurship and Regional Development*, 18 (2), 151–183.

Yoder, J.D. (1994), Looking beyond numbers: the effects of gender status, job prestige, and occupational gender-typing on tokenism processes. *Social Psychology Quarterly*, 57 (2), 150–159.

3. Gender congruency theory, experience of discrimination and access to finance

Natalie Sappleton

INTRODUCTION

Since the 1970s, there has been a massive upsurge in business ownership among women. In the United States, women now own around 28 per cent of all privately held, non-agricultural businesses (Center for Women's Business Research, 2009). In 2008, American women started over 400 new enterprises a day – twice the rate of other groups (that is, male-owned and jointly owned); their firms generated $1.9 trillion in sales and employed more than 13 million people (Center for Women's Business Research, 2009). According to the latest available data (US Census Bureau, 2011b), women own some 10.1 million businesses, representing more than a 25-fold increase since records began in 1972 (Center for Women's Business Research, 2009). Between 1985 and 2000, the number of female-owned sole proprietorships grew at a faster rate than their male-owned and jointly owned counterparts; their business receipts grew at more than twice the rate of male-owned sole proprietorships; and their profits increased at an average annual rate of 6.9 per cent, compared with a 3.9 per cent average annual growth rate for male-owned sole proprietorships (Lowrey, 2005).

In spite of this impressive record, women-owned businesses are overwhelmingly crowded into a narrow segment of the economy, particularly in retail and services. US Census Bureau statistics from 2007 (the latest available data) show that, at the two-digit industry classification,[1] women are over-represented in healthcare and social assistance, and educational services, and under-represented in construction and the primary sectors. Men are under-represented in the sectors in which women are most commonly found, but form a majority in most industries. As with occupational segregation, the level of segregation is even more extreme when six-digit industry classifications are considered. Using Statistics of Income data, Lowrey (2005) assessed the distribution of male- and female-owned sole traders across the business activities in which most small firms were engaged from the period 1985–2000.[2] Of the top ten activities, most were heavily sex-segregated. Carpentry and floor contractors and miscellaneous special trade contractors were heavily male-dominated, while beauty shops and child daycare were heavily female-dominated.

The self-employed work that many women do – cleaning homes, caring for children, mending clothes and so on – are effectively commercial replications of the unpaid work that women perform in the home (Sappleton, 2009). Typically, these businesses are smaller than those owned by men (Burke et al., 2002), are more likely to be organized as sole traders rather than as larger corporations (Coleman, 2002), occupy lower-status portions of the job market, cater to local rather than global markets (Bates, 2002), and are generally less profitable (Verheul et al., 2009), less sustainable, and have lower levels of growth and turnover than businesses in typically male sectors (Morris et al., 2006). The most lucrative industry segments – high-technology and construction – have yielded far less to the new invasion, effectively remaining male monopolies (Parker, 2010).

Given the differences in the size, performance and status of many women-owned firms, entrepreneurial segregation may undermine the progress that has been made in women's uptake of entrepreneurship. Indeed, there is evidence that entrepreneurial segregation contributes to inequality in similar ways to sex segregation in employment (Marlow et al., 2008). Women earn less than men in self-employment and business ownership, with segregation making a significant contribution to earnings disparities (Hundley, 2001; Lowrey, 2005; Budig, 2006; Lechmann and Schnabel, 2012). The industries in which women tend to be found have higher rates of firm turnover (Robb, 2002), and firms in sectors like manufacturing, construction and computer services have better chances of survival than those in the competitive retail and services industries (Brüderl and Rolf, 1992; Brüderl and Preisendorfer, 1998; Dahlqvist et al., 2000; Schmidt and Parker, 2003; Bird and Sapp, 2004). Indeed, the major industrial classification with the single greatest concentration of women-owned enterprises – personal services – is also the least profitable major industry subgroup in the US (US Census Bureau, 2011a).

Given the link between segregation and earnings differentials in self-employment, a valuable research question is: why has women's entry into business ownership in male-dominated sectors not kept pace with women's migration into entrepreneurship as a whole? Or, posed differently: when women decide to strike out on their own, why do they opt to establish themselves in the most stereotypically female business domains? There is surprisingly little empirical literature that has explicitly addressed this question. The purpose of this chapter, therefore, is to examine the role of two potential antecedents of entrepreneurial segregation: discrimination and access to finance. Specifically, it is conjectured that women are drawn into self-employment and business ownership in stereotypically female fields because they experience heightened levels of discrimination and lack access to financial support to establish themselves in male-dominated sectors.

There are two reasons for examining the role of financial access. First, a review of the literature suggests that women entering non-traditional sectors perceive less support from family, friends and financial and other institutions than women entering more traditional female sectors (Anna et al., 2000; McAdam and Marlow, 2010; Orser et al., 2011). In particular, women entering non-traditional sectors appear to suffer heightened levels of discrimination and are perceived as less credible business owners (Chesser, 1998; Coyle and Flannery, 2005; Verwey, 2005). Second, longitudinal analyses have shown that capital endowments at start-up are strongly associated with value of assets, number of employees and sales turnover many months or even years later (Carter and Rosa, 1998; Dahlqvist et al., 2000; Bird and Sapp, 2004; Alsos et al., 2005), and undercapitalization is said to be the greatest cause of business failure amongst small firms (Blake, 2006).

The rest of this chapter is organized as follows: the next section describes the theoretical framework guiding the study: gender role congruency theory. A review of the literature on gender, self-employment and business ownership, and financial access follows. The fourth section describes the methodology. After the findings are discussed, the chapter concludes with an appeal to scholars to account for gender segregation in business ownership in future analyses and discussions of research findings.

GENDER ROLE CONGRUENCY THEORY

Gender role congruency theory provides a model for understanding the relationship between the perceived fit between an individual and their occupational role, and ensuing social outcomes. Linton (1936) famously defined a 'role' as a performance: a cluster of expected behaviour patterns and obligations attached to a particular social status in which expectations are culturally and socially defined and individuals are pressured, rewarded and punished to adopt certain roles and to reject others. West and Zimmerman (1987) argued that gender is one such role, and individuals 'do' gender by acting in accordance with commonly accepted sex-appropriate behaviours. In articulating gender role congruency theory,

Nieva and Gutek (1980) argued that performing gender-typed tasks is one way in which the sexes meet these expectations. Trust and legitimacy arise between actors if stereotypically held inferences about the behaviour of each are empirically met. The punishment for violating the expected patterns of behaviour for a gender role is negative evaluation. Thus, where a task is male-typed, men receive more favourable evaluations than women. Where a task is female-typed, women are judged as more competent than men. As noted by Feldman-Summers et al. (1980, p. 312):

> One might expect a woman who expressed an opinion about childcare facilities to be seen as more knowledgeable about that issue than a man. If the woman were seen as more knowledgeable than the man, she is likely to be seen as more credible and consequently, should be able to exert greater influence on the audience than her male counterpart.

To support gender role congruency theory, Nieva and Gutek (1980) presented evidence that both men and women suffer when applying for sex-incongruent jobs, and that studies showing that men are favoured over women in certain jobs or tasks all tended to use male-typed situations (for example, manager, scientist, professor). In fact, the theory is often articulated in relation to occupation because, like sex, it is one of the most basic levels of human categorization ('What do you do?' is often one of the first questions newly introduced people ask each other), and since occupation and sex are generally correlated, they tend to be used together in the development of descriptive and prescriptive stereotypes. Because individuals have many roles (gender, race, family status and so on), only the role that is most salient in a given situation is used to make inferences about their suitability for, and capabilities with respect to, a particular role. Where occupations are heavily sex-segregated, sex is the most readily observable and salient characteristic of the occupation, and is thus used to denote expectations about the behaviour of the incumbents of the occupation. In other words, incongruency makes the incumbent's sex more salient as a basis for evaluation. This is what Kram and Hampton (1998) refer to when they talk of women entrepreneurs being trapped in a 'visibility–vulnerability spiral'. When women are unusual and form a numerical minority in their role – 'an X in a series of Os' (Kanter, 1977) – they are subject to greater levels of visibility and, therefore, scrutiny:

> Gender specific expectations are likely to result in negative attributions of women leaders, particularly in highly prescriptive organizational cultures in which appropriate sex role behaviour is clearly – and narrowly – delineated. This combination of dynamics means that, in general, a woman's performance in a role is more likely to be negatively evaluated than a man's, especially

in male-dominated organizations where the evaluators are likely to be male. (Kram and Hampton, 1998, p. 216)

Evidence to support gender role congruency theory is abundant in non-business contexts. For instance, studies on debate and discussion have found that a match between sex of speaker and the sex-type of discussion topic increases the speaker's status and influence (Ellyson et al., 1992). In one empirical study, Baron (2001) showed that male scientists exhibited greater confidence and influence than women (who were also experts and established scholars in their – male-typed – field) during professional debates at conferences. In laboratory experiments using mixed-sex groups men display greater power and influence when discussing male-typed tasks, such as changing car oil (Dovidio et al., 1988), while women exhibit greater influence in the discussion of 'feminine' issues such as personal safety (Feldman-Summers et al., 1980). In addition, research has found that men exhibit greater influence when discussing sex-neutral topics because 'sex serves as a primary status cue when there is no other information indicating competence and power differences among interactants' (Dovidio et al., 1988, p. 582).

Gender role congruency theory has not been empirically tested in the business context, but there are some indications that women entrepreneurs in male-dominated contexts face unique challenges (Heilman and Chen, 2003). For example, Coyle and Flannery's (2005) interviews with women business owners in male-dominated industries offer some empirical support for this proposition. They report that women experienced a much higher incidence of discrimination and prejudice when dealing with clients than they did when dealing with employees. This was particularly true of male customers. When dealing with male clients, the women were afforded less power and status, and their credibility and expertise was questioned. Male clients expressed scepticism about the quality of their products and workmanship, or questioned their ability to take on a project because of family responsibilities; at other times they refused to recognize them as legitimate owners of their own firms, or treated their ventures as hobbies. Some women even encountered flirting, innuendos or inappropriate touching from male clients. The authors concluded that it was the women based in the most densely male-dominated fields that experienced the greater number of gender-related barriers. However, the authors did not interview women based in traditionally female industries, thus it is not possible to say definitively whether this level of discrimination is industry-related.

Bates (2002) argued that women-owned firms encounter buyer discrimination when they seek out markets beyond the (female) household clientele.[3] Analysing the US Census Bureau Characteristics of Business

Owners data, Bates found that even when variables representing capacity for serving business and government clients were statistically controlled, women-owned businesses were less likely to sell to other firms and government agencies than male-owned firms. Bates (2002, p. 321) concluded that these women experienced buyer discrimination (even in skilled services, construction and goods industries, the industries most easily able to penetrate business–government markets), and 'capacity notwithstanding, owner gender by itself is a major factor shaping market access'. Anecdotal evidence from Coolidge (1998) lends support to Bates's findings, and qualitative research indicates that restricted market access may be related to the shortage of women in large corporate and government procurement and contracting offices (Brush, 1997).

Another scenario in which role congruency has been tested is the supervisor–subordinate relationship. In a comprehensive meta-analysis of papers on gender and leader effectiveness, Eagly et al. (1995) concluded that men and women are perceived as equally effective leaders, unless the role itself is gendered. In male-dominated roles, evaluations of women are prejudiced because being able to do the job well is strongly associated with male characteristics. Experimental studies on the sex-role congruency of leaders in the workplace are few, and many are now outdated (e.g. Rosen and Jerdee, 1973). For example, in one experiment, male students worked under a supervisor who was male or female, and who possessed a congruent or incongruent job title (Cohen et al., 1978). Where supervisors were female and incongruent, reactions by subordinates were unfavourable. Another empirical study of men and women upper-level managers found that women experienced greater stress levels in male-typed sectors, with women in these sectors reporting high levels of perceived discrimination (Gardiner and Tiggemann, 1999). Similarly, a review by Eagly and Karau (2002) concludes that women in incongruent fields suffer from prejudice.

Applying the results of these studies of the entrepreneurial context, it is hypothesized that:

H1: Women business owners in male-dominated fields suffer greater levels of perceived discrimination than women business owners in female-dominated fields.

WOMEN, BUSINESS OWNERSHIP AND ACCESS TO FINANCE

Although there is little consensus in the literature, many researchers have presented copious evidence of perceived discrimination against women entrepreneurs by banks, venture capitalists and other financiers. This is an important observation because business activities rely heavily on financial resources; without them, transition is less likely to occur and, where it does occur, discontinuation is a real possibility (Sena et al., 2012). Longitudinal analyses have shown that capital endowments at start-up are strongly associated with asset values, number of employees, and sales turnover many months or even years later (Carter and Rosa, 1998; Dahlqvist et al., 2000; Bird and Sapp, 2004; Alsos et al., 2005), and undercapitalization is said to be the greatest cause of business failure amongst small firms (Blake, 2006).

Some studies have found that women are more likely to be turned down for a loan than men (Schwartz, 1976; Hisrich and O'Brien, 1981; Pellegrino and Reece, 1982; Loscocco et al., 1991; Carter and Cannon, 1992; Verheul and Thurik, 2001; Muravyev et al., 2009; Gicheva and Link, 2013) and, therefore, are forced to rely more heavily on friends and family, savings and/or bootstrapping as funding sources (Brophy, 1989; Johnson and Storey, 1993; McClelland et al., 2005). Where women are able to obtain bank loans, they are required to pledge personal guarantees (Carter and Cannon, 1992), or personal collateral (Riding and Swift, 1990) more often than men, and face more restrictive covenants, higher capital and credit enhancement requirements, tighter repayment terms and higher credit costs than their male counterparts[4] (Wu and Chua, 2012). One paper concluded that all-female teams (as opposed to sole traders) obtain lower levels of financial capital than male sole traders (Carter, 1997). Brush et al. (2002) discovered that just 2.4 per cent of venture capital investments made between 1957 and 1998 were in women-led businesses. Alsos et al. (2005) found statistically significant differences between the levels of financial capital that females and males were able to raise, even when funding perceptions and activity in applying for loans were controlled. Most of these studies have attributed women's difficulty in securing finance to the prejudiced attitudes held by financiers; lenders have been described as 'unsympathetic, and patronizing' (Goffee and Scase, 1985, p. 636), with a 'reputation for failing to give women's businesses the credibility they deserve' (Allen and Truman, 1992, p. 122).

Others have found no evidence of discrimination: Carter and Rosa's (1998) examination of 600 firms in hotel and catering, textiles and clothing manufacturing and business services revealed that more men than women owners admitted to being refused finance by an institution, and there were no sex patterns in the number of guarantees required by lenders. In an analysis of the financial fortunes of over 4000 Canadian firms, sex of owner was not a significant predictor of the level of total debt to total assets, the level of externally acquired debt or the likelihood of applying for, or being approved for, a bank loan (Coleman, 2002). In another Canadian study, Haines et al. (1999) found no sex differences in loan size, collateral requirements or interest rates after controlling for firm characteristics. In analyses of debt, lease and supplier financing, Orser et al. (2006) found no sex differences in turndown rates, and the differential rates at which women and men owners applied for debt, lease and supplier financing disappeared when size and sector of firm were controlled. Buttner and Rosen (1989) reported that loan officers were equally likely to approve male and female entrepreneurs' loan applications; they were also equally likely to make a counter-offer to owners of both sexes, and there was no significant difference in the value of the counter-offer.

Analysing data from the 1998 Survey of Small Business Finances, Mitchell and Pearce (2005) uncovered evidence of race discrimination but not sex discrimination by lenders. In the Australian context, Watson (2006) did find that female-headed small and medium-sized enterprises (SMEs) acquired less external funding than male-headed SMEs, but that sex differences were greater for older, rather than younger firms, undermining the notion that the differences are caused by systematic discrimination. Later research by Watson and colleagues also found no evidence that the finance gap between male and female owner operators is driven by supply-side factors (Watson et al., 2009).

What could possibly account for the inconsistencies in these findings? In assessing the risks and costs associated with investing in or extending a loan to a small business, financiers supposedly base their decisions on a set of generalized, objective criteria (Read, 1998; Haines et al., 1999). These criteria include the characteristics of the firm (such as sector, size and stage of business cycle) as well as characteristics of the owner (such as age, experience and assets). Given information asymmetries and time constraints (Haines et al., 1999 estimate that the average account manager in a Canadian bank has little more than one working day to spend with each client), decision-makers may rely on cultural stereotypes when making lending decisions. Examining the literature, it could be possible that the inconsistent findings have arisen because sector of firm is rarely controlled. Industry is important because 'gendered beliefs about the proper roles for women may discourage bankers from lending capital to women in nontraditional industries' (Godwin et al., 2005, pp. 30–31). Back in 1989, Brophy (1989, p. 73) argued that women's financing difficulties have:

> been due to attitudes held by representatives of male-dominated institutions – and often reinforced by businesswomen themselves – regarding the proper role of women in business. That role has been seen as staff or part-time employee or

business hobbyist, and – if an entrepreneur at all – one confined to businesses traditionally run by women: retail and service businesses for the most part.

A more recent quote from a venture capitalist that specializes in financing computing firms indicates that this view has not dissipated: 'I would never invest in a women-led business. Don't get me wrong, women are great for day care centers and have done a lot for customer service, but as an investor, you can't take a chance that they might leave to get married or pregnant' (cited in Brush et al., 2004, p. 72).

Among such a vast number of empirical studies, it is quite surprising that few researchers have explicitly examined whether there is an interaction between sex of finance seeker and gender-typicality of business venture. For example, Buttner and Rosen (1989) reported no evidence of sex discrimination in their study of loan decisions given by 51 commercial loan officers (40 of whom were male) and 69 undergraduates (34 males). Interestingly, the hypothetical business plan that the subjects were asked to evaluate was in a patently male-typed sector (toxic waste disposal) and the sex of the decision-maker was not examined as an intervening variable. Research from the early 1980s found that businesswomen in manufacturing and other male-dominated industries faced more difficulties in obtaining external finance than women in retailing and services (Hisrich and O'Brien, 1981). One-quarter of the women in Borooah et al.'s (1997, p. 86) study of Northern Irish business owners described their gender as hindering their access to external finance; many complained that banks 'took them seriously only when the chosen business was in "women's" area'. However, these results should be treated with caution because business ownership amongst women is somewhat uncustomary in conservative Northern Ireland, and the findings were based on a relatively low survey response rate of 22.4 per cent. Marlow and Strange (1994, p. 181) contended that 'bank managers are still reluctant to fund female ventures, particularly those which stray beyond traditional feminized occupations'.

It is also possible that women may face difficulties securing finance through the regular channels (that is, bank loans) because their business profile – typified by small, low-growth firms – is less favourable to investors (Shane and Cable, 2002). For instance, Greene et al. (2001) noted that most venture capital investments are made in industries that offer the best risk–reward ratios. In 2003, 90 per cent of venture capital dollars went to organizations in just nine industries: telecommunications; software; biotechnology; medical devices and equipment; semiconductors; media and entertainment; computers and peripherals; information technology (IT) services; and industrial energy. These are the least female-typed industries (Brush et al., 2004). So, 'the predominant industry choices of female entrepreneurs appear to be mismatched with the industry preferences of venture capitalists' (Greene et al., 2001, p. 68). Although the proportion of venture capital investments made in women-led firms appears to be growing, up until 1998 no investments had yet been made in women-led firms in construction, public administration, or finance, insurance and real estate (Greene et al., 2001).

In one simulated experiment, male and female undergraduates evaluated a hypothetical loan application and business plan (Buttner and Rosen, 1988). Sex of entrepreneur and sector of business were manipulated. The results indicated that male decision-makers were more supportive of women seeking finance for a traditionally female firm, and more supportive of males establishing a traditionally male company. Female decision-makers, on the other hand, supported entrepreneurs of both sexes regardless of the gender typicality of the sector. The authors concluded that non-traditional women business owners are disadvantaged when seeking start-up capital, and recommended that they seek out a female financier. This study was a laboratory experiment and undergraduates are not decision-makers. However, in interviews with male and female bankers, Blake (2006) found further evidence that certain sectors (such as construction) were seen as more appropriate for male owners while other sectors were deemed more suitable for women. She concluded that 'to succeed at securing a business loan in these environments women must . . . be starting a business that is perceived as needed within the local context, but which is not perceived to be something that "men do"' (Blake, 2006, p. 196). A male loan officer in that study cited the example of a female who began a cleaning firm with a loan from his bank. Despite the applicant's previous job in auto repair, the banker admitted that he would have had 'a greater degree of difficulty granting the loan to her if she had wanted to start a business as a mechanic' (Blake, 2006, p. 196). This example is important because it belies the notion commonly held by financiers that prior experience is an important prerequisite to venture success. Blake (2006) argues that because lenders see the firm and the owners as one and the same, loan officers consider the legitimacy of the individual concurrently with the legitimacy of the enterprise:

> Women's participation in entrepreneurship, especially in traditionally male-dominated sectors, is likely to challenge notions held by bank loan officers and others regarding definitions of who is an entrepreneur. Women are therefore subject to a kind of gendered legitimacy that men do not face as they start and run their businesses. When there is confusion regarding the legitimacy of a person for an activity that they are undertaking . . . doubt is likely to be cast over the legitimacy of the whole enterprise. (Blake, 2006, p. 188)

To summarize, there is a now a vast body of literature that has sought to examine whether women business owners experience discrimination in seeking out loans and other types of finance. These studies have had mixed and often contradictory results. However, these studies have rarely taken account of industry. Gender role congruency theory predicts that stereotypes about women's abilities in sex-typed fields will affect lenders' decisions about whether to extend finance to women entrepreneurs. External resource holders may capitulate to stereotypes in making the decision to invest time, capital or other resources in an organization, particularly if a firm has little by way of track record by which outsiders can evaluate its quality and potential. Thus, women that operate firms in traditionally male sectors may be viewed as illegitimate players, and denied the funding they seek. Therefore:

H2a: Women owners of firms in male-dominated sectors experience greater perceived discrimination from financiers than women owners of firms in female-dominated sectors.

H2b: Women owners of firms in male-dominated sectors experience greater difficulty in obtaining external finance than women owners of firms in female-dominated sectors.

METHOD

Data

The data for this study came from a wider study of women and men business owners in gender-typical and gender-atypical business sectors (Sappleton, 2013). Female and male business owners of 700 randomly selected firms in the construction (male-dominated), sound recording (male-dominated), childcare (female-dominated) and publishing (integrated) sectors in New York City were contacted three times by email with a request to complete an online survey by clicking a hyperlink. The business owners were identified through the Dun & Bradstreet's Selectory and ReferenceUSA databases. Email addresses were purchased from ReferenceUSA or located through an online search. The 57-item survey instrument was posted on the Bristol Online Surveys system, provided by the Institute for Learning and Technology at Bristol University, and ran for seven months. Of the 700 emails, 49 bounced back and five respondents actively refused to participate. Completed and usable questionnaires were submitted by the owners of 255 businesses, equivalent to a response rate of 38.1 per cent.

The analysis presented below is restricted to 87 women-owned firms, 56 in male-dominated industries (sound recording and engineering, and construction) and 31 in the female-dominated childcare industry. Descriptive characteristics for the sample are presented in Table 3.1.

Table 3.1 Descriptive data

	Female-dominated sector (n = 31)	Male-dominated sectors (n = 56)
Mean age (years)	43.0	42.8
Ethnicity (%):		
Asian/Asian-American	6.5	21.4
Middle Eastern	12.9	0
Black/African-American	6.5	10.7
White/Caucasian	71.0	53.6
Hispanic/Latino	3.2	3.6
Other ethnicities*	0	10.7
Run a firm before (%)	54.8	64.3
With degree or above (%)	83.3	64.3
Mean hours of work	45.1	47.7
Married or cohabiting (%)	78.6	57.1
With children** (%)	60.7	28.6
Legal status (%):		
Sole trader	22.6	10.7
Partnership	0	3.6
LLC	22.6	10.7
Corp	54.8	75.0
Stage in life-cycle (%):		
New start-up	0	3.6
Young	19.4	32.1
Well established	80.6	64.3
Ownership (%):		
Set up firm	71.0	57.1
Acquired firm	29.0	42.9
Growth expectations (%):		
Expand	32.3	50.0
Stay the same	67.7	46.4
Get smaller	0	3.6
Has employees (%)	83.9	64.3
Mean no. of employees	7.10	17.89
Mean firm age (months)	134.81	128.54

Note: * Includes Indian, Native American, and 'Other' categories; ** Under 18 and living at home.

Measures

Sex-domination of sector
The samples of women business owners in the construction and sound recording sectors were pooled and coded as male-dominated '1'. The sample of women business owners in the childcare industry was coded as female-dominated '2'.

Discrimination
Respondents were asked, 'Thinking just about your commercial relationships, have you or your business ever experienced discrimination because of your gender? Please indicate below all sources of this treatment.' The six possible sources were: customers and clients, staff, colleagues, suppliers, financial institutions, and other. If a respondent perceived discrimination, this was coded as '1'; no perceived discrimination was coded as '0'.

Acquisition of finance
Respondents were asked, 'Can you think of anyone who has provided this firm with a loan, investment funds or other type of finance?' After answering this question, respondents were asked whether: they had received this resource from a man or a woman; they were unsuccessful in their search for finance; or this was a resource they did not require (not applicable). They were also asked to indicate their relationship to the person providing the resource from a number of choices (spouse or partner, family member, friend, employees, client or customer, supplier, accountant, bank manager or other consultant, business organization member, other business owner – same industry, other business owner – different industry, or other), and how well they knew the provider of the resource on a five-point Likert scale.

In addition to these main outcome measures, data was requested on the respondent's age, marital status, ethnicity and sexual orientation. In order to ascertain firm size, respondents were asked whether they employed others and, if so, the number of employees. To gauge firm maturity, respondents were asked to indicate the age of the firm in months, and their subjective view of the firm's stage in the business cycle (the categories available were 'planning stage', 'new', 'young' or 'well-established'). However, no respondents selected the 'planning stage' and, for purposes of analysis, the 'new' and 'young' categories were recoded as one). Two measures of human capital are also included in the analysis: holding a degree (0 = no degree, 1 = Bachelor's degree or above), and prior experience running a firm (0 = no, 1 = yes).

Method of Analysis

The data are first analysed descriptively, exploring differences between women in the female- and male-dominated sectors on demographic and firm-level characteristics. Pearson chi-square is used to test for differences in discrimination and acquisition of finance between the subsamples.

FINDINGS

Descriptive Data

The descriptive data is reported in Table 3.1. There are some interesting differences between women business owners in the female- and male-dominated sectors. Although the samples are similar in terms of age, a far greater proportion of women in the female-dominated sector (78.6 per cent) are married, or cohabiting, compared to women in the male-dominated sector (57.1 per cent). While the full sample is diverse in terms of ethnicity, a greater proportion of women in the male-dominated sectors are from ethnic minorities, while 71 per cent of the women in the female-dominated sector describe their ethnicity as White/Caucasian. More non-traditional women have previous experience running a firm, but more traditional women have a degree. The businesses of the women in the male-dominated sectors are younger, both in terms of age and stage in the business life-cycle, but these firms are also more likely to be organized as corporations and in general employ more staff.

Discrimination and Access to Finance

Discrimination

For each subsample, Table 3.2 reports the raw percentages of respondents that indicated they had experienced discrimination on the basis of their gender from each of the six sources listed (customers, staff, colleagues, suppliers, financial institutions and other). The raw data shows that women business owners in the male-dominated sectors experienced higher levels of discrimination from all six sources compared to women business owners in the female-dominated sectors. Therefore, hypothesis 1 is supported.

Within the male-dominated sectors 71.4 per cent of women owners reported experiencing discrimination from financiers, compared to 16.1 per cent of women owners in the female-dominated sector. Therefore, hypothesis 2a is supported.

Table 3.2 *Proportion reporting experience of discrimination, by source and sample*

	% saying 'Yes'					
	Customer	Staff	Colleagues	Suppliers	Financial institutions	Other
Female-dominated (n = 31)	16.1	0	3.2	3.2	16.1	0
Male-dominated (n = 56)	71.4	21.4	50.0	53.6	71.4	17.9
χ^2	24.44***	7.71**	19.65***	22.05***	24.44***	6.26**

Note: ** $p < 0.01$; *** $p < 0.001$

Acquisition of finance

A greater proportion (96.3 per cent) of owners in the female-dominated sector than women in the male-dominated sectors (69.2 per cent) said they had successfully managed to secure a loan or other form of investment from a network member,[5] and the difference is statistically significant ($\chi^2 = 7.71$, $p < 0.01$). Based on the odds ratio, the odds of a business owner successfully securing a loan or investment from a network member are 11.56 times higher if they were based in a female-dominated sector than if they were in a male-dominated sector. Therefore, hypothesis 2b is supported. It is perhaps worth noting, as a final point, that of the 36 non-traditional women that did receive financial support, 24 (66.7 per cent) received the finance from a spouse or partner, family member or friend, and 34 (94.4 per cent) received the finance from a man.

DISCUSSION

Why, given the increasing migration of women into business ownership, does entrepreneurial segregation persist? There are a number of possible causes shaping women's apparent preference for typically female sectors: sex differences in human capital investments; educational, occupational and technical expertise; personal career goals and objectives; and family responsibilities. There are also a number of other potential intervening variables that may encourage women and men to develop businesses in segregated areas of the economy. Two such variables (discrimination and access to finance) were the focus of this study, which differentiated between the experiences of women in female- and male-dominated sectors.

Women owners of childcare firms, a stereotypically female business sector, reported fewer incidents of discrimination by customers, suppliers, employees, colleagues, financial institutions and from other sources. Moreover, they were more than 11 times more successful in obtaining a loan or investment in their firm than women operating businesses in the male-dominated construction and sound recording industries.

It is possible, therefore, that the under-representation of women business owners in male-dominated sectors could – at least partially – be attributed to the discrimination they face and their inability to secure the finance they need. The capital requirements for business start-up differ by industry, with many female-typed firms requiring little by way of start-up and ongoing finance. Firms in manufacturing and high technology require high levels of initial capital to finance physical materials and facilities, and to cover initial losses because they are faced with long lead times in developing and bringing products to market. On the other hand, service-oriented firms have lower facilities, equipment and inventory requirements, and since production and consumption often coincide, costs can be recouped almost immediately. This means that it may be easier to start firms in the service industries using just bootstrapping strategies or personal savings (Read, 1998; Carter et al., 2003; Brush et al., 2004). Using longitudinal data from the 1984 Survey of Income and Program Participation, for example, Bates (1995) found empirical evidence that financial capital (measured by levels of household wealth) is relatively unimportant for self-employed entry into the skilled services, but predicts entry into the manufacturing and wholesale sectors. Lack of wealth was found to be less of a barrier to entry 'when the line of self-employment being entered generates very low levels of profits' (Bates, 1995, p. 1440).

Although Bates did not provide results disaggregated by gender, it could be surmised from this research that because of their lower earnings and levels of personal income (Blau et al., 2006), women are constrained to sectors that require limited initial capital endowments. Thus, for women, 'the choice of business can be seen in terms of high motivation to immediate independence tempered by economic rationality rather than a conscious desire to operate a "female-type" business' (Watkins and Watkins, 1984, p. 286).

As women comprise a growing proportion of business owners, the stereotype that women do not assume leadership of organizations may be weakening. Gender role congruency theory predicts that legitimacy is tied up with a 'fit' between the sex of an individual and the sex-type of the activity they are undertaking. The persistence of entrepreneurial segregation may mean that women undertaking male-typed entrepreneurship will be viewed as less legitimate than a woman undertaking female-typed entrepreneurship. The reaction of customers, financiers and others to gender role incongruence is likely to be discriminatory. As the results of the analysis above show, women owners of firms in typically male sectors report greater levels of discrimination than women owners of firms in sectors that are congruent with their sex.

Research suggests that an individual's non-conformance with the activities predominant among members of their own sex reduces their ability to acquire legitimacy. Hanson and Blake (2009) illustrate the differences between two distinct forms of legitimacy with the example of the family. Families can and do take many forms, but the model that is most recognized in Western society consists of a heterosexual couple and biological children: the nuclear family. Polygamous families do exist and, therefore, can be imagined, giving them cognitive legitimacy, but because polygamy is generally considered unacceptable, this family model lacks socio-political legitimacy. So, whether an institution is viewed as legitimate depends on the model that existing institutions follow. In the same way, the sex of a firm's leader could affect perceptions of legitimacy in industries where owner-operators have typically been of one sex. In Hanson and Blake's (2009, pp.138–9) words, because 'practices are performed by people who have a gender, class and ethnic identification, for example, these aspects of social identity become wrapped up in the process of the legitimization of a particular activity or practice'. Since stakeholders use legitimacy as a signal of merit, they may withhold resources from individuals they perceive as illegitimate. This explains why, for example, women job seekers receive tips about female-typed jobs but rarely about male-typed jobs (Hanson and Pratt, 1991; Huffman and Torres, 2002).

Much of the extant literature on women's entrepreneurship highlights the fact that the increased representation of women in entrepreneurial undertakings has not been matched by a reduction in discrimination against them. Sociologists have attributed discrimination against women entrepreneurs to the endurance of a 'think-manager-think-male mentality' (Schein, 2001; Gupta et al., 2009) and the representation of the concept of 'entrepreneur' as a masculine one (Bruni et al., 2004). The results presented here suggest that there may be differences in such experiences depending on the perceived 'fit' between the woman business owner and the gender-type of her firm and industry. Although business ownership remains male-dominated, in societies such as the US (where it is no longer unusual to see a woman in a leadership position) it is possible that the association between entrepreneurship and a generic masculine stereotype may have weakened (Powell et al., 2002). Labelling business ownership itself as a non-traditional activity for women now seems almost archaic given that women represent 40 per cent of US business owners. However, the significant levels of discrimination perceived by women owners in the non-female-dominated sector identified in this study lends credence to the suggestion that the general stereotype regarding women in business may be being replaced by more specific stereotypes regarding the type of business that men and women should own and operate.

The message from this explorative study, therefore, is that rather than focusing on two-group comparisons of sex differences, researchers in entrepreneurship should address within-category differences between groups of female and male business owners. The sex-as-a-variable approach that has been prevalent in entrepreneurship research may have served to mask the considerable differences between groups of women (and men) business owners. Previously, findings derived from undifferentiated samples have been extrapolated to the wider entrepreneurial population without misgivings. In particular, in examining female entrepreneurs, the 'dominant service sector characteristic often mask[s] the nature and achievement of women in high-growth and nontraditional areas such as finance, insurance and real estate, wholesale trade, manufacturing, transport' (Moore, 1999, p. 372). If, when conducting their analyses, researchers combine all types of women owners and all types of women-owned firms into one category and report the averages, the characteristics of women who own and operate firms in sectors that are not typical for their sex are masked. This tendency to treat women business owners as one homogeneous subset of the wider entrepreneurial population, and as one that differs from men business owners, may have distorted previous research findings. The conflicting findings in the literature on financial discrimination may be linked to such a singular approach. Future research on women entrepreneurs should be undertaken on an industrially differentiated basis; entrepreneurs should be recognized as a diverse and complex group of individuals with varied backgrounds, circumstances and world-views. Distinguishing business owners in this way is important because, as Mirchandani (1999, p. 225) notes:

> while there has been some reflection on the difference which the sex of business owner makes, this reflection has not been contextualized within theoretical understandings of the ways in which entrepreneurial work is situated within gendered processes which form, and are formed through, relationships between occupation, organizational structure and the sex of the worker.

NOTES

1. The North American Industry Classification System (NAICS) is a hierarchical schema consisting of two- to six-digit industry classifications. The number of industries ranges from 20 two-digit industries to 1175 six-digit industries. Most analyses take place on the two-digit

classification because this data is most commonly reported in Census Bureau statistics. However, as is the case with occupational segregation, segregation in business ownership becomes more extreme as the level of classification becomes more detailed (Anker, 1998).
2. During this time period, 51.9 per cent of female and 28.4 per cent of male sole proprietorships were found in just ten activities: carpentering and floor contractors; miscellaneous specialty trade contractors; door-to-door sales; real estate agents and brokers; beauty shops; miscellaneous personal services; janitorial and building-related services; other business services; child daycare; and consulting and research.
3. The 1994 Federal Acquisition Streamlining Act set a 5 per cent goal for government procurement for woman-owned businesses, but government departments are at liberty to determine strategies to meet this goal. For example, the US Air Force deployment of the 'Rule of One' – that at least one woman-owned enterprise is solicited for every competitive contract tender – increased woman-owned business participation in Air Force contracts by 25 per cent over two years (see DeLuca, 1997).
4. Until the passing of the Women's Business Ownership Act 1988, it was legal for banks to refuse to lend money to women entrepreneurs unless a man offered a co-signature.
5. These proportions exclude those respondents who did not actively seek finance.

REFERENCES

Allen, S. and Truman, C. (1992), 'Women, business and self-employment: a conceptual minefield', in S. Arber and N. Gilbert (eds), *Women and Working Lives: Divisions and Change*, New York: St Martin's Press, pp. 162–174.

Alsos, G., Isaksen, E. and Ljunggren, E. (2005), 'Access to new venture financing and subsequent business growth in men- and women-led ventures', Twenty-Fifth Annual Research Conference, Babson College, Wellesely, MA.

Anker, R. (1998), *Gender and Jobs: Sex Segregation of Occupations in the World*, Geneva: International Labour Office.

Anna, A.L., Chandler, G.N., Jansen, E. and Mero, N.P. (2000), 'Women business owners in traditional and non-traditional industries', *Journal of Business Venturing*, 15 (3), 279–303.

Baron, B. (2001), 'Arguing among scholars: female scientists and their shaping of expertise', in Baron, B. and Kotthoff, H. (eds), *Gender in Interaction: Perspectives on Femininity and Masculinity in Ethnography and Discourse*, Amsterdam: John Benjamins Publishing Company, pp. 211–246.

Bates, T. (1995), 'Self-employment entry across industry groups', *Journal of Business Venturing*, 10 (2), 143–156.

Bates, T. (2002), 'Restricted access to markets characterizes women-owned businesses', *Journal of Business Venturing*, 17 (4), 313–324.

Bird, S.R. and Sapp, S.G. (2004), 'Understanding the gender gap in small business success', *Gender and Society*, 18 (1), 5–28.

Blake, M.K. (2006), 'Gendered lending: gender, context and the rules of business lending', *Venture Capital*, 8 (2), 183–201.

Blau, F., Ferber, M.A. and Winkler, A.E. (2006), *The Economics of Women, Men and Work*, Upper Saddle River, NJ: Pearson Prentice Hall.

Borooah, V.K., Collins, G., Hart, M. and McNabb, A. (1997), 'Women and self-employment: an analysis of constraints and opportunities in Northern Ireland', in Deakins, D., Jennings, P. and Mason, C. (eds), *Small Firms: Entrepreneurship in the Nineties*, London: Paul Chapman Publishing, pp. 72–88.

Brophy, D.J. (1989), 'Financing women-owned entrepreneurial firms', in Hagan, O., Rivchun, C. and Donald, S. (eds), *Women-Owned Businesses*, New York: Praeger, pp. 55–75.

Brüderl, J. and Preisendorfer, P. (1998), 'Network support and success of newly founded businesses', *Small Business Economics*, 10 (2), 213–225.

Brüderl, J. and Rolf, P.Z. (1992), 'Survival chances of newly founded business organizations', *American Journal of Small Business*, 57 (2), 227–242.

Bruni, A., Gherardi, S. and Poggio, B. (2004), 'Entrepreneur-mentality, gender and the study of women entrepreneurs', *Journal of Organizational Management Change*, 17 (3), 256–268.

Brush, C. (1997), 'Women-owned businesses: obstacles and opportunities', *Journal of Developmental Entrepreneurship*, 2 (1), 1–24.

Brush, C., Carter, N.M., Gatewood, E., Greene, P.G. and Hart, M.M. (2004), *Clearing the Hurdles: Women Building High-Growth Businesses*, Upper Saddle River, NJ: Financial Times Prentice Hall.

Brush, C.G., Carter, N.M., Greene, P.G., Hart, M. and Gatewood, E. (2002), 'The role of social capital and gender in linking financial suppliers and entrepreneurial firms: a framework for future research', *Venture Capital*, 4 (4), 305–323.

Budig, M.J. (2006), 'Gender, self-employment, and earnings: the interlocking structures of family and professional status', *Gender and Society*, 20 (6), 725–753.

Burke, A.E., FitzRoy, F.R. and Nolan, M.A. (2002), 'Self-employment wealth and job creation: the roles of gender, non-pecuniary motivation and entrepreneurial ability', *Small Business Economics*, 19 (3), 255–270.

Buttner, E.H. and Rosen, B. (1988), *The Influence of Entrepreneur's Gender and Type of Business on Decisions to Provide Venture Capital*, Atlanta, GA: South Management Association.

Buttner, E.H. and Rosen, B. (1989), 'Funding new business ventures: are decision makers biased against women entrepreneurs?', *Journal of Business Venturing*, 4 (4), 249–261.

Carter, N. (1997), 'Entrepreneurial processes and outcomes: the influence of gender', in Reynolds, P.D. and White, S.B. (eds), *The Entrepreneurial Process: Economic Growth, Men, Women, and Minorities*, Westport, CT: Quorum, pp. 163–117.

Carter, N.M., Brush, C.G., Greene, P.G., Gatewood, E. and Hart, M.M. (2003), 'Women entrepreneurs who break through to equity financing: the influence of human, social and financial capital', *Venture Capital*, 5 (1), 1–28.

Carter, S. and Cannon, T. (1992), *Women as Entrepreneurs: A Study of Female Business Owners, their Motivations, Experiences and Strategies for Success*, London: Academic Press.

Carter, S. and Rosa, P. (1998), 'The financing of male- and female-owned businesses', *Entrepreneurship and Regional Development*, 10 (3), 225–241.

Center for Women's Business Research (2009), 'Key facts about women-owned businesses, 2008–09 update', McLean, VA: Center for Women's Business Research.

Chesser, M.L. (1998), 'Overcoming structures of inequality: a study of the personal networks of minority and female hi-tech business owners', PhD Thesis, Austin, TX: University of Texas at Austin.

Cohen, S.L., Bunker, K.A., Burton, A.L. and McManus, P.D. (1978), 'Reactions of male subordinates to the sex-role congruency of immediate supervision', *Sex Roles*, 4 (2), 297–311.

Coleman, S. (2002), 'Constraints faced by women small business owners: evidence from the data', *Journal of Developmental Entrepreneurship*, 7 (2), 151–173.
Coolidge, S.D. (1998), 'Ms. Boss', *Christian Science Monitor*, 90, 15–16.
Coyle, H.E. and Flannery, D.D. (2005), 'Gendered contexts of learning female entrepreneurs in male-dominated industries within the United States', Summer Institute of the National Center for Curriculum Transformation Resources on Women, Turkey.
Dahlqvist, J., Davidsson, P. and Wiklund, J. (2000), 'Initial conditions as predictors of new venture performance: a replication and extension of the Cooper et al. study', *Enterprise and Innovation Management Studies*, 1 (1), 1–17.
DeLuca, A.J. (1997), 'Women-owned business and access to markets', Proceedings of the OECD Conference on Women Entrepreneurs in SMEs: A Major Force in Innovation and Job Creation, Paris, 16–18 April.
Dovidio, J.F., Brown, C.E., Heltman, K., Ellyson, S.L. and Keating, C.F. (1988), 'Power displays between women and men in discussions of gender-linked tasks: a multichannel study', *Journal of Personality and Social Psychology*, 55 (4), 580–587.
Eagly, A.H. and Karau, S.J. (2002), 'Role congruity theory of prejudice toward female leaders', *Psychological Review*, 109 (3), 573–598.
Eagly, A.H., Karau, S. and Makhijani, M. (1995), 'Gender and the effectiveness of leaders: a meta-analysis', *Journal of Personality and Social Psychology*, 117 (1), 125–145.
Ellyson, S.L., Dovidio, J.F. and Brown, C.E. (1992), 'The look of power: gender differences and similarities in visual dominance behavior', in Ridgeway, C.L. (ed.), *Gender, Interaction and Inequality*, New York: Springer-Verlag, pp. 50–80.
Feldman-Summers, S., Montano, D.E., Kasprzyk, D. and Wagner, B. (1980), 'Influence attempts when competing views are gender-related: sex as credibility', *Psychology of Women Quarterly*, 5 (2), 311–320.
Gardiner, M. and Tiggemann, M. (1999), 'Gender differences in leadership style, job stress and mental health in male- and female-dominated industries', *Journal of Occupational and Organizational Psychology*, 72 (3), 301–315.
Gicheva, D. and Link, A.N. (2013), 'Leveraging entrepreneurship through private investments: does gender matter?', *Small Business Economics*, 40 (2), 199–210.
Godwin, L.N., Stevens, C.E. and Brenner, N.L. (2005), 'Forced to play by the rules? Theorizing how mixed-sex founding teams benefit women entrepreneurs in male-dominated contexts', *Entrepreneurship: Theory and Practice*, 30 (5), 623–642.
Goffee, R. and Scase, R. (1985), *Women in Charge: The Experiences of Female Entrepreneurs*, London: Allen & Unwin.
Greene, P.G., Brush, C.G., Hart, M.M. and Saparito, P. (2001), 'Patterns of venture capital funding: is gender a factor?', *Venture Capital*, 3 (1), 63–83.
Gupta, V.K., Turban, D.B., Wasti, S.A. and Sikdar, A. (2009), 'The role of gender stereotypes in perceptions of entrepreneurs and intentions to become an entrepreneur', *Entrepreneurship: Theory and Practice*, 33 (2), 397–417.
Haines, J.G.H., Orser, B.J. and Riding, A.L. (1999), 'Myths and realities: an empirical study of banks and the gender of small business clients', *Canadian Journal of Administrative Sciences*, 16 (4), 291–307.
Hanson, S. and Blake, M. (2009), 'Gender and entrepreneurial networks', *Regional Studies*, 43 (1), 135–149.

Hanson, S. and Pratt, G. (1991), 'Job search and the occupational segregation of women', *Annals of the Association of American Geographers*, 81 (2), 229–253.

Heilman, M.E. and Chen, J. (2003), 'Entrepreneurship as a solution: the allure of self-employment for women and minorities', *Human Resource Management Review*, 13 (2), 347–364.

Hisrich, R.D. and O'Brien, M. (1981), 'The woman entrepreneur from a business and sociological perspective', in Vesper, K. (ed.), *Frontiers of Entrepreneurship Research*, Wellesley, MA: Babson College, pp. 21–39.

Huffman, M. and Torres, L. (2002), 'It's not only "who you know!" that matters: gender, personal contacts, and job lead quality', *Gender and Society*, 16 (6), 793–813.

Hundley, G. (2001), 'Why women earn less than men in self-employment', *Journal of Labor Research*, 22 (4), 818–828.

Johnson, S. and Storey, D. (1993), 'Male and female entrepreneurs and their businesses: a comparative study', in Allen, S. and Truman, C. (eds), *Women in Business: Perspectives on Women Entrepreneurs*, London, Routledge, pp. 70–85.

Kanter, R.M. (1977), *Men and Women of the Corporation*, New York: Basic Books.

Kram, K.E. and Hampton, M.M. (1998), 'When women lead: the visibility–vulnerability spiral', in Klein, E., Gabelnick, F. and Herr, P. (eds), *The Psychodynamics of Leadership*, Madison, CT: Psychosocial Press, pp. 193–218.

Lechmann, D.S. and Schnabel, C. (2012), 'What explains the gender earnings gap in self-employment? A decomposition analysis with German data', IZA Discussion Paper No. 6435, Institute for the Study of Labor.

Linton, R. (1936), *The Study of Man*, New York: Appleton-Century.

Loscocco, K.A., Robinson, J., Hall, R.H. and Allen, J.K. (1991), 'Gender and small business success: an inquiry into women's relative disadvantage', *Social Forces*, 70 (1), 65–87.

Lowrey, Y. (2005), *US Sole Propriertorships: A Gender Comparison 1985–2000*, Washington, DC: Small Business Administration Office of Advocacy.

Marlow, S., Carter, S. and Shaw, E. (2008), 'Constructing female entrepreneurship policy in the UK: is the USA a relevant benchmark?', *Environment and Planning C: Government and Policy*, 26 (2), 335–351.

Marlow, S. and Strange, A. (1994), 'Female entrepreneur – success by whose standards?', in Tanton, M. (ed.), *Women in Management: A Developing Presence*, London: Routledge, pp. 172–184.

McAdam, M. and Marlow, S. (2010), '"All by myself": the female high-technology entrepreneur', in Brush, C., de Bruin, A., Gatewood, E.J. and Henry, C. (eds), *Women Entrepreneurs and the Global Environment for Growth*, Cheltenham, UK and Northampton, MA, USA: Edward Elgar, pp. 72–85.

McClelland, E., Swaill, J., Bell, J. and Ibbotson, P. (2005), 'Following the pathway of female entrepreneurs: a six country investigation', *International Journal of Entrepreneurial Behaviour and Research*, 11 (2), 84–107.

Mirchandani, K. (1999), 'Feminist insight on gendered work: new directions in research on women and entrepreneurship', *Gender, Work and Organization*, 6 (4), 224–36.

Mitchell, K. and Pearce, D.K. (2005), 'Availability of financing to small firms using the survey of small business finances', S.B. Advocacy. Washington, DC.

Moore, D.P. (1999), 'Women entrepreneurs: approaching a new millenium', in

Powell, G.N. (ed.), *Handbook of Gender and Work*, Thousand Oaks, CA: Sage, pp. 371–389.

Morris, M.H., Miyasaki, N.N., Watters, C.E. and Coombes, S.M. (2006), 'The dilemma of growth: understanding venture size choices of women entrepreneurs', *Journal of Small Business Management*, 44 (2), 221–244.

Muravyev, A., Talavera, O. and Schafer, D. (2009), 'Entrepreneurs' gender and financial constraints: evidence from international data', *Journal of Comparative Economics*, 37 (2), 270–286.

Nieva, V.F. and Gutek, B.A. (1980), 'Sex effects on evaluation', *Academy of Management Review*, 5 (2), 267–276.

Orser, B., Riding, A. and Stanley, J. (2011), 'Perceived career challenges and response strategies of women in the advanced technology sector', *Entrepreneurship and Regional Development*, 24 (1–2), 73–93.

Orser, B.J., Riding, A.L. and Manley, K. (2006), 'Women entrepreneurs and financial capital', *Entrepreneurship: Theory and Development*, 30 (5), 643–666.

Parker, B.J. (2010), 'A conceptual framework for developing the female entrepreneurship literature', *Journal of Research on Women and Gender*, 1 (2), 169–190.

Pellegrino, E.T. and Reece, B.L. (1982), 'Perceived formative and operational problems encountered by female entrepreneurs in retail and service firms', *Journal of Small Business Management*, 20 (2), 15–24.

Powell, G.N., Butterfield, D.A. and Parent, J.D. (2002), 'Gender and managerial stereotypes: have the times changed.' *Journal of Management*, 28 (2), 177–193.

Read, L. (1998), *The Financing of Small Business: A Comparative Study of Male and Female Business Owners*, London, UK and New York, USA: Routledge.

Riding, A.L. and Swift, C.S. (1990), 'Women business owners and terms of credit: some empirical findings of the Canadian experience', *Journal of Business Venturing*, 5 (5), 327–340.

Robb, A.M. (2002), 'Entrepreneurial performance by women and minorities: the case of new firms', *Journal of Developmental Entrepreneurship*, 7 (4), 384–397.

Rosen, B. and Jerdee, T.H. (1973), 'The influence of sex-role stereotypes on evaluations of male and female supervisory behavior', *Journal of Applied Psychology*, 57 (1), 44–48.

Sappleton, N. (2009), 'Women non-traditional entrepreneurs and social capital', *International Journal of Gender and Entrepreneurship*, 1 (3), 192–218.

Sappleton, N. (2013), 'When the "manny" is the boss. An exploratory study into discrimination and preferential treatment perceived by men childcare business owners', *Recherches Sociologiques et Anthropologiques*, 44 (2), 93–113.

Schein, V.E. (2001), 'A global look at psychological barriers to women's progress in management', *Journal of Social Issues*, 57 (4), 675–688.

Schmidt, R. and Parker, C. (2003), 'Diversity in independent retailing: barriers and benefits – the impact of gender', *International Journal of Retail and Distribution Management*, 31 (8), 428–439.

Schwartz, E.B. (1976), 'Entrepreneurship: a new female frontier', *Journal of Contemporary Business*, 5 (1), 47–76.

Sena, V., Scott, J. and Roper, S. (2012), 'Gender, borrowing patterns and self-employment: some evidence for England', *Small Business Economics*, 38 (4), 467–480.

Shane, S. and Cable, D. (2002), 'Network ties, reputation, and the financing of new ventures', *Management Science*, 48 (3), 364–381.

US Census Bureau (2011a), 'Economic census. All sectors 2007. Economy-wide statistics', Washington, DC: US Census Bureau.

US Census Bureau (2011b), 'Survey of business owners – women-owned firms: 2007. Summary of findings', Washington, DC: US Census Bureau.

Verheul, I., Caree, M. and Thurik, R. (2009), 'Allocation and productivity of time in new ventures of female and male entrepreneurs', *Small Business Economics*, 33 (3), 273–291.

Verheul, I. and Thurik, R. (2001), 'Start-up capital: "does gender matter?"', *Small Business Economics*, 16 (4), 329–345.

Verwey, I.V. (2005), 'A comparative analysis between South Africa and USA women entrepreneurs in construction', Pretoria: University of Pretoria.

Watkins, J.M. and Watkins, D.S. (1984), 'The female entrepreneur: her background and some determinants of business choice – some British data', *International Small Business Journal*, 2 (4), 21–31.

Watson, J. (2006), 'External funding and firm growth: comparing female and male-controlled SMEs', *Venture Capital: An International Journal of Entrepreneurial Finance*, 8 (1), 33–49.

Watson, J., Newby, R. and Mahuka, A. (2009), 'Gender and the SME "finance gap"', *International Journal of Gender and Entrepreneurship*, 1 (1), 42–56.

West, C. and Zimmerman, D.H. (1987), 'Doing gender', *Gender and Society*, 1 (2), 125–151.

Wu, Z. and Chua, J.H. (2012), 'Second-order gender effects: the case of US small business borrowing cost', *Entrepreneurship Theory and Practice*, 36 (3), 443–463.

4. Female entrepreneurship in rural Vietnam: an exploratory study
Cuc Nguyen, Howard Frederick and Huong Nguyen

INTRODUCTION

During the last few decades female entrepreneurship has been expanding in most parts of the world (Driga et al., 2009) and is considered one of the fastest-growing entrepreneurial populations worldwide (Brush et al., 2009). This development is seen as particularly important for low-income countries (Bushell, 2008). For example, both the Micro-Credit Summit in Washington in 1997 and the Global Microcredit Summit in Canada in 2006 emphasized the need to enable female entrepreneurs (and their families) to gain access to credit for self-employment and to other financial and business services as a means of lifting hundreds of millions of people out of extreme poverty (Bushell, 2008). Similarly, female entrepreneurship development is also a part of 'ongoing national efforts to alleviate poverty in developing countries in relation to the Millennium Development Goals' (Tambunan, 2009, p.27). In rural areas, the growing number of female new business founders is contributing to the utilization of an untapped source of productivity for the local economy (Anthopoulou, 2009) and to the development of new income sources on the farm (Bock, 2004). The aim of this chapter, therefore, is to attempt to find answers to two important questions:

1. What contextual facilitators support rural women engaging in entrepreneurial activities?
2. What contextual constraints exist that prevent or inhibit rural women from engaging in entrepreneurial activities?

As female entrepreneurship in rural regions is generally under-researched, and this is particularly true of rural Vietnam, we expect the results from this study to contribute to a better understanding of the environmental factors influencing entrepreneurial participation among rural women in Vietnam. It should also be noted that, unlike much of the prior research which has generally been survey-based (Brush et al., 2003), this study uses the ethnographic interview method. The study aims to develop a model of entrepreneurship that will be useful in enabling rural women in Vietnam (and South East Asia, more generally) to be successfully involved in entrepreneurial activities.

The chapter begins by providing the background to this research project, including a review of the existing literature concerning the importance of entrepreneurship, and female entrepreneurship in particular, to rural development, and some background to the economic context in Vietnam, particularly with respect to women in rural Vietnam. We then discuss a number of entrepreneurship frameworks that we believe are useful in understanding female entrepreneurship in rural Vietnam, and consider how these conceptual frameworks were used in the current study. Next we describe our research method and the results of analysing the responses from our in-depth interviews with six rural female microentrepreneurs and six rural female non-entrepreneurs. A discussion of our findings and their implications, together with the study's limitations, concludes the chapter.

RESEARCH BACKGROUND

The Importance of Entrepreneurship in Rural Development

The importance of rural entrepreneurship has been well recognized in developed countries and is considered a key tool for stimulating diversified and endogenous growth in rural development policy (OECD, 2006). In the United States, for example, Dabson (2001) argues that entrepreneurship is important for tackling deep-rooted economic problems in low-income communities and distressed regions within rural areas. Henderson (2002) notes that entrepreneurship facilitates the diversification of (and the synergies associated with) local services, and helps to retain local populations by creating local career alternatives. Henderson (2002) suggests that rural entrepreneurship increases local incomes and wealth, and helps to connect the community to the wider (global) economy. Macke and Markeley (2006) and Gladwin et al. (1989) emphasize the importance of rural entrepreneurship when they argue that entrepreneurial-based development can play an important part in revitalizing rural areas in the USA through its significant role in stimulating human development, rural vitality, civic entrepreneurship development and economic development policy priorities.

Further, Driga et al. (2009) argue that entrepreneurship contributes more to rural development than simply economic and employment growth. In rural Europe, for example, entrepreneurship is considered an important mechanism for overcoming barriers to the development of peripheral rural areas (Labrianidis, 2006) and a source of income to make the rural economies and societies of Central and Eastern European countries viable (Davis and Pearce, 2001). In developing nations, rural entrepreneurship accounts for around 25 per cent of full-time rural employment and 40 per cent of rural incomes. Thus, entrepreneurship obviously plays a crucial role in sustaining rural populations and offers an important economic alternative to the rural poor (Haggblade et al., 2002).

The Importance of Female Entrepreneurship in Rural Development

Female entrepreneurship is consistently viewed as beneficial to rural communities. It is seen as a potential vehicle for alleviating the relative hardship of women in rural areas and as a means of utilizing the untapped economic development potential of rural women (Anthopoulou, 2009; Driga et al., 2009). Furthermore, entrepreneurship is expected to bring women economic independence and, as such, is an important key to both the emancipation of women and national development (Chitsike, 2000). Recent research has drawn attention to the contribution of female entrepreneurs to economic development in developing countries; for example, a Malaysian study has found that women's entrepreneurship is increasingly being promoted as a way of creating growth and development (Franck, 2012). Interestingly, a study of six Arab countries (Weeks, 2009) found that women were operating across a range of business sectors and, in some cases, with employment levels ahead of most women-owned firms in Western Europe and North America. Furthermore, the study found that most of the women surveyed were trading internationally and were growth-oriented.

Vietnam's Economic Context

Vietnam is a densely populated developing country located in South East Asia with around 90 million people. After the introduction of the Đổi Mới (renovation) policy in 1986, Vietnam moved to implement the structural reforms needed to modernize its economy and to produce more competitive export-driven industries. Vietnam joined the World Trade Organization (WTO) in January 2007, and is part of the Trans-Pacific Partnership trade agreement created in 2010. In 2010, with a gross domestic product (GDP) (purchasing power parity) of US$276.6 billion, Vietnam was ranked 42nd in the world and, with a GDP per capita of US$3100 it was ranked 166th in the world (Central Intelligence Agency, 2011).

Vietnam's economy and its achievements are reviewed by Fan et al. (2004) through three time periods: 1975–1980 (reunified, with a centrally planned economy), 1980–1988 (modified planned economy) and subsequent to 1989 (economy in transition, striving for industrialization and international integration). In the first period, the Vietnamese economy experienced stagnation due to a number of problems, such as the improper government-administered supply of physical inputs and outputs, a lack of business autonomy and the absence of factor markets, highly regulated goods and services markets, an investment bias towards heavy industry, and having a passive financial system with a single government bank. The second period witnessed significant micro-economic reforms, such as the 'Three-Plan System' for state-owned enterprises; and the 'Contract System' for the agricultural sector. These breakthroughs in Vietnam's economic policies resulted in a high rate of economic growth and led to the country becoming food self-sufficient in 1985. The third period started with the adoption of a radical and comprehensive reform package aimed at stabilizing the economy, opening up the economy, enhancing freedom of choice for economic units and increasing competition. The significant achievements in this last period include the introduction of macroeconomic stabilization policies, enhanced private sector development, the reform of state-owned enterprises, and reforms in the agricultural, trade and investment, and banking sectors. During the 1990s Vietnam became one of the fastest-growing economies in the world, albeit from a very low base, with an average GDP growth rate of around 7 per cent per capita.

Rural Vietnam

Rural Vietnam is best seen in three contexts – agriculture, rural development and rural livelihoods – with each of these having both positive and negative indicators (Powell et al., 2011). With respect to agriculture, successful economic development over the past 20 years has facilitated the transition of Vietnam's economy from largely agriculture-based to more industry-based. Despite various challenges (such as market price fluctuations, natural disasters and epidemics) the production of agriculture, forestry and aquaculture has increased significantly in recent times. Statistics from the study by Powell et al. (2011) indicate that between 2000 and 2007 cereal production increased by 5.5 million tonnes, animal husbandry's annual production increased by 7–8 per cent, fish farming (catch capacity and productivity) doubled, deforestation reduced and the actual forest area increased by almost 40 per cent, and exported agricultural products grew by 16.8 per cent per year. The widespread application of new technology not only improved productivity but also maintained the sustainability of the entire agricultural sector.

In terms of rural development, Powell et al. (2011) note that investment in infrastructure in rural areas is continuing. For example, the improvement in irrigation and drainage capacity has increased, which has resulted in good conditions for agricultural production (while preventing natural disasters) and has contributed to an improvement in the livelihoods of rural residents. The networks providing electricity, schools, local markets, medical centres and telecommunication services now cover almost all rural areas. Statistically, the national electricity grid provides electricity to almost all communities and to 97 per cent of all households in the country. Almost 100 per cent of communities have primary schools, 91 per cent have high schools, and 88 per cent have kindergartens. Local markets are available in most communities. Ninety-nine per cent of communities have a medical clinic and 55.6 per cent have a pharmacy. All communities have telephone lines and 85 per cent have a postal service. Significantly, 70 per cent of households have clean water for domestic use. Many industrial zones, businesses and urbanized centres are also being established in rural areas.

Turning to rural livelihoods, Powell et al. (2011) note that rural people account for over 70 per cent of the total population in Vietnam, with 54 per cent of the rural population employed in agriculture, forestry or aquaculture. The number of agricultural, forestry and aquaculture co-operatives has increased to over 7000, providing farmers with irrigation, plant protection and electricity services. The average income of rural people has increased almost threefold in recent years, with the average household savings having doubled between 2001 and 2006, and the number of poor households having reduced from 35.6 per cent in 2002 to 18 per cent in 2007. Rural people have also gained more entitlements to medical treatment, and rural students are more able to participate in higher education through the provision of student loans at favourable interest rates. As a result, the level of education and professional skills in rural Vietnam is also improving.

Although Vietnam's agricultural sector has achieved good growth in recent times, Powell et al. (2011) point to a number of issues and difficulties that need addressing. First, crop production still dominates the sector's total production (57 per cent); the other subsectors are either developing slowly or are ineffectively managed. Second, an imbalance between production and environmental management has resulted in increased environmental pollution, and this improper exploitation of natural resources is threatening future development. Third, the total area available for agriculture is being reduced, the rural labour force continues to decline and the price of agricultural inputs continues to increase. Finally, the agriculture sector in Vietnam is particularly vulnerable to global climate change and natural disasters. For example, statistics from Germanwatch Climate Risk Index 2009 (Harmeling, 2008) indicate that Vietnam is one of the top ten countries most affected by extreme climatic events.

Powell et al. (2011) also note that development has not yet been built into Vietnam's strategic planning process and, as a result, the development of infrastructure has been slow and this, together with weak labour skills and inappropriate supporting policies, has made rural areas less attractive for investment. Income diversification activities are also limited, with the majority of rural households relying on agriculture. Similarly, social services (such as education, medical treatment and insurance), although available, are still poorly provided in rural areas and, consequently, rural residents face numerous problems. In summary, low incomes, low quality of social services (such as healthcare and education), a lack of access to markets and information, and environmental pollution are all contributing to a reduction in the welfare of the rural population in Vietnam, and are expanding the gap between rural and urban areas. Further, Hang (2008) argues that more practical efforts are required to address gender inequality issues in Vietnam because the gap between verbal commitments to gender equality and actual practice is sizable. It seems that, in Vietnam, the rate of female participation in power at all levels is much lower than that of men, and this is particularly true in rural areas.

The Livelihoods of Rural Women in Vietnam

The 2009 National Population Census (Central Population and Housing Census Steering Committee, 2010) indicated that women accounted for 54 per cent of the rural population in Vietnam. Similarly, the Vietnam Women Entrepreneurs Council (2007) reported that over 60 per cent of Vietnamese women worked in agriculture in 2002, and Hang (2008) found that 76 per cent of female workers in Vietnam were concentrated in agriculture, forestry and fish farming. The urbanization and rural mechanization process in Vietnam has created dramatic changes in rural areas, leading to changes in the livelihoods of rural women. The most significant of these changes has been the conversion of large amounts of farming land to industrial zones, tourism sites or new urban areas. This, in turn, has led to a significant increase in the rate of unemployment in rural Vietnam (Hoang, 2010). As a result, a growing number of males and a large proportion of the youth population have left their families to earn a living in urban areas or industrial zones. This trend in migration has exposed rural families and rural communities to substantial structural changes. It has resulted in 'feminised agriculture' (that is, women are in charge of almost all agricultural production), an 'aging rural sector' (that is, the majority of villagers are now middle-aged or elderly) and 'women household heads' (that is, the males have migrated to urban areas) (Hoang, 2010, Thanh et al., 2005).

According to the World Bank (2011), around 90 per cent of the poor in Vietnam live in rural areas, and the International Fund for Agricultural Development (IFAD, 2010) suggests that the poorest people in Vietnam include members of ethnic minority groups, residents in remote upland areas, residents in coastal areas with a poor natural resource base and prone to adverse climatic events, households headed by women, households with disabled members, landless people, and migrants. Further, Hoang (2010) found that rural women have higher rates of poverty than rural men and urban women.

POTENTIAL FRAMEWORKS FOR ANALYSING FEMALE ENTREPRENEURSHIP IN A RURAL SETTING

One of the dilemmas of novel research is to establish a framework, or lens, through which to view, and analyse, the phenomenon in question. Morris et al. (2001) wrote an excellent article on how to understand entrepreneurship through frameworks that could help organize the field of entrepreneurship in a systematic way. A framework provides a blueprint that converts abstraction into order, allows prioritization of variables (or issues) and helps to identify relationships. Below we review three frameworks that we feel potentially provide a useful conceptual basis for the examination of female entrepreneurship in rural Vietnam.

The Concept of 'Necessity' versus 'Opportunity' Entrepreneurship

The Global Entrepreneurship Monitor (GEM) framework presented in various GEM reports highlights the concept of 'necessity' versus 'opportunity' entrepreneurs. GEM refers to 'necessity entrepreneurs' as individuals who view entrepreneurship as the best option available but not necessarily their preferred option (Kelley et al., 2012). Such individuals are considered to have been 'pushed' into entrepreneurship. By way of contrast, 'opportunity entrepreneurs' engage in entrepreneurship out of choice to exploit a business opportunity. Such individuals are considered to have been 'pulled' into entrepreneurship (Bosma, 2006). Prior to GEM, Das (1999)

Table 4.1   Categories of female entrepreneur by reason/motivation for starting a business

Category	Main Reason/Motivation
'Chance' entrepreneurs	To keep busy
	Was hobby/special interest
	Family/spouse had business
'Forced' entrepreneurs	Financial/needed the money
	Control over time/flexibility
	Challenge, try something on one's own
	Show others I could do it
'Created' or 'pulled' entrepreneurs	To be independent
	Self satisfaction
	Example to children
	Provide employment for others/do something worthwhile

Source: Adapted from Das (1999, p.154, Table 3).

categorized female entrepreneurs into three types: 'chance', 'forced', and 'created' or 'pulled' entrepreneurs, as depicted in Table 4.1. 'Chance' entrepreneurs often started their business as a hobby, then, as their friends and relatives started purchasing some of their products, the hobby slowly grew into a fully fledged business operation. 'Forced' entrepreneurs are pushed into entrepreneurial activity because they need money (what GEM would describe as 'necessity' entrepreneurs). 'Created' or 'pulled' entrepreneurs (what GEM would describe as 'opportunity' entrepreneurs) have a desire to become independent, take a challenge and show others that 'I can do this'. In this study our focus is on 'necessity' or 'forced' entrepreneurs. Given the conditions facing women in rural Vietnam, becoming a 'necessity' entrepreneur could be seen as a solution to their financial difficulties and could provide them with individual empowerment. However, although women entrepreneurs in Vietnam may be chiefly necessity-driven, research has shown that their motives change over time, with many women who originally entered entrepreneurship out of necessity becoming more opportunity-driven (Williams, 2009).

The GEM Model of Entrepreneurship

A recent GEM report (Kelley et al., 2011) groups countries into one of three categories according to a World Competitiveness Index: factor-driven, efficiency-driven and innovation-driven. From the GEM category descriptions, Vietnam can be classified as a factor-driven country that is in transition to the efficiency-driven group. Many (particularly female) entrepreneurs in Vietnam are characterized by the need to satisfy basic requirements and, as such, Vietnam's economy ranges from subsistence agriculture to the extraction of natural resources. More recently, however, entrepreneurs in Vietnam have sought to create scale-intensive models to advance development and, therefore, Vietnam is in the process of transitioning to an efficiency-driven economy.

To gain an understanding of the entrepreneurship process in any country (regardless of its level of development) Kelley et al. (2011, p. 15) suggest that one needs to start by considering the socio-cultural and political context of the country concerned. Thus, in order to encourage rural women to become involved in entrepreneurship (and to contribute to their personal empowerment and the development of their rural communities) it is first necessary to study the contextual setting in which these women reside.

Community Context

Another framework that we believe is particularly salient to our study (because it helps to analyse the contextual setting of rural women in Vietnam) is provided by Hindle (2010), who argues that 'Community Context' affects the entrepreneurial process through both 'Generic Structural Factors' and 'Generic Human Factors'. These are considered independent variables that characterize the community context and facilitate the 'Entrepreneurial Process'. Hindle (2010) further suggests that entrepreneurship 'Facilitation and Programs' and 'Task Specific Tools' moderate the interaction between the 'Structural' and 'Human' factors.

In collecting the primary data for this study, we focused on several attributes from the GEM and Hindle models (such as social and cultural norms, social networks, governance and physical resources available) that related to two key constructs, namely socio-cultural influences and governmental support policies. The first construct embraces issues concerning current social changes occuring in rural communities and the cultural norms affecting rural women in Vietnam. The second construct deals with the support provided by government for female entrepreneurship in rural Vietnam. Our purpose was to describe the community context through a synthesis of its various components. The end-goal was to articulate any required facilitation initiatives or programmes and any task-specific tools that might be required as fundamental prerequisites to improving female entrepreneurial participation in rural Vietnam.

METHODOLOGY

We adopted a qualitative research design aimed at examining the cultural phenomena that give meaning to, and guide entrepreneurial participation by, rural women in Vietnam. Our primary purpose was to identify and describe the potential barriers to, and facilitators of, female entrepreneurship in this setting.

Sample Selection

Vietnam is commonly divided into seven regions, which include the Northern Uplands, Red River Delta, North Central Coast, Central Highlands, Central Coast, South East and Mekong Delta. The first three regions are considered 'the North' while the last four are considered 'the South' (Van de Walle and Cratty, 2004). Due to our familiarity with the culture in North Vietnam, our sample of rural female entrepreneurs and non-entrepreneurs was selected from three rural communities in this region: Trang Minh precinct (Kien An, Hai Phong), Dong Mai commune (Thanh Oai, Ha Tay) and Phu Luong commune (Dong Hung, Thai Binh).

While acknowledging the many different types of entrepreneurial activities female entrepreneurs might engage in, the focus of this study was on female 'micro-entrepreneurship'. This term can be used interchangeably with 'self-employed' female individuals who seek to survive, or to increase their income, through informal self-employment (Tambunan, 2009). Our focus on micro-entrepreneurship is due to the limited individual (as well as regional) resources typically available in rural settings such that micro-entrepreneurship is more prevalent than small or medium enterprises in these regions.

During the period 2009–2010, we conducted in-depth interviews (using a semi-structured questionnaire) with four women (two entrepreneurs and two non-entrepreneurs) in each of the three rural locations noted above. A convenience sampling approach was adopted to identify potential interviewees, and we used a filter question to ensure the interviewees were aged between 28 and 50. The entrepreneurs we interviewed were also required to have been engaged in their entrepreneurial activities for more than 12 months. Other demographic questions included the interviewee's name (optional), location, business type and age of business (for entrepreneurs only), marital status and number of family dependants. The interviews with the entrepreneurs were conducted at their place of business, while the interviews with the non-entrepreneurs were conducted in their homes. Each interview lasted about 30 to 45 minutes. Tables 4.2 and 4.3

Table 4.2 Code name and demographic details for the female entrepreneurs

Code	Location	Business type	Age of business	No. of employees	Marital status	No. of dependants
E1	Trang Minh, Kien An, Hai Phong	Waste recycling dealer	2 years	2	Widowed	4
E2	Trang Minh, Kien An, Hai Phong	Home-based herbalist, Traditional medicine manufacturer	15 years	5	Widowed	0
E3	Dong Mai, ThanhOai, Ha Tay	Home-based local convenient store; motorbike wash services	10 years	2	Married	2
E4	Dong Mai, ThanhOai, Ha Tay	Fish and poultry trader	5 years	0	Married	4
E5	PhuLuong, Dong Hung, Thai Binh	Construction materials trader and transport service provider	7 years	2	Single	1
E6	PhuLuong, Dong Hung, Thai Binh	Confectionery manufacturer and seller	10 years	3	Married	2

Table 4.3 Code name and demographic details for the female non-entrepreneurs

Code	Location	Marital status	No. of dependants
N.E1	TrangMinh, Kien An, Hai Phong	Married	2
N.E2	TrangMinh, Kien An, Hai Phong	De facto	2
N.E3	Dong Mai, ThanhOai, Ha Tay	Married	3
N.E4	Dong Mai, ThanhOai, Ha Tay	Married	2
N.E5	PhuLuong, Dong Hung, Thai Binh	Married	1
N.E6	PhuLuong, Dong Hung, Thai Binh	Married	0

summarize the demographic details for the female entrepreneurs and non-entrepreneurs, respectively.

The questionnaire items used in our study were selected from previously conducted research on female entrepreneurship in other countries, and were obtained either by directly contacting the researchers involved or from appendices in the journal articles they had published. The items were translated and then reworded to make them more easily understood by rural women in Vietnam. Field notes were also made during the time the researchers conducted the interviews at the three locations.

RESULTS

Responses from the Rural Female Entrepreneurs

Motivations
In answering the question 'Why did you decide to start this business?' all of the women stated that the main reason for them starting their business was to earn more income for their family.

E1 frankly shared: *You know, I do not have an official job like those in the city. I also have four kids. Three of my children are now working in footwear companies; their incomes are low so they are still not totally independent financially. The smallest one now is at school. I have to pay him in many ways. You see, I can't rely on my farm, it is just enough for our rice in every day's meals. Now I have to think out a way to do something. Otherwise, we will starve.*

E4 was a little shy to tell about her motivation for entering business, but stated that: *My family is poor, and my husband's family is poor, they were not able to give us anything when we moved out. My husband has no stable job, just a casual house builder. Now he is working with his relatives in house-building sites in Hanoi. He just came home once or twice a month, but the salary is very limited, he could give me very little after his rent, food, and travel fees sometimes. All the domestic work and responsibilities are left for me. You know, my three kids are at school. There are also a number of remembrance services we have to attend in both of the family sides, which cost me a huge amount of money. I need to earn more money apart from my agricultural work to handle all of them.*

Training
When asked about the training they undertook before starting their business, all the women stated that they had not been involved in any training

prior to starting their ventures. Interestingly, some of the women were even surprised when the need for training was raised.

E1 was surprised and laughed: *No, I did not have any training, but I don't think waste-recycling business needs any training.*

E4 shared: *This is quite simple work, if you saw someone doing it, even for the first time, you also can do it.*

However, E2 and E6 mentioned the importance of training when their businesses grew bigger and their reputation developed. In both cases they found and paid for the training courses themselves; no government help was provided.

E2 seriously stressed: *Training is very important for me in this business. I am too old to study, but I tried my best to take part in three training courses in herbal medicine organized by the Municipal Traditional Medicine Association. Even though it cost me quite a large amount of money, I think it is useful. Only with proper training, I can offer more effective medicines to patients so that they will believe in me and come to buy them.*

E6 also shared: *I make cakes and sell, but if I sell the same kind of cakes every day, the customers will be fed up. So I need to learn to make them different sometimes, not too much, but some other flavours would be good. It will be better if I can learn about many ways to make them different.*

Raising capital
When asked about government policies designed to help them develop their businesses, all the women mentioned two organizations: the Farmers' Union and the Women's Union. The women seemed very happy with these two organizations because of the financial support they provided in the form of two-year loans. Although these organizations only provided a small amount of credit (from US$400 to US$900) it was not too difficult to obtain. Further, provided the applicant was a registered member of the organization, and had a National Identity Card (*Chứng minh thư nhân dân*) and Household Registration Book (*Sổ hộ khẩu*), the funds were generally available in about a week.

E2 also stated that, in Hai Phong city, there were some other associations available for female entrepreneurs (such as the Small Traders Association and the Veterans Association), which could assist in raising funds for individuals involved in entrepreneurial activities. A number of the interviewees also referred to *hụi* or *vào họ*. This is an informal savings plan whereby a group of women contribute a certain amount of money monthly to a fund holder (*chủ họ*). This person then organizes for those funds to be allocated to one of the contributors (*rút họ* or *bốc họ*) with some interest being paid to the other contributors. This process is repeated over time until all the contributors have had their savings returned. This informal process was seen as another way of raising funds to start a new venture. Although this is an illegal and potentially risky method of fund raising, because of the personal trust the women have with each other and the fund holder it is quite commonly practised in Vietnam. The interviewees noted that this method of fund raising could provide more funds than would normally be available through the associations referred to previously. Further, the monthly contribution plan also provides some interest income for the individuals and a motivation for better managing their money (savings).

Relationships and networking

When asked 'What was most difficult for you in setting up your business?' the two most frequent factors mentioned by the women were 'relationships' (the networks of customers) and 'information' (about potential target markets). When asked whether they had a networking system (support system) with other businesswomen (or businessmen) to help develop their business, the answer was almost always 'no'.

E2 honestly said: *No, we do not have any official networking system with other businesswomen yet. Anyway, we do different things so there is nothing to share.*

E4 stressed: *We do selling in different places, and are busy all day. I do not associate with anyone about the business things.*

E6 revealed: *Some of my relatives are also making cakes, but different types. They share with me sometimes their experience, but they will not share with outsiders.*

Societal expectations of women

When asked about their role in terms of domestic work (meaning household services for the family), all of the women stated that their role was important. Interestingly, the views expressed by the interviewees appeared to reflect societal expectations and, further, our interviewees did not appear to have a problem with the assumption that, as women, they were expected to carry the major share of domestic responsibilities.

E3 said: *My business here is home-based, so I am very busy. I manage my business and my domestic work at the same time. I can't leave all the domestic work for my husband; he is a man, people will laugh at our family if men have to do housework.*

E5 said: *I only do this in the daytime, from 9am to 11am, then 1pm to around 4pm. I still have to manage my domestic work such as cooking, cleaning, feeding the animals. My mother is too weak now; she cannot help.*

E4 also shared: *All of my three kids are at school now, they need to do homework, but if I do not push them, they will not work. I have to spend my evening staying around them to make sure that they finish their work for school. My husband is away most of the time, when he returns, sometimes he helps to take care of the kids, but he hit them many times, he can't push them to study properly.*

When asked 'What does your husband or family say when you can earn more than or the same as your husband?' the women had quite different responses.

E6 said: *It does not matter much. He finds it alright. He helps me sometimes in the business, so in front of neighbours or relatives, I must say that it is him who does most of the work.*

E4 said: *He is not happy, of course. No man is happy when his wife does better. When he is drunk, he mentions this. Anyway, he has no choice and he is away most of the time, he does not care, as long as his children and his family are fine.*

E3 said: *He supports my work basically. But he said that no matter what I do, I have to pay my most attention to my domestic work.*

Responses from the Rural Female Non-Entrepreneurs

The set of questions prepared for the non-entrepreneurs was shorter than that for the entrepreneurs. We asked them the questions about governmental support but we also focused on the reasons why they had not been (or felt hesitant to be) involved in entrepreneurial activities. All of the interviewees were well aware of the support provided by the Women's Union and Farmers' Union in terms of their micro-credit schemes. However, there were some differences in the responses provided by the non-entrepreneurs (compared to the entrepreneurs) concerning the role of these two associations. In contrast to the entrepreneurs, the rural female non-entrepreneurs generally did not consider the loans easy to obtain.

NE5 commented: *In our commune's Women's Union meetings, we do voting for the loans from the Union. Normally, only those who are the poorest will be considered to get the loans.*

When answering the question concerning the potential barriers to entrepreneurial activities, our group of non-entrepreneurs pointed to a lack of time, training, infrastructure (land or natural resources) and personal self-efficacy.

NE2 said: *Agricultural and domestic work takes almost all of my time. I even do not think about that.*

NE6 said: *I know some rural women entrepreneurs; they can do entrepreneurship because they were trained before.*

NE5 said: *I believe that entrepreneurs are some people with gifted characteristics, I don't think I have. I could only raise animals and grow vegetables.*

NE2 said: *I think younger women should start entrepreneurship as it is easier for them to get training.*

NE5 said: *I know the neighbouring commune is promoting the enterprising activities among women. However, the land is wider there so that women can do larger scale fish farming; pig or poultry growing. In our commune, the land allocation for each individual is very limited, we can't make the place the farmland.*

There was a diversity of views expressed by the non-entrepreneurs when asked about the likely views of their husbands if they were to consider being involved in an entrepreneurial venture.

NE5 said: *I think he will support me if I can do it. It is good for the family though.*

NE6 said: *He is just worried about my health, he said that doing entrepreneurship will make me very tired.*

NE1 said: *I talked to him sometimes about the intention, but he said that I may not have enough time.*

NE2 said: *He does not believe that I could do it. He said that I'd better concentrate on my farm and domestic work. It is less risky.*

DISCUSSION AND CONCLUSION

The results from our interviews with rural female entrepreneurs in Vietnam suggest they were 'necessity-driven' or 'forced' entrepreneurs. For them it was a question of survival and reflected a desire to earn extra income to cover family expenses. There was no evidence to suggest that any of our female entrepreneurs had been 'pulled' into their new venture.

There also appeared to be a notable lack of information and/or training programmes available to these rural women. It was not until they began to grow their ventures that some of the women recognized a need for training. In these cases the women paid for their own training, as they were not aware of any government-sponsored programme available. This finding suggests that either training programmes targeting rural female entrepreneurs are not widely available or information about programmes that are available has not been widely publicized. On further inquiry we discovered that there was a Vietnam Women Entrepreneurs Council (VWEC) (*Hội Doanh nhân nữ Việt Nam*) which formed part of the Vietnam Chamber of Commerce and Industry (VCCI) (*Phòng Công nghiệp và Thương mại Việt Nam*). Although this Council was established in 2001, its effectiveness appears to have been rather limited when it comes to rural entrepreneurs; none of the interviewees made any reference to this body. However, the VWEC created the Gender Economic Development Working Group on 11 November 2011, and this working group is expected to expand the role of the Council to include rural areas. Despite this initiative by the VWEC, we would suggest that the provision of targeted training courses for rural women interested in establishing a new venture might be a useful government initiative to further aid the development of rural communities. The availability of such training courses might also help to overcome the low entrepreneurial self-efficacy exhibited by the rural women we interviewed. Moreover, it might be helpful if the training programmes included sessions involving partners (or their family members) so that they might better understand (appreciate) the challenges facing women starting new ventures and how to support them in their business activities.

In terms of financing a new venture, both interview groups (the entrepreneurs and non-entrepreneurs) were familiar with the Vietnam Women's Union and the Farmers' Union, indicating the effectiveness of these organizations in providing financial support to rural female entrepreneurs. However, the funds provided by both these micro-credit schemes were relatively limited, and it seems that preference was given to the poorest women. This suggests that, with government support, these schemes could be expanded to provide both a greater level of funding and wider access for both business start-up and subsequent growth.

Apart from the limited financing initiatives, it would appear that the provision of other supporting activities (such as networking opportunities) is also limited in rural Vietnam. Again this suggests a role for government support agencies if Vietnam is serious about continuing its rapid rate of economic development.

The responses from the interviewees concerning socio-cultural issues indicated that, in Vietnam (as in many other countries), domestic work is assumed to be a woman's job. Interestingly, this assumption was also held by the women we interviewed and was not seen (or at least it was not raised) as a major inequity. Nevertheless, this 'saving face' philosophy (whereby it would be considered inappropriate, culturally, to expect a man to undertake domestic duties) may well be holding back many rural women in Vietnam from undertaking entrepreneurial initiatives. On a positive note, however, there did not appear to be any serious community concern about rural women, through their entrepreneurial endeavours, being able to earn more money than their husbands.

In terms of limitations, it is important to acknowledge that our small sample size means that our results cannot be generalized and, therefore, further research with larger samples and in other regions is needed to validate our findings. Nevertheless, we believe our findings provide a useful first step to a better understanding of the contextual facilitators and constraints impacting women wishing to engage in entrepreneurial activities in rural Vietnam. As such, our findings should be of interest to government policymakers and fellow researchers with an interest in rural entrepreneurship.

ACKNOWLEDGEMENT

This chapter was previously published in the *International Journal of Gender and Entrepreneurship*.
© Emerald Group Publishing, *International Journal of Gender and Entrepreneurship*, 6 (1), 2014.

REFERENCES

Anthopoulou, T. 2009. Rural women in local agrofood production: Between entrepreneurial initiatives and family strategies. A case study in Greece. *Journal of Rural Studies*, 26, 394–403.

Bock, B.B. 2004. Fitting in and multi tasking: Dutch farm women's strategies in rural entrepreneurship. *Sociologia Ruralis*, 44, 245–260.

Bosma, N. 2006. Global Entrepreneurship Monitor: GEM 2006 summary results. London: London Business School.

Brush, C.G., de Bruin, A. and Welter, F. 2009. A gender-aware framework for women's entrepreneurship. *International Journal of Gender and Entrepreneurship*, 1, 8–24.

Brush, C.G., Duhaime, I.M., Gartner, W.B., Stewart, A., Katz, J.A., Hitt, M.A., Alvarez, S.A., Meyer, G.D. and Venkataraman, S. 2003. Doctoral education in the field of entrepreneurship. *Journal of Management*, 29, 309–331.

Bushell, B. 2008. Women entrepreneurs in Nepal: What prevents them from leading the sector? *Gender and Development*, 16, 549–564.

Central Intelligence Agency. 2011. *The World Factbook* [Online]. Available: https://www.cia.gov/library/publications/download/download-2011/index.html, accessed 16 October 2012.

Central Population and Housing Census Steering Committee. 2010. *The 2009 Vietnam population and housing census: Completed results* [Online]. Statistical Publishing House. Available: http://vietnam.unfpa.org/webdav/site/vietnam/shared/Census%20publications/3_Completed-Results.pdf, accessed 22 September 2011.

Chitsike, C. 2000. Culture as a barrier to rural women's entrepreneurship: Experience from Zimbabwe. *Gender and Development*, 8, 71–77.

Dabson, B. 2001. Supporting rural entrepreneurship. *Exploring Policy Options for a New Rural America*. Available from IDEAS virtual data bank, http://ideas.uqam.ca.

Das, M. 1999. Women entrepreneurs from southern India: An exploratory study. *Journal of Entrepreneurship*, 8, 147–163.

Davis, J. and Pearce, D. 2001. The rural non-farm economy in central and eastern Europe. In: Lerman, Z. and Csaki, C. (eds), *The Challenge of Rural Development in the EU Accession Process*, Washington DC: World Bank.

Driga, O., Lafuente, E. and Vaillant, Y. 2009. Reasons for the relatively lower entrepreneurial activity levels of rural women in Spain. *Sociologia Ruralis*, 49, 70–96.

Fan, S., Huong, P.L. and Long, T.Q. 2004. Government spending and poverty reduction in Vietnam. Project report prepared for the World Bank funded project 'Pro-poor spending in Vietnam', by International Food Policy Research Institute, Washington DC, and Central Institute for Economic Management, Hanoi.

Franck, A.K. 2012. Factors motivating women's informal micro-entrepreneurship: Experiences from Penang, Malaysia. *International Journal of Gender and Entrepreneurship*, 4, 65–78.

Gladwin, C.H., Long, B.F., Babb, E.M., Beaulieu, L.J., Moseley, A., Mulkey, D. and Zimet, D.J. 1989. Rural entrepreneurship: One key to rural revitalization. *American Journal of Agricultural Economics*, 71, 1305–1314.

Haggblade, S., Hazell, P.B.R. and Reardon, T.A. 2002. Strategies for stimulating poverty-alleviating growth in the rural nonfarm economy in developing countries. Environment and Production Technology Division, International Food Policy Research Institute (IFPRI), and Rural Development Department, World Bank EPTD Discussion Paper No. 92.

Hang, T.T.T. 2008. Women's leadership in Vietnam: Opportunities and challenges. *Signs*, 34, 16–21.

Harmeling, S. 2008. Global climate risk index 2009. *Germanwatch*, Berlin, available at www.germanwatch.org.

Henderson, J. 2002. Building the rural economy with high-growth entrepreneurs. *Economic Review-Federal Reserve Bank of Kansas City*, 87, 45–75.

Hindle, K. 2010. How community context affects entrepreneurial process: A diagnostic framework. *Entrepreneurship and Regional Development*, 22, 599–647.

Hoang, B.T. 2010. Rural employment and life: Challenges to gender roles in Vietnam's agriculture at present. Paper presented at the FAO-IFAD-ILO Workshop on Gaps, trends and current research in gender dimensions of agricultural and rural employment: differentiated pathways out of poverty Rome, 31 March–2 April 2009, available at http://www.fao-ilo.org/fileadmin/user_upload/fao_ilo/pdf/Papers/16_march/Thinh_final.pdf.

IFAD. 2010. Enabling poor rural people to overcome poverty in Vietnam: International Fund for Agricultural Development.

Kelley, D.J., Bosma, N. and Amorós, J.E. 2011. *Global Entrepreneurship Monitor: 2010 Global Report* [Online]. London: Global Entrepreneurship Research Association, London Business School, London. Available: http://www.gemconsortium.org/download/1321407603438/GEM%20GLOBAL%20REPORT%202010rev.pdf, accessed 20 October 2011.

Kelley, D.J., Singer, S. and Herrington, M. 2012. *Global Entrepreneurship Monitor: 2011 Global Report* [Online]. London: Global Entrepreneurship Research Association, London Business School, London. Available: http://www.gemconsortium.org/docs/download/2201, accessed 25 April 2012.

Labrianidis, L. 2006. Fostering entrepreneurship as a means to overcome barriers to development of rural peripheral areas in Europe. *European Planning Studies*, 14, 3–8.

Macke, D. & Markeley, D. 2006. Entrepreneurship and rural America. *Rural Research Report*, 17, 1–6.

Morris, M.H., Kuratko, D.F. and Schindehutte, M. 2001. Towards integration: Understanding entrepreneurship through frameworks. *The International Journal of Entrepreneurship and Innovation*, 2, 35–49.

OECD. 2006. *The New Rural Paradigm: Policies and Governance* [Online]. OECD Report, Directorate for Public Governance and Territorial Development. Available: http://www.oecd.org/document/7/0,3343,en_2649_33735_37015431_1_1_1_1,00.html, accessed 20 April 2010.

Powell, N., Swartling, Å.G. & Minh Ha, H. 2011. The national policy landscape: The legacy and the present situation. In: Powell, N., Swartling, Å.G. & Minh Ha, H. (eds), *Stakeholder Agency in Rural Development Policy: Articulating Co-governance in Vietnam*. Hanoi, Vietnam: World Agroforestry Centre ICRAF.

Tambunan, T. 2009. Women entrepreneurship in Asian developing countries: Their development and main constraints. *Journal of Development and Agricultural Economics*, 1, 27–40.

Thanh, H.X., Anh, D.N. and Tacoli, C. 2005. *Livelihood diversification and rural-urban linkages in Vietnam's Red River Delta* [Online]. International Food Policy Research Institute (IFPRI), discussion paper No. 193. Available: http://ideas.repec.org/p/fpr/fcnddp/193.html, accessed 20 October 2011.

Van de Walle, D. & Cratty, D. 2004. Is the emerging non farm market economy the route out of poverty in Vietnam? *Economics of Transition*, 12, 237–274.

Vietnam Women Entrepreneurs Council. 2007. *Women's entrepreneurship development in Vietnam* [Online]. Vietnam Chamber of Commerce and Industry (VCCI) and the International Labour Organization (ILO) report. Available: http://www.ilo.org/wcmsp5/groups/public/@asia/@ro-bangkok/documents/publication/wcms_100456.pdf, accessed 22 September 2011.

Weeks, J.R. 2009. Women business owners in the Middle East and North Africa: A five-country research study. *International Journal of Gender and Entrepreneurship*, 1, 77–85.

Williams, C.C. 2009. Informal entrepreneurs and their motives: A gender perspective. *International Journal of Gender and Entrepreneurship*, 1, 219–225.

World Bank. 2011. *Rural development & agriculture in Vietnam* [Online]. Available: http://web.worldbank.org/WBSITE/EXTERNAL/COUNTRIES/EASTASIAPACIFICEXT/EXTEAPREGTOPRURDEV/0,,contentMDK:20534368~menuPK:3127821~pagePK:34004173~piPK:34003707~theSitePK:573964,00.html, accessed 25 October 2011.

5. Women entrepreneurs in Asia: culture and the state in China and Japan
Kathryn Ibata-Arens

Women hold up half the sky (妇女能顶半边天), Mao Zedong, 1968 (Gao, 2010)

INTRODUCTION

An assumption about Asian economies is that women play more traditional roles and are not motivated to pursue entrepreneurial careers. In culture-based explanations, such as Hofstede (1980), Asian countries are often labeled as 'masculine' societies. The challenges that women face within systems with a gender bias (for example, discrimination by banks) are said to limit female entrepreneurs to the 'most ambitious' (Lituchy et al., 2003). However, Global Entrepreneurship Monitor (GEM) data indicates that both the overall entrepreneurship rate and the rate for female entrepreneurs varies across countries within Asia in a pattern similar to the variation in other world regions (Kelley et al., 2011; Kelley et al., 2012). Furthermore, women in Asian countries such as Singapore and Thailand have entrepreneurship rates on a par with their male counterparts, and these countries create as many new firms, proportionately, as the United States and other Western countries (Kelley et al., 2011, Kelley et al., 2012).

Highlighting the experiences of women entrepreneurs in both China and Japan, this chapter explores the potential impact of state policies and culture on the incidence of women's entrepreneurship in Asian countries. China and Japan exhibit a significant variation in the occurrence of female entrepreneurship (high in China and low in Japan), not due to state intervention per se, but rather because of the nature of such intervention. Unfortunately, the retreat of the state from market intervention in China in recent decades appears to have led to an increase in gender discrimination, while in Japan it appears to have presented an opening for women entrepreneurs.

The remainder of this chapter comprises three sections. First, the debate between the cultural and statist approaches to understanding the presence (or absence) of women entrepreneurs in Asia is reviewed. Second, two original case studies of female 'opportunity' entrepreneurs, one in China and one in Japan, are used to provide a lens with which to view the broader trends in society and public policy in these countries and, in particular, their apparent effect on female entrepreneurship. The chapter concludes with implications for the study of female entrepreneurship in Asia and elsewhere.

CULTURAL VERSUS STATIST APPROACH

The Culture Thesis

Research on Asia has often referred to cultural differences, including Confucian ideas about the role of women in the economy and society. These societies are said to prioritize a hierarchical order in relationships, persistence, thrift and shame avoidance (Deng et al., 2011). The work of Hofstede (1980) is cited in a number of these studies (Thomas and Mueller, 2000; Gerrard et al., 2003). Interestingly, Asian countries with a Confucian history, such as China (where the philosophy originated), Singapore and Thailand, rank at least 30 percent higher on gender equity than countries such as Japan, India and Korea (World Economic Forum, 2012). The latter countries fall below the top 100 in this regard, and even lower in terms of the economic participation and opportunities afforded to women. Japan and Korea rank the lowest among all 59 Global Entrepreneurship Monitor (GEM) countries in terms of the perceived entrepreneurial capabilities, opportunities and intentions of women (Kelley et al., 2011). Although Japanese women increased their entrepreneurial activity threefold between 2001 and 2011 (from 1 percent to 3 percent of the working-age population), their rate of entrepreneurial activity remains the lowest in Asia.

By way of contrast, excluding Iceland and Sweden, China's women fare better than all 22 'innovation-driven' economies in recent GEM surveys (surpassing countries such as Finland, the United States and the United Kingdom) (Kelley et al., 2011; Kelley et al., 2012). In 2010, for example, the rate of female entrepreneurial activity in China was greater than 22 percent; more than twice the rate in the United States and seven times higher than Japan. Thailand is another Asian country with a high rate of female entrepreneurial activity: just below China in 2010 with 21 percent. Singapore also does well compared to other countries in Asia (7 percent).

The high rate of female entrepreneurial activity in China is largely driven by 'necessity', with women becoming entrepreneurs primarily due to an absence of other employment options (GEM, 2011; Kelley et al., 2013). In contrast, Japan and Singapore lead Asian economies in terms of the ratio of women pursuing 'opportunity'-driven entrepreneurship. Research suggests that specific country contexts can significantly influence the rate of female entrepreneurship (Greene et al., 2003). For example, women entrepreneurs in Asia have struggled to obtain venture finance (Kitching et al., 2005; Muravyev et al., 2009; Kelley et al., 2011), and to achieve a desirable balance in terms of work–family duties that include childcare (Kitching and Jackson, 2002; Shastri and Sinha, 2010; Ghosh and Cheruvalath, 2007; Kim and Ling, 2001; Alam et al., 2011) while leading growth firms (Malaya, 2006). Interestingly, in a study of 41 countries, Baughn et al. (2006) found that (overall) the environment for entrepreneurship within a country impacts female entrepreneurship more than a lack of gender equity does. This suggests that, in promoting female entrepreneurship, policy measures targeting gender equity might be less effective than policies designed to improve societal attitudes towards entrepreneurship, regardless of gender.

The State Intervention Thesis

Research also suggests that the state has played a significant role in the evolution of business in Asian countries by affecting the prevalence of new business start-ups including opportunities for women (Agarwala, 2010). Gerschenkron (1962) argued that late-developing countries required high levels of state intervention in order to catch up to the levels of industrialization in European countries. This intervention in Asian countries (such as Japan and South Korea) included the establishment of state-owned banks to fund industrial development in targeted sectors, primarily manufacturing. The so-called 'developmental state' guided economic growth through public–private collaboration with large corporations, particularly those engaged in the process of developing incremental innovations with respect to technology imported from Western countries, such as the United States. Vertically integrated production structures facilitated rapid process innovations. However, there have been two potential negative outcomes from this developmental process. First, it has resulted in limited new product innovations in large firms. Second, it has reduced the Schumpetarian 'creative destruction' process (Schumpeter, 1942) responsible for the emergence of new sectors and firms as old, innovatively weak, firms die off (Ibata-Arens, 2005). One reason for this is that Asian developmental states, particularly Japan, have propped up moribund large companies at the expense of new small firms (Brooke, 2002). Estrin and Mickiewicz (2009) found that countries having a large state sector (with high taxes and welfare supports) have fewer female entrepreneurs. The authors reason that women have an incentive to seek entrepreneurially derived profit in the absence of government-provided welfare supports, which are available in higher-tax systems. The legacies of state intervention, in mitigating or reinforcing culture, are the subject of the following section, which focuses on the economies of China and Japan through case study analysis with reference to survey and other supporting data.

CASE STUDIES OF FEMALE 'OPPORTUNITY' ENTREPRENEURS IN CHINA AND JAPAN

Study Parameters and Methods

The study herein of female entrepreneurs in Asia is focused in two ways. First, in keeping with the themes of the Diana Project (Gatewood et al., 2003), the emphasis is on 'opportunity' entrepreneurs (in contrast to the 'necessity' entrepreneurs prevalent in most developing economies). Entrepreneurs are defined, herein, as individuals who have brought new products and services to market via establishing new firms (Kelley et al., 2011). Opportunity entrepreneurs recognize a market opportunity and choose to start new businesses even though they have alternative employment options. Compared to necessity entrepreneurs – who have no other potential source of income – opportunity entrepreneurs tend to be more educated, have work experience in the formal sector, and have well-developed professional networks (Kelley et al., 2011). Secondly, the focus is on China and Japan, which have the two largest economies in Asia, and the second- and third-largest in the world, respectively. Although they are geographically and culturally similar, these two countries have a wide variation in terms of their rate of entrepreneurial activity. For example, while China's entrepreneurship rate (including the rate of female entrepreneurship) is on a par with that of the United States, Japan's entrepreneurship rate (for either gender) is among the lowest in the industrialized world. Meanwhile, the national governments in these countries have, in recent years, enacted policies to encourage entrepreneurship education to stimulate opportunity entrepreneurship. In some of these instances these policies have particularly targeted women (Development Bank of Japan, 2012; Zhou and Xu, 2012).

Two case studies of women entrepreneurs (one in China and one in Japan) form the focus of the remainder of this chapter. Firm-level case study observations can provide potential generalizations at the economy level and can complement the extent to which deductions can be made from aggregate quantitative data (Eisenhardt, 1989). The two case studies discussed were selected from 11 questionnaire survey-based interviews that were conducted in China (3) and Japan (8) in November and December 2012, with the women entrepreneurs having multiple employees and operating in a variety of fields (including information technology, finance and manufacturing). The interviews were conducted in Chinese, English and Japanese, depending on the respondent's native language. Respondents were asked a series of questions about their start-up history and the environment for female entrepreneurs in their country (including government support and perceptions of gender discrimination). Subjects were selected using a snowball approach (introduction by other female entrepreneurs) and the interviews were supplemented with information from newspapers and other publicly available data on the subject firms. Due to space constraints, only one case study from each country (China and Japan) is discussed in detail in the chapter, although specific insights provided by some of the other cases are also highlighted.

There are three important limitations to the use of case study data that should be acknowledged. First, a low number of cases can mean that anecdotal findings may not be representative of all women opportunity entrepreneurs in a particular country. Second, the concentration of cases in two large cities (Shenzhen, China and Tokyo, Japan) might limit implications beyond urban environments. Third, though care was taken to identify women from a variety of industrial fields, convenience samples can limit subjects to like-minded individuals. Nevertheless, the stories shared by the women entrepreneurs interviewed appear to be indicative of the general perceptions concerning the environment for women entrepreneurs (and entrepreneurship more generally) in their respective countries.

China: Women Entrepreneurs and their Environment – Xiuzhen Zhang Taiyuanli Investment Guarantee Co, Ltd

Zhang was a government engineer in Tibet for more than ten years in the 1990s and was fortunate to be posted there with her husband who, like her, was also a government engineer. Employment in the country's civil service is touted as a 'Golden Rice Bowl', providing a lifetime of lucrative benefits (such as full urban residency, generous social welfare benefits, access to subsidized medical care and the right to buy an apartment at below market price).

After some time working in Tibet, Zhang decided to move to Shenzhen to provide her daughter with a better education. Unfortunately, in addition to giving up her 'Golden Rice Bowl' job, she had to live in Shenzhen without her spouse. Now that she was living as a single mother she began selling insurance to provide for her and her daughter. Zhang worked in insurance for over ten years and during that time she not only developed a deep knowledge of insurance policies and bank services but also built a wide professional network. As the Chinese economy continued to churn out more entrepreneurial start-ups, Zhang witnessed many entrepreneurs finding it difficult to get financing from banks. As such, Zhang had identified a market need (opportunity) that she believed she could fill.

Zhang decided to start her own credit guarantee company: 'I want to do business when there are few people doing [so] and when regulation is weak. That's where the opportunities are' (Zhang, 2012). A credit guarantee company offers help to small and medium-sized enterprises to obtain bank loans by pledging to repay the loans if the borrower defaults. Of course this is risky, as Zhang is doing business in a space where Chinese banks fear to tread. On the other hand, Zhang is able to charge a higher premium to mitigate potential defaults.

Zhang provided a number of reasons as to why her clients had been unable to obtain loans from banks. For example, a lack of collateral, need for short-term cash flow, having reached their credit limit, and a poor credit score were among the top reasons for failed bank loan applications. In addition, small businesses do not bring sizable profits to the banks, but the banks still incur many of the same overhead costs in lending to these firms as they do when lending to much larger businesses. As a result, banks are less willing to lend to small businesses. The small firms are also burdened with similar amounts of paperwork and the same long waiting times for funds that apply to larger businesses. Zhang currently has five employees and raises capital from banks and high-net-worth individuals. Though business is good, it is not without its challenges. Even with collateral many banks are unwilling to lend money to her to pass on to her clients.

When it comes to gender differences, Zhang thinks that women are more dependable and trustworthy because women tend to be cautious while men are 'bold and impulsive'. Zhang also indicated that she is seeing an increasing number of women bank directors nowadays and they are 'doing great' in the financial world, demonstrating equal (if not better) financial acumen than their male counterparts.

When Zhang first came to Shenzhen she did not understand why most of the companies did not hire women older than 35 years of age. According to Zhang, employers assume that women over 35 years of age are not as passionate about their job as younger women and are likely to prioritize their families, including childcare. A number of studies have found that older women in China are part of an 'unlucky' generation of workers who fail to compete with much younger, more skilled, and internationalized university graduates. Zhang's observations of discrimination against women are reflected in the changing attitudes towards women entrepreneurs in China.

Since the 1950s, women have been encouraged to work in China as part of its industrialization strategy. In 1956, the National Programme for Agricultural Development specified the number of days (80 to 180 days) that every woman was required to work each year. By 2002, 38 percent of working adults were women and this rose to 45.4 percent by 2006, almost reaching the level expressed in Mao Zedong's statement that women 'hold up half the sky' (see Gao, 2010). However, married Chinese women spend (on average) one more hour per day than their husbands in household work and child tutoring (while Japanese men spend even less time on family chores). Further, gender discrimination still exists when it comes to hiring decisions and promotion. According to a survey on the social status of women in China in 2010 (Project Group, 2011), 61.6 percent of men and 54.6 percent of women agree that the domain for men is public, while that for women is private. Compared to the year 2000, these percentages have increased by 7.7 percent and 4.4 percent, respectively. It seems that both Chinese men and women perceive there to be less gender equity in 2010 compared to a decade earlier. In other words, China is moving backwards in this regard.

In a Forbes article on Chinese women entrepreneurs, interviewees noted that traditional Chinese culture encourages women to create a stable family (Flannery, 2013). Consequently, many private investors prefer to invest in technology companies established primarily by men. According to Zhang, the percentage of Chinese women board members in public companies has grown slightly in the past decade, from 3.7 percent in 1997 to 4 percent in 2010; and the percentage of Chinese women chief executive officers (CEOs) in public companies has increased from 4.6 percent in 1997 to 5.6 percent in 2010 (which compares well to the barely 1 percent of women in Japan who hold any kind of executive position) (Matsui et al., 2010).

Research in China suggests that women face far fewer barriers to entrepreneurship than in many other countries, even in high-technology fields. Communist Party state leaders promoted gender equity in both their words and their deeds. Measures included universal education with gender-blind admissions criteria; although some of the advancement of women in China can be attributed to the 'one child' policy (preventing parents from having the choice between investing in male versus female siblings). However, in comparison to Western countries, China is considered to have relatively few formal legal supports for women business owners. Consequently, specific policies supporting women in business do not necessarily translate directly into increasing female entrepreneurship rates in China (Scott et al., 2010; Ye, 2010).

According to a survey conducted in 2011 by the Shenzhen Women's Federation (All-China Women's Federation, 2011), 42 percent of women in China had encountered gender discrimination while looking for jobs, and 50 percent, 34 percent and 12.4 percent of women had experienced discrimination in terms of promotion, salary and training, respectively.[1] Although it is illegal to post any gender, age or place of birth requirements on job descriptions, the lack of enforcement measures (and the absence of any official department in charge of monitoring and enforcement) results in no punishment for violations. In order to promote gender equity, Shenzhen passed a policy referred to as the Shenzhen Special Economic Zone Act to Promote Gender Equality (the Act) prohibiting companies from discriminating based on gender. The Act became effective on 1 January 2013. With the aim of making government policies concerning gender equity more effective, the Act included specific rules with respect to the employment of women, domestic violence and sexual harassment (All-China Women's Federation, 2011).

In a 2001 study of women entrepreneurs in China, Pistrui (2001) surveyed 56 retail and technology entrepreneurs and found that, upon starting their firms, women business owners were younger, slightly less educated and had fewer years of experience than their male counterparts. Kitching and Jackson (2002) found that women entrepreneurs in China are motivated by increased independence and socio-economic status, but perceived there to be rising rates of gender discrimination in the workplace. This is echoed in other research reporting that women in China view entrepreneurship as a means to personal autonomy and a way of escaping gender discrimination in their jobs (Kitching and Woldie, 2004).[2] The fact that gender discrimination appears to have increased in post-Communist societies in market transition points to the prior efficacy of affirmative action policies in these countries. Further, Kitching and Woldie (2004) note that, relative to other countries, perceptions of discrimination in China are more likely to be associated with the country's culture.

Research on business in China often identifies the importance of interpersonal networks (*guanxi*) and, not surprisingly, this also applies to women entrepreneurs. Chinese *guanxi* networks are governed by the norms of mutual trust and reciprocity. *Guanxi* networks are distinct from inter-firm networks (and the concurrent notion of social capital) in the

West in that Chinese individuals tend to have more family members in their professional networks (Scott et al., 2012). *Guanxi* networks have been found (through mentoring relationships) to help women develop business skills.

Haiyan Gong, founder of Jiayuan.com (in English: Beautiful Destiny), China's largest online dating platform, noted the role of friends and family networks in her firm's early success (Gong, 2012). Gong started Jiayuan in 2003 in her university dorm room as a more efficient way to meet potential marriage partners than using China's traditional match-makers (usually hired by parents). In 2011, Jiayuan went public on the NASDAQ (ticker 'DATE'), and Gong earned approximately $70 million from the sale. The company employed 500 people in 2013 (Jiayuan.com, 2013).

Further, in utilizing their local *guanxi* networks, women entrepreneurs are found to draw from international networks as well. For example, Alon et al. (2011) analyzed 12 'high-profile' Chinese women, half of whom had studied and/or worked abroad, and found that returnee women had more education and were able to rise to executive leadership positions at a younger age than 'domestic' women. Further, returnee women cited international relationships and ideas as sources of their success. Zhang's experience as a woman entrepreneur echoes that of other women entrepreneurs in China and reflects the increasing gender discrimination evident in a post-Communist economy. While previous Communist state policies promoting gender equity appear to have had a positive impact on women's entrepreneurship, unfortunately the retreat of the state in recent years appears to have led to a reversal of fortunes for women. *Guanxi*, particularly international business networks, have partly compensated for the decline in gender equity in China and the negative impact this has had on women's ability to acquire professional and business skills.

As the following discussion on Japan shows, Japanese women entrepreneurs are more likely to point to gender discrimination as the main impediment to their career success; although, ironically, workplace discrimination appears to be a key factor in stimulating their desire to become entrepreneurs. Paradoxically, and unlike in China, the retreat of the Japanese state may have increased the potential for entrepreneurship, including women entrepreneurs.

Japan: Women Entrepreneurs and their Environment – Makiko Fukui Harmony Residence

Makiko Fukui is the founder of Harmony Residence, an executive head-hunting and recruiting service that specializes in highly qualified mid-career women. Fukui graduated in 1991 with a degree in economics from Yokohama National University and was one of 30 new women recruits (out of 400 new hires) at a major securities firm. In 1986 the Japanese government enacted the Equal Employment Opportunity Law and, as a result, for the first time women began to be hired for career track employment (Fackler, 2007). Fukui was assigned to the Bond Trading Department; she was the first and only woman at the time to be employed by that department.

Fukui recalled: 'We had high expectations that women may have a chance to get promoted, but seeing the first generation females it was difficult to see them as role models.' They were the type of women who were never going to get married. The work schedule was grueling. All new employees lived together in corporate dorms, were woken up by a bell at 5:30 in the morning, ate the same food, and went to the office together. Also, all new recruits were expected to go out drinking after work with their bosses. Fukui was frustrated:

> I quit after less than a year, I just thought I would waste time there; it would be totally impossible, due to the working hours and drinking habits. Unless you go out drinking late at night with your boss (*nomikai*), you do not get the work related information, and you do not get promoted. As a student, I did not know that. I wish that some adult had explained the reality beforehand. I was very naïve; I believed that if you work hard and you are smart enough, you would get promoted. (Fukui, 2012)

Fukui's new husband was soon transferred to New York in what turned out to be the first of several overseas assignments in New York. While in New York, Fukui earned a paralegal degree from New York University (NYU) and worked in a boutique law firm. In addition to professional mentoring, Fukui learned how to run a small business. By 1999, Fukui had given birth to a daughter.

After her husband's New York assignments ended, the family returned to Tokyo, and given Japan's shortage of daycare facilities, it took Fukui more than six months (on various waiting lists) to find a daycare place for her daughter.[3] Women often struggle to find placements because they must first have a job in hand before they can apply for childcare.[4] Once her daughter began primary school (in 2003), Fukui was able to find work at a Tokyo law firm, where she remained until she left to start Harmony Residence in 2007.

Fukui decided to create Harmony Residence after having an 'aha moment' with her mother. Due to her husband's onerous work hours, he was never able to do his part to take care of their daughter, let alone any housework. She was feeling like she was a single mother. Fukui had been complaining that she was overloaded with three huge responsibilities: work, childcare and housework. It was then that her mother said something really meaningful: 'It is not *taihen* [fraught with difficulty] for you, look at the single moms. You work because you want to work; they work because they must work. You have the luxury, you could quit; they cannot.'

Fukui started to research the situation for working mothers (especially single mothers) and found that even at low levels of income it is impossible to obtain sufficient welfare and childcare support.[5] At the same time, there are many well-educated, experienced women who have much to offer Japanese firms. Further, single mothers (unlike their married counterparts with the luxury of quitting if it gets to be 'too much') are highly motivated to do an excellent job. Promotions mean higher income, and quitting is not an option. Fukui saw a market opportunity.

Harmony Residence became the first recruiting company to provide corporate clients with a large talent pool of more than 700 career women, with each having at least ten years of business experience in fields including marketing, finance and law. Many are multilingual and have degrees from top universities, including Kyoto University and Waseda University. Within five years of establishing Harmony, Fukui had placed women in more than 100 companies, and Harmony Residence has been featured in two NHK *Close Up Gendai* (a leading national business news program) telecasts (Nikkei Morning, 2012).

According to Fukui, most working women find themselves in a lose–lose scenario once they become pregnant. Supervisors do not want to promote them, as they assume they will not want to work extra hours and expect they will eventually quit anyway. Consequently, working women find themselves left out of management mentoring opportunities. As the prospects for advancement fade, these women leave the workforce.

So far, most Japanese corporations have 'invested in the hardware' of maternity leave programs. However, most women never return to work (despite the maternity laws) because bosses often refuse to allow the women to return. Instead, Fukui believes that companies should invest in the 'software' of the employee, so that talented women can remain and move up the company ladder and be an inspiration for other women.

However, Fukui is against the government creating programs to encourage women to become entrepreneurs, because most of these women will 'fail' and afterwards will never be hired for full-time employment elsewhere. Fukui referred to the government trying to increase the number of lawyers by opening up law schools all over Japan in 2004. The reality is that half of the graduates from these programs have never found work. After spending all that time and money on their law degree, graduates who fail to pass the bar three times cannot become attorneys (because of the 'three strikes and you are out' rule). They end up working in a series of dead-end part-time jobs with no company health and other benefits. Likewise, offering support to women to leave their very good jobs to become entrepreneurs is irresponsible. If anything, in Fukui's opinion, the bar should be even higher so that only the very serious consider an entrepreneurial career: those who are passionate about their business idea and cannot imagine doing anything else with their lives. While Fukui's experience with gender discrimination in Japan soured her impression of corporate Japan, her time in New York as a paralegal provided her with critical business skills that she would have been unable to gain working in a Japanese firm. Other research on women entrepreneurs in Japan confirms Fukui's observations about the need for gender equity in existing firms in order to stimulate the creation of new women-owned firms (Futagami and Helms, 2009; Cooke, 2010; Steinberg and Nakane, 2012).

Gender discrimination in the workplace remains endemic in Japan (Futagami and Helms, 2009) and, in contrast to China in the 20th century, the Japanese state has been instrumental in preventing women from rising to leadership positions in business. Ironically, the lack of (cultural and societal) expectations that Japanese women should pursue a corporate business career has freed them to be more experimental and risk-taking than their male counterparts.

Japan's industrialization during the Meiji Restoration after 1868 was coupled with political rhetoric – espoused at all levels, from national media to primary school classrooms – which stated a 'rich nation, strong army' should be supported by 'good wives and wise mothers'. These attitudes survived the imposition of democracy by the American Occupation, despite the fact that the post-war Japanese constitution was written mostly by an American woman (Russell, 2013). Notably, Equal Opportunity Laws did not exist in Japan until the late 1980s, and even today are rarely enforced.

In a study comparing China, Japan, India and South Korea, Cooke (2010) found that the enforcement of equal opportunity laws in each country was largely ineffective and this has no doubt made it difficult for women to acquire the business skills necessary to be a successful entrepreneur in those countries. Further, Japan's weak childcare system means that women who want to pursue a career of any kind face a dilemma: they either have to choose to have a career or choose to have a family. While conservative commentators in Japan cite low birth rates as a reason to keep women out of the workforce, international comparative analysis by the International Monetary Fund (IMF) debunks this political rhetoric.

A 2012 NHK television program, *Close Up Gendai*, addressed some of the issues facing women in Japan and asked the question: 'Can women save Japan?' (NHK, 2012). The show, featuring Christine Lagarde (Managing Director of the IMF), highlighted the findings of a study comparing the economic participation of women across 22 Organisation for Economic Co-operation and Development (OECD) countries. The results from the IMF study concurred with other research that places Japanese women at the bottom of the advanced economies in terms of childcare provision, management-level positions and spousal household contribution. The study concluded that in order to make up for the labor shortfall and productivity decline caused by a declining population, Japan needed to initiate two policies: first, it must increase the number of career-track female employees; and second, it must provide better support for working mothers (Steinberg and Nakane, 2012).

The IMF study also estimated that an 8 percent increase in women's labor market participation (to put Japan on track with other G7 economies) would translate into a 4 percent 'permanent' boost in Japan's gross domestic product (GDP) per capita. In short, facing an aging society and falling birth rates, Japan needs 'womenomics' (an economic system that harnesses the potential contributions of women in the labor force; Steinburg and Nakane, 2012).

Meanwhile, Keidanren (the leading Japanese business association which comprises large corporations like Mitsubishi, Sony and Toyota) conducted an internal study on recruitment and hiring that was presented to a group of visiting policymakers and academics in 2011. The report indicated that if all new hires in member firms (representing the major corporations in Japan) were gender-neutral, more than 70 percent of the expected hires in 2012 would be women. However, when asked how many of the new hires in 2012 would in fact be women, the response was: 'we are aiming for fifteen percent' (Keidanren, 2011). This lack of opportunity to train young female talent in existing firms affects both the number and the quality of nascent women entrepreneurs in Japan.

A 2010 survey conducted by the Ministry of Economy, Trade and Industry of thousands of start-ups found that female-owned firms were less likely to earn a profit than male-owned firms. However, a slightly higher percentage of female entrepreneurs than male entrepreneurs were optimistic about their future business prospects; although the female entrepreneurs were 20 percent less likely than their male counterparts to have plans to expand their businesses. While the male entrepreneurs surveyed had an average of ten years of prior business experience, the female entrepreneurs had (on average) less than eight years. Further, while virtually all the men were full-time employees prior to starting their businesses, only about half the women had full-time work experience. Likewise, about a third of the women (compared to 14 percent of men) reported that their current venture had nothing to do with their prior business experience. Further, while 80 percent of men reported they had help from their spouses in running their business, the same only applied to about half of the women entrepreneurs. Not surprisingly, more women reported a worsening of work–life balance after starting their firms. Like their Chinese counterparts, the Japanese women were younger than the Japanese men when starting their businesses (35 years old compared to 40 years old) and slightly less educated (Ministry of Economy, Trade and Industry, 2011). Finally, although some inroads have been made in the last decade, women entrepreneurs still struggle to obtain start-up finance in Japan's collateral-based bank loan system (which is embedded within a tradition of patrilineal property ownership).

Despite the difficulties they face, there have been a number of very successful female entrepreneurs in Japan. Fujiyo Ishiguro, the founder of NetYear Group, and Tomoko Namba of DeNA are two examples (Nakada, 2000). Fujiyo Ishiguro founded Netyear Group in 1999 as a 'strategic internet professional services' company. Ishiguro had previously worked in Silicon Valley as the CEO of an information technology (IT) consulting firm after obtaining her MBA from Stanford University. The company grew quickly, and by 2008 Netyear was listed on the Mothers exchange (market of the high-growth and emerging stocks) in Tokyo and, as of 2012, the company had 225 employees. Ishiguro cited the business experience she gained, and the professional network she established, while studying and working in California as major factors in her venture's ultimate success.

Tomoko Namba started DeNA in 1999 after leaving a lucrative position as a partner in the multinational consultancy firm McKinsey & Co. Namba and her team quickly moved the company from an e-commerce (bidding) platform to include mobile and other social gaming in its repertoire of products and services. By 2013 (largely through leveraging Namba's international professional networks established at McKinsey) DeNA had expanded to more than ten countries including China, South Korea, Singapore, the United States, Canada and the United Kingdom. DeNA has more than 2000 employees and is traded on the Tokyo Stock Exchange.

Ishiguro and Namba followed a path forged decades earlier by Merle Okawara. Okawara (relying on her American business networks developed as a student in the United States) brought the frozen pizza concept to Japan in the mid-1960s. By the 1970s, Okawara had become the first woman in Japan to head a publicly listed company (JC Comsa). Other Japanese women entrepreneurs have been effective in harnessing the more 'gender-neutral' internet in developing growth businesses (Futagami and Helms, 2009; Nakada, 2000).[6] At the same time, many Japanese women entrepreneurs have experienced difficulties in establishing business networks (Debroux, 2003) in Japan. From the evidence provided by the Japanese women interviewed for this study, it would appear that those with foreign study and/or working experience, particularly in the United States, have benefitted significantly from the professional networks they were able to develop as part of their international experience. Akin to the importance of women's *guanxi* in China, professional (particularly international) networks are an important element in developing a business for Japanese women entrepreneurs.

Summary of Case Studies: Networks and Mentoring

The preceding discussion has illuminated women's entrepreneurship in both China and Japan, which could be indicative of similar patterns in other Asian countries. Almost all of the respondents reported using social networking sites and Twitter as a way of attracting clients and customers. However, there are significant differences in how Chinese and Japanese women perceive the environment for entrepreneurship in their home countries and their experiences with gender discrimination.

The successful Japanese women entrepreneurs had substantial international experience, through university study and/or work, prior to establishing their businesses. The women used the business skills and professional networks they had gained while overseas to help them develop their businesses. Further, it seems that Japanese women entrepreneurs rely on international networks in the absence of strong domestic professional networks. Several respondents noted that once they had left their previous Japanese employer, any business networks they might have had were severed, along with their employment. This reflects the insular nature of Japanese business networks, which typically are not only confined within firms but also within age cohorts.

By way of contrast, Chinese women entrepreneurs rely on both international and domestic professional networks in developing their businesses. These findings (particularly the role of *guanxi* networks) are supported by other studies (see, e.g., Scott et al., 2012). Further, Chinese women entrepreneurs are less likely to report that they had experienced gender discrimination; although attitudes in this regard seem to have regressed in recent times with China's move to an open market system. This move appears to have been associated with a decrease in gender equity.

CONCLUSION

The findings reported in this chapter (based on interviews with Chinese and Japanese women entrepreneurs and the associated literature) indicate that variations in entrepreneurship by gender appear to have more to do with institutional barriers than with culture. In particular, the lack of enforcement of equal opportunity laws and limited childcare facilities appears to be hampering would-be women entrepreneurs in both countries. Moreover, the Chinese and Japanese women entrepreneurs interviewed indicated that nascent female entrepreneurs would benefit from greater levels of business experience and mentoring prior to establishing their new firms.

A number of interesting questions for further study arise from this research. For example, additional hypothesis testing on the legacy of Communist gender equity policies in various post-Communist societies might be of interest. More broadly, it may be that the specific nature of state intervention (rather than proxy measures such as the size of government) is more effective in explaining the factors behind the emergence of significant numbers of successful women 'opportunity' entrepreneurs in Asian countries. Research in the United States has found that the amount of prior business experience is the strongest predictor of entrepreneurial firm-level success. If this finding proves true across economies, supply-side measures attempting to stimulate the number of new firm start-ups are likely to be less successful than the enforcement of equal opportunity laws, in conjunction with quality on-the-job mentoring for women within existing firms.

NOTES

1. Shenzen is one of the largest cities in China, located near the border with Hong Kong. It is a major center of manufacturing and finance. Shenzhen enacted the first gender equity local statute in mainland China (Sznews.com, 2012).
2. Scott et al. (2010) cite research indicating the diminishing power of state intervention; for example, in the *danwei* organizational system combining 'productive and reproductive' functions.
3. The Japanese daycare system is divided into the higher-level kindergarten (*hoikuen*) and ordinary daycare (*yochien*) facilities.
4. Most facilities are subsidized by the government on a sliding price scale based on income.
5. The relative poverty rate for single-parent households with children in Japan is the highest among OECD countries; 10 percent higher than in the United States (Steinberg and Nakane, 2012).
6. See also Martin and Wright (2005) for an analysis of the information and communication technology (ICT) industry and reviews by Honjo (2012) of women leading high-tech start-ups in Japan and elsewhere.

REFERENCES

Agarwala, T. (2010), 'India', in Fielden, S.L. and Davidson, M.J. (eds), *International Research Handbook on Successful Women Entrepreneurs*, Cheltenham, UK and Northampton, MA, USA: Edward Elgar Publishing, pp. 84–97.
Alam, S., Jani, M. and Omar, N. (2011), 'An empirical study of success factors of women entrepreneurs in Southern Region in Malaysia', *International Journal of Economics and Finance*, 3 (2), 166–175.
All-China Women's Federation (2011), 'One year on: China's first local gender equality regulation in Shen Zhen', http://www.womenofchina.cn/html/womenofchina/report/168921-1.htm (accessed 13 January 2014).
Alon, I., Misati, E., Warnecke, T. and Zhang, W. (2011), 'Comparing domestic and returnee female entrepreneurs in China: is there an internationalisation effect?', *International Journal of Business and Globalisation*, 6 (3), 329–349.
Baughn, C., Chua, B. and Neupert, K. (2006), 'The normative context for women's participation in entrepreneurship: a multicountry study', *Entrepreneurship Theory and Practice*, 30 (5), 687–708.
Brooke, J. (2002), 'They're alive! They're alive! Not!; Japan hesitates to put an end to its "zombie" businesses', *New York Times*, 22 October, http://www.nytimes.com/2002/10/29/business/they-re-alive-they-re-alive-not-japan-hesitates-put-end-its-zombie-businesses.html?pagewanted=all&src=pm (accessed 16 March 2013).
Cooke, F.L. (2010), 'Women's participation in employment in Asia: a comparative analysis of China, India, Japan and South Korea', *International Journal of Human Resource Management*, 21 (12), 2249–2270.
Debroux, P. (2003), *Human Resource Management in Japan: Changes and Uncertainties: A New Human Resource Management System Fitting to the Global Economy*, Aldershot: Ashgate Publishing.
Deng, S., Wang, X. and Alon, I. (2011), 'Framework for female entrepreneurship in China', *International Journal of Business and Emerging Markets*, 3 (1), 3–20.
Development Bank of Japan (2012), 'Announcement of the winners and finalists of the first annual Development Bank of Japan (DBJ) new business plan competition for women, June 19, 2012', http://www.dbj.jp/ja/topics/dbj_news/2012/html/0000010265.html (accessed 19 March 2013).
Eisenhardt, K.M. (1989), 'Building theories from case study research', *Academy of Management Review*, 14 (4), 532–550.
Estrin, S. and Mickiewicz, T. (2009), 'Do institutions have a greater effect on female entrepreneurs?', IZA Discussion Papers, No. 4577, Institute for the Study of Labor (IZA).
Fackler, M. (2007), 'Career women in Japan find a blocked path', *New York Times*, 6 August, http://www.nytimes.com/2007/08/06/world/asia/06equal.html?_r=0 (accessed 19 March 2013).
Flannery, R. (2013), 'Forbes China 30 under 30 List: women entrepreneurs face more hurdles than men in China', http://www.forbes.com/sites/russellflannery/2013/03/15/forbes-china-30-under-30-list-women-entrepreneurs-face-more-hurdles-than-men-in-china/ (accessed 25 March 2013).
Fukui, M. (2012), 'Harmony Residence', interview 21 November.
Futagami, S. and Helms, M.M. (2009), 'Emerging female entrepreneurship in Japan: a case study of Digimom workers', *Thunderbird International Business Review*, 51 (1), 71–85.

Gao, X. (2010), 'Hold up "half the sky"', *Chinese Women News, Jiayuan.com*, http://www.jiayuan.com/master/approachmaster/ (accessed 20 February 2013).

Gatewood, E.G., Carter, N.M., Brush, C.G., Greene, P.G. and Hart, M.M. (2003), *Women Entrepreneurs, Their Ventures, and the Venture Capital Industry: An Annotated Bibliography*, Stockholm: ESBRI.

Gerrard, P., Schoch, H. and Barton Cunningham, J. (2003), 'Values and skills of female entrepreneurs in Vietnam: an exploratory study', *Asia Pacific Business Review*, 10 (2), 139–159.

Gerschenkron, A. (1962), *Economic Backwardness in Historical Perspective, a Book of Essays*, Cambridge, MA: Belknap Press of Harvard University Press.

Ghosh, P. and Cheruvalath, R. (2007), 'Indian female entrepreneurs as catalysts for economic growth and development', *International Journal of Entrepreneurship and Innovation*, 8 (2), 139–148.

Global Entrepreneurship Monitor (GEM) (2011), '2007 report on women and entrepreneurship', http://www.gemconsortium.org/docs/download/281 (accessed 4 January 2014).

Gong, H. (2012), 'Get to know the little Dragon Maiden, CEO of Jiayuan', jiayuan.com, http://en.zgc.gov.cn/2013-02/04/content_16199450.htm (accessed 20 February 2013).

Greene, P., Hart, M., Gatewood, E., Brush, C. and Carter, N. (2003), 'Women entrepreneurs: moving front and center: an overview of research and theory', USASBE White Papers, United States Association for Small Business and Entrepreneurship.

Hofstede, G. (1980), *Culture's Consequences: International Differences in Work-Related Values*, Vol. 5, Newbury Park, CA: Sage Publications.

Honjo, Shuji (2012), 本荘修二 『日本の閉塞感を打ち破れるのは女性起業家だ！男性にはない自由さと生命エネルギーに要注目』　インキュベーションの虚と実、2012年10月29日 http://diamond.jp/articles/-/26952 (accessed 20 February 2013).

Ibata-Arens, K. (2005), *Innovation and Entrepreneurship in Japan*, Cambridge: Cambridge University Press.

Jiayuan.com (2013), http://www.jiayuan.com/master/approachmaster/ (accessed 20 February 2013).

Keidanren (2011), anonymous interview, March.

Kelley, D., Brush, C., Greene, P. and Litovsky, Y. (2011), *Global Entrepreneurship Monitor: 2010 Women's Report*, Babson Park, MA: Global Entrepreneurship Research Consortium (GERA), Babson College.

Kelley, D., Brush, C., Greene, P. and Litovsky, Y. (2013), GEM 2012 Women's report, *Global Entrepreneurship Monitor*, http://www.gemconsortium.org/docs/2825/gem-2012-womens-report (accessed 16 October 2013).

Kelley, D., Singer, S. and Herrington, M. (2012), *Global Entrepreneurship Monitor 2011 Global Report*, Global Babson Park, MA: Entrepreneurship Research Consortium (GERA), Babson College.

Kim, J. and Ling, C. (2001), 'Work–family conflict of women entrepreneurs in Singapore', *Women in Management Review*, 16 (5), 204–221.

Kitching, B. and Jackson, P. (2002), 'Female entrepreneurs in a transitional economy: businesswomen in China', *International Journal of Entrepreneurship and Innovation*, 3 (2), 145–155.

Kitching, B., Mishra, R. and Shu, X. (2005), 'Female entrepreneurs in transitional economies: a comparative study of women in the business workplace in India and China', ABERU Discussion Paper.

Kitching, B. and Woldie, A. (2004), 'Female entrepreneurs in transitional economies: a comparative study of businesswomen in Nigeria and China', Hawaii International Conference on Business, 21–24 June, Honolulu, Hawaii.

Lituchy, T., Bryer, P. and Reavley, M. (2003), 'Small business in the Czech Republic and Japan: successes and challenges of women entrepreneurs', *Globalization and Entrepreneurship: Policy and Strategy Perspectives*, Cheltenham, UK and Northampton, MA, USA: Edward Elgar Publishing, pp. 152–179.

Malaya, M. (2006), 'A gender-based analysis of performance of small and medium printing firms in Metro Manila', *Journal of International Women's Studies*, 8 (1), 88–100.

Martin, L. and Wright, L. (2005), 'No gender in cyberspace? Empowering entrepreneurship and innovation in female-run ICT small firms', *International Journal of Entrepreneurial Behaviour and Research*, 11 (2), 162–178.

Matsui, K., Suzuki, H., Eoyang, C., Akiba, T. and Tatebe, K. (2010), 'Japan: portfolio strategy, Womenomics 3.0 the time is now', Goldman Sachs, 1 October.

Ministry of Economy, Trade and Industry (2011), '2010 report on conditions for female entrepreneurs', Ministry of Economy, Trade and Industry, March.

Muravyev, A., Talavera, O. and Schäfer, D. (2009), 'Entrepreneurs' gender and financial constraints: evidence from international data', *Journal of Comparative Economics*, 37 (2), 270–286.

Nakada, G. (2000), 'Japan's female netpreneurs: breaking through', Japan Inc., 19 November, http://www.japaninc.com/article.php?articleID=307 (accessed 25 March 2013).

NHK (2012), http://www.nhk.or.jp/gendai/kiroku/detail02_3261_1.html (accessed 25 March 2013).

Nikkei Morning (2012), http://www.harmonyresidence.co.jp/wordpress/wp-content/uploads/20121010_Nikkei-Morning.pdf (accessed 19 March 2013).

Pistrui, D. (2001), 'Entrepreneur', *Family Business Review*, 14 (2), 141–152.

Project Group of the 3rd Survey on the Status of Chinese Women (2011), 'Executive report of the 3rd Survey on the Status of Chinese Women', *Collection of Women's Studies*, 6 (108), 5–15.

Russell, C. (2013), 'The American woman who wrote equal rights into Japan's Constitution', *Atlantic*, 5 January, http://www.theatlantic.com/sexes/archive/2013/01/the-american-woman-who-wrote-equal-rights-into-japans-constitution/266856/ (accessed 20 March 2013).

Scott, J., Harrison, R., Hussain, J. and Millman, C. (2012), 'The role of guanxi networks in the performance of women-led firms in China', Joint Australian Centre for Entrepreneurship Research Exchange (ACERE) and DIANA International Conference, Queensland University of Technology, Fremantle, Western Australia.

Scott, J., Hussain, J., Harrison, R. and Millman, C. (2010), 'China', in Fielden, S.L. and Davidson, M.J. (eds), *International Research Handbook on Successful Women Entrepreneurs*, Cheltenham, UK and Northampton, MA, USA: Edward Elgar Publishing, pp. 49–59.

Schumpeter, J. (1942), *Capitalism, Socialism and Democracy*, New York: Harper & Row.

Shastri, R. and Sinha, A. (2010), 'The socio-cultural and economic effect on the development of women entrepreneurs (with special reference to India)', *Asian Journal of Business Management*, 2 (2), 30–34.

Steinberg, C. and Nakane, M. (2012), 'Can women save Japan?', IMF Working Paper 12/248, Asia and Pacific Department, International Monetary Fund.

Sznews.com. (2012), 'Shenzhen enacted the first gender equity local statute in mainland China', http://www.sznews.com/news/content/2012–06/29/content_6892354_4.htm (accessed 29 March 2013).

Thomas, A. and Mueller, S. (2000), 'A case for comparative entrepreneurship: assessing the relevance of culture', *Journal of International Business Studies*, 31 (2), 287–301.

World Economic Forum (2012), 'The Global Gender Gap Report 2012', http://www.weforum.org/reports/global-gender-gap-report-2012 (accessed 4 January 2014).

Ye, W. (2010), 'Chinese women development and contribution in the century', Beijing: Social Science in China Press. 叶文振 中国女性百年发展与贡献 《中国社会科学报》 2010年3月5日

Zhang, X. (2012), Taiyuanli Investment Guarantee Co., interview 24 December.

Zhou, M. and Xu, H. (2012), 'A review of entrepreneurship education for college students in China', *Administrative Sciences*, 2 (1), 82–98.

PART II

Meso: firm-level analysis

6. Gender differences in innovation among US entrepreneurs
Alicia Robb and Susan Coleman

INTRODUCTION

Innovation and entrepreneurship have been recognized as important contributors to the US economy (Audretsch, 2002; Wong et al., 2005). Over recent decades, there have been major waves of innovation in such disparate industries as technology, healthcare, manufacturing, retailing, education and national defense. Some innovations have involved the development of new products and services, while others have occurred in the area of delivery systems and processes. For example, in the area of product innovation, artificial knees and hips have dramatically increased the mobility and longevity of many senior citizens. At the other end of the age spectrum, the iPod has become a regular feature in the ears, hands and book bags of almost every teen and college student. From the standpoint of service, most firms now provide an online service option to supplement or even replace in-store service personnel, enabling goods to be purchased, returned and repaired online. Fast food restaurants are another example of service innovation. Recognizing that working professionals and parents may not have time for a leisurely meal, restaurants such as McDonald's, D'Angelos and Subway cater to their need for fast service and increasingly healthy choices.

One of the most important areas of innovation in recent years has been in the area of delivery systems and processes. These innovations do not necessarily introduce new products or services, but are alternatively geared toward improving the processes for producing and delivering products and services. Amazon.com is a powerful example of an innovator in the area of delivery systems. Founder Jeff Bezos started by selling books electronically and has transformed the firm into a retailing powerhouse that targets the needs and interests of customers in a broad range of categories. Many product, service and process innovations are developed by existing companies seeking to expand market share or reduce costs. Often, however, important innovations develop in new and entrepreneurial firms.

New firms are not plagued by the problem of structural inertia, nor are they bound to the past by internal politics, company norms, or existing structures and processes. Rather, they are free to 'start from scratch' and innovate in any or all of the areas highlighted above.

In light of the important role played by innovation, likely questions might be: 'Who are the innovators?' and 'How do they innovate?' In this chapter we will provide a gendered perspective on innovation using a sample of almost 200 US entrepreneurs. In particular, we will explore the extent to which women entrepreneurs innovate, and whether their level of innovation is comparable to that of men. We will also explore the types of innovations that women pursue and compare them with those pursued by men. Finally, we will explore potential barriers to innovation for women entrepreneurs and conclude with recommendations for addressing and removing those barriers.

PRIOR RESEARCH

Surprisingly, relatively little research has been carried out on the topic of gender and innovation. Although a number of articles and studies have compared women and men in specific industries typically associated with innovation – that is, information technology and bioscience – almost none has compared the attitudes of women and men toward innovation in general, or their specific approaches to innovation in particular. From the standpoint of human capital, women are much less likely to have degrees in STEM disciplines (science, technology, engineering and math), which serve as a locus for the development of many new products and services (Zafar, 2009). In particular, women are less likely to have experience working in technology firms. Prior research reveals that these firms are typically very male-dominated and are often perceived as a hostile and unwelcoming environment for women (Treanor et al., 2010). Women are also less likely to have prior entrepreneurial experience or high-level management experience in innovative firms, and are more likely to be clustered in the ranks of middle management (Cross and Linehan, 2006; Tai and Sims, 2005).

Prior research also indicates that women are less likely to be involved in innovative networks or networks that could provide resources for the development of new products and services. Researchers associated with the Diana Project have noted that only 5 percent of venture capital funding, which is often critical in the launch of technology-based and growth-oriented firms, goes to women-owned firms (Brush et al., 2002, 2004). Other qualities typically associated with innovation and entrepreneurship include self-confidence and a willingness to assume risks that may accompany failure. Prior research attests to gender differences in both of these dimensions (Koellinger et al., 2008; Minniti, 2010). In terms of self-confidence, women are often seen, or even describe themselves, as less confident in their own abilities than men (Allen et al., 2008; Catalyst, 2000). Similarly, prior research has often found that women lag men in the area of self-efficacy or 'the self-confidence that one has the necessary skills to succeed in creating a business' (Wilson et al., 2007, p. 388). From the standpoint of risk aversion, a number of studies have similarly identified the fear of failure as a major impediment to the launch and growth of women-owned firms (Allen et al., 2008; Canizares and Garcia, 2010; Cliff, 1998; Sexton and Bowman-Upton, 1990; Watson and Newby, 2005). Taken together, much of this previous literature suggests that women are less likely to be involved in innovative types of industries and activities. However, a new and growing stream of research contends that our definitions of innovation tend to be gendered and biased towards the types of industries (such as information technology and manufacturing) typically dominated by men (Blake and Hanson, 2005; Eriksson and Aromaa, 2012; Ranga and Etzkowitz, 2010; Sjogren and Lindberg, 2012). Thus, women appear to be less innovative in comparison to men. This research suggests that we often measure innovation in terms of the creation of new products, often involving some type of intellectual property, and have not focused as much on innovations in the service industry, where women dominate, or on process rather than product innovations. Blake and Hanson (2005), in particular, stress that we need to consider the contexts in which women operate when we evaluate the extent and nature of their innovative activities. Shaw et al. (2009, p. 37) assert that the 'problem, it appears, is not the existence of gender differences, but the lack of an appreciation of the differing contribution that women entrepreneurs make to society'.

This contention is consistent with observations regarding the gendered nature of entrepreneurship in general. In reviewing a sample of 81 research articles, Ahl (2006, p. 595) found 'a tendency to recreate the idea of women as being secondary to men and of women's businesses being of less significance'. Similarly, Brush et al. (2009, p. 19) argued that, for women, context affects the ways in which the entrepreneurial process unfolds as well as on 'growth prospects or even novelty of the venture'.

In this chapter, we seek to extend this line of inquiry by examining the extent to which women entrepreneurs are involved in innovation. We will also compare the ways in which women and men define and pursue innovative activities.

DATA AND CHARACTERISTICS

Data were drawn from a study on innovation in women-owned firms sponsored by the United Nations Commission on Trade and Development (UNCTAD). A survey was administered electronically using Survey Monkey in November of 2010. Participants were drawn from a variety of groups targeting entrepreneurs, small firms and women business owners. These included the National Association of Women Business Owners, the Women's Business Enterprise National Council, the Women Presidents' Organization and Xconomy.com. Firms were also drawn from the US Small Business Administration's Dynamic Small Business Search listing, and recruited through social networking sites such as Facebook, LinkedIn, and Twitter. A total of 196 usable surveys were returned, 69 from men, and 127 from women.

Table 6.1 summarizes the characteristics of firm owners included in our sample. It reveals that women were somewhat older than their male counterparts. This may reflect the fact that some women wait to launch their firms until after they have had children. Conversely, however, our findings reveal that women business owners were less likely to be married (66.7 percent vs. 77.9 percent) and more likely to be separated or divorced than men (16.7 percent vs. 10.3 percent). This suggests that women may turn to entrepreneurship as a means for supporting themselves and their families. These findings also reinforce the findings of prior research suggesting that work–life balance is more of a challenge for women entrepreneurs than for men (Brush et al., 2001; Walker et al., 2008). Our results indicate that both women and men entrepreneurs were well educated; over 80 percent completed a college or postgraduate degree program. However, men were more likely to have completed a masters, doctorate, or other graduate degree than women (58 percent vs. 49.6 percent). In terms of their race or ethnicity, the women owners in our sample were less likely to be Caucasian, and more likely to be black than men (84 percent vs 88.2 percent, and 8.8 percent vs. 2.9 percent, respectively). Male owners, however, were more likely to be immigrants or children of immigrants (14.5 percent vs. 3.2 percent, and 10.1 percent vs. 5.6 percent). Table 6.1 also reveals that, in spite of their impressive educational attainments, women entrepreneurs were less likely to have human capital in the form of prior senior management experience (31.7 percent vs. 41.2 percent). This finding is consistent with prior research indicating that, in spite of gains in the workplace, women have still not fully penetrated the senior ranks of management (Becker-Blease et al., 2010; Boden and Nucci, 2000; Carter et al., 1997; Nixdorff and Rosen, 2010). This has implications for their ability to develop skills in the area of overall firm strategy and senior-level decision-making.

Table 6.1 Owner characteristics

Questions and responses	Female (%)	Male (%)
What is your current age?		
25–34	3.2	11.6
35–44	26.2	20.3
45–54	30.2	24.6
55–64	31.7	33.3
65 or older	8.7	10.1
What is your marital status or living arrangement?		
Never married	13.5	11.8
Married/Living with a partner	66.7	77.9
Separated/divorced	16.7	10.3
Widowed	3.2	0.0
What is the highest level of education you have achieved?		
Primary school or less	0.8	0.0
Secondary school or less	0.8	0.0
Some college or similar	16.5	14.5
Bachelor's degree	33.1	27.5
Postgraduate degree	49.6	58.0
What is your race or ethnicity (or national origin)?		
Caucasian	84	88.2
African descent	8.8	2.9
Asian/Pacific islander	4.0	5.9
Hispanic/Latino	2.4	5.9
Native American/Alaska Native	0.8	0.0
Other	4.0	5.9
Did you or one or both of your parents immigrate to the US from another country?		
No	88.1	71.0
Yes, I did	3.2	14.5
Yes, one or both my parents did	5.6	10.1
Yes, myself and one or both parents did	3.2	4.3
Which one of the following best describes the position you held immediately prior to starting this business?		
Executive/senior management in another business/organization	31.7	41.2
Middle management	25.2	22.1
Professional (doctor, attorney, etc)	17.1	13.2
Technical/clerical/service position	6.5	8.8
Student or teacher	7.3	8.8
Out of the workforce	3.3	1.5
Owner of another business	8.9	4.4
Other (please specify)	4.1	2.9

Table 6.2 summarizes the characteristics of firms included in our sample and reveals that, consistent with prior research, women-owned firms were smaller than men-owned firms in terms of both sales and number of employees (Coleman, 2002; Fairlie and Robb, 2009; Robb and Wolken, 2002). About 40 percent of women-owned firms had revenues of less than $50000 per year, compared with about 30 percent of firms owned by men. Similarly, a higher percentage of men-owned firms had revenues in excess of $1 million, compared with women-owned firms (17.6 percent vs. 11.3 percent). Women entrepreneurs were also more likely to have no employees aside from themselves (36.2 percent vs. 23.2 percent). In contrast, men-owned firms were about ten times as likely as women-owned firms to have more than 50 employees (11.6 percent vs. 1.6 percent). Our findings also show that women were much more likely to be the sole owners of their firms than men (68.8 percent vs. 33.8 percent). This has implications for the level of resources available to the firm in the form of human and financial capital. It stands to reason that multiple owners would provide a broader and possibly deeper range of education and experience. Finally, as in prior studies, our survey results revealed noteworthy gender differences in industry concentration (Anna et al., 2000; Du Rietz and Henrekson, 2000; Kalleberg and Leicht, 1991; Loscocco et al., 1991; Robb and Wolken, 2002). In particular, women-owned firms were less likely to be in the fields of manufacturing; information and communication; and professional, scientific and technical activities. Conversely, they were more likely to be in retail and service industries as well as finance and insurance. Since the information and communication, and professional, scientific and technical fields tend to provide fertile ground for product and service innovations, one might surmise from these results that men-owned firms would be more involved in activities typically defined as innovative.

GENDER DIFFERENCES IN APPROACHES TO INNOVATION

One important gender difference in attitudes and approaches to innovation relates to the entrepreneur's original motivation for launching their firm. As Table 6.3 reveals, men were more likely to state that they started their firm for the expressed purpose of developing an entirely new product or service (38.5 percent vs. 19.7 percent). In contrast, women owners were more likely to focus on innovation in their marketing and management practices than men. Women were also more likely to express the belief that their company was not innovative (7.7 percent vs. 1.5 percent).

Table 6.3 also highlights gender differences in defining the term

Table 6.2 Business characteristics

Questions and responses	Female (%)	Male (%)
What were the approximate sales of your business in 2009?		
Under $50 000	39.1	30.9
$50 000–$99 999	14.8	8.8
$100 000–$249 999	13.0	14.7
$250 000–$499 999	6.1	4.4
$500 000–$999 999	11.3	13.2
$1 000 000–$4 999 999	11.3	17.6
$5 000 000 or more	4.3	10.3
How many full-time equivalent employees (including part-time and contract workers) does your primary business currently employ, not including yourself?		
None in addition to myself	36.2	23.2
1–4 employees	37.0	31.9
5–9 employees	11.8	15.9
10–49 employees	13.4	17.4
50+ employees	1.6	11.6
In what industry is your business?		
Manufacturing	5.5	11.1
Water supply; sewerage, waste management and remediation activities	1.8	0.0
Construction	2.7	4.8
Wholesale and retail trade	4.5	1.6
Transportation and storage	2.7	0.0
Accommodation and food service activities	1.8	4.8
Information and communication	8.2	25.4
Finance and insurance	6.4	1.6
Real estate activities	3.6	1.6
Professional, scientific and technical activities	25.5	31.7
Administrative support service activities	6.4	0.0
Education	3.6	0.0
Human health and social work activities	5.5	4.8
Arts, entertainment, recreation	3.6	4.8
Other service activities	18.2	7.9

'innovation' within the context of the firm. Not surprisingly, the majority of both women and men associated entrepreneurship with the introduction of new products or services. Other definitions of innovation included commercializing opportunities created by new knowledge and new ideas, recognizing the value of new information, investing in new technologies or

Table 6.3 Business intentions/innovations

Questions and responses	Female (%)	Male (%)
Some businesses are started with the intention of bringing a new or improved product or service to the market. Most others start for a myriad of reasons, but some then develop creative ways to manage or market existing products or services. In thinking about your own business, do any of the following describe your business' activities or what has made your business different from others?		
My firm was started with the express purpose of developing and selling an entirely new product or service in my market	19.7	38.5
My firm was started with the express purpose of making a significant improvement to an existing product or service	41.9	43.1
My firm deals with an existing product or service, but markets it in a new or substantially different way	32.5	26.2
While my firm is not innovative in terms of products or services, I've developed new management practices within my company that are innovative	20.5	18.5
I don't think my company is innovative	7.7	1.5
What does the word 'innovation' mean to you in the context of your business? (Check as many as apply)		
Investing in new technologies or processes	48.8	50.7
Introducing or developing new products or services	75.6	84.1
Introducing a new method of production	35.4	46.4
Entering a new market	49.6	52.2
Introducing changes in the practice of organizational or management behavior	58.3	49.3
Introducing changes in marketing process	59.1	44.9
Recognizing the value of new, external information, and applying it to commercial ends	64.6	69.6
Exploiting the opportunities provided by new knowledge and ideas that are not fully commercialized by existing firms	63.0	81.2
High level of risk taking	14.2	24.6
Has your company implemented any of the following innovations in the past three years? (Check as many as apply)		
New or significantly improved product or service	71.5	77.6
New or significantly improved production or delivery process	37.4	43.3
New business practices	57.7	53.7
New marketing practices	68.3	58.2

processes, entering a new market, or introducing changes in organizational or management practices. Table 6.3 also shows that men were more likely to associate innovation with new methods of production (46.4 percent vs. 35.4 percent), possibly because they were more heavily represented in the fields of manufacturing and information technology. Men were also more likely to associate innovation with the commercialization opportunities that accompany new knowledge and new ideas (81.2 percent vs. 63 percent). Conversely, women were more likely to associate innovation with changes in marketing processes (59.1 percent vs. 44.9 percent), and with changes in organizational or management behavior (58.3 percent vs. 49.3 percent). These differences might lead us to surmise that men tend to have a harder definition of innovation, associating it with the development and eventual sale of new products and services, while women are more likely to have a softer definition of innovation in that they are more likely to associate it with changes in marketing or management processes and practices. Men were also much more likely to associate innovation with risk-taking than women (24.6 percent vs. 14.2 percent), possibly at least partially due to the different ways in which they characterized innovation.

Finally, Table 6.3 illustrates that, in terms of their own experience with innovation, a high percentage of both women and men reported that they had implemented innovations in their companies within the previous three years. Consistent with their responses to the previous question, a higher percentage of men indicated that they had introduced a new or significantly improved product, service, means of production or delivery system. Conversely, women were more likely to state that they had introduced new business practices (57.7 percent vs. 53.7 percent) or new marketing practices (68.3 percent vs. 58.2 percent).

One measure of the level of innovative activity is the extent to which firms make use of intellectual property protection. Our data revealed that male business owners were more likely to have patents than women business owners (35.6 percent vs. 12.5 percent). Similarly, male business owners were significantly more likely to have industrial design rights and licenses. However, women-owned businesses were more likely to hold copyrights than men-owned businesses (58.9 percent vs. 46.7 percent). These differences in intellectual property between men and women business owners may be a reflection of the types of industries in which their firms operate, that is, male-dominated industries such as manufacturing and technology, versus female-dominated industries such as education, marketing and the arts.

Another manifestation of the level of innovative activity is the extent to which the entrepreneur is willing to reinvest firm revenues in the pursuit of innovation. Interestingly, here we find that men were less likely than women to invest in innovation (56.0 percent vs. 40.4 percent). Our findings reveal, however, that women were more likely to invest in informal efforts rather than in formal research (10.2 percent vs. 19.6 percent); again, possibly a reflection of the personal and industry contexts in which women operate.

A third indication of the level of innovative activity may be the entrepreneur's attitude toward risk. With any new or enhanced product, service or delivery system there is the risk of failure. Thus, we might assume that business owners who are less willing to take risks, and have a greater fear of failure, might be less willing to innovate. Surprisingly, our findings indicate that while there were more women than men who hesitated when it came to taking risks (6.3 percent vs. 2.9 percent), there were also more women than men who enjoyed taking risks (26.2 percent vs. 22.1 percent), even if they did not know what the outcome would be.

In spite of their expressed willingness to take risks, our findings revealed that women business owners had fewer failure experiences than men. Women were more likely to respond that they had no failure experiences (28.3 percent vs. 14.5 percent). At the other extreme, men were more likely to respond that they had more than three failure experiences (30.4 percent vs. 11.8 percent). This finding may suggest, consistent with interviews conducted by the authors, that women are more likely to take calculated risks and develop contingency plans if events do not transpire as anticipated (Coleman and Robb, 2012). Another possible explanation for this finding is that women are more reluctant to define a business setback as a failure. Alternatively, they may view it as an inevitable part of their learning process. The women and men business owners in our sample also exhibited different responses to failure experiences. Whereas both women and men responded that their own hard work was the major factor in recovering from a failure (43.9 percent and 37.9 percent), men were much more likely to attribute their recovery to self-confidence than women (33.3 percent vs. 17.5 percent). Consistent with prior research, women appear to rely more heavily on family support than men (7.9 percent vs. 1.5 percent). Women were also more willing to turn to external advisors (7.9 percent vs. 4.5 percent) to help them recover from a failure experience.

We conclude this section with Table 6.4, which summarizes the respondents' attitudes and beliefs about innovation. These reveal similarities between women and men as well as some important differences. Both women and men business owners felt that innovation and creativity were important for their business, and neither particularly felt that innovation was too costly or that it was easier for large firms. In contrast, women business owners were much more likely to strongly or somewhat agree with the statement that they have innovative ideas but do not know how

Table 6.4 Attitudes and beliefs about innovation

	Strongly agree (%)	Agree somewhat (%)	Disagree somewhat (%)	Strongly disagree (%)	I don't know (%)
Here are some statements that business owners have made concerning their views on innovation and creativity. For each one, please tell us if you strongly agree, agree somewhat, disagree somewhat, or strongly disagree.					
Females:					
Innovation and creativity are important tenets of my business' operation.	73.2	23.6	3.1	0.0	0.0
Being innovative takes too much time and money, and is not very important to my business at this time.	0.0	4.0	17.6	76.8	1.6
It's much easier for larger businesses to be innovative than for smaller firms.	6.3	15.7	24.4	53.5	0.8
I have some innovative ideas, but I don't know how to implement them.	4.8	35.7	27.8	32.5	0.8
I could be more innovative in my business if I had more examples or role models, from other businesses or by participating in an educational program.	8.1	30.6	29.0	29.8	4.8
Males:					
Innovation and creativity are important tenets of my business' operation.	73.5	25.0	1.5	0.0	0.0
Being innovative takes too much time and money, and is not very important to my business at this time.	0.0	2.9	14.7	82.4	0.0
It's much easier for larger businesses to be innovative than for smaller firms.	1.5	11.8	22.1	64.7	0.0
I have some innovative ideas, but I don't know how to implement them.	4.5	21.2	24.2	48.5	1.5
I could be more innovative in my business if I had more examples or role models, from other businesses or by participating in an educational program.	4.4	26.5	22.1	41.2	5.9

to implement them (40.5 percent vs. 25.7 percent). Similarly, women were more likely to strongly or somewhat agree with the statement that they could be more innovative if they had greater access to role models or educational programs (38.7 percent vs. 30.9 percent). We will explore these differences more fully in our multivariate analysis below.

MULTIVARIATE ANALYSIS

Although our descriptive statistics reveal similarities as well as differences between women and men in both their attitude and approach to innovation, some of our differences may be driven by firm and owner characteristics such as firm size, industry selection and the owner's human capital, rather than by innate gender differences. To explore this possibility, we constructed a series of multivariate models using various measures of innovation as the dependent variable. Independent variables included measures of owner age, educational level, firm size, firm age, industry, gender and growth expectations. These variables were selected because our descriptive statistics revealed gender differences in these areas. Specifically, women business owners tended to be somewhat older and were less likely to have graduate degrees. Their firms were also smaller, newer and more likely to be in non-professional industries (service and retail). Logistic regression was used for our multivariate analysis since the dependent variables were dichotomous rather than continuous.

Our first logistic regression model used intellectual property as the dependent variable (a dummy variable coded 1 if the respondent had some form of intellectual property protection, otherwise 0). One typically associates intellectual property, or the creation of new ideas, with innovative firms. Further, our descriptive statistics revealed large differences between women and men in their types of intellectual property protection. However, the results of our multivariate analysis presented in Table 6.5 reveal that when we control for growth expectations, industry, owner age and education, firm age and size, there are no significant differences between women and men in terms of their intellectual property. Thus, controlling for other variables, the women entrepreneurs in our sample were just as likely to have and protect innovative ideas as men. The only independent variable that was significant in this model was the variable representing high growth. Thus, firm owners who aspire to higher levels of growth for their firms also have a significantly greater likelihood of having intellectual property protection.

Our second logistic regression model examined the extent to which women felt they were able to develop their innovative ideas (a dummy

Table 6.5 The relationship between gender and intellectual property protection

Independent variables	Coefficient	z-score	P>|Z|
Female[1]	−0.4272300	−1.23	0.220
High growth expectations[2]	0.6905727	1.66	0.098
Industry[3]			
Non-professional	0.0486893	0.12	0.906
Professional	0.3058834	0.68	0.493
Age[4]			
<35 years	−0.0146570	−0.02	0.983
45–54 years	0.4453232	1.04	0.297
55–64 years	0.6623159	1.38	0.166
65+ years	0.0529458	0.08	0.936
Education[5]			
College degree	0.2006000	0.41	0.682
Postgraduate +	−0.4363370	−0.98	0.327
Firm age[6]			
6–10 years	0.5282389	1.20	0.231
11–15 years	−0.7611270	−1.33	0.182
>15 years	−0.3616880	−0.72	0.472
Revenue[7]			
100–250K	0.7076124	1.42	0.157
250–500K	0.0370982	0.05	0.959
500K–1 million	−0.5720340	−1.07	0.283
>1 million	0.5949773	1.20	0.231
Constant	0.0785796	0.12	0.907

Log likelihood: −125.0119
Prob> chi2: 0.1237
Pseudo R2: 0.0871

Notes:
1. A dummy variable coded 1 if the respondent was female, otherwise 0.
2. A dummy variable coded 1 if the respondent's goal was to grow their firm into a large entity, otherwise 0.
3. Industry unknown has been excluded.
4. 35–44 years age group has been excluded.
5. Less than a college degree has been excluded.
6. Less than 5 years has been excluded.
7. Less than 100K has been excluded.

variable coded 1 if the respondent agreed or somewhat agreed with the statement 'I have some innovative ideas, but I don't know how to implement them', otherwise 0). This was another area where gender differences were revealed in our descriptive analysis. As was the case in our first logistic regression model, the results presented in Table 6.6 show no significant differences between women and men business owners when we control for other factors. Thus, women entrepreneurs felt they were just as capable of developing their innovative ideas as men. In this model, the variable

Table 6.6 *The relationship between gender and the propensity to develop/ implement innovative ideas*

Independent variables	Coefficient	z-score	P>|Z|
Female[1]	−0.5218780	−1.48	0.139
High growth expectations[2]	0.0661616	0.17	0.868
Industry[3]			
Non-professional	0.8583852	2.09	0.037
Professional	0.2513501	0.58	0.559
Age[4]			
<35 years	−0.5102360	−0.72	0.470
45–54 years	−0.0498010	−0.12	0.907
55–64 years	0.0600646	0.13	0.899
65+ years	0.0535263	0.08	0.936
Education[5]			
College degree	−0.2349650	−0.48	0.633
Postgraduate +	−0.1857880	−0.41	0.681
Firm age[6]			
6–10 years	−0.5139310	−1.22	0.221
11–15 years	0.0159030	0.03	0.979
>15 years	−0.4150320	−0.84	0.403
Revenue[7]			
100–250K	0.4711722	0.95	0.344
250–500K	1.0843000	1.26	0.206
500K–1 million	0.0720384	0.14	0.892
>1 million	0.4399525	0.91	0.362
Constant	0.5638656	0.83	0.408

Log likelihood: −125.22569
Prob> chi2: 0.6548
Pseudo R2: 0.0536

Notes:
1. A dummy variable coded 1 if the respondent was female, otherwise 0.
2. A dummy variable coded 1 if the respondent's goal was to grow their firm into a large entity, otherwise 0.
3. Industry unknown has been excluded.
4. 35–44 years age group has been excluded.
5. Less than a college degree has been excluded.
6. Less than 5 years has been excluded.
7. Less than 100K has been excluded.

representing non-professional firms was significant and positive. This suggests that owners of firms in industries such as service and retail, where women are heavily represented, feel less confident in their ability to develop innovative ideas. This finding further suggests that innovative behavior may be at least partially driven by industry selection rather than by gender.

Our third model examined the importance of role models and educational opportunities in helping business owners develop innovative ideas (a dummy variable coded 1 if the respondent agreed or somewhat agreed with the statement 'I could be more innovative if I had role models or education', otherwise 0). Our descriptive statistics revealed that women business owners were more likely to agree or strongly agree with the statement that they could be more innovative if they had more role models or education. As in our previous logistic regression models, however, we again found no significant gender differences when we controlled for other variables (see Table 6.7). In this model, we did find that the variables representing the oldest two groupings of entrepreneurs (55–64 and 65+ years of age) were significant and positive. Thus, older entrepreneurs were less confident in their ability to innovate without additional support from role models or educational programs. Similarly, the variables representing older firms and higher-revenue firms were significant and negative at the 0.10 level. This result suggests that larger, well-established firms have developed a strategy for developing innovative ideas over time. Finally, the variable representing non-professional firms was significant and positive at the 0.10 level. As was the case in the previous model, owners of firms in industries such as service and retail are less confident in their abilities to develop innovative ideas without external support.

Our final logistic regression model examines the relationship between the gender of a business owner and their growth expectations (a dummy variable coded 1 if the respondent's goal was to grow their firm into a large entity, otherwise 0). Highly innovative firms are often associated with significant growth and profitability. Prior research, however, suggests that women entrepreneurs are less likely than men to be motivated by firm growth. Alternatively, several researchers have suggested that women prefer moderate and controlled growth (Morris et al., 2006; Orser and Hogarth-Scott, 2002). Further, some researchers theorize that women are more concerned than men with the risks associated with rapid growth (Cliff, 1998). Our findings, as shown in Table 6.8, confirm this hypothesis. The women entrepreneurs in our sample were significantly less likely than the men to state that their goal was to grow their firm into a large entity. Older firms (>15 years) were also less likely to cite growth as a goal, while larger firms (revenue >1 million) were significantly more likely to pursue growth.

Table 6.7 The relationship between gender and the importance of role models and education to the development of innovative ideas

Independent variables	Coefficient	z-score	P>|Z|
Female[1]	−0.2236977	−0.64	0.521
High growth expectations[2]	0.7131157	1.69	0.090
Industry[3]			
Non-professional	0.4749788	1.14	0.254
Professional	0.1923502	0.43	0.666
Age[4]			
<35 years	0.1499840	0.21	0.830
45–54 years	0.5288750	1.24	0.214
55–64 years	0.8550752	1.78	0.075
65+ years	1.9661200	2.58	0.010
Education[5]			
College degree	0.1314201	0.26	0.794
Postgraduate +	−0.0872856	−0.19	0.848
Firm age[6]			
6–10 years	0.3384848	0.78	0.433
11–15 years	0.6585990	1.04	0.299
>15 years	−0.9196584	−1.78	0.076
Revenue[7]			
100–250K	−0.0079599	−0.02	0.987
250–500K	0.4158626	0.52	0.602
500K–1 million	−0.9776225	−1.81	0.071
>1 million	0.6522448	1.27	0.205
Constant	−0.4931960	−0.72	0.469

Log likelihood: −122.4321
Prob> chi2: 0.0464
Pseudo R2: 0.1022

Notes:
1. A dummy variable coded 1 if the respondent was female, otherwise 0.
2. A dummy variable coded 1 if the respondent's goal was to grow their firm into a large entity, otherwise 0.
3. Industry unknown has been excluded.
4. 35–44 years age group has been excluded.
5. Less than a college degree has been excluded.
6. Less than 5 years has been excluded.
7. Less than 100K has been excluded.

SUMMARY AND CONCLUSIONS

This chapter summarizes the results of survey responses from approximately 200 US entrepreneurs concerning their attitudes and behaviors

Table 6.8 The relationship between gender and high growth expectations

Independent variables	Coefficient	z-score	P>|Z|
Female[1]	−0.7491929	−1.85	0.064
Industry[2]			
Non-professional	−0.5586081	−1.08	0.278
Professional	−0.2121011	−0.39	0.695
Age[3]			
<35 years	0.6161463	0.83	0.405
45–54 years	−0.3158118	−0.62	0.537
55–64 years	0.0217538	0.04	0.969
65+ years	−0.1929056	−0.21	0.835
Education[4]			
College degree	0.1390789	0.22	0.823
Postgraduate +	0.4414175	0.78	0.435
Firm age[5]			
6–10 years	0.1435183	0.29	0.768
11–15 years	−0.7076288	−0.98	0.329
>15 years	−1.9066780	−2.51	0.012
Revenue[6]			
100–250K	0.2737406	0.45	0.649
250–500K	0.3173478	0.35	0.728
500K–1 million	0.4358875	0.63	0.531
>1 million	1.6320010	2.85	0.004
Constant	−0.8408944	−1.06	0.290

Log likelihood: −90.371764
Prob> chi2: 0.0367
Pseudo R2: 0.1319

Notes:
1. A dummy variable coded 1 if respondent was female, otherwise 0.
2. Industry unknown has been excluded.
3. 35–44 years age group has been excluded.
4. Less than a college degree has been excluded.
5. Less than 5 years has been excluded.
6. Less than 100K has been excluded.

toward innovation and the development of innovative ideas in their firms. Our descriptive results reveal many similarities but also noteworthy differences between women and men in both their innovative attitudes and behaviors. In particular, men were more likely to state that they started their firms to develop an entirely new product or service, while women were more likely to innovate in the areas of marketing or management practices. Men were also much more likely than women to have intellectual property (IP) protection in the form of patents, industrial design rights, and licenses, while women were more likely to have IP protection in the form of copyrights. Women were more likely to agree or strongly agree that they had innovative ideas but did not know how to implement them. Further, women were more likely to agree or strongly agree with the statement that they could be more innovative if they had more role models or educational programs. Taken together, these descriptive results seem to suggest that women business entrepreneurs are less innovative and less engaged in innovation than men.

However, multivariate analysis allows us to gain some additional insight from these survey results. In particular, when we control for owner and firm characteristics such as owner age, educational level, firm age, firm size as measured by revenues, industry and growth expectations, we find no significant gender differences in terms of: (1) intellectual property protection; (2) knowing how to implement innovative ideas; or (3) needing additional support in the form of role models and educational programs. Thus, our multivariate results indicate that women entrepreneurs are just as innovative and as capable of implementing innovations as men. Our findings also suggest that gender differences noted in our descriptive results may be driven by differences in variables such as owner age, firm age, firm size and industry selection rather than by inherent gender differences in a desire or ability to innovate. Specifically, the women entrepreneurs in our sample tend to be somewhat older, while their firms are younger, smaller and more likely to be clustered in retail and service industries.

Our results suggest the need to broaden our definition of innovation to encompass the types of innovative activities in which women engage. Prior research suggests that our current narrow definition of innovation may have the effect of devaluing or ignoring the contributions of women and their firms (Ahl, 2006; Blake and Hanson, 2005; Sjogren and Lindberg, 2012). These contributions include innovations in the service, retail, healthcare and education industries (where women dominate), as well as process rather than product types of innovations. A broader definition of innovation would also recognize the industries and contexts of which women are a part (Brush et al., 2009). Our findings reveal that in spite of industry, size and other differences, the majority of business owners in our survey, women as well as men, regarded themselves as innovators within the context of their firms.

Consistent with prior research, our multivariate results show that women entrepreneurs are significantly less likely to have expectations of high growth for their firms (Cliff, 1998; Morris et al., 2006; Orser and Hogarth-Scott, 2002). This may cause them to shy away from the types of innovations that would lead to explosive growth firms or gazelles, which start out small but grow very rapidly. Further qualitative research into the motivations of both growth-oriented and non-growth-oriented entrepreneurs could shed additional light on this distinction. However, the results of our study add value by pointing out that, contrary to prior research (Cross and Linehan, 2006; Ranga and Etzkowitz, 2010; Tai and Sims, 2005) but consistent with the views of Ahl (2006), there may be more similarities than differences in the innovative attitudes, beliefs and practices of women and men entrepreneurs.

REFERENCES

Ahl, H. (2006), 'Why research on women entrepreneurs needs new directions', *Entrepreneurship Theory and Practice*, 30 (5), 595–621.

Allen, I.E., Elam, A., Langowitz, N. and Dean, M. (2008), 'Global entrepreneurship monitor 2007 report on women and entrepreneurship', Wellesley, MA: Babson College.

Anna, A., Gaylen, L., Chandler, N., Jansen, E. and Mero, N.P. (2000), 'Women business owners in traditional and non-traditional industries', *Journal of Business Venturing*, 15 (3), 279–303.

Audretsch, D.B. (2002), 'The dynamic role of small firms: evidence from the US', *Small Business Economics*, 18 (1–3), 13–40.

Becker-Blease, J.R., Elkinawy, S. and Stater, M. (2010), 'The impact of gender on voluntary and involuntary executive departure', *Economic Inquiry*, 48 (4), 1102–1118.

Blake, M.K. and Hanson, S. (2005), 'Rethinking innovation: context and gender', *Environment and Planning*, 37 (4), 681–701.

Boden, R.J. Jr. and Nucci, A.R. (2000), 'On the survival prospects of men's and women's new business ventures', *Journal of Business Venturing*, 15 (4), 347–362.

Brush, C.G., Carter, N.M., Gatewood, E., Greene, P.G. and Hart, M.M. (2004), 'Gatekeepers of venture growth: a Diana project report on the role and participation of women in the venture capital industry', Kansas City, MO: Kauffman Center for Entrepreneurial Leadership.

Brush, C.G., Carter, N.M., Greene, P.G., Hart, M.M. and Gatewood, E. (2002), 'The role of social capital and gender in linking financial suppliers and entrepreneurial firms: a framework for future research', *Venture Capital*, 4 (4), 305–323.

Brush, C.G., de Bruin, A. and Welter, F. (2009), 'A gender-aware framework for women's entrepreneurship', *International Journal of Gender and Entrepreneurship*, 1 (1), 8–24.

Brush, C.G., Greene, P.G. and Hart, M.M. (2001), 'From initial idea to unique advantage: the entrepreneurial challenge of constructing a resource base', *Academy of Management Executive*, 15 (1), 64–78.

Canizares, S.M.S. and Fuentes Garcia, F.J. (2010), 'Gender differences in entrepreneurial attitudes', *Equality, Diversity and Inclusion: An International Journal*, 29 (8), 766–786.

Carter, N.M., Williams, M. and Reynolds, P.D. (1997), 'Discontinuance among new firms in retail: the influence of initial resources, strategy, and gender', *Journal of Business Venturing*, 12 (2), 125–145.

Catalyst, Center for Education of Women at the University of Michigan and

University of Michigan Business School (2000), 'Women and the MBA: gateway to opportunity', http://www.catalystwomen.org.

Cliff, J.E. (1998), 'Does one size fit all? Exploring the relationship between attitudes toward growth, gender, and business size', *Journal of Business Venturing*, 13 (6), 523–542.

Coleman, S. (2002), 'Characteristics and borrowing behavior of small women-owned firms: evidence from the 1998 survey of small business finances', *Journal of Business and Entrepreneurship*, 14 (2), 151–166.

Coleman, S. and Robb, A.M. (2012), *A Rising Tide: Financing Strategies for Women-Owned Firms*, Stanford, CA: Stanford University Press.

Cross, C. and Linehan, M. (2006), 'Barriers in advancing female careers in the high tech sector: empirical evidence from Ireland', *Women in Management Review*, 21 (1), 28–39.

Du Rietz, A. and Henrekson, M. (2000), 'Testing the female underperformance hypothesis', *Small Business Economics*, 14 (1), 1–10.

Eriksson, P. and Aromaa, E. (2012), 'Co-construction of innovation and gender: a critical review of research articles', paper presented at the Gender, Work, and Organization Conference, June, Keele University, UK.

Fairlie, R. and Robb, A. (2009), 'Gender differences in business performance: evidence from the characteristics of business owners survey', *Small Business Economics*, 33 (4), 375–395.

Kalleberg, A.L. and Leicht, K.T. (1991), 'Gender and organizational performance: determinants of small business survival and success', *Academy of Management Journal*, 34 (1), 136–161.

Koellinger, P., Minniti, M. and Schade, C. (2008), 'Seeing the world with different eyes: gender differences in perceptions and the propensity to start a business', Tinbergen Institute Discussion Paper TI 2008-035/3.

Loscocco, K.A., Robinson, J., Hall, R.H. and Allen, J.K. (1991), 'Gender and small business success: an inquiry into women's relative disadvantage', *Social Forces*, 70 (1), 65–85.

Minniti, M. (2010), 'Female entrepreneurship and economic activity', *European Journal of Development Research*, 22 (3), 294–312.

Morris, M.H., Miyasaki, N.N., Watters, C.E. and Coombes, S.M. (2006), 'The dilemma of growth: understanding venture size choices of women entrepreneurs', *Journal of Small Business Management*, 44 (2), 221–244.

Nixdorff, J.L. and Rosen, T.H. (2010), 'The glass ceiling women face: an examination and proposals for the development of future women entrepreneurs', *New England Journal of Entrepreneurship*, 13 (2), 71–87.

Orser, B. and Hogarth-Scott, S. (2002), 'Opting for growth: gender dimensions of choosing enterprise development', *Canadian Journal of Administrative Sciences*, 19 (3), 284–300.

Ranga, M. and Etzkowitz, H. (2010), 'Athena in the world of techne: the gender dimension of technology, innovation and entrepreneurship', *Journal of Technology Management and Innovation*, 5 (1), 1–12.

Robb, A.M. and Wolken, J. (2002), 'Firm, owner, and financing characteristics: differences between female- and male-owned small businesses', FEDS Working Paper No. 2002–18, http://www.federalreserve.gov/.

Sexton, D.L. and Bowman-Upton, N. (1990), 'Female and male entrepreneurs: psychological characteristics and their role in gender-related discrimination', *Journal of Business Venturing*, 5 (1), 29–36.

Shaw, E., Marlow, S., Lam, W. and Carter, S. (2009), 'Gender and entrepreneurial capital: implications for firm performance', *International Journal of Gender and Entrepreneurship*, 1 (1), 25–41.

Sjogren, F. and Lindberg, M. (2012), 'Gendering innovation', paper presented at the Gender, Work, and Organization Conference, June, Keele University, UK.

Tai, A.R. and Sims, R.L. (2005), 'The perception of the glass ceiling in high technology companies', *Journal of Leadership and Organizational Studies*, 12 (1), 16–23.

Treanor, L., Henry, C. and Miahj, F. (2010), 'Supporting women-led new venture creation in the bio-sciences: the role of the incubator', paper presented at the 2010 Diana International Conference on Women's Entrepreneurship, Banff, Alberta, 3–4 August.

Walker, E., Wang, C. and Redmond, J. (2008), 'Women and work–life balance: is home-based business ownership the solution?', *Equal Opportunities International*, 27 (3), 258–275.

Watson, J. and Newby, R. (2005), 'Biological sex, stereotypical sex-roles, and SME owner characteristics', *International Journal of Entrepreneurial Behavior and Research*, 11 (2), 129–143.

Wilson, F., Kickul, J. and Marlino, D. (2007), 'Gender, entrepreneurial self-efficacy, and entrepreneurial career intentions: implications for entrepreneurship education', *Entrepreneurship Theory and Practice*, 31 (3), 387–406.

Wong, P.K., Ping Ho, Y. and Autio, A. (2005), 'Entrepreneurship, innovation and economic growth: evidence from the GEM data', *Small Business Economics*, 24 (3), 335–350.

Zafar, B. (2009), 'College major choice and the gender gap', Federal Reserve Bank of New York, Staff Report No. 364.

7. A gender perspective on family business succession: case studies from France

Janice Byrne and Salma Fattoum

INTRODUCTION

In family business research, studies have shown that daughters are less likely to be chosen as successors (Ip and Jacobs, 2006; Martin, 2001; Dawley et al., 2004; Vera and Dean, 2005; Wang et al., 2008). More research on gender and succession is required (Martinez Jimenez, 2009; Wang, 2010; Constantinidis and Nelson, 2009) and different contextual settings may offer new insights. In this chapter, we further explore the role of gender in family business succession. We begin by reviewing the literature for explanations of women's under-representation as successors in family business. We posit that extant research largely takes an essentialist viewpoint and explains gender imbalance either through individual characteristics of women and/or broader environmental factors which differentially impact men and women. We then document five case studies of family business succession in France. We examine whether the explanatory factors offered in the literature are reflected in our case studies. We show how a broader understanding of gender can lend a more nuanced view of family business succession.

THEORETICAL GROUNDING

Family Business Research: Succession and Gender

Numerous authors have attempted to define the family firm (Lank, 1997). Our understanding of the family firm is 'an organization where members of an emotional kinship group dominate policy-making and ownership' (Carsrud, 1994, p. 40). The question of succession management in family business is perhaps one of the most important topics today (De Massis et al., 2008). Research has found that daughters are less likely to be considered as viable succession candidates (Ip and Jacobs, 2006; Martin, 2001; Dawley et al., 2004; Vera and Dean, 2005; Wang et al., 2008) and the phenomenon of 'primogeniture', whereby first-born sons are favored for succession, still largely prevails (Curimbaba, 2002; Dumas, 1992, 1998; Haberman and Danes, 2007; Keating and Little, 1997). The issue of daughter exclusion remains an under-researched area, especially when compared to the overall attention given to understanding succession within the family business field (Ip and Jacobs, 2006). We need to understand why so few women currently lead family businesses (Vera and Dean, 2005). Without such research, there is a danger that gender bias will lead to potential successors being ignored or undervalued (Martinez Jimenez, 2009) which could create a situation where worthy successors are not 'groomed' and failure of succession becomes inbuilt (Wang et al., 2008). We posit that, thus far, researchers have offered limited explanations as to why fewer daughters take over the family business, centering attention instead on mainly individual or firm-related environmental factors.

Individual Explanations

Some researchers have focused on the attributes, characteristics and behaviors of women to explain their under-representation as successors in family business. Women are said to possess 'limiting attitudes' toward their own potential and role in family business (Salganicoff, 1990). Questions are raised about women's interest and motivation to become successors. In general, women reportedly do not plan a career in the family business, do not aspire to ownership and see their work as a job rather than as a career (Dumas, 1989; Dumas et al., 1995; Vera and Dean, 2005). In a study of 91 women, only 27 percent expected to enter the family business (Salganicoff, 1990). Researchers have also examined women's reasons for wanting to join the family firm. Varying reasons included emotional ties to the family firm, a feeling of wanting to help the family, filling a position that nobody wanted, or being dissatisfied in another job (Salganicoff, 1990; Constantinidis, 2010). However, issues of ambition and family business careers have rarely been investigated. Once working in the family firm, women may experience challenges that prevent them from assuming a leadership role. They may experience role confusion and identity ambiguity (Freudenberger et al., 1989) and thus may be uncertain about how to behave and position themselves. Research found that daughters are often reluctant to upset their fathers or wound their fathers' pride by suggesting that their father retire and so may avoid the subject (Dumas, 1998).

Women in family business may fear being seen as unfeminine if they are aggressive in business (Freudenberger et al., 1989, p. 51).

Largely, research has dealt with gender issues in succession from an essentialist point of view, where 'women are like this and men are like that' (Bradley, 2007). Women are said to have different communication styles within family businesses (Danes et al., 2005) and a better ability to openly express themselves and communicate compared to men (Haberman and Danes, 2007). Some family business researchers maintain that women communicate and problem-solve differently from men and they prioritize life experiences differently (Danes et al., 2005; Dumas, 1989, 1998; Francis, 1999; Haberman and Danes, 2007). Constructing men and women as different means that one understands men and women to be essential, unitary concepts, which limit the repertoire of both sexes (Ahl, 2006).

An example of an exception to that rule is the work of Cole (1997). In her study of nine family businesses in the United States, Cole found that as many men as women in family business seemed comfortable playing the nurturing and peacekeeping role – a role usually associated with female members of the family. Cole's (1997) research pointed to the heterogeneity of women's experiences in family business. She asserted that the differences between women in family business were as important as their similarities. Research participants held different views about how far they wanted to advance in the company and varying perspectives on the issue of childcare (Cole, 1997). However, researchers taking account of women's heterogeneity, or recognizing the limits of an essentialist approach to explaining gender inequality in family business, have remained relatively rare over the last decades. Indeed, as in entrepreneurship research, perhaps this search for difference between men and women is more willingly received by publishers than that of findings of 'sameness' (Ahl, 2002). We gain inspiration from those entrepreneurship researchers who understand gender as being about what one 'does' and not what one 'is' (Ahl, 2002, 2006; Hughes et al., 2012). Gender is a continuum, where masculine and feminine actions and behaviors can be performed (by either sex) to a lesser or stronger degree in different circumstances (Butler, 1990). Such an understanding yields a richer picture of gender, allowing for a more nuanced understanding of successor selection.

Environmental Explanations

Some family business researchers have explored the role of the environment and, more particularly, socialization in explaining gender inequality in succession. Socialization is the processes by which families, schools, workplaces, the mass media and literature transmit the rules and norms of gender-appropriate behavior for men and women (Oakley, 1981). Indeed, it is such socialization which explains how it is that 'one is not born, one becomes a woman' (De Beauvoir, 1973, p. 301). Garcia-Alvarez et al. (2002) identified how the potential successor's interest in the family business develops (or not) during early family socialization. This phase depends largely on the predecessors (Garcia-Alvarez et al., 2002). Differences in the extent and degree of socialization of sons and daughters in the family business have been identified as a key contributory factor to the under-representation of women successors. Daughters and sons are socialized differently, with daughters found to spend less time in the business and to receive less frequent encouragement than their fraternal counterparts (Iannarelli, 1992). Families often neglect to envisage daughters as potential successors in a family business and fail to make the necessary preparation or provision for them to assume a potential successor role (Dumas, 1990; Constantinidis, 2010). Next-generation family members are influenced from an early age in their decision to participate in the family firm (Dumas, 1998). While sons are encouraged to join the family business for an apprenticeship, daughters are encouraged to train for other careers (Keating and Little, 1997). Female offspring do not receive the same encouragement, opportunity and education as male offspring – a double standard which prevents women from attaining an executive or ownership position in the business (Rosenblatt et al., 1985; Constantinidis, 2010). Again, in terms of research emphasis, an exception is Cole's (1997) study, that found that many women felt supported by male family members. Most expressed satisfaction with their positions in the family business and the rule of primogeniture was not automatic; indeed 'sisters appeared to be moving ahead as fast as or faster than their brothers' (Cole, 1997, p. 366). Unfortunately, previous studies emphasizing the role of socialization do not examine cases where daughters have become successors in family firms against the odds (that is, without appropriate family socialization). This means that the agency of individual actors to overcome the structures in which they are embedded has not been fully explored. In line with this, we assert that the diversity of women's socialization experiences in family business is not accounted for.

Looking beyond the family role in socialization, research has also addressed how broader social norms can impact on succession. On a positive note, Dumas (1992) noted how societal conditioning of women as natural 'collaborators' and 'negotiators' may be advantageous in some instances. Daughters have been found to be able to successfully work with their fathers to take over the family firm because they had been socialized to collaborate throughout their lives (Dumas, 1992). However, generally, the stereotyping and discrimination against women in family business is said to be the result of prejudice in society as a whole (Salganicoff, 1990) and is damaging to potential daughter successors. People often assume that men are more competent than women (Carli, 1990), and women in family business are not valued in the same way as men (Francis, 1999; Gillis-Donovan and Moynihan-Bradt, 1990). Many women feel 'invisible' in a family business because they are not viewed by others, whether inside or outside the business, in the same way as male members (Hollander and Bukowitz, 1990). Daughter successors often experience conflict with non-family business members (Vera and Dean, 2005) as well as a lack of legitimacy in the eyes of suppliers and clients (Dumas, 1998; Vera and Dean, 2005; Constantinidis, 2010).

Research from the broader management domain indicates that the beliefs people hold about the sexes are derived from observations of the role performances of men and women and thus reflect the sexual division of labor and gender hierarchy of the society (Eagly et al., 2004). Characteristics of traditional leaders – individualism, control, assertiveness, skills of domination and advocacy – are socially ascribed to men in Western culture and generally understood as masculine (Acker, 1990; Calas and Smirich, 1993). It is often more difficult for women to become leaders and to achieve success in leadership roles (Eagly and Karau, 2002). This limits their leadership potential. In entrepreneurship research, the likelihood of women engaging in entrepreneurial activity is linked to the societal norms regarding women and labor force participation more generally (Delmar and Holmquist, 2003). An interesting research agenda, thus far neglected, would address how family and societal norms regarding gender roles impact family business succession.

RESEARCH OBJECTIVES AND CONTEXT

In the above paragraphs we sought to summarize and critically reflect on previous research addressing gender and succession in family business. Building on this, we clarify our primary research question: what role does gender play in succession? We look at this issue in the French context. In France, women represent 50 percent of the working population and are often more qualified than men (Belghiti-Mahut, 2004), but there is still a relatively low number who manage to break the 'glass ceiling'. French women rarely occupy top management positions in companies and represent only 7 percent of large companies' top executives (Cox and Harquail, 1991; Lewis, 1992; Laufer, 2004). But what are their experiences in family business? Are they held back by their own limiting attitudes and/or ambitions? Are they socialized differently to their male siblings? Are there other factors explaining the lower number of daughter successors? To answer such questions, we engaged in case study research involving French family firms which were involved in (or had recently completed) the succession process. We will begin by explaining in more detail our methodological choices and procedure.

METHOD AND SAMPLE

The human dynamics surrounding succession decisions and choices are complex and, thus, researchers greatly benefit from using in-depth qualitative methodologies. Qualitative research is excellent for addressing 'how' questions and for understanding the world from the perspective of those studied (that is, informants) as well as for examining and articulating processes (Pratt, 2009). A qualitative research method is thus particularly valuable for understanding and tackling aspects that are intrinsic to the process of succession (Cadieux et al., 2002). This study was part of a larger research project of 11 in-depth case studies of family business succession in France. Case study analysis enables us to have a 'rich picture' of complex processes and choices (Thomas, 2011). We identified the family businesses through our personal networks as well as the local Chamber of Commerce. In this chapter, we chose five different cases of family business succession. By using 'maximum variation' in purposeful sampling (Patton, 1980), the researcher can have more confidence in common patterns that emerge, while being able to describe the unique variation. Variation in the cases allows for replication, theory extension and consideration of alternative explanations (Yin, 1994). It also increases the robustness of findings (Eisenhardt and Graebner, 2007). We sought instances of diversity not only in family composition and final successor choice but also in the type of business. Thus, this sample includes a variety of male–female sibling configurations. We had one single case of father–daughter succession from all 11 cases and include that here as well as four other cases of father–son succession. Figure 7.1 shows the family composition in genogram format. In one of our families, there were three sons.

The family businesses in our sample came from various different sectors of activity: construction, industrial spare parts, restaurants and catering, dairy farming and manufacturing. The businesses also varied in age, size and turnover. See Table 7.1 for an overview of each of the five family business cases chosen for this study. We also indicate the interviewees with whom we met in each case.

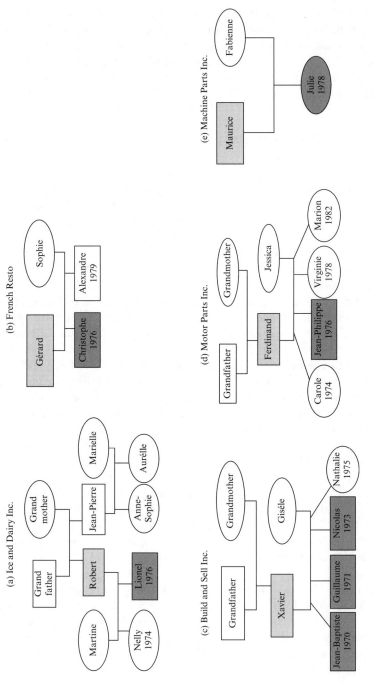

Figure 7.1 Family composition

Table 7.1 Overview of family business cases

Name	Sector of activity	Year founded	Number of Employees	Revenue (millions of euros)	Generation	Family composition	Successor	Successor's birth order	Interviewees
Ice & Dairy Inc.	Dairy/Ice cream Production	1898	520	94	4th	1 daughter and son	Son	2nd	Successor (Lionel) Sister of successor (Nelly)
French Resto	Restaurant and brasserie business	1972	110	32	2nd	2 sons	Son	1st	Predecessor (Gérard) Successor (Christophe)
Build & Sell Inc.	Construction and real estate	1945	250	80	3rd	3 sons and 1 daughter	3 sons (rotating directorship)	1st, 2nd and 3rd	Predeccessor (Xavier) Successor (Nicolas)
Motor Parts Inc.	Spare parts (vehicles)	1948	400	48	3rd	1 son, 3 daughters	Son	2nd	Predecessor (Ferdinand) Successor (Jean Philippe)
Machine Parts Inc.	Industrial small parts	1993	150	31	2nd	1 daughter	Daughter	Only child	Successor (Julie) (Predeccesor; Maurice, deceased)

Data Collection and Analysis

We gathered contextual information about the organizations from primary and secondary sources. We visited the physical site in each instance and gained insight into how each business functioned and got a sense of the prevailing company culture. We consulted company documentation and websites to familiarize ourselves with business operations. We believe that these data sources allowed us to have a good understanding of each business and the family members working there. We then conducted semi-structured interviews with family business members (eight male and two female) from our five different cases. The interview protocol included: introduction to the firm; open questions about participants' involvement and role in business; open questions about how the succession process came about and how it was developing. The interviews varied in length from 45 to 90 minutes and were all conducted face-to-face. All interviews were recorded, transcribed and subsequently uploaded to the NVivo 10 software package for further analysis. In four of the five cases, we held interviews with at least two family members (the one exception is the family firm Machine Parts Inc. where we spoke only with the daughter, Julie (the successor), after the premature death of her father ('the predecessor', Maurice). Interviews took place at the family business site.

Our analysis involved a content analysis of interview transcripts with family business members as well as our in-depth knowledge of each case. We used NVivo 10 to record, identify and categorize the participants' written and verbatim accounts. We began by reading and rereading the data to become thoroughly familiar with them and identify patterns, themes and/or surprising features (Hammersley and Atkinson, 1983). We first adopted a strategy of weak prestructured coding. Two broad a priori categories, derived from the literature review, were used to code the data: individual and environmental factors. The two researchers independently identified relevant phrases and sentences from data relating to succession and assigned them to one of the two overarching categories. Our secondary coding stage was carried out without consultation between the two researchers in order to avoid influencing the other's coding procedure. During this stage, each researcher revisited the two broad category themes and developed subcategories within each broad category theme. Following this, the two researchers met to discuss their subcategories. Mutual agreement on the subcategories of the individual and environmental factor themes was reached by further discussion and collaboration.

FINDINGS

Individual Factors

Interest

Our case studies echo to some extent the previous literature findings where daughters have indicated a lack of interest in taking on the family business, particularly when there is a brother in the family (Constantinidis, 2010). In the case of Ice & Dairy Inc., Nelly clearly indicated her lack of interest in working in the family firm. While she did work in the company for a short period following her studies, she made it quite clear that it was not a career path that she had in mind for herself. She left after six months to rejoin her boyfriend in another region of France and set up her own hotel business. Her brother, Lionel, joined the firm later and is now the designated successor. He maintains he had expressed interest in the firm at a young age, while his cousins declined and he explained how it 'didn't suit' his sister. In French Resto Inc., Christophe talked of how his father had successfully 'passed on his passion' for working in the restaurant business to him and how he could not imagine doing anything else. It was something Christophe always 'knew' he wanted to do. The second son joined the firm after some time abroad. Their father emphasized how both came to work in the family business of their own accord. In the case of Build & Sell, Nicolas explains how he was working elsewhere when his father approached him and advised him to join the business now under his guidance. He saw it as an opportunity that he could not turn down. Xavier (the predecessor at Build & Sell Inc.) evokes notions of an unpleasant power struggle between his three sons who rotate the leadership role. In Motor Parts Inc., the son successor, Jean-Philippe, described his sisters' lack of interest in taking on the family firm. His father, Ferdinand, recalls how he asked one of his daughters if she was interested in taking on the family firm and she replied, 'Are you kidding, Dad?!' as if the idea were an absurdity. In the case of Machine Parts Inc., succession did not feature at all in Julie or her father's plans. In fact, Julie had planned to start her own architecture and interior design business for the luxury goods sector. Succession only became a reality due to Maurice's illness, his very sudden decline, and premature death. This correlates with previous findings (Dumas, 1989; Constantinidis, 2010) that daughters often become successors as a last resort or in the case of a family crisis.

Ability

The literature states that parents often doubt their daughter's ability or competence to take on the successor role (Barnes, 1988; Dumas, 1989, 1998;

Keating and Little, 1997). In our case studies, we encountered some explicit 'surface'-level opinions of the lack of capability of the daughters concerned. In Motor Parts Inc., the predecessor (father), Ferdinand, clearly states how 'girls are less daring', while in Build & Sell Inc., Xavier deems his daughter 'less intelligent' than her brothers. Her brother implies it is for the best that she does not have the 'worries' of the family business. The sons in both Build & Sell and Motor Parts all followed higher education in the broad area of their father's business (construction, engineering and mechanical engineering as well as business studies) and so deemed themselves capable of taking on responsibility in the family firm. Interestingly, daughters in both families went on to set up and run their own successful businesses.

A broader understanding of gender can show how predecessors choose between siblings based on 'gendered' perceptions of leadership style and perceived competencies as opposed to biological sex. For example, Nelly from Ice & Dairy Inc. attests to her father's preference for her to assume the role of successor. She explains her father's preference for her as a function of her personality: an impulsive, dynamic, action-oriented person who makes decisions. Hence here we have an example of a father who does not doubt his daughter's ability (Nelly herself, however, believes that she is better suited to working in a smaller business with more opportunities for contact with clients) and who conforms to masculine notions of leadership according to him: charismatic, takes decisions and acts fast. A couple of years later, her younger brother assumed the role. Nelly presents her brother Lionel as 'quite shy' and points out that his way of managing is much more human and collaborative than her father's. Nelly moreover told us that his father sometimes disagreed with her brother's approach. This way of managing – relational and collaborative – is often equated with a more feminine style of leadership (Fletcher, 2004).

A broader understanding of gender can help us understand how Gerard (French Resto) chooses between his two sons, Christophe and Alexandre. Gerard portrays Alexandre as the weaker of the two sons, he is a 'good little Daddy', who is 'not a winner' and is happy to 'back up his brother'. Alexandre is not portrayed as a strong man with leadership skills. It is his brother, Christophe, who is successor today. Gerard admires Christophe's dynamism and confidence, while Alexandre plays a supporting role and is more of a 'family man'. Gerard separates and ranks his two sons, positioning the son who 'does gender well' (Mavin and Grandy, 2012, p. 218), conforming to traditional masculine notions of strength and competition. Indeed, this example demonstrates well how some forms of masculinity and modes of behaviour are privileged in organizations (Broadbridge and Simpson, 2011). Illustrative quotations for two subcategories of individual factors ('interest' and 'ability') are presented in Table 7.2.

Table 7.2 Individual factors explaining succession

	Interest	Abilities
Ice & Dairy Inc.	'I didn't like the work in the family business' (Nelly)	'I am a saleswoman and I am made for small structures' (Nelly)
	'about 15 years ago my father had a meeting with my uncle, his two daughters, me and my sister . . . he asked, "Who wants to take it on? Who's interested in the business?" And I said I was interested. And there was no clear answer from the others. The girls. And very quickly, in fact, my uncle's two daughters said they weren't interested. And my sister had a go in the company but it didn't suit her at all' (Lionel)	'My father did not like the idea that I leave the firm . . . I have the same temperament as him, while my brother is more thoughtful. I think that he counted more on me than on my brother' (Nelly)
		'My dad said "You have travelled a good bit, you have commercial sales training, it could suit you . . . it could be a good opportunity for you, a good opening"' (Lionel)
		'Lionel . . . is more about feelings . . . he doesn't see the bad in people, he is still young and naive.' (Nelly)
French Resto	'I did not imagine doing something other than the restaurant business because my father passed on his passion' (Christophe)	'I did two years of preparatory school and three years at business school . . . so all that learning on the job I know . . . washing up, I know that. The kitchens and how it's organized, I know that . . . so all that groundwork, I didn't need to go back over it, I had already done it . . . so straight away I started in the head office . . . heading up finance, so financial director' (Christophe)
	'One day Christophe came to me . . . and said "I'm a bit bored, can I come work with you a while?" I said OK, you can have the office with Rodger the finance director . . . With the other [son], it was the same . . . he went to London for a year and a half because he had failed his hospitality diploma and . . . when he came back he said to me "Can I come to work?" I said "You can work in the restaurants as a head waiter", and that's how it all started' (Gerard)	'Christophe is General Director and Alexandre is Assistant Director . . . It's Christophe who manages . . . he has good interpersonal skills, he's a leader . . . Alexandre is less of a manager than Christophe . . . He hides behind his brother, he never comes to see me. But that doesn't bother me' (Gerard)

149

Table 7.2 (continued)

	Interest	Abilities
Build & Sell Inc.	'At the start, I wasn't completely certain that I wanted to come [and work at Build & Sell Inc.], so I pursued an independent career . . . it was useful to see other careers, other ways of working' (Nicolas)	'Succession is very difficult with three children . . . for example, it causes a problem with their sister, because there is a fourth one . . . She is 31 and has a lot of problems. First of all, she's less intelligent, the neurons don't work so well, and she had a horse accident a few years back and so lost the use of her arm' (Xavier)
	'My father didn't exactly give me an ultimatum . . . but he said to me either you come and work at Build & Sell now under my supervision or you'll come later and have to negotiate that with your brothers [smiles]. And so . . . I thought about it a lot . . . and I said to myself that giving it a go at Build & Sell was really worth it' (Nicolas)	'I am the third and then we have a little sister who is . . . who is younger obviously and she is in a whole other profession entirely . . . She [sister] is involved in horse-riding. So she doesn't have the worry of estate agency and construction' (Nicolas)
	'My three sons joined the business seven or eight years ago now, and they grumble because the succession isn't finalized. Some want the power, and say so' (Xavier)	'My two other brothers, one worked in construction and my oldest brother worked both in construction and in insurance' (Nicolas)
Motor Parts Inc.	'There's three girls and one boy and my sisters aren't at all interested in this business' (Jean Philippe)	'My son did a masters in the US . . . no, there was nobody else who could have taken over . . . not my daughters, they wouldn't have been able to . . . If I may say so, there's something about girls that makes them less daring, in general' (Ferdinand)
	'I said to my eldest daughter, "Don't you want to take on the business?" she said, "Dad, you must be kidding!", so it was settled in two seconds flat' (Ferdinand)	'I completed a scientific high school diploma, then a degree in mechanical engineering . . . so I was already

		mechanics oriented. I went to business school and I completed my studies with an MBA' (Jean Philippe)
	'I really became interested when I had more challenging things to do... it was when I did a whole complete year of an internship' (Jean Philippe)	'It's me who asked him to come... if I thought he wasn't sufficiently competent, I wouldn't have even tried. We would have talked about it' (Ferdinand)
Machine Parts Inc.	'I had a start-up project in mind but which was rather in the architecture and design sector... marketing for the big companies such as Louis Vuitton... where the store is really a strong symbol of communication. I wanted to create an agency in this domain' (Julie)	'I am an architect... in 2000 I was in exchange Erasmus in Italy so I was very far from all that... All my internships had been in the luxury domain... I was far removed from the industrial environment' (Julie)
	'I took it as a big opportunity to be able to take over a company... it suited my father too. Thus we said "OK, we'll do it like that"... I am a candidate for succession' (Julie)	'My personal psyche has always been really independent, solitary, go it alone, a seemingly "hard" personality. When people don't know me, they say that I am quite hard and authoritarian... some doubt my humanity' (Julie)

Environmental Factors

Socialization: family business initiation and expectations

Similar to the relevant literature, our case studies showed that daughters and sons were socialized differently (Iannarelli, 1992; Dumas, 1998), with the sons spending more time in the business. Christophe (successor, French Resto Inc.) talked of his early involvement in the restaurant business, often accompanying his father on his rounds of the restaurants and helping out on weekends as a waiter when it was busy. Nicolas (Build & Sell Inc.) remembers from a very young age being presented as a future successor to employees in his father's company. In Motor Parts Inc., Jean-Philippe (successor) first visited his father's company at the age of eight. He worked there in the summer months while at school and later completed his college internships in the family business. Lionel (Ice & Dairy Inc.), from the age of eight, woke early on Sunday mornings to do the rounds of the dairy farms with his father. At the age of 12, he assisted on the factory assembly line. Later he worked each summer in the family business and helped out with farm machinery or maintenance. Nelly, his sister, never went to the factory as a young girl and instead accompanied her mother when she went to help out at her grandparent's jewelry store. Julie (Machine Parts Inc.) very seldom visited her father's company as a young child and it was never envisaged that she would join the family business until the rapid demise of her father due to his illness. Indeed, Maurice had planned to sell his company before he learned of his illness.

We found that perceptions of family expectations of encouragement and succession 'obligation' varied. It cannot be said that all fathers actively encouraged their sons, but where there were daughters it does appear that they were guided in an alternative direction. In French Resto, where there were two sons and no daughters, Christophe (the oldest son) describes it as a natural evolution that he would one day lead the family business. His father Gerard (predecessor, French Resto), however, did not see it as a 'given' that his sons would come to work with him, saying to them, 'you will be my heirs but not necessarily my successors'. In Build & Sell, Nicolas also expressed a feeling of filial responsibility in continuing the family business. He talks of how he and his two brothers were often introduced over the years as the 'next generation' of leaders for the company. He believes that his father (Xavier), did not completely discount the possibility of his sister joining, but Xavier never described that. Xavier is preoccupied with the issue of equity. He does not think his oldest son Jean Baptiste is 'physically or mentally' up to the job; he thinks his second son has 'middle child' issues and is wary of the power struggle between them. Today he gains immense pleasure from helping his daughter in her horse-riding business. In Motor Parts Inc., Ferdinand describes the family tradition of being in mechanics and his son Jean Philippe indicates that his father 'succeeded' in passing on his 'love of machinery'.

Of course expectations (as a component of socialization) do not explain all eventualities. Ice & Dairy Inc. is the one case where a father had expectations for his daughter to succeed the family business (as opposed to his son). Nelly recalls how her father encouraged her to join the family firm once she finished her studies. Her boyfriend at the time also advised her that she should 'seize the opportunity'. She worked for six months in the company before leaving, much to her father's disappointment. Perhaps it is the time Nelly spent in her grandparent's jewelers which explains why she sees herself as 'made for small structures' and 'more of a sales person' as opposed to joining her father's ice cream and dairy production enterprise. Today Nelly runs a successful hotel business with her husband, which she set up herself.

Equally, socialization fails to explain Julie's success (successor at Machine Parts Inc.), as she was not socialized into the family business. Her prior education and work experience were in the luxury and design industry, and as her father did not bring her to the firm, the employees did not know her. She nonetheless accepted the role of managing director when her father's sudden illness meant that his plans to sell the company prior to retirement never materialized. As her father's illness progressed, Julie made a dramatic career move and applied for an MBA in family business management at a top French business school in in preparation to take over. Her father died before she had completed her MBA. Upon graduating, she took over the family business and accepted a year of working in a 'small, corner office' to which the acting company director allocated her. She 'took her time' to make allies and 'observe' before forming her own management team and firing those who blocked her path to real leadership. Within three years Julie had built a steady, reliable management team and boosted the organization's financial performance. Focusing on socialization denies the power of agency, that is, the individual's power to act (Bradley, 2007). To better understand the context of succession in each family firm of our sample, we need to recognize both the agency of the individual and the power relations that structures can impose. Thus, while subjectivity and external pressures define 'what it is possible to be' (Belsey, 1985), individuals can circumvent expectations.

Family roles

We found evidence of broader societal patterns of behavior which could help further explain the lower incidences of daughter successors. Many of our respondents (including the women themselves) reflected traditional views of family structures and childcare arrangements, accepting a lesser role for women in the family business as a consequence of this. Our interviewees describe very traditional views with regard to women's roles in their description of family structures: family members from Ice & Dairy, Motor Parts Inc., Machine Parts Inc., Build & Sell Inc. and French Resto Inc. all had family arrangements where the mother stayed at home to mind the children while the father worked in the family business. It was the norm that 'mothering' was seen to be a woman's primary responsibility. For example, Gerard and Christophe (predecessor and successor, French Resto) speak little about their mother's role in the business, despite the fact that she worked alongside her husband for the first ten years. She left after the birth of her second son, and following that her role was in the home while Gerard spent his time in the family business that they had started together. Nelly (Ice & Dairy Inc.) described how it was taken for granted that her female cousin who had a family early in life would not be a potential successor. She also made many comments about her mother's devotion to looking after the family while her father worked. She views her as a good mother and an 'excellent' wife. In Build & Sell, Xavier (the predecessor) worried that his son's wife was not supportive enough. He feared she wanted a husband who did not work at weekends, but he believed this was a norm that should be expected.

In the French Resto case, Gerard talks of how it is difficult to be both a good father and a good businessman; for him, it is impossible to be both. Hence his second son's characterization as a 'good little daddy' excludes him from the leadership role. In Ice & Dairy Inc. and Machine Parts Inc., we see women's role in family business as one of support and counsel. Nelly, while no longer involved in the company actively, sits on the board and regularly acts as a sounding board for her father and brother. Julie described how her mother 'listens to her at the end of the day, when you need a sympathetic ear'. She adds, 'she knows everything'. Thus, the women in the family business conform to the societal norms of women as being 'naturally' caring, collaborative and good listeners.

Exclusion and separation
No group ever sets itself up as 'the one' without at once setting up 'the other' against itself (de Beauvoir, 1973). As such, we see a separation and hierarchical ranking of men and women emerge through our interviewees' accounts of doing business. The 'separation' of men and women, and 'hierarchical ranking' or prioritizing (men being allowed to do certain things while women are not) reflects postmodern feminist ideas of how women's inequality in society is achieved and perpetuated (Ahl, 2002, 2006). This separation and hierarchical ranking limits women's access to

certain domains where business is discussed; that is, late at night in the office, or during male-only sporting or leisure activities. In French Resto, a distinct separation between masculine and feminine roles was described where men discussed work while hunting or 'over a cigar in the office in the evening' (Christophe, French Resto Inc.). Women in French Resto are also excluded from business discussions at family dinners, as the men usually sit together and join the women once work-related discussion is over. In Build & Sell, Xavier (predecessor) talks of the difficulty of succession when there are 'three children' (even though he has four, the other 'child' being his daughter). He also mentions his issues with Jean Baptiste's wife; he presents her as 'a problem' and considers her to be interfering in affairs that are not her concern. This exclusion of women was even formalized in Ice & Dairy Inc. where a 'pact' was made which enforced the non-participation of wives in the family business. Doing so, according to Nelly, is necessary because it 'limits problems'. Nelly also described how her uncle, a senior manager in the family business, 'didn't make it easy for his daughters to work in the company'. Julie (successor of Machine Parts Inc.) also described such a gender separation. She reflected how 'I was a young woman in an environment which in itself was not very feminine'. Julie raised issues of legitimacy she faced as a result of the gender difference. She talked of how difficult it was to gain the respect and credibility of her peers upon entering the 'very industrial world' of Machine Parts Inc. She attributes this as being due not only to her different background (her elitist 'grade ecole' education and experience in the luxury and design sectors) but also to her gender. Although, interestingly, she feels that her gender benefitted in her relations externally while it was more problematic internally. Illustrative quotations for three subcategories of environmental factors ('socialization', 'family roles' and 'exclusion and separation') are presented in Table 7.3.

DISCUSSION

Through our literature review, we found that previous research largely adopts an essentialist approach to understanding gender inequality: that is, that man and women are distinct groupings which can be compared and contrasted on the basis of biological sex. Some researchers have labeled women as a group who possess 'limiting attitudes' to their own advancement in family business (Salganicoff, 1990). Our findings show that such an understanding denies the heterogeneity of women as a group and levels blame at them for their lesser roles in family business, and also underestimates their ambition and career potential. While an obvious limitation of

Table 7.3 Environmental factors explaining succession

Case	Socialization (initiation and expectations)	Family roles	Exclusion and separation
Ice and Dairy Inc.	'When I was a little kid, I remember going with my class to visit my father's firm. I have other memories . . . every Sunday my father went to the factory to look around and I went with him as a young lad. It may seem trivial, but that was how my feelings for it grew. It was a matter of always being around the business' (Lionel) 'I think that my father saw me working with him more than my brother . . . it is true that he counted on me at first' (Nelly)	*Mother was a stay-at-home house wife. Helped out in her parents' business. No involvement in husband's business.* 'Mom took care of us even if she regularly went to work in my grandparents' jewelry store and my father was in charge . . . For my father the firm is his whole life' (Nelly.) 'we have a really great mother . . . and she is an excellent wife . . . to have done all she has done over the years' (Nelly)	'It was a partners' pact between dad and his brother: the wives do not work in the company . . . and they were right to do that, because often afterwards with the problems it's harder to manage' (Nelly) 'Anne Sophie [cousin] would have been able to go into the company, but I don't know if I should say this, but I think that Jean Pierre [Nelly's uncle] didn't make it easy for his daughters to work in the company' (Nelly)
French Resto	'You have to understand that since a very young age, I was always in the firm. I always followed my father at the weekends. I accompanied him when he made his rounds of the restaurants, in the	*Mother was a stay-at-home house wife, Gerard's wife worked in the family business for the first 10 years. After the birth of their second child she became a stay-at-home housewife.*	'During family meals, the women are on one side, and we are there, we discuss . . . women talk between themselves and we discuss between ourselves and at the end of two minutes we have dealt with all the work issues' (Christophe)

156

| Build and Sell Inc. | 'At the weekend, over the hunting season, we'd go hunting and its a two hour drive to get there, so, in the car on the way we would just talk about work' (Christophe)

'We spend our evenings . . . I was here at 8 o'clock and he comes in, he hadn't finished his cigar. He smokes the cigar and we're off . . . we talk about work, we talk strategy. We left here and it was 11 pm and he says, "Will we have a little something to eat?" and we continued in a restaurant and when we finished it was one in the morning. And we chat. And we talk about work, only work. Business' (Christophe)

'It's very difficult to hand on a business when there are three children' (Xavier – he actually has four children, the fourth is his daughter)

'and then there was the problem of his [Jean Baptiste] wife . . . she only thinks of her holidays and I said to myself "If she doesn't help him, if she doesn't support him, he won't manage"' (Xavier) | 'He worked all his life, it's his life. Us? We didn't see him at home . . . it was him who couldn't sleep for all those years when the company wasn't going well, you know what I mean? My mother, she doesn't work anymore since the birth of my brother' (Christophe)

'So she [wife] took care of the children and I continued alone. After all, that's life, we are not always at home . . . It is true that I was not maybe a very good dad, because it is hard to make a success of both' (Gerard)

'Alexandre is a good little Daddy: he's not a winner, but he tries' (Gerard)

Mother was a stay-at-home house wife. No family business involvement.

'So I said to her [Jean Baptiste's wife] . . . you want a husband who . . . doesn't have any worries, who sleeps at night, but what if your husband is the boss and he doesn't sleep at night and brings home work at the weekends? It won't be like before' (Xavier) | evening we'd find ourselves in a restaurant and I sometimes helped out' (Christophe).

'Me, with my kids, I never asked them to come work for me . . . I always said go work where you want, be happy, you will be my heirs but not necessarily my successors' (Gerard)

'We were regularly introduced as potential successors in the company. Even when we were young, well, I remember . . . my father talking in public in front of the company staff when we were there and he introduced us (the three sons) as potentially the next generation' (Nicolas) |

Table 7.3 (continued)

Case	Socialization (initiation and expectations)	Family roles	Exclusion and separation
Motor Parts Inc.	'I entered the business by doing internships, summer jobs first of all. The first time I went to the company I was 8 years old, and then there were summer jobs to earn a bit of money when I was 15, 16, 17. The business always interested me . . . my father succeeded in making me want to do the same as him from an early age' (Jean Philippe) 'One day I said to him [my son], "If you don't want to take over the company, there is no point in keeping it, I'm fed up, I don't want to work anymore." I was 67, so he came, and he hasn't done too badly at all' (Ferdinand)	*Mother was a stay-at-home house wife. No family business involvement. Father impressed that his daughters actually completed third-level studies. Son's succession was considered 'natural' progression.*	'I have three daughters and a nephew but he doesn't have the level of education' (Ferdinand – no mention of nieces, daughters grouped together as one)

158

Machine Parts Inc.	'The employees didn't know me… I was a long way away from this industrial environment… I did not go with him so often as that to the company' (Julie)

'I came from HEC thus it is attractive but it is the diploma which is badly seen by people without qualifications, and what's more I had work experiences in the luxury sector!' (Julie) | *Mother was a stay-at-home house wife. No physical involvement in business (moral support role).*

'She [Julie's mother] is not at all involved in the operational side of things but she has a very human and emotional insight [into the succession/business]' (Julie)

'She [Julie's mother] knows the story as I tell her my worries. We need a friendly ear when we are the manager, because we take decisions alone' (Julie) | 'There was a shock of cultures, between the luxury environment and the factory' (Julie)

'So I had doors closed (on me) with the director general letting me see only the things that he wanted me to see … everything was closed off … I had a terrible time getting an office in my own factory, then they found me a little one in a corner' (Julie)

'From a client and external relations point of view, I think there were lots of people who were touched by my situation: a young woman who doesn't come from this sector and who takes on a firm which is seen as a bit old fashioned, hardware/machinery, it's not very high tech so people were touched and wanted to help me' (Julie) |

our research is that we do not have all daughters' accounts or perceptions of the succession process, we do know that in the three cases in which the daughters did not succeed to the family business they set up and managed new successful entrepreneurial ventures. Hence, questions or doubts about their ability to run the family business are less credible.

A more postmodern view – where gender is viewed as being about 'doing' rather than 'being' – allows for a richer understanding of successor selection in family business than the essentialist 'male versus female' approach. Many family business members still conceptualize the role of successor in masculine terms making it more difficult (but not impossible) for women to identify with this role. In the French Resto case, the son who is presented as a doting father is not considered suitable successor material; he is the less masculine of the two brothers. Similarly, Lionel was not the preferred successor for Ice & Dairy Inc. and he is said to exhibit more feminine qualities such as timidity, collaboration and human skills. Julie, the only daughter successor, evokes her own 'masculine' qualities, being seen as 'hard' and 'authoritarian', as contributory to her success. Thus, we encourage researchers to go beyond essentialist categorization and consider gendered actions and behaviors. We believe that it is not always helpful to divide men and women into binary categories and then investigate their different experiences, as is largely the case in extant research. As a group, women have diverse and varied interests, abilities and behaviors (as do men).

While we found broad support for the idea that daughters were socialized differently to their male siblings and encouraged to take other careers, we maintain that socialization only partly explains succession choices and outcomes. We believe more attention should be paid to agency, where individual actors overcome structure. We observed the instance of Julie, the young woman who was not socialized for succession and experienced credibility issues in relation to her management team, business partners and suppliers, yet today she successfully manages the industrial small parts company that her father had developed. We propose that to better understand the lower number of female successors as a product of family socialization alone is to understate the role of deeply embedded institutional norms in reproducing inequality. Practices of 'exclusion and separation' and taken-for-granted norms of 'role division' in the family impact on women's potential to be considered as successors. All our families exhibited very traditional domestic arrangements. Our case studies revealed how women are often 'subjectified' as primary care giver or home maker – a role which is implied to be incompatible with the responsibility of succession and, hence, justifies their exclusion from certain aspects of family business. There were no role models of successful women leaders in these businesses. Instead the women were either invisible supporters or 'listeners' in the family business and/or 'good mothers'. Identities are co-constructed by the individuals, groups and institutions in which they are embedded.

Practices of exclusion and separation may also influence actors' choices and opportunities. Even if a daughter aspires to leadership, failing to receive validation for one's leadership attempts diminishes self-confidence as well as the motivation to take on a leadership role (Ely et al., 2011).We saw how women were excluded from decision-making through explicit means: wives were prevented from participating via the formal family 'pact' in Ice & Dairy. We also witnessed more subtle arrangements: physical space (an office 'in the corner' for Julie), and segregated activities (family meals, hunting and cigars), which had the same effect of excluding women from decision-making and information sharing. Gender discrimination is not always obvious and so it is more difficult to identify when and how it is contributing to inequality.

CONCLUSION

Our case studies illustrate the significant role that gender plays in successor selection in French family businesses. Among siblings, the path to succession is gendered. To say that an analytical unit is gendered means that advantage and disadvantage, exploitation and control, action and emotion, meaning and identity are patterned through a distinction between male and female, masculine and feminine (Acker, 1990). Today many women are in gender denial (Broadbridge and Simpson, 2011), whereby they believe that their gender does not prevent them from succeeding. Gender is no longer seen as salient, yet it continues to shape culture in significant ways (Kelan and Dunkley Jones, 2010). Through our research we seek to show how gender inequality manifests itself in discreet, yet complex ways in family business succession, and while women may be unaware of its ubiquity, they may be strongly impacted by its presence.

REFERENCES

Acker, J. (1990), Hierarchies, jobs, bodies: a theory of gendered organizations, *Gender and Society*, 4 (2), 139–158.
Ahl, H. (2002), *The Making of the Female Entrepreneur: A Discourse Analysis of Research Texts on Women's Entrepreneurship*, Sweden: Jönköping International Business School.

Ahl, H. (2006), Why research on women entrepreneurs needs new directions, *Entrepreneurship Theory and Practice*, 30 (5), 595–623.
Barnes, L.B. (1988), Incongruent hierarchies: daughters and younger sons as company CEOs, *Family Business Review*, 1 (1), 9–21.
Belghiti-Mahut, S. (2004), Les déterminants de l'avancement hiérarchique des femmes cadres, *Revue Française de Gestion*, 151, 145–160.
Belsey, C. (1985), *The Subject of Tragedy: Identity and Difference in Renaissance Drama*, London: Methuen.
Bradley, H. (2007), *Gender, Key Concepts*, Cambridge: Polity Press.
Broadbridge, A. and Simpson, R. (2011), 25 years on: reflecting on the past and looking to the future in gender and management research, *British Journal of Management*, 22 (3), 470–483.
Butler, J. (1990), *Gender Trouble: Feminism and the Subversion of Identity*, London: Routledge.
Cadieux, L., Lorrain, J. and Hugron, P. (2002), Succession in women-owned family businesses: a case study, *Family Business Review*, 15 (1), 17–30.
Calas, M. and Smircich, L. (1993), Dangerous liasons: the feminine in management meets globalization, *Business Horizons*, 3, 73–83
Carli, L. (1990), Gender, language and influence, *Journal of Personality and Social Psychology*, 59, 941–951.
Carsrud, A.L. (1994), Meanderings of a resurrected psychologist, or lessons learned in creating a family business program, *Entrepreneurship: Theory and Practice*, 19 (1), 39–48.
Cole, P.M. (1997), Women in family business, *Family Business Review*, 10 (4), 353–372.
Constantinidis, C. (2010), Entreprise familiale et genre: Les enjeux de la succession pour les filles, *Revue Française de Gestion*, 200, 143–159.
Constantinidis, C. and Nelson, T. (2009), Intégrer les problématiques de la succession et du genre selon la perspective de la fille dans l'entreprise familiale: une enquête transnationale, *Management International*, 14 (1), 43–54.
Cox, T.H. and Harquail, C.V. (1991), Career paths and career success in the early career stages of male and female MBAs, *Journal of Vocational Behavior*, 39, 54–75.
Curimbaba, F. (2002), The dynamics of women's roles as family business managers, *Family Business Review*, 15 (3), 239–252.
Danes, S., Haberman, H. and McTavish, D. (2005), Gendered discourse about family business, *Family Relations*, 54 (1), 116–130.
Dawley, D., Hoffman, J. and Smith, A. (2004), Leader succession: does gender matter? *Leadership and Organisation Development Journal*, 25 (8), 678–690.
De Beauvoir, S. (1973), *The Second Sex*, New York: Vintage Books.
De Massis, A. Chua, J.H. and Chrisman, J.J. (2008), Factors preventing intra-family succession, *Family Business Review*, 21 (2), 183–199.
Delmar, F. and Holmquist, C. (2003), 'Female entrepreneurship: issue and policies', OECD report, presented at the 21st session of the Working Party on Small and Medium-Sized Enterprises and Entrepreneurship, Paris.
Dumas, C. (1989), Understanding of father–daughter and father–son dyads in family-owned businesses, *Family Business Review*, 2 (1), 31–46.
Dumas, C. (1990), Preparing the new CEO: managing the father–daughter succession process in family business, *Family Business Review*, 3 (2), 169–181.

Dumas, C. (1992), Integrating the daughter into family business management, *Entrepreneurship Theory and Practice*, 16 (4), 41–55.
Dumas, C. (1998), Women's pathways to participation and leadership in the family-owned firm, *Family Business Review*, 11 (3), 219–228.
Dumas, C., Dupuis, J.P., Richer, F. and St-Cyr, L. (1995), Factors that influence the next generation's decision to take over the family farm, *Family Business Review*, 8 (2), 99–120.
Eagly, A.H. and Karau, S.J. (2002), Role congruity theory of prejudice toward female leaders, *Psychological Review*, 109 (3), 573–598.
Eagly, A.H., Beall, A. and Sternberg, R.S. (2004), *The Psychology of Gender*, 2nd edn, New York: Guilford Press.
Eisenhardt, K.M. and Graebner, M.E. (2007), Theory building from cases: opportunities and challenges, *Academy of Management Journal*, 50 (1), 25–32.
Ely, R., Ibarra, H. and Kolb, D. (2011), Taking gender into account: theory and design for women's leadership development programs, *Academy of Management Learning and Education*, 10 (3), 474–493.
Fletcher, J.K. (2004), The paradox of post heroic leadership: an essay on gender, power and transformational change, *Leadership Quarterly*, 15 (5), 647–661.
Francis, A. (1999), *The Daughter Also Rises: How Women Overcome Obstacles and Advance in the Family-Owned Business*, San Francisco, CA: Rudi Publishing.
Freudenberger, H.J., Freedheim, D.K. and Kurtz, T.S. (1989), Treatment of individuals in family business, *Psychotherapy*, 26 (1), 47–53.
Garcia-Alvarez, E., Lopez-Sintas, J. and Saldana Gonzalvo, P. (2002), Socialization patterns of successors in first to second generation family businesses, *Family Business Review*, 15 (3), 189–203.
Gillis-Donovan, J. and Moynihan-Bradt, C. (1990), The power of the invisible women in the family business, *Family Business Review*, 3 (2), 153–167.
Haberman, H. and Danes, S.M. (2007), Father–daughter and father–son family business management transfer comparison: family FIRO model application, *Family Business Review*, 20 (2), 163–184.
Hammersley, M. and Atkinson P. (1983), *Ethnography: Principles in Practice*, London: Routledge.
Hollander, B.S. and Bukowitz, W.R. (1990), Women, family culture and family business, *Family Business Review*, 3 (2), 141–145.
Hughes, K.D., Jennings, J.E., Brush, C., Carter, S. and Welter, F. (2012), Extending women's entrepreneurship research in new directions, *Entrepreneurship Theory and Practice*, 36 (3), 429–442.
Iannarelli, C. (1992), The socialization of leaders: a study of gender in family business, unpublished Doctoral dissertation, University of Pittsburgh.
Ip, B. and Jacobs, G. (2006), Business succession planning: a review of the evidence, *Journal of Small Business and Enterprise Development*, 13 (3), 326–350.
Keating, N.C. and Little, H.M. (1997), Choosing the successor in New Zealand family farms, *Family Business Review*, 10 (2), 157–171.
Kelan, E.K. and Dunkley Jones, R. (2010), Gender and the MBA, *Academy of Management Learning and Education*, 9 (1), 26–43.
Lank, A.G. (1997), Entreprises familiales: echapper au syndrome Dallas, L'art d'entreprendre, Les Echos, dossier n°6, octobre.
Laufer, J. (2004), Femmes et carrières: la question du plafond de verre, *Revue française de gestion*, 151, 117–127.
Lewis, G.B. (1992), Men and women toward the top: backgrounds, careers, and

potential of federal middle managers, *Public Personnel Management*, 21 (4), 473–491.
Martin, L. (2001), More jobs for the boys? Succession planning in SMEs, *Women in Management Review*, 16 (5), 222–231.
Martinez Jimenez, R. (2009), Research on women in family firms: current status and future directions, *Family Business Review*, 22 (1), 53–64.
Mavin, S. and Grandy, G. (2012), Doing gender well and differently in management, *Gender in Management: An International Journal*, 27 (4), 218–231.
Oakley, A. (1981), *Subject Women*, Oxford: Martin Robertson.
Patton, M.Q. (1980), *Qualitative Evaluation Methods*, Beverly Hills, CA: Sage.
Pratt, M.G. (2009), For the lack of a boilerplate: tips on writing up (and reviewing) qualitative research, *Academy of Management Journal*, 52 (5), 856–862.
Rosenblatt, P.C., De Mik, L., Anderson, R.M. and Johnson, P.A (1985), *The Family in Business*, San Francisco, CA: Jossey-Bass.
Salganicoff, M. (1990), Women in family businesses: challenges and opportunities, *Family Business Review*, 3 (2), 125–137.
Thomas, G. (2011), *How to do your Case Study: A Guide for Students and Researchers*, London: Sage.
Vera, C.F. and Dean, M.A. (2005), An examination of the challenges daughters face in family business succession, *Family Business Review*, 18 (4), 321–345.
Wang, C. (2010), Daughter exclusion in family business succession: a review of the literature, *Journal of Family and Economic Issues*, 31 (4), 475–484.
Wang, C., Barrett, R., Walker, E.A. and Redmond, J. (2008), Who gets the nod? Gender issues in successor selection, ISBE: Institute for Small Business and Entrepreneurship, 5–7 November, Belfast, Ireland.
Yin, R.K. (1994), *Case Study Research: Design and Methods*, 2nd edn, Beverly Hills, CA: Sage Publishing.

8. Gender-based differences in the performance of Slovenian high-growth companies
Karin Širec and Dijana Močnik

INTRODUCTION

Researchers, practitioners and policymakers alike emphasize firm growth as an indication of business success, yet existing research offers little consensus about entrepreneurial success. Policy programmes designed to stimulate and assist individual firms' growth are commonplace, presumably in the hope that this will result in increased employment and tax revenues (Storey, 1994). However, entrepreneurship is recognized as a complex phenomenon involving individuals, firms and the environment in which it occurs (Begley, 1995). Extant research also reveals a clear picture of a gender gap in venture creation and ownership activity. In almost all participating Global Entrepreneurship Monitor (GEM) countries, the structure by gender reveals that men are more entrepreneurially active than women.[1] In Slovenia, females account for only 24 per cent of entrepreneurs (Rebernik et al., 2013). Pursuing either an entrepreneurial or employed occupational career is determined by many factors, including biography (Müller, 2001), age (Mondragon-Velez, 2009), gender (Minniti and Nardone, 2007), education (Van der Sluis et al., 2008), personality (Müller and Gappisch, 2005) and motivations (Locke and Baum, 2007). The gender perspective is important given the limited understanding of the gendered influences of economic development that entrepreneurship activity undoubtedly has on society. A partial explanation for this phenomenon might be found in companies' growth patterns. Therefore, the current chapter examines gender-mediated dimensions regarding the performance of Slovenian high-growth companies (that is, 'gazelles').

This chapter investigates the impact of various firm-specific factors on firm growth among a sample of 782 Slovenian high-growth firms from 2008 to 2009.[2] Firm growth is critical to economic development and the creation of wealth and employment. Surprisingly, and despite its economic upside potential, growth research has focused predominantly on 'normal' to 'high' growth rates (5 per cent to 20 per cent) while overlooking formidably high growth or 'hyper growth' (measured by hundreds to thousands of percentages; in our case, a firm's five-year sales growth rate ranges from 382 per cent to 10 240 per cent). A similar approach was adopted by Roper (1999) and Niskanen and Niskanen (2007), although most studies in the field have investigated growth in employment. We chose sales because firms rarely select employment growth as their goal per se. It could also be argued that our sample of Slovenian firms justifies this choice even more due to the excessively high labour cost imposed on local employers; a major barrier for small firms seeking to increase their number of employees.

This chapter's fundamental research question is: Is Slovenian high-growth companies' ('gazelles') performance dependent on firm size, profitability, indebtedness and labour costs and, in addition, mediated by gender (male owner versus female owner)? A framework for entrepreneurship conceptualization that incorporates measures for investigating gender-related dimensions in high-growth companies was developed, which involved refining the previously proposed, but inadequately tested, theoretical constructs into an empirically testable framework. Additional questions are: Does firm growth relate to companies' industry, legal form, and/or governance structure? To our knowledge, this is one of the rare texts investigating the impact of determinants on firm growth for small and medium-sized (SME) high-growth firms from a variety of industries.

The remainder of the chapter is divided into five sections. The second section presents the theoretical background and previous research. The third describes research hypotheses. The fourth section presents the data and models. The fifth explains the regression results. The sixth section presents the discussion and conclusion.

THEORETICAL BACKGROUND AND PREVIOUS RESEARCH

Several decades ago, David Birch used the term 'gazelles' to refer to a small group of high-growth companies that generated a disproportionately large share of new jobs in the economy (Landström, 2005, p. 170). High-growth firms have been shown to be a key factor for economic growth and structural change (Teruel and de Wit, 2011). They contribute to the economy via a variety of different channels: they facilitate the dynamics of the economy; facilitate the introduction of innovation and the growth of labour productivity; generate a large proportion of employment (Henrekson and Johansson, 2010); and are believed to act as an inspiring role model for existing or nascent entrepreneurs (Bosma et al., 2011). Given the evident importance of high-growth firms to the economy, these firms have drawn increasing attention from policymakers as well as academics during the past two decades (Storey, 1994; Schreyer, 2000; Delmar et al., 2003; Autio, 2007; Hölzl, 2009; Henrekson and Johansson, 2009, 2010). Yet, surprisingly, little empirical evidence is available (Henrekson and Johansson, 2010, p. 230), perhaps due to the lack of suitable data, the cost of conducting such studies, and the relatively recent interest in these questions (Henrekson and Johansson, 2009, p. 12).

Entrepreneurship research and practice emphasize company growth as a measure of entrepreneurial success. In many cases, researchers give growth a central role, with some researchers even seeing growth as the very essence of entrepreneurship (Sexton, 1997; Steffens et al., 2009). According to Davidsson (1991), firm growth is an indication of continued entrepreneurship (Gundry and Welsch, 2001, p. 455). Penrose (1959) argued that growth-oriented firms might be more likely to attract extraordinary management talent as well as financial support from investors, allies and competitors. As such, growth is assumed to be beneficial and something that entrepreneurial firms should seek to achieve (Markman and Gartner, 2002, p. 66).

Gender is also an influential factor determining the differences related to a company's growth patterns. Women start ventures that grow at a slower rate than those owned by men (Hisrich and Brush, 1984), although more recent studies have highlighted differences as well as similarities in growth decisions between the genders. Morris et al. (2006) suggested that women have a clear sense of the costs and benefits of growth and make careful trade-off decisions. Studies examining growth aspirations among female and male entrepreneurs in Slovenia revealed that, although women are on average less likely to be involved in entrepreneurship than men, their growth aspirations do not differ significantly from those of men (Tominc and Rebernik, 2006, 2007). Širec et al. (2010) identified a positive relationship between the intensity of applied new technologies and growth aspirations among Slovenian SMEs as well as certain gender differences regarding their growth aspirations. Other researchers have claimed that gender influences a company's growth: being female negatively affects growth, and female entrepreneurs rarely become 'growth entrepreneurs' (Kjeldsen and Nielsen, 2004).

Women lag behind men in entrepreneurship in most countries (Kelley et al., 2011). To better understand the identified gender gap, additional circumstances should be considered. Slovenia, as a Central and Eastern European country, is facing a still-incomplete transition process. Transitional countries share many common features with regard to female participation in the labour force, including the average level of education and gender wage gap. Women's participation in the Slovenian labour market (60.9 per cent) is still generally lower than men's (67.7 per cent). The choice of education in Slovenia shows an over-representation of women in 'typical' female fields (for example, education) and men in 'typical' male fields (for example, engineering). Overall, Slovenian women tend to be somewhat more educated than men, especially among 25- to 44-year-olds, which includes twice as many women with higher postgraduate degrees than men (16.6 per cent of women versus 8.6 per cent of men). Yet women earn on average only 93 per cent of men's average gross monthly salary (Statistical Office of the Republic of Slovenia, 2009).

The transition process has affected both men and women, creating a loss in job security and employment costs; however, women seem to have addressed a larger share of the adjustment costs (Ruminska-Zimny, 2003). Transition changes have also had important and often negative effects on women's position in society (Stoyanovska, 2001). After the fall of the communist regime, structural inequalities between men and women became evident (Tominc, 2002). Yet female entrepreneurs in Slovenia for the most part do not encounter prejudice in their entrepreneurial careers. Indeed, no legal barriers restrict women from the ownership of enterprises. Thus, female entrepreneurship in Slovenia shows considerable reserve. Gender can be one important characteristic influencing high-growth-oriented enterprises. In light of the question about the link between entrepreneurs' or managers' gender and growth of their companies, our empirical research aims to identify micro-level factors of firm growth.

RESEARCH HYPOTHESES

To generate economic growth and added value, it is important to support and promote companies' growth. Job gains are significantly concentrated among rapidly expanding firms, making it of immediate interest to identify these firms' important drivers of growth (Schreyer, 2000, p. 16). Previous academic research on firm growth suggests substantial heterogeneity in a number of factors characterizing firm growth, including industry, size, region, age, capital (labour) intensity, high- or low-technology, stage of life-cycle and personality type (Širec and Močnik, 2012a; Gundry and Welsch, 2001, p. 454). The intent herein is to examine gender-dependent linkages between the growth of Slovenian high-growth companies and their size, profitability, indebtedness and labour costs.

Early studies in the manufacturing industry found a relationship between growth and size, suggesting that this relationship is a stochastic phenomenon: an idea known as Gibrat's law (Gibrat, 1931). According to Gibrat's law, the firm's size at a given point in time is the product of a series of random growth rates in the firm's history. Yet Evans (1987) found that firm growth decreases with firm size in 89 out of 100 industries of the manufacturing sector analysed. In addition, Hall (1987) found a negative relationship between size and growth for large firms in the US manufacturing sector from 1976 to 1983. More recently, Mata (1994) and Becchetti and Trovato (2002) identified the same negative relationship between growth and size, implying that smaller firms grow faster than larger firms. Širec and Močnik (2012b) also empirically confirmed the negative relationship between firm growth and firm size among Slovenian high-growth firms from various industries.

Despite the lack of a common consensus on how likely male and female entrepreneurs desire their business growth, there appear to be important differences with respect to how they wish to expand. Cliff's (1998) findings suggest that female entrepreneurs are more likely to establish maximum business size thresholds beyond which they would prefer not to expand; these thresholds are smaller than those set by their male counterparts. Female entrepreneurs also seem to be more concerned than male entrepreneurs about the risks associated with fast-paced growth and tend to deliberately adopt a slow and steady rate of expansion (Cliff, 1998). Thus, our first research hypothesis is:

H1: A firm's size moderated by gender is significantly and negatively related to firm growth.

Although several theories suggest that profitability drives growth, available empirical evidence does not support the existence of a general, positive relationship between growth and profitability. The assumption that sales growth is positively associated with profitability has appeared in various studies (Gupta, 1981; Besanko et al., 2004). However, little empirical support exists for a strong and general growth–profitability relationship. In studies reporting the association between growth and profitability measures, correlations range from relatively substantially positive to those that are weakly positive yet statistically significant, and those that find no statistically or practically significant relationship (Davidsson et al., 2009).

Numerous comparative studies have examined the performance of male- versus female-controlled SMEs, generally finding that female-controlled SMEs underperform male-controlled SMEs (e.g., Kalleberg and Leicht, 1991; Fischer et al., 1993; Rosa et al., 1996; Fasci and Valdez, 1998; Du Rietz and Henrekson, 2000). However, Robb and Watson (2012) suggested that female- and male-controlled firms should perform equally well. Thus, the empirical evidence is inconclusive, leading to our empirical assessment of this relationship. Our second research hypothesis is:

H2: A firm's profitability mediated by gender is significantly and positively related to firm growth.

Numerous surveys have suggested that SMEs in particular are willing to finance their growth internally. Carpenter and Petersen (2002) found that SMEs' growth is constrained by internal finances. According to Storey (1994), the most important external barriers for UK firms are the availability and cost of funding. SMEs face specific constraints in raising external financing (Berger and Udell, 1998); they find it difficult to obtain small amounts of outside capital and, when they can, it is at high interest rates (Storey, 1994). Access to external financing is one of the highest barriers to growth in all companies, but particularly companies managed by women (Coleman, 2002). Prior studies have suggested that men can obtain more generous external financing than women; consequently, their companies grow more rapidly (Alsos et al., 2006). Other authors (Coleman, 2000; Arenius and Autio, 2005) have detected no differences in access to external financing, but did identify differences stemming from the firm's age as well as size and type of business (Coleman, 2000). In our model, we tested the impact of debt financing on growth. We propose a negative and gender-mediated association between indebtedness and a firm's growth. Our third research hypothesis is:

H3: A firm's gender-mediated indebtedness is significantly and negatively related to firm growth.

Extensive evidence, at both the country and individual levels, indicates that education is associated with productivity. Generally speaking, countries that invest the most in education also tend to be the richest and have the highest rates of growth of per capita output, and grow faster. Education, including formal schooling, job training and work experience, has clear benefits for individuals. Numerous studies have demonstrated that each year of school tends to raise one's wages by 5 per cent to 7 per cent, on average. The numbers vary depending on the quality of school, the type of education, and so on, but there is little doubt that more highly educated workers are better paid and – unless firms are throwing their money away – more productive (e.g., Tominc and Rebernik, 2012; de Wit and Teruel, 2011; Močnik and Širec, 2010).

Millan et al. (2011) recently demonstrated that more education positively affects the average entrepreneur's performance. When profitable opportunities for new economic activities exist, individuals with a higher level of human capital should more effectively identify and develop them. Higher labour costs positively affect the firm's productivity and, consequently, growth. Women differ from men in their experience because they hold different occupations (often less appropriate for self-employment and entrepreneurship), and have different on-the-job routines, social relationships and daily lives; they also identify business opportunities differently and try to exploit them differently (Širec and Močnik, 2012a). Thus, our final research hypothesis is:

H4: Labour costs mediated by gender are significantly and positively related to firm growth.

DATA AND MODELS

Data

Our empirical study examined Slovenia's fastest-growing companies using a dataset provided by the newspaper company Dnevnik and collected primarily by the company Bisnode Ltd. Dnevnik publishes a list of Slovenia's 500 fastest-growing companies, ranking firms by sales growth over a five-year period in all standard industry classification (SIC) categories. The selected companies had to generate a profit in the balance of the previous year, with at least €220 500 in revenues from sales in the base year; operate all 12 months in both index years; and make profits in the preceding year. The dataset is checked and verified by certified public accountants. Unlike small-scale, regional or survey-based studies, the sample is not only large enough to be meaningful, but also provides a five-year longitudinal perspective on companies from around the country.

The statistical population identified for this study (that is, high-growth gazelle firms in Slovenia) consists of two firm cohorts: firms on the 500 fastest-growing gazelles list 2008 (sales growth difference from 2003 to 2007) and firms on the 500 fastest-growing gazelles list 2009 (sales growth difference from 2004 to 2008). We used the polled dataset for 2008 and 2009 ($N = 782$). To avoid repeated measures, data were retained only for the last year a firm appeared on the list. Table 8.1 presents the sample description.

The data's cross-sectional nature precludes the inference of causality and might be a limitation of our study.

Table 8.1 Sample description

		Males		Females		Total	%
		Frequency	%	Frequency	%		
Industry	Manufacturing, mining and agriculture	131	21.7	23	17.6	154	21.0
	Construction	97	16.1	27	20.6	124	16.8
	Trade	178	29.5	44	33.6	222	30.2
	Services	198	32.8	37	28.2	235	32.0
	Total	604	100.0	131	100.0	735	100.0
Legal form	Limited	551	91.2	106	80.9	657	89.4
	Unlimited	53	8.8	25	19.1	78	10.6
	Total	604	100.0	131	100.0	735	100.0
Governance structure	Independent	535	88.6	120	91.6	655	89.1
	Subsidiary	61	10.1	10	7.6	71	9.7
	Parent and subsidiary	8	1.3	1	0.8	9	1.2
	Total	604	100.0	131	100.0	735	100.0
Size regarding number of employees	Micro	395	65.4	95	72.5	490	66.7
	Small	141	23.3	26	19.8	167	22.7
	Medium	42	7.0	5	3.8	47	6.4
	Large	26	4.3	5	3.8	31	4.2
	Total	604	100.0	131	100.0	735	100.0

Methodology

Using a stepwise multiple least square dummy variable (LSDV) regression, we assessed the relationship between a firm's ratio of five-year sales growth (the dependent variable) to assets and four independent variables: firm size, profitability, indebtedness and labour costs. The three control variables were used to improve the model: industry (construction, trade and services as opposed to manufacturing), legal form (limited as opposed to unlimited) and governance structure (parent and subsidiary, or subsidiary, as opposed to independent). Only the trade dummy proved to be a significant determinant; thus, we added the interaction terms between the trade dummy and the four independent variables to the model and dropped the other control variables.

Dependent Variable

Regarding firm growth as a dependent variable, in this study, we use the ratio of the difference of a firm's five-year sales revenues (2003–2007 and 2004–2008) to assets in 2008 and 2009.

Independent Variables

In the models described later in the chapter, we use four main independent variables: firm size, profitability, indebtedness and labour costs.

Firm size
Firm size is calculated as the sum of logarithms of assets and squared assets. Most studies assume a linear growth size relationship; we also added the square of this variable to capture the possible non-linear shape of the firm growth–size relationship suggested in, for example, Evans (1987) and Niskanen and Niskanen (2007). The scatterplot between the natural logarithm of squared assets and firm growth proved to be quadratic, but is not included in the chapter due to space limitations.

Profitability
We used the ratio of EBITDA (earnings before interest, taxes, depreciation and amortization) to sales in 2008 and 2009 to measure profitability.

Indebtedness
Indebtedness is the ratio of total debts to assets in 2008 and 2009.

Labour costs
Labour costs are calculated as the ratio of labour costs to employees in 2008 and 2009.

Control Variables

We expanded the investigation of the relationship between the four main determinants and a firm's growth with three additional control variables: the impact of an industry, the legal form of the firm, and governance structure on a firm's growth.

Industry
Industry affiliation is another factor potentially affecting companies' growth patterns. Analyses of firm growth patterns indicate that an industry might have an important effect on firms' growth rates and profitability (Camp et al., 1999; Sexton et al., 2000). Almus and Nerlinger (1999) categorized their sample into high-tech, medium-tech and low-tech industry firms. Dunne and Hughes (1994) included 19 industry dummies in their investigation; and Harhoff et al. (1998) used a sample of firms in the manufacturing, construction, trade and service industries. We divided our sample into four industry subgroups: manufacturing, mining and agriculture; construction; trade; and services.

Legal form
Businesses can operate under several different legal forms, but the main differentiating factor, as far as growth is concerned, is whether or not the legal form offers the owners limited liability. Previous studies using German (Harhoff et al., 1998; Almus and Nerlinger, 1999; Niskanen and Niskanen, 2007) and Swedish data (Davidsson et al., 2002; Niskanen and Niskanen, 2007) show that firms with limited liability grow faster than firms with unlimited liability, implying that limited liability firms' owners are more willing to invest in risky ventures that might foster firm growth. Harhoff et al. (1998) also found that limited liability firms are more likely to become insolvent than comparable full liability firms. We used a dummy variable to indicate whether or not the firm is operating under an unlimited liability legal form.

Governance structure
Business governance structure can also affect firm growth. Davidsson et al. (2002) used dummy variables for parent companies, subsidiaries and independent firms, finding that independent firms grow faster than firms with parent corporate relationships. In our regression model, we included

two dummy variables: one for a parent and subsidiary and the other for a subsidiary only.

Models

Male model
We first estimated the relationship between the four independent variables and the dependent variable using the male model (M1):

$$Firm\ Growth_i = a + b_1\ Firm\ Size_i + b_2\ Firm\ Size_i^2 + b_3\ Profitability_i + b_4\ Indebtedness_i + b_5\ Labour\ costs_i + e_i \qquad (M1)$$

where firm growth is the ratio of the difference of a firm's five-year sales revenues (2003–2007 and 2004–2008) to assets in 2008 and 2009; a is a regression constant; b_j are regression coefficients ($j = 1, 2, 3, 4$); firm size is calculated as the sum of logarithms of assets and squared assets; profitability is the ratio of EBITDA to sales in 2008 and 2009; indebtedness is the ratio of total debts to assets in 2008 and 2009; labour costs are the ratio of labour costs to employees in 2008 and 2009; e is an error term of the regression; and i is the index for the number of cases.

After obtaining the results, we extended the model (M1) by incorporating different dummy variables for construction, trade, services, unlimited legal form, subsidiary, parent and subsidiary to determine whether we could improve the model. Only the dummy variable for trade (1 if a firm belongs to a trade industry; 0 otherwise) proved to significantly increase the R^2.[3] Thus, we next added the trade dummy variable and its interactions between the four independent variables from model (M1). Model (M2) for estimation reads:

$$Firm\ Growth_i = a + b_1\ Firm\ Size_i + b_2\ Firm\ Size_i^2 + b_3\ Profitability_i + b_4\ Indebtedness_i + b_5\ Labour\ costs_i + d\ Trade_i + c_1\ Trade_i \times Firm\ size_i + c_2\ Trade_i \times Firm\ size_i^2 + c_3\ Trade_i \times Profitability_i + c_4\ Trade_i \times Indebtedness_i + c_5\ Trade_i \times Labour\ costs_i + e_i \qquad (M2)$$

where the description of variables is the same as in model (M1); d is the regression coefficient of the trade dummy for which the value of the regression constant a for trade firms changes; and c_k is the regression coefficients of interaction terms.

Female model
We first estimated the relationship between the four independent variables and the dependent variable using model (F1):

$$\text{Firm Growth}_i = a + b_1 \text{ Firm Size}_i + b_2 \text{ Firm Size}_i^2 + b_3 \text{ Profitability}_i + b_4$$
$$\text{Indebtedness}_i + b_5 \text{ Labour costs}_i + e_i \quad \text{(F1)}$$

where the description of the variables is the same as in model (M1), except that they hold for female firms. We made further calculations by adding the control (dummy) variables as we did for the male sample, but model (F1) proved to be the correct one.

FINDINGS

We analysed the results of the male model (M2) and the female model (F1). We first discuss the data's descriptive statistics.

Descriptive Statistics

The quotient of the ratio of a male firm's five-year sales difference to assets (dependent variable) amounts to 1.76; thus, on average, growing sales revenues exceed the average value of assets by 76 per cent. For females, this figure is even higher at 84 per cent. The average value of a male firm's assets in 2008 and 2009 amounted to €2 186 910. For a female's firm, this figure is slightly smaller at €1 885 493. The average profitability in 2008 and 2009 was 10.8 per cent for males and 10.9 per cent for females; thus, on average, a firm's EBITDA represents 10.8 per cent of sales revenue for males and 10.9 per cent for females. The mean value of the labour costs was €23 990 for males and €23 011 for females; thus, in 2008 and 2009 on average, an employee caused such an amount of labour costs per male/female employer. Furthermore, on average, short- and long-term debts represented 71 per cent of total assets for both genders, which is a fairly high level of indebtedness. The interaction term is excluded from Table 8.2. Independent sample *t*-tests (not included in the chapter) showed that differences of the independent variables between genders were not significant.

Regression Results

The estimation of regression coefficients was conducted using the stepwise LSDV regression with SPSS 19.0. Table 8.2 presents the results of the seventh step for the male regression and the third step for the female regression. The calculations were based on 596 male cases (firms) and 128 female cases for which all data were available. As Table 8.2 indicates, three independent variables proved to be statistically significant. Only the indebtedness variable is not significant in both cases.

Table 8.2 Multiple regression (dependent variable: firm growth; method of estimation: stepwise OLS)

	Males			Females		
	Step 7	t	VIF[2]	Step 3	t	VIF
a Constant	7.528**	12.353		8.318**	5.697	
b_1 Firm size	−0.414**	−9.686	1.083			
b_2 Firm size squared				−0.232**	−4.396	1.135
b_3 Profitability	−3.567**	−6.869	1.247	−5.622**	−4.646	1.025
b_5 Labour costs	2.092E-5**	5.061	1.073	3.686E-5**	3.512	1.114
c_2 Trade × Firm size squared	0.037**	6.561	2.268			
R^2	0.340			0.303		
R^2 Adjusted	0.334			0.286		
Number of cases	596			128		
F	60.664**			17.962**		
DW[1]	2.067			1.848		

Notes:
** significant at the 0.01 level.
1 DW = Durbin Watson; we can accept the hypothesis of no positive or negative autocorrelation in the models ($DW_U < DW < DW_{L*}$; $DW_{L*} = 4 - DW_U$; Males: 1.715 < 2.067 < 2.285; Females: 1.799 < 1.848 < 2.201).
2 VIF = variance inflation factor. As no VIF is higher than 2.268 (according to the critical value of 10), the models do not suffer the multicollinearity problem.

Table 8.2 indicates that, altogether, 33.4 per cent and 28.6 per cent of the variability of the firm growth (the dependent variable) is explained by the firm size, profitability and labour costs for the male and female case, respectively. Firm growth is negatively associated with firm size for males and firm size squared for females (males: $b_1 = -0.414$; $p = 0.000$; females: $b_2 = -0.232$; $p = 0.000$) and profitability (males: $b_3 = -3.567$, $p = 0.000$; females: $b_3 = -5.622$, $p = 0.000$) and positively with labour costs (males: $b_5 = 2.209\text{E-}5$; $p = 0.000$; females: $b_5 = 3.686\text{E-}5$; $p = 0.001$). The interaction term between the trade dummy and firm size squared is also positively

Table 8.3   Model summary

Step	Males [Model (M2)]			Females [Model (F1)]		
	R^2 Change	F Change	F	R^2 Change	F Change	F
1	0.161	113.990**	113.990**	0.166	25.162**	25.162**
2	0.089	70.276**	98.780**	0.067	10.945**	19.046**
3	0.044	36.683**	82.044**	0.069	12.337**	17.962**
4	0.030	26.003**	70.632**			
5	0.010	8.498**	58.922**			
6	0.008	7.383**	50.864**			
7	−0.002	1.570	60.664**			

Note: **significant at the 0.01 level.

and significantly related to firm growth in the male sample ($c_2 = 0.037$, $p = 0.000$). This value decreases the negative coefficient for firm size for trade male firms. In other words, when a firm size increases by a unit, firm growth decreases by 0.414 units for male (0.377 units for trade male) and 0.232 units for female firms. When profitability increases by a unit, firm growth decreases by 3.567 units for male firms and 5.622 units for female firms. When labour costs increase by, for example, €10 000, firm growth increases by 0.21 units for male and 0.37 units for female companies.

The comparison between males and females shows that the direction of the regression coefficients is the same. However, the impact is greater for females in both directions. In both cases, profitability explains the greatest share of variability in firm growth (males: 16.1 per cent; females: 16.6 per cent) (see Table 8.3). The second-largest share (8.9 per cent) in male firms is firm size, whereas in female firms it is labour costs (6.9 per cent). This variable ranks third in importance for males (4.4 per cent). For females, firm size explains the least variability of firm growth (6.7 per cent). Thus, labour costs and firm size explain almost identical shares of the variability of female firms' growth; while in male firms, firm size explains almost twice as much variability in firm growth compared to labour costs.

No problem of multicollinearity or autocorrelation occurred in the models as indicated by variance inflation factors (VIFs) and the Durbin–Watson (DW) statistic in Table 8.1. We tested the regression results' robustness using the Chow test (Gujarati, 2004, pp. 274–278).[4] Based on the results, we rejected the null hypothesis of parameter stability among genders (i.e., structural change).

We confirmed our first research hypothesis (H1), which states that firm size moderated by gender is a significant factor in explaining the negative relationship with firm growth. Our findings suggest that female entrepreneurs are more likely than males to establish maximum business size thresholds beyond which they would prefer not to expand.

We did not confirm our second research hypothesis (H2), which argues that a firm's profitability mediated by gender positively relates to firm growth. Our result assumes that high-growth firms (male or female controlled) resist the temptation to encourage rapid growth before securing a sound level of profitability. Table 8.3 (first step) shows that profitability explains most (more than 16 per cent) of firm growth variability for males as well as females.

We also did not confirm our third hypothesis (H3), which states that a firm's indebtedness mediated by gender is a significant factor explaining the negative relationship with firm growth. We confirmed our fourth research hypothesis (H4): namely, labour costs mediated by gender are significant in explaining the positive relationship with firm growth.

DISCUSSION AND CONCLUSION

With two multiple least square dummy variable regressions, one for the male and one for the female sample of firms, we assessed the relationships between firm growth as a dependent variable and four main determinants: namely, the independent variables: companies' size, profitability, indebtedness and labour costs. The models were further refined by the addition of three control variables: industry, legal form and governance structure.

The results showed that firm size and profitability are negatively related to firm growth for male and female firms, while labour costs are positively related. However, the negative/positive relationships are greater for female firms. Indebtedness is an insignificant determinant of firm growth. In addition, all control variables proved to be insignificant determinants of the growth of Slovenian gazelles in the observed period, except for the trade variable in its interactions with firm size for male firms.

Using the empirical results, we confirmed our first research hypothesis, which states that firm size mediated by gender is negatively related to firm growth. For male firms from the trade industry, this regression coefficient is slightly less negative. We did not confirm our second research hypothesis, which argues that a firm's profitability mediated by gender is positively related to firm growth. This result does not support the existence of a generally presupposed positive relationship between growth and profitability, which is also not supported in the majority of other empirical studies (e.g., Chandler and Jansen, 1992; Cox et al., 2002, cited in Davidsson et al.,

2009). Our results assume that high-growth firms resist the temptation to encourage rapid growth before securing a sound level of profitability; even more so for female firms.

We did not confirm our third research hypothesis, which states that a firm's indebtedness mediated by gender is negatively related to firm growth. We found an insignificant regression coefficient for indebtedness. Thus, generally debts do not represent a constraint for high-growth firms, which concurs with the result related to the association between profitability and growth. We confirmed our fourth research hypothesis, which argues that labour costs mediated by gender are positively related to firm growth through higher productivity (e.g., de Wit and Teruel, 2011).

Given that women remain an unexploited source of entrepreneurship, establishing effective mechanisms for the promotion of female entrepreneurship could be an important source of entrepreneurial ideas in Slovenia. Future studies could be enriched in several ways. First, policies and programmes supporting female entrepreneurship should stem from a diagnosis of the motives of prospective female small business owners, focusing on strengthening pull motives, to serve as a basis for more viable and innovative entrepreneurial activities. In addition to the personal characteristics and motivational factors necessary for devising programmes and policies supporting female Slovenian entrepreneurs during the start-up phase, it would be interesting to conduct further research related to skills and competences needed not only for start-ups, but also for the development and growth of the business.

NOTES

1. The GEM was created in 1997. Focusing primarily on entrepreneurship, it studies determinants affecting national levels of entrepreneurial activity and economic growth. See www.gemconsortium.org.
2. In the sample, 282 firms were examined in 2008, and 500 firms in 2009.
3. R^2 with main independent variables is 0.291; R^2 with the added dummy variable for trade and its interactions with independent variables is 0.34. From F tables, we find that for 5 and 585 df the 1 per cent critical F value is 3.02, whereas our calculated F value amounts to 16.86. Therefore, the probability of obtaining an F value as much as or greater than 16.86 is much smaller than 1 per cent. Thus, we chose the model M2 as the correct one.
4. We calculated the residual sum of squares (RSS) of the pooled (restricted) regression (RSS_{pooled} = 1184.035) and separately for males (RSS_{males} = 926.183) and females ($RSS_{females}$ = 230.094). We calculated the unrestricted RSS as the sum of RSS_{males} and $RSS_{females}$, which amounts to 1156.277 and consecutively the F restricted value of 3.03. From the F tables, for 6 and 758 df, the 1 per cent critical F value is 2.90. Therefore, the probability of obtaining an F value of as much as or greater than 3.03 is much smaller than 1 per cent.

REFERENCES

Almus, M. and Nerlinger, E. (1999), 'Growth of new technology-based firms: which factors matter?', *Small Business Economics*, 13 (2), 141–154.
Alsos, G.A., Isaksen, E.J. and Ljunggren, E. (2006), 'New venture financing and subsequent business growth in men- and women-led businesses', *Entrepreneurship Theory and Practice*, 30 (5), 667–686.
Arenius, P. and Autio, E. (2005), 'Financing of small businesses: are Mars and Venus more alike than different?', *Venture Capital*, 8 (2), 93–107.
Autio, E. (2007), *Global Entrepreneurship Report, 2007, Report on High-Growth Entrepreneurship*, London: London Business School and GERA.
Becchetti, L. and Trovato, G. (2002), 'The determinants of growth for small and medium sized firms. The role of the availability of external finance', *Small Business Economics*, 19, 291–306.
Begley, T. (1995), 'Using founder status, age of firm and company growth rate as the basis for distinguishing entrepreneurs from managers of smaller businesses', *Journal of Business Venturing*, 10 (3), 249–263.
Berger, A. and Udell, G.F. (1998), 'The economics of small business finance: the roles of private equity and debt markets in the financial growth cycle', *Journal of Banking and Finance*, 22, 613–673.
Besanko, D., Dranove, D. and Shanley, M. (2004), *Economics of Strategy*, 3rd edn, New York: Wiley.
Bosma, N.S., Hessels, S.J.A., Schutjens, V.A.J.M., Van Praag, C.M. and Verheul, I. (2011), 'Entrepreneurship and role models', *Journal of Economic Psychology*, 21, 455–472.
Camp, S.M., Nenide, B., Pricer, R.W. and Sexton, D.L. (1999), 'Predicting financial performance in firm growth: problems associated with and recommendations for using large databases', paper presented at the Babson Entrepreneurship Research Conference, Columbia, SC, May.
Carpenter, R. and Petersen, B. (2002), 'Is the growth of small firms constrained by internal finance?', *Review of Economics and Statistics*, 84, 298–309.
Chandler, G.N. and Jansen, E. (1992), 'The founder's self-assessed competence and venture preformance', *Journal of Business Venturing*, 7 (3), 223–236.
Cliff, J.E. (1998), 'Does one size fit all? Exploring the relationship between attitudes towards growth, gender and business size', *Journal of Business Venturing*, 13 (6), 523–542.
Coleman, S. (2000), 'Access to capital and terms of credit: a comparison of men- and women-owned small businesses', *Journal of Small Business Management*, 38 (3), 37–53.
Coleman, S. (2002), 'Access to capital and terms of credit. A comparison of men and women-owned small businesses', *Journal of Small Business Management*, 8 (3), 37–52.
Cox, L.W., Camp, S.M. and Ensley, M.D. (2002), 'Does it pay to grow? The impact of growth on profitability and wealth creation', paper presented at the Babson College/Kauffman Foundation Entrepreneurship Research Conference, Boulder, CO.
Davidsson, P. (1991), 'Continued entrepreneurship: ability, need, and opportunity as determinants of small firm growth', *Journal of Business Venturing*, 6, 405–429.
Davidsson, P., Delmar, F. and Wiklund, J. (2002), 'Entrepreneurship as growth:

growth as entrepreneurship', in M.A. Hitt, R.D. Ireland, S.M. Camo and D.L. Sexton (eds), *Strategic Entrepreneurship, Creating a New Mindset*, Oxford: Blackwell Publishers, pp. 26–44.

Davidsson, P., Steffens, P. and Fitzsimmons, J. (2009), 'Growing profitable or growing from profits: putting the horse in front of the cart?', *Journal of Business Venturing*, 24, 388–406.

De Wit, G. and Teruel, M. (2011), 'Determinants of high-growth firms', Scales Research Reports H201107, EIM Business and Policy Research, available at: http://www.entrepreneurship-sme.eu/pdf-ez/H201107.pdf (accessed June 2012).

Delmar, F., Davidsson, P. and Gartner, W.B. (2003), 'Arriving at the high-growth firm', *Journal of Business Venturing*, 18 (2), 189–216.

Du Rietz, A. and Henrekson, M. (2000), 'Testing the female underperformance hypothesis', *Small Business Economics*, 14 (1), 1–10.

Dunne, P. and Hughes, A. (1994), 'Age, size, growth and survival: UK companies in the 1980s', *Journal of Industrial Economics*, 42 (2), 115–140.

Evans, D.S. (1987), 'The relationship between firm growth, size and age: estimate for 100 manufacturing industries', *Journal of Industrial Economics*, 35, 567–581.

Fasci, M.A. and Valdez, J. (1998), 'A performance contrast of male- and female-owned small accounting practices', *Journal of Small Business Management*, 36 (3), 1–7.

Fischer, E.M., Reuber, R.A. and Dyke, L.S. (1993), 'A theoretical overview and extension of research on sex, gender, and entrepreneurship', *Journal of Business Venturing*, 8 (2), 151–168.

Gibrat, R. (1931), *Les Inegalités Economiques*, Applications: Aux Inégalités des Richesses, a la Concentration des Entreprises, Aux Populations des Villes, Aux Statistiques des Familles, etc., d'une Loi Nouvelle: La Loi de l'Effect Proportionnel, Paris: Sirey.

Gujarati, D. (2004), *Basic Econometrics*, 4th edn, Boston, MA: McGraw-Hill.

Gundry, L.K. and Welsch, H.P. (2001), 'The ambitious entrepreneur: high growth strategies of women-owned businesses', *Journal of Business Venturing*, 16 (5), 453–470.

Gupta, V. (1981), 'Minimum efficient scale as a determinant of concentration', *Manchester School of Economic and Social Studies*, 49, 153–164.

Hall, B. (1987), 'The relationship between firm size and firm growth in the US manufacturing sector', *Journal of Industrial Economics*, 35, 583–606.

Harhoff, D., Stahl, K. and Woywode, M. (1998), 'Legal form, growth and exit of West German firms – empirical results for manufacturing, construction, trade and service industries', *Journal of Industrial Economics*, 46, 453–489.

Henrekson, M. and Johansson, D. (2009), 'Competencies and institutions fostering high-growth firms', *Foundations and Trends in Entrepreneurship*, 5, 1–80.

Henrekson, M. and Johansson, D. (2010), 'Gazelles as job creators: a survey and interpretation of the evidence', *Small Business Economics*, 35, 227–244.

Hisrich, R. and Brush, C. (1984), 'The woman entrepreneur: management skills and business problems', *Journal of Small Business Management*, 22, 31–37.

Hölzl, W. (2009), 'Is the R&D behaviour of fast-growing SMEs different? Evidence from CIS III data for 16 countries', *Small Business Economics*, 33, 59–75.

Kalleberg, A.L. and Leicht, K.T. (1991), 'Gender and organizational performance: determinants of small business survival and success', *Academy of Management Journal*, 34 (1), 136–161.

Kelley, D., Bosma, N. and Amoros, J.E. (2011), *Global Entrepreneurship Monitor, 2010 Global Report*, Babson, MA: Babson College, Universidad del Desarrollo, London Business School, and GERA.
Kjeldsen, J. and Nielsen, K. (2004), 'Growth creating entrepreneurs: what are their characteristics and impact, and can they be created?', in M. Hancock and T. Bager (eds), *Global Entrepreneurship Monitor Denmark 2003*, Copenhagen: Borsens Forlag, pp. 195–211.
Landström, H. (2005), *Pioneers in Entrepreneurship and Small Business Research*, New York: Springer.
Locke, E.A. and Baum, J.R. (2007), 'Entrepreneurial motivation', in Baum, J.R., Frese, M. and Baron, R.A. (eds), *The Psychology of Entrepreneurship*, SIOP Organizational Frontiers Series, Mahwah, NJ: Lawrence Erlbaum, pp. 93–112.
Markman, G.D. and Gartner, W.B. (2002), 'Is extraordinary growth profitable? A study of Inc. 500 high-growth companies', *Entrepreneurship Theory and Practice*, 27 (1), 65–75.
Mata, J. (1994), 'Firm growth during infancy', *Small Business Economy*, 6 (1), 27–40.
Millán, J.M., Congregado, E., Román, C., van Praag, M. and van Stel, A. (2011), 'The value of an educated population for an individual's entrepreneurship success', EIM Business and Policy Research, Zoetermeer, the Netherlands, http://www.tinbergen.nl/discussionpapers/11066.pdf (accessed June 2012).
Minniti, M. and Nardone, C. (2007), 'Being in someone else's shoes: the role of gender in nascent entrepreneurship', *Small Business Economics*, 28 (2–3), 223–238.
Močnik, D. and Širec, K. (2010), 'The determinants of Internet use controlling for income level: cross-country empirical evidence', *Information Economics and Policy*, 22 (3), 243–256.
Mondragon-Velez, C. (2009), 'The probability of transition to entrepreneurship revisited: wealth, education and age', *Annals of Finance*, 5 (3–4), 421–441.
Morris, M.H., Miyasaki, N.N., Watters, C.E. and Coombes, S.M. (2006), 'The dilemma of growth: understanding venture size choices of women entrepreneurs', *Journal of Small Business Management*, 44, 221–244.
Müller, G.F. (2001), 'Biographical factors of occupational independence', *Psychological Reports*, 89, 309–314.
Müller, G.F. and Gappisch, C. (2005), 'Personality types of entrepreneurs', *Psychological Report*, 96, 737–746.
Niskanen, M. and Niskanen, J. (2007), 'The determinants of firm growth in small and micro firms – evidence on relationship lending effects', http://ssrn.com/abstract=874927 (accessed June 2012).
Penrose, E. (1959), *The Theory of the Growth of the Firm*, Oxford: Oxford University Press.
Rebernik, M., Tominc, P., Crnogaj, K., Širec, K. and Bradač-Hojnik, B. (2013), *Nezaznane priložnosti: GEM Slovenija 2012* (Unperceived opportunities: GEM Slovenia 2012), Slovenian Entrepreneurship Observatory, Maribor: Faculty of Economics and Business, University of Maribor.
Robb, A.M. and Watson, J. (2012), 'Gender differences in firm performance: evidence from new ventures in the United States', *Journal of Business Venturing*, 27 (5), 544–558.

Roper, S. (1999), 'Modelling small business growth and profitability', *Small Business Economics*, 13, 235–252.
Rosa, P., Carter, S. and Hamilton, D. (1996), 'Gender as a determinant of small business performance: insights from a British study', *Small Business Economics*, 8 (6), 463–478.
Ruminska-Zimny, E. (2003), 'Women's entrepreneurship and labour market trends in transition countries', *Women's Entrepreneurship in Eastern Europe and CIS Countries*, Geneva: United Nations, pp. 1–16.
Schreyer, P. (2000), 'High-growth firms and employment', OECD Science, Technology and Industry Working Papers, OECD Publishing, http://www.sour ceoecd.org/vl=3995978/cl=11/nw=1/rpsv/cgi-bin/wppdf?file=5lgsjhvj7mtd.pdf (accessed June 2012).
Sexton, D.L. (1997), 'Entrepreneurship research needs and issues', in Sexton, D.L. and Smilor, R.W. (eds), *Entrepreneurship 2000*, Chicago, IL: Upstart Publishing Company, pp. 401–408.
Sexton, D.L., Pricer, R.W. and Nenide, B. (2000), 'Measuring performance in high-growth firms', paper presented at Babson Entrepreneurship Research Conference, Wellesley, MA, June.
Statistical Office of the Republic of Slovenia (2009), *Statistical Yearbook of the Republic of Slovenia, 2009*, Ljubljana: Statistical Office of the Republic of Slovenia.
Steffens, P., Davidsson, P. and Fitzsimmons, J. (2009), 'Performance configurations over time: implications for growth and profit-oriented strategies', *Entrepreneurship Theory and Practice*, 33 (1), 125–148.
Storey, D. (1994), *Understanding the Small Business Sector*, London, UK and New York, USA: Routledge.
Stoyanovska, A. (2001), *Jobs, Gender and Small Enterprises in Bulgaria*, Geneva: ILO.
Širec, K. and Močnik, D. (2012a), 'Gender specifics in entrepreneurs' personal characteristics', *Journal of East European Management Studies*, 17 (1), 11–39.
Širec, K. and Močnik, D. (2012b), 'Determinants of the level of entrepreneurial growth: empirical evidence from Slovenian high-growth firms', paper presented at RENT XXVI conference, Lyon, France, November.
Širec, K., Tominc, P. and Rebernik, M. (2010), 'Gender differences in the growth aspirations and technology orientation of Slovenian entrepreneurs', in Brush, C.G. (ed.), *Women Entrepreneurs and the Global Environment for Growth: A Research Perspective*, Cheltenham, UK and Northampton, MA, USA: Edward Elgar, pp. 323–343.
Teruel, M. and De Wit, G. (2011), 'Determinants of high-growth firms. Why have some countries more high-growth firms than others?', EIM Research Reports, H201107.
Tominc, P. (2002), 'Some aspects of the gender wage gap in Slovenia', *Društvena istraživanja*, 11 (6), 879–896.
Tominc, P. and Rebernik, M. (2006), 'Female entrepreneurial growth aspirations in Slovenia: an unexploited resource', in Brush, C.G., Carter, N.M., Gatewood, E., Greene, P.G. and Hart, M.M. (eds), *Growth-Oriented Women Entrepreneurs and their Businesses: A Global Research Perspective*, New Horizons in Entrepreneurship, Cheltenham, UK and Northampton, MA, USA: Edward Elgar, pp. 330–347.
Tominc, P. and Rebernik, M. (2007), 'Gender differences in early-stage entrepre-

neurship in three European post-socialist countries', *Društvena istraživanja*, 16 (3), 589–611.

Tominc, P. and Rebernik, M. (2012), 'Gender differences in entrepreneurial education and entrepreneurial activity in part of the Danube region', *Aktual. Probl. Ekon.*, 12 (138), 496–505.

Van der Sluis, J., van Praag, M. and Vijverberg, W. (2008), 'Education and entrepreneurship selection and performance: a review of the empirical literature', *Journal of Economic Surveys*, 22 (5), 795–841.

9. Growth process of small and medium-sized manufacturing in developing countries: a study of women-owned firms in Bangladesh

Mosfeka Jomaraty and Jerry Courvisanos

INTRODUCTION

In developing countries, small and medium-sized enterprises (SMEs) are seen as crucial for endogenous growth and development, as is evident in the fast-developing Asian economies; yet little is known about the role of women entrepreneurs in these environments (Tambunan, 2009). Bangladesh is an example of an Asian economy with dismal underdevelopment and a lowly 3.7 per cent economic growth measured in annual gross domestic product (GDP) during the 1980s. However, since the onset of the 1990s it started to grow at an accelerating rate with average annual GDP jumping to 4.8 per cent in the 1990s and accelerating in the decade of the 2000s to an average of just under 6 per cent. This was accompanied by a more than 5 per cent per capita income rise that represents a threefold increase compared to the 1980s (Osmani, 2010, p. 37). The role that women have played in the development of Bangladesh is little understood, which is surprising given that 47 per cent of all Bangladeshi women-owned firms are in manufacturing, a sector that has been the driver of growth in most economies (Zohir and Greene, 2012). Therefore, in this chapter we explore the growth experiences of women-owned urban-based manufacturing SMEs in Bangladesh.

Specifically, the focus of this chapter is to better understand women entrepreneurship in the context of Dhaka (the capital city of Bangladesh) by adopting the epistemological stance of pragmatism and viewing a businesswoman's 'belief', 'habit' and 'doubt' as critical for researching gender-related issues in entrepreneurship. A conceptual framework is used to examine various growth aspects associated with women-owned manufacturing SMEs with the aim of addressing two neglected issues in relation to female entrepreneurship. One is the scarcity of studies on women entrepreneurs in developing countries, especially in the context of the Diana International Project. The other is to focus, in the context of a strong male-dominated Islamic nation, on very successful (high-growth) women-owned firms (the 'outliers').

This study adopts a framework developed out of the Diana International Project for the investigation of Bangladeshi women-owned businesses. In order to evaluate the growth process itself, the framework is modified with the addition of two variables, growth resources and actions; as proposed by Edith Penrose in her 1959 seminal book *The Theory of Growth of the Firm*. This allows for the investigation of the effects of managerial and entrepreneurial abilities on growth, and the identification of how firms achieve growth.

UNDERSTANDING THE GROWTH OF WOMEN-OWNED FIRMS

Although firm growth has been a central issue in entrepreneurial studies, the growth of women-owned firms has received very little attention. In the academic field, research on female entrepreneurship is still insignificant (Gatewood et al., 2003; de Bruin et al., 2006; Holmquist and Carter, 2009). Although there has been some conceptualization and explanation of growth aspects of women-owned enterprise since the Diana Project was established in 1999, a major Diana Project study noted that an understanding of the factors affecting growth is largely still absent (Brush et al., 2006, p.4). Ahl (2006) argues for major change in current practices of entrepreneurship studies where women are considered as secondary to men and their businesses less important. Ahl (2006, p. 613) goes on to state that 'the growth ideal is therefore another gendered attribute that merits a closer look and more research'.

Growth of Women-Owned Small Firms in Developing Countries

The number of women-owned businesses is increasing in developing countries but, significantly, they tend to be relatively small and limited in their capacity to grasp growth opportunities (Woldie and Adersua, 2004; Mitra, 2002; Bushell, 2008). A number of studies examine the obstacles to growth of such smaller women-owned firms in the developing world. Among the obstacles identified are: lack of resources for improving firm capabilities (Chea, 2008); an inability to access funding (Halkias et al., 2011; Abzug, 2002; Chea, 2008); and lack of time after housework is prioritized (Kevane and Wydick, 2001). Robinson et al. (2007) draw attention to the influence of culture and social structure on African American women's business experiences and highlight the importance of context (including the individual's personal history, social networks and personal values) when assessing firm performance. In particular, poverty, violence, bias towards men, and sexual harassment have been identified as major factors acting against the growth of women-owned firms (Woldie and Adersua, 2004).

Family support, informal networking and freedom to meet people can play a vital role in enterprise development (Roomi, 2009). In Islamic countries like Pakistan, religious, social and cultural constructs put many restrictions on women (Mathew, 2010; Roomi, 2009; Tambunan, 2007). In addition, women in Islamic nations are frequently poor in human and technological resources, and face business restrictions, as well as social and cultural barriers (Tambunan, 2007). Welter and Smallbone (2008) identify the contextual importance for successful women's entrepreneurship, and that government regulations and institutional bottlenecks hinder growth opportunities.

There are, however, some positive reports of growth in women-owned firms. Chirwa (2008) reports rapid employment growth of women-owned Malawi firms compared to their male counterparts. From regression results of survey data, education is identified as one of the most important success factors for Malawian women entrepreneurs. Other research has identified family support (Halkias et al., 2011) and management training and business networking (Bushell, 2008).

Tambunan (2009) identifies three types of women entrepreneurs in Asian developing countries: 'chance', 'created' and 'forced' entrepreneurs. Chance and created entrepreneurs are motivated by 'pull' factors relating to opportunities identified and exploited. Forced entrepreneurs are compelled by 'displacement' circumstances. Financial motivation, such as the loss of employment (and/or a husband's unemployment), can create 'push' factors that motivate women to embark on an entrepreneurial career. In the context of developing countries, Das (2000) finds 'push' factors to be more influential for Asian women entrepreneurs than 'pull' or 'chance' factors. Tambunan (2009) also finds that most Asian women entrepreneurs fall into the category of 'forced' entrepreneurs, and that the 'push' factors that motivated these women to become entrepreneurs can also limit their growth aspirations. Given that most Asian women appear to be 'pushed' into entrepreneurship, there is limited research available specifically focusing on Asian women who have been 'pulled' into entrepreneurship.

Further, it is evident from the literature that gender plays a role when it comes to business performance as it can influence an entrepreneur's ability to achieve business growth, particularly in the context of developing economies. Women-owned firms in developing economies typically start with little capital and often face difficulties in accessing bank loans. In such circumstances, financial and emotional support provided by family can significantly impact the performance of women-owned firms (Tambunan, 2009). Given there can be substantial differences among groups of women in terms of their backgrounds and how they grow their businesses, it is important to recognize these contextual differences if the complexities of the growth process are to be properly understood. This chapter, therefore, focuses on the role of 'pull' factors in the growth of women-owned urban-based businesses within a developing-country context (Bangladesh).

THE CONTEXT OF WOMEN-OWNED SMEs IN BANGLADESH

The traditional Islamic society of Bangladesh has identified women for their reproductive role. Their activities in the socio-cultural setting are primarily domestic in nature. In Bangladesh, gender inequality prevails in the overall structure of society. Women are typically restricted from engaging in public conduct and various forms of paid employment. The legal status of women, their rights, as well as their role in society, are shaped largely by the law of the country and members of society. Despite the fact that Section 27 of the Constitution of the People's Republic of Bangladesh reads, 'All citizens are equal before law and entitled to equal protection of law', norms of female subordination are still prevalent in the social structure of Bangladesh (Islam and Sultana, 2006).

In Bangladesh, women comprise 48.9 per cent of the total population, but 86 per cent of women live in rural areas (Schwab, 2011). Women in rural areas have inadequate access to the law due to a lack of legal literacy, information and resources, as well as a lack of awareness of their human rights. In rural areas, there are often community groups of influential people who tend to set and control the normative codes of conduct for the community. These rules result in discrimination against women by putting them in a disadvantageous position (Islam and Sultana, 2006). In urban areas, however, the influence of these community groups no longer exists. In urban areas there is a substantial variety in the beliefs, norms and values regarding women's role within and outside the family, determined largely by the socio-economic background of the family. The increase in higher education and improved awareness among women has changed their gender role (Parvin et al., 2012). In this context, women's economic role and their contribution has increasingly been acknowledged in addition to their contribution as home-makers (Huq and Moyeen, 2011). A growing number of urban women are involved in various salaried occupations in both the public and private sectors. Women also participate in the mainstream economy through their economic contributions as business owners.

As reported in the Economic Census 2001–2003, women own 2.83 per cent of all enterprises in Bangladesh, with women entrepreneurs constituting 6 per cent of the total micro, small and medium-sized enterprises of the country (Daniels, 2003). Women-owned businesses are mostly found in the production and marketing of agricultural and consumer goods, and the provision of services for domestic and international markets (ADB, 2012). Women entrepreneurs in urban areas are mostly involved in craft manufacturing, fashion apparel making and boutiques, fabric printing, bakery and fast food shops, interior decoration and design, beautification and healthcare centres, training centres, and leather goods manufacturing. There is an emerging group of educated, urban-based, middle-to-upper-class women motivated by 'pull' factors in their ownership of small and medium-sized businesses (Huq and Moyeen, 2011).

THE CONCEPTUAL FRAMEWORK

The conceptual framework used in this chapter incorporates components derived from seminal works in the field. The growth model developed by Brush et al. (2010) forms the foundation for evaluating the factors influencing the growth of individual women-owned firms. As shown in Figure 9.1, the elements of (1), (3), (4) and (5) were adapted from Brush et al. (2010) and focus on factors influencing women-owned businesses. The Brush et al. (2010) framework was modified and expanded with the addition of element (2) from Penrose (1959), in order to incorporate the impact of entrepreneurial, managerial and technical abilities on firm growth, and with the expansion of element (5) to identify how firms achieve this growth via the resources they have available and the actions they take. In this study, the external environmental context (3) relates to a specific group of successful women-owned firms that have experienced strong growth in the urban-based city of Dhaka. This framework is flexible as it allows variations, depending on the external environment, to be used for the evaluation of any region with successful firm growth.

Element 1: Individual Factors and Family Context

An entrepreneur's individual characteristics and family context are the starting element in this framework. Each entrepreneur possesses a unique

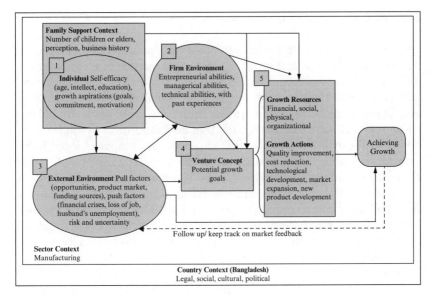

Sources: adapted from Brush et al. (2010) and Penrose (1959).

Figure 9.1 Conceptual framework of women-owned SME growth

bundle of individual characteristics related to self-efficacy (age, intellect and education) and growth aspirations (goals, commitment and motivation). An owner's level of education and knowledge tend to be positively associated with firm success (Langowitz and Minniti, 2007). The potential for business growth is also influenced by the owner's individual growth ambitions. Women tend to differ from men in their entrepreneurial aspirations (Širec et al., 2010) and motivation for success (Treanor and Henry, 2010), with less immediate urgency and a longer term perspective.

Greater emphasis has recently been placed on the need for contextualizing women's entrepreneurship at the family level (Brush et al., 2010). Every entrepreneur is embedded within a family context, which has a 'greater impact on women than men in the entrepreneurial process' (Brush et al., 2010, p.4). In Figure 9.1 the individual characteristics of women entrepreneurs are captured within the outer circle of her family context. Family context may include the number of children or elders to be taken care of, the family's perception of women entrepreneurs, and the family's business history.

Element 2: Internal (Firm) Environment

This element is made up of the entrepreneurial, managerial and technical capabilities of the owner that are brought to the internal firm environment. The owner's entrepreneurial versatility is formed from her imaginative efforts, sense of timing, ability to make decisions and ability to recognize demand in the market (Penrose, 1959). The entrepreneur needs to build this entrepreneurial capability within the firm because growth depends on the ability of the owner to perceive and act upon opportunities for profitable growth, experiment with new ideas, and be prepared (and able) to move the business into new geographical areas. Managerial capabilities are made up of administrative abilities, including the insertion of resources into the firm, and the application of appropriate actions. These qualities are needed for transforming ideas into realities and have practical implications for growing the firm (Penrose, 1959). Vigorous and creative managerial capabilities allow the firm to alter the range of products and expand the total output, even in unfavourable market conditions. Technical capabilities can be achieved through specialized training, as well as industry-specific knowledge. Previous work experiences in similar fields help the entrepreneur to accumulate the necessary business and management skills that are important for creating the firm environment for growth. The differing experiences of women compared to men impact on the way the three capabilities are built into the firm environment (Kevane and Wydick, 2001).

Element 3: External Environment

This element is specific to the external environment and includes both 'pull' and 'push' factors. 'Pull' factors strongly drive product markets, opportunities and funding sources. The ability of the firm to grow depends, in large part, on the external opportunities available to it. The larger the opportunity set, the larger the growth potential (McKelvie and Wiklund, 2010). A firm's competence to cater to a large market will facilitate its growth potential. Access to external funding sources, including financial institutions or equity providers, is also important for firm growth and may differ for men- and women-owned business. Women are frequently 'pushed' to start and run their own business due to a financial crisis (such as losing their job, or their husband's unemployment). In these cases entrepreneurs may not initially seek high growth because of the risks and uncertainty involved. The chances of failure can be reduced by estimating the risk and unavoidable uncertainty attached to various courses of actions. Women tend to be better at self-screening, which makes women able to reduce risk by doing what they know (Ljunggren and Kolvereid, 1996).

Element 4: Venture Concept

The venture concept consists of the products or services that the firm provides (Bhidé, 2000). It includes breakthrough ideas, unique solutions to a vital problem, or inventions of a product with few substitutes. These ideas and innovations are transformed into a concept that is defined by the activities of the firm. Brush et al. (2010) clearly indicate that women's selection of their appropriate venture concept is based on different priorities, but it is this selection that determines the firm's potential growth goals.

Element 5: Growth Resources and Actions

Firm resources transform ideas into products and services and make them available to customers (Penrose, 1959). The set of resources required to grow the business includes social, organizational, physical and financial resources (Brush et al., 2010). Social resources are crucial for obtaining access to opportunities and other resources, as well as establishing connection with sources of advice and support. Social resources evolve from norms, relationships and social structures, and include a firm's contact network, reputation and ability to acquire necessary resources (Aldrich, 1999). Organizational resources include structures, relationships and information. Human resources are central to the continuation of the enterprise and are based on education, industry knowledge, business experience and appropriate training of the firm's workforce. Physical resources include land and natural resources, as well as plant, equipment, raw materials, technology and other physical assets of the business. Financial resources include the monetary assets of the business, which often comprise the owner's personal savings (Bygrave, 1992). Firm growth is also a function of the growth strategy and actions adopted. Selecting actions for growth depends on the mode of growth, which might be organic or acquisitive. This research concentrates only on growth within the firm and excludes acquisitions, mergers, licensing and franchising.

Resources can be viewed as a bundle of available assets that can be applied to the productive operations of the firm. In order to understand and explain the growth actions and operations of a particular firm, it is essential to identify the nature and extent of its productive opportunities and its ability to make resource decisions. These decisions include actions related to improving product or service quality, reducing costs, technological advancements, market expansion and the introduction of new products in the market.

Operationalizing the Framework

It is difficult to decide which factor(s) should be placed in which internal/ external element of the framework. For example, Davidsson (1991) and Chandler and Hanks (1994) view opportunity as an external factor, whereas Davidsson (2004) mentions opportunity as being the same as 'business idea' and views this as an internal factor. Consistent with the literature, recognizing a particular factor's impact on growth is more important than classifying it as either internal or external, provided particular allocations are held constant throughout the study. The conceptual framework in this study allows a specific internal or external allocation of factors based on what we believe would be the priorities from women's perspective.

The five elements combine (as shown by the arrows in Figure 9.1) to determine the nature and extent of firm growth. The framework consists of both one-way and two-way arrows. One-way arrows demonstrate the unidirectional influences, whereas two-way arrows emphasize bi-directional influences of one factor of growth on the other. This framework is interactive with an iterative nature, such that firm growth acts as feedback via market signals for women entrepreneurs to re-evaluate various aspects of their ventures to relatively quickly address changes in the external environment (Element 3), which can then feedback to individual goals (Element 1), and the internal environment (Element 2).

The conceptual framework recognizes that the growth process of an individual women-led firm is a combined result of the multifaceted interplay of all the determinants of growth. Potential growth of the firm is also directly influenced by its sector (in this case manufacturing) and country (Bangladesh) context (Carter and Allen, 1997). Competitive and congested sectors limit a firm's ability to grow. The country context explains how the role of women is socially constructed. In Bangladesh, like many other non-Western countries, the arena of entrepreneurship is male-dominated and gender stereotyping affects the performance of women-owned businesses (Aslanbeigui et al., 2010). These represent potential growth hurdles for women-owned firms that need to be understood when investigating the growth of female-owned firms.

METHODOLOGY

The conceptual framework depicted in Figure 9.1 largely determined the methodological approach adopted in this study with respect to the collection and analysis of data. The framework aims to identify the influential factors behind firm growth and to explore the growth processes using the five elements in the conceptual framework.

Female entrepreneurship studies, like Brush et al. (2009), argue that although the individual personal characteristics of female entrepreneurs within a male-dominated capitalist system are important, there is a need to concentrate more on process developments. By focusing on process development, this study aims to better understand the growth process in women-owned firms.

The study takes the epistemological stance of pragmatism, embracing both objective and subjective points of view (Tashakkori and Teddlie, 1998). Pragmatism has its roots in mid-19th-century American reform philosophy, but has only recently (compared to traditional philosophies like positivism and constructivism) been adopted as a modern research philosophy. Yet, pragmatism has already proved its applicability as a competing paradigm (Tashakkori and Teddlie, 1998).

Pragmatism is important as it encompasses norms, beliefs and habits (Peirce, 1855). According to Yefimov (2003), reality and knowledge depend on habits and beliefs that are created within an institutional context. We have already identified that women's entrepreneurship is socially embedded, and the importance of context in researching women's entrepreneurship. In this context, the Brush et al. (2010) framework considers individual women owners to be embedded within the family context, which has a larger impact on women than men in the entrepreneurial process.

From the epistemological stance of pragmatism, this study follows the ontological assumption of 'accepting the external reality and selecting the explanations that best produce desired outcomes' (Tashakkori and Teddlie, 1998, p. 23). As such, this study assumes the external world is operating independently of our minds, while knowledge claims cannot be totally abstracted from contingent beliefs and interests.

Unit of Analysis

Individual firm cases were developed on the basis of in-depth interviews and supporting documents. These interviews were based on the framework outlined in Figure 9.1 and aimed to identify growth factors and the growth processes involved in women-owned businesses. To identify the unit of analysis for this project, it is essential to provide a definition of SMEs in the context of Bangladesh. The Government of Bangladesh revised the definition of SMEs in the circular for the Bank of Bangladesh of 26 May 2008. Small enterprises in the manufacturing sector are defined either by the value of their resources (other than land and factory buildings) being between 0.05 million and 15 million Bangladeshi taka (BDT) or having 50 or less employees. Medium-sized enterprises in the manufacturing sector are defined by the value of their resources being between 15 million and 200 million BDT or having between 51 and 150 employees.

The study follows Davidsson et al. (2005, p. 3) who state that the prototypical growth firm is one that experiences relatively stable growth in sales over a considerable time period, and this growth in sales is, at least to some extent, accompanied by an accumulation of employees and assets, so that organizational and managerial complexity increase with growth. The unit of analysis for this study is a successfully growth-oriented manufacturing SME in Dhaka that is owned and run by a woman.

Sample Selection

This chapter reports on eight SMEs made up of four small and four medium-sized firms. Growth-oriented firms have been selected through purposive sampling, as having no less than a 10 per cent increase in sales and employees over a period of three years (2008–2010). The owners were successful women entrepreneurs who have been recognized with awards such as the National SME Women Entrepreneurship Award, Bangladesh Women Chamber of Commerce and Industry-EBL Progressive Award and Outstanding Women of the Year in Business of 2008–10. These women have firms that have been independently identified as successful 'outliers' and, thus, their success can inform our conceptual framework in terms of the specific decisions and actions taken (Taleb, 2008, pp. 51–61). Therefore, the sample selection criteria we adopted was fundamentally based on its relevance to the research topic, as advocated by Flick (1998).

Data Collection and Analysis

All interviewees were asked the same questions (see Box 9.1). The responses from interview participants were audio-recorded, or notes were taken if the interviewee requested no recording. Interview transcripts were coded and saved as a separate Word file. Codes were used to maintain participants' confidentiality and anonymity. Interview data was supported by organizational documents, such as annual financial reports, internal management reports, existing secondary data analyses, organization websites, and published news from media.

For the purpose of maintaining the confidentiality of research participants and their firms, no real names of either the participants or their firms are disclosed. For ease of understanding, same size firms from the same

BOX 9.1 SEMI-STRUCTURED INTERVIEW SCHEDULE

Firm name:
Starting time: Finishing time:
Date: Address:

Demographic description
Year of establishment
Type of business: Probe – Products, services
Sales
Employees

Internal firm environment
Individual

- Age
- Level of education
- Previous experience

Family

- Number of children/ elders: Probe – Do you need to take care of them? Does it affect your business?
- Perception of family members: Probe – Husband's perception, children's perception, encouragement, support, sharing work load
- Business history in family: Probe – Father, husband, other family member or near friend doing business

External environment
Reason for choosing particular business: Probe – Opportunities, product market
Relationship with supplier: Probe – Quality, promptness, efficiency
Perception on customers: Probe – Demanding, loyal
Did you get any loan for starting or growing?
How do you assess risk? To what extend do you take risk?

Venture concept
Growth plans/goals for next three years: Probe

> **Resources**
> What were the resources in order to grow the business? Were they adequate?: Probe – Organizational, physical, financial resources
> How did you acquire any resource necessary for growing your business?
>
> **Growth actions**
> How did you reach your growth goal?
>
> - Improving the quality of product/service? How?
> - Reducing cost of production? How?
> - Developing the process of production/service? Change or addition in process? Using what advanced technology?
> - Introduce new product/service in the market? How?
> - Expanding existing market? How?
> - Please specify if any other strategies have been taken to achieve growth of your business.

industry were identified with identical letters (for example, medium-sized manufacturing firms are prefaced by the letters MM) and then numbered subsequently (1, 2, 3 and 4) in the order in which they were executed. The interviewees who were the owners of the respective firms have been prefaced by the letter RMM and then numbered subsequently (1, 2, 3 and 4) in the order in which they were interviewed. Data from in-depth interviews and supporting documents were used to build individual firm narratives within the theoretical framework.

Themes were identified, categorized and compared against the framework elements. Each of the eight firm narratives identifies factors within the framework elements assisting the growth and the growth process of each firm. Patterns were identified across each of the four cases within one context (small or medium-sized) and then across both contexts. Patterns were then matched with the conceptual framework for recognizing the influential growth factors and growth processes undertaken. The influence of these growth factors to each firm was categorized into very low, low, moderate, high and very high: 'very low' denotes no support for business growth with all negative influences; 'low' represents minimum level of support for growth with some negative influences; 'moderate' denotes equal amounts of positives and negatives for business growth; 'high' signifies a strong level of support with few negative impacts for growth;

and 'very high' represents the maximum level of support for firm growth without any negative influence.

RESULTS

A short narrative on each firm is presented in this section in order to gain a perspective on successful women-owned firms in manufacturing.

Section 1: Four Medium-Sized Manufacturing Firms

Case 1
MM1 is a printing press company, established in 1982 and has experienced growth since 1986. The firm has gone through two growth phases. The early growth phase was from 1986 to 1993. MM1 established a strong position in the local market before exporting. Over time, business relationships with bigger clients were strengthened and a good market position was established with a strong customer base. The second phase of growth occurred between 1998 and 2010, with exports to Italy and the UK. RMM1's creative and artistic approach formed the base for the second growth phase. In 2011 MM1 functioned with eight printing machines; 80 permanent employees, including six technicians, four electricians and three engineers; as well as 20 part-time non-permanent workers.

Case 2
MM2 was formed during the early 1980s as an export-oriented garments manufacturing firm. Initially the export volume was very small. Due to the use of low-skilled workers, the production quality was very basic. The owner, RMM2, arranged comprehensive overseas training for the workers and managers for skill development. Reliance on imported materials and their costs were reduced with local sourcing of raw materials. The use of commission agents was eliminated, and direct sales relationships were established with foreign buyers, which increased the growth of MM2. As of 2011 the firm employed 147 workers and is considered one of the most successful women-owned medium-sized manufacturing firms in the country.

Case 3
In 2003, MM3 began as one of the very few leather products manufacturing firms created and owned by a women leather technologist. As of 2011, it employed 110 workers, with a production capacity per month of 500 jackets, 6000 wallets or bags, and 600 pairs of footwear. With an

innovative combination of materials, RMM3 was successful in differentiating MM3's product from the rest of the market, which provided the first phase of MM3's growth. Growth was also achieved through the annual product promotion of MM3 at International Trade Fairs.

Case 4

MM4 is a decorative and architectural art glass manufacturing company. Its success is based on RMM4's ambitions and creative skills in this form of art. It began as a small enterprise in 1998 with two workers in a small 400 square foot studio. Initially it produced simple forms of architectural glass but later increased its product range from simple to sophisticated designs. In 2000 MM4 moved into a 2200 square foot studio with a retail sales showroom. Massive demand in the local market led MM4 to open a second showroom. With two grand showrooms in the country's two largest cities, MM4 is now considered Bangladesh's leading crafted art glass designer, producer and supplier and holds nearly 40 per cent of the total market.

Common Patterns across the Medium-Sized Manufacturing Firms

It is important to note that each of the four women-owned firms has achieved substantial sales growth either domestically or internationally, and two of them (MM1 and 4) were the first-movers in their industry. The common patterns in MM1, 2, 3 and 4, based on our framework of analysis, are summarized in Table 9.1 and discussed below.

From Table 9.1 it can be seen that the owner's self-efficacy and growth aspirations were consistently rated very highly in terms of their importance to firm growth. All four owners were highly motivated to develop and grow their businesses and three of the owners had strong family support from a spouse or in-laws. However, RMM3 was not supported by her family and had to leave her family home while starting the business. All the women came from upper-class Bangladesh society, which although providing strong financial and cultural backing to aid firm growth, nevertheless presented a challenge for these women as they attempted to enter successful male power domains.

The internal firm environment element from Penrose (1959) also played a significant role in the success of these women entrepreneurs. The prosperous growth operations of these firms were the result of their owners' entrepreneurial abilities. All of them were successful in identifying opportunities in the market. The growth of these firms increased the complexity of decision-making and highlighted the difficulties associated with managing growth. RMM4 was the only owner with prior managerial

Table 9.1 Framework elements into business growth of four women-owned medium-sized manufacturing firms

Framework element \ Cases	MM1	MM2	MM3	MM4
Individual factors				
Self-efficacy	****	****	*****	*****
Growth aspirations	*****	*****	*****	*****
Family support	*****	*****	*	*****
Internal firm environment				
Entrepreneurial ability	*****	*****	*****	*****
Managerial ability	*	*	*	*****
Technical ability	*****	*	*****	*****
External environment				
Product market	*****	*****	*****	*****
Opportunities	*****	*****	*****	*****
Government support	**	*****	**	**
Growth resources				
Financial	****	*****	***	*****
Social	***	*****	***	*****
Human	***	***	*****	***
Growth actions				
Product quality improvement	*****	*****	*****	*****
Cost reduction	*****	*****	*****	*****
Technological development	*****	****	*****	*****

Note: * denotes 'very low', ** 'low', *** 'moderate', **** 'high' and ***** 'very high' level of input into the growth processes.

abilities, which she gained from working in a handicraft organization as a manager. In the other firms (MM1, 2 and 3), in an effort to address the increasing complexities brought on by growth, the owners recognized their own weaknesses and recruited skilled and experienced management staff. Technical abilities were common among three of the firm owners (RMM1, 3 and 4), learnt either from family business or from professional training. RMM3 and RMM4 were also trained in specific production processes and had artistic skills in leather and glass, respectively.

From an external environment perspective, all of the women were pulled into the market by opportunities created from existing product market demands, but the owners leveraged incremental innovation using their skill and creativity (in Element 2) to grow their businesses. Crucially, opportunity identification attracted their entry into this area of male-dominated businesses. For MM1, after a decade of independence from Pakistan, there was a need to retain the nation's authenticity. Consequently, there was a demand for publishing as well as printing in the local language. MM1 seized this opportunity for a number of years following its inception. Another action taken by MM1 to enhance growth was a proactive scanning of the international market to identify opportunities, which opened the door to cater to a larger market. For MM2, a change in global apparel production location created the opportunity for her to start up in the garment industry. MM2's low-cost labour force and simple technology production supported further expansion. For MM3, a large domestic market for leather products and a lack of qualified designers in the leather industry provided an opportunity for MM3 to grow. For MM4, the lack of a local producer in the art glass industry created an opportunity and provided a strong base for growth.

Government support was another important factor within the external environment. The policy level support provided by the government facilitated the growth of MM2. As a part of the government's Ready-Made Garments (RMG) promotion policy, a meeting was organized for garments manufacturers, foreign buyers and agents. This ensured that RMM2 was acquainted with overseas apparel buyers and agents. RMM2 received her first work order from, and then started manufacturing for, a USA-based buying agent. Although none of the remaining firms (MM1, 3 and 4) received any industry-specific support from government (because their industries were not identified as high priority industries) there were some small government support programmes available to these firms.

Firm resources were also seen as important for the growth of all four MM firms. In particular, the owners' personal savings and family resources were an important source of financial support for the growth of all four MMs. The influential positions the owners' families occupied within society also played a significant role in establishing social networks and achieving business growth. RMM2 and RMM4 had a greater advantage compared to the other two women owners in this respect. Human resources in the form of well-trained, experienced and low-cost workers and managers also created a positive influence for the growth of all four firms. MM3 hired skilled and experienced workers from the market who did not require further training. However, overseas training occurred at an extra cost for firms MM1, 2 and 4.

Finally, the growth actions of these firms seemed to differ depending on their industry context. For example, while training workers and managers was seen as important for improving product quality, the owners of MM1, 2 and 4 arranged regular overseas training, whereas MM3 arranged local training. Similarly, while cost reduction through sourcing raw materials locally was used by MM2, 3 and 4 to significantly influence firm growth, MM1 used a low-cost machine (instead of an expensive machine) without affecting quality and productivity to achieve cost reductions and increase growth. The importance of technological advancement was also highlighted as being significant for the growth of all four MMs. MM2 implemented advanced technological systems that linked orders and inventory to streamline order processing, production and stock keeping capabilities. Technological change had an impact on the productive capacity of MM1's machine operators. Newer machines significantly outperformed older technologies and complemented the creative team of artists that was formed within MM1. A unique combination of materials provided a different form of product for MM3. MM4 signed an international franchise agreement for achieving a higher technology level of production. Equipment was upgraded and a new management style was implemented to meet the franchise agreement.

Section 2: Four Small Manufacturing Firm Studies

Case 1
SM1, formed in 2004, is one of the first recycled-metal producers in Bangladesh. Initially the firm applied simple forms of production, carried out by four workers with two machines in a small metal factory. Gradually, RSM1 and the workers moved into more complicated forms of production. The handicrafts they produced from the recycled materials were appreciated by international buyers; since 2006 SM1 has exported to Sweden, Germany, Norway and Denmark. Growing demand in the international market led SM1 to add a product line of recycled glass. With improved skills and experienced workers, SM1 created a strong technological base and differentiated its products from the market. This fast-growing craft manufacturer employed a total of 45 people in 2011.

Case 2
SM2 is a manufacturing firm that uses fibreglass to cater mainly for the domestic demands of sanitary ware traders. In 2006 it started manufacturing fibreglass bathroom fittings of shower trays and corner trays, later expanding their production to large waste bins, bathtubs and as a by-product, bonsai containers. SM2 emerged as a developing and growth-oriented venture through the modernism and innovativeness of its owner RSM2. She was recognized for the local production of fibreglass materials, which earlier had been imported from China and South Korea. Production capacity of SM2 includes 200 bathtubs and 350 other items a month. As of 2011 the firm employed 35 workers.

Case 3

SM3 began in 2002 as a domestic-based themed fashion clothing manufacturer. More recently it has specialized in traditional and authentic apparel and accessories. Initially, SM3 produced and sold outfits only. Within a short time, however, it became very popular among consumers and in 2005 SM3 opened a second showroom. Craftsmen were hired and trained for jewellery making. Traditional jewellery was added to the product line and a third showroom was opened in 2008. With a team of 50 people employed in the factory and showrooms, over the last ten years, SM3 has become one of the leading fashion houses in Bangladesh.

Case 4

SM4 is a boutique launched in 2005 with a vision to popularize Bangladesh's traditional art and crafts among the fashion conscious in Bangladesh. Reflecting the ideas of the owner, SM4 created its own designs and materials; handwoven materials were naturally dyed and block-printed to create unique products. Exceptionally creative outfits were successful in attracting consumers. In 2008, ornaments, footwear and decorative items were added to the product line. Starting with one small factory, in 2011 SM4 operated one production facility and two showrooms in Dhaka with a team of 45 workers and a monthly production capacity of 1000 outfits, 200 footwear products, and 200 jewellery and home decorating items.

Common Patterns across Small Manufacturing Firms

Significant sales and employee growth were achieved by each of the four small women-owned manufacturing firms; three through local markets and one through foreign markets as well as local markets. Two of these firms (SM1 and SM2) were first-movers in their industry. The common patterns of SM1, SM2, SM3 and SM4 are outlined in Table 9.2.

The growth of all four SMs has been due to a combination of the owners' individual aspirations and both internal and external factors. The strong educational background of RSM1, 3 and 4 is notable; and the strong self-efficacy of all four owners meant they were highly motivated to grow their businesses. All had strong family support for creating and developing their businesses and one of them (RSM1) had a family background in business.

The owners' entrepreneurial capabilities and their influence on the successful operations of their businesses were important for the growth of their firms (internal firm environment). All of the owners were capable of identifying unseen prospects and acting upon opportunities. Two of them

Table 9.2 Framework elements into business growth of four women-owned small-sized manufacturing firms

Framework element \ Cases	SM1	SM2	SM3	SM4
Individual factors				
Self-efficacy	*****	***	*****	*****
Growth aspirations	*****	*****	*****	*****
Family support	*****	*****	*****	*****
Internal firm environment				
Entrepreneurial ability	****	*****	****	*****
Managerial ability	****	***	**	****
Technical ability	*****	*****	*****	*****
External environment				
Product market	*****	*****	****	****
Opportunities	*****	*****	*****	*****
Government support	**	**	**	**
Growth resources				
Financial	*****	****	*****	****
Physical	*****	*****	*****	*****
Human	*****	***	*****	***
Growth actions				
Product quality improvement	*****	*****	*****	*****
Cost reduction	*****	****	****	****
Technological development	*****	****	****	****

Note: * denotes 'very low', ** 'low', *** 'moderate', **** 'high' and ***** 'very high' level of input into the growth processes.

(RSM1 and 4) had managerial abilities, as they had previously worked in managerial positions. All four owners had professional training in specific production processes that then built strong technical capabilities in their firms. Three of them (RSM1, 3 and 4) graduated in Fine Arts with early career experience in craft-making and graphic design.

Growth resources in the form of financial resources came from the owner's personal savings (RSM1), their husband's savings (RSM3) and bank loans (RSM2, 4). Well-trained, inexpensive workers, as well as experienced management staff, were important human resources for RSM1, 3 and 4. Physical resources in the form of low-cost local materials had a positive influence on the growth of all four firms.

The successful growth of these four firms in a relatively short time was based on their owners' creative abilities. RSM1's innovative transforming of metal and glass recycled items into decorative products was a successful growth action for SM1. RSM2's innovative idea of producing bathroom fittings from fibreglass provided a strong impetus for SM2's growth. The creative abilities of RSM3 and RSM4 enabled their products to be differentiated from the market. RSM1 and RSM2's careful control over expenditures, combined with a focus on quality production, was also important for the growth of SM1 and SM2.

DISCUSSION

The growth patterns for the eight women-owned medium-sized and small manufacturing firms investigated in this study are illustrated in Figures 9.2 and 9.3, respectively. The horizontal (X) axis in each figure represents the years of business operation and the vertical (Y) axis represents the annual sales for each firm in AUS$ million.

Figure 9.2 illustrates how the four medium-sized manufacturing firms have grown consistently over a long period of time, except the oldest firm (MM1) which has experienced two separate phases of growth since its inception. Although the starting points and growth rates varied considerably, there are some commonalities among them. Three of the firms (MM1, 2 and 4) had a matching period of steady growth in annual sales since 2000 (MM3 was not in operation until 2004). All four MMs show fairly similar strong growth paths since 2006, despite the fact that three of them had been in existence for quite a while.

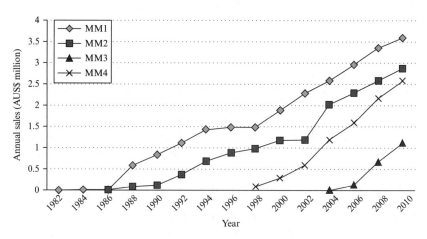

Figure 9.2 Growth of four medium-sized manufacturing firms

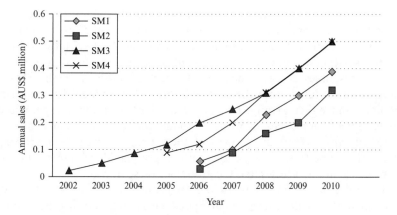

Figure 9.3   Growth of four small manufacturing firms

Similarly, Figure 9.3 illustrates how the four small manufacturing firms have grown, over a shorter period of time, and with similar starting points for three of the businesses (SM1, 2 and 4). Among the four firms, SM3 grew over the longest period of time (from 2002) and experienced stable growth in annual sales throughout.

A comparison of the growth patterns across these eight cases has been complicated because of the diversity of starting points and different operational areas. Differences in growth patterns were noted on the basis of the nature and condition of the specific industries involved. In analysing the growth patterns of these firms it is evident that, regardless of size and nature of the enterprise, women's entry into entrepreneurship and subsequent firm growth appears to be related to a number of factors, including self-efficacy, growth aspirations, family support, entrepreneurial abilities and market opportunities. All these factors appear to be comparable in terms of their impact on firm growth. Six women owners had high levels of education, receiving at least ten years of education to Secondary School Certificate, two years to Higher Secondary School Certificate and four years to graduation. Although they exhibited a diverse range of motivations for venture creation, high-growth aspirations appear to be common among all of them. Further, the growth experiences of the SMEs we studied were largely shaped by the owner's family context. Seven of the owners had strong family support for their business in the form of both financial support and carrying out family responsibilities.

The elements of growth, incorporated from Penrose (1959) and added to the Brush et al. (2010) framework, help to explain the growth processes in a developing economy like Bangladesh. All the owners were successful in identifying opportunities in the market. In all eight firms, external conditions were productively exploited. Evident from the cases is that all the owners were 'created' entrepreneurs who were 'pulled' into business by market opportunities. The successful organization and utilization of growth resources ensured their achievement of strong growth. This is despite the evidence from the cases that four of them lacked managerial abilities and either arranged managerial training or hired experienced management employees. Low-cost labour and the availability of raw materials also helped the growth of these firms. A large and growing domestic market in conjunction with a gradual development in the national economy accelerated the growth of these firms.

The financial resources to fund firm growth largely appear to have been provided by the entrepreneurs' personal savings and by other family members. Six of the eight owners were reluctant to take bank loans. They relied on their personal and family savings for starting their businesses and then reinvested their profits to fund the growth of their firms. Support provided by the government facilitated the growth of only one business (a medium-sized ready-made garment factory); none of the other firms received any specific government support.

CONCLUSION

The research aim of this study was to identify the influential factors behind firm growth and explore the growth process mechanism in the context of the developing economy of Bangladesh. The patterns that emerge support the five elements that underpin the conceptual framework adopted in this chapter. The firms examined were not typical firms, but were successful growth 'outliers' that can be used to inform the framework through an analysis of the specific decisions and actions taken by their owners (Taleb, 2008). These firms are among the most successful firms in their respective industries. They have been developed and grown by women in an Islamic male-dominated society. The owners' individual self-efficacy and their growth aspirations were strong elements underpinning the growth of their firms. Also, well-thought-out growth actions were linked with the owners' growth aspirations to drive firm success. The positive influence of strong growth aspirations (as an individual factor) and various growth action factors was evident in all eight successful firms.

Three final remarks provide the basis for understanding successful firm growth experiences in developing economies. The first is the success of 'pull'-driven women-owned firms, founded by educated, family-oriented, urban-based, middle-to-upper-class females. Their strong self-efficacy and aspirations were matched by internal and external environmental factors together with appropriate resources and effective decision-making to provide a solid foundation for firm growth. This research contrasts with much previous research, which has focused on women engaging in entrepreneurship in developing economies out of necessity ('push' factors) due to poverty and unemployment. Necessity entrepreneurs (generally microcredit and agricultural-based) typically exhibit minimal firm growth and generally lack the potential to contribute significantly to the broader economic growth of their communities.

The second remark is specifically related to the Islamic context of this research. Islamic developing economies have generally ignored women as strong economic constituents. What this study shows is that given the opportunity within the family, the community and the general body politic, talented and educated women can emerge from the home to be significant and different entrepreneurs.

Finally, the size differences between the small and medium-sized firms merely reflect the longer time period that the medium-sized firms have had to grow, as the small firms appear to be growing at a similar rate to the medium firms. This finding should encourage the Bangladesh government to abandon the garments export-only business development policy, which is too dependent on one highly exploitative industry.

REFERENCES

Abzug, C. (2002), *Impact of SAPs on the Female Gender in North Ghana*, Accra, Ghana: Worldwide Press.
Ahl, H. (2006), 'Why research on women entrepreneurs needs new directions', *Entrepreneurship Theory and Practice*, 30 (5), 595–621.
Aldrich, H. (1999), *Organizations Evolving*, Thousand Oaks, CA: Sage.
Asian Development Bank (ADB) (2012), *Key Indicators for Asia and the Pacific*, No. 44, Manila: Asian Development Bank.
Aslanbeigui, N., Oakes, G. and Uddin, N. (2010), 'Assessing microcredit in Bangladesh: a critique of the concept of empowerment', *Review of Political Economy*, 22 (2), 181–204.
Bhidé, A. (2000), *The Origin and Evolution of New Businesses*, Oxford: Oxford University Press.
Brush, C.G., Carter, N.M., Gatewood, E.J., Greene, P.G. and Hart, M.M. (eds) (2006), *Growth-oriented Women Entrepreneurs and their Business: A Global Research Perspective*, Cheltenham, UK and Northampton, MA, USA: Edward Elgar.
Brush, C.G., de Bruin, A., Gatewood, E.J. and Henry, C. (2010), 'Introduction: women entrepreneurs and growth', in Brush, C.G., de Bruin, A. and Gatewood, E.J. (eds), *Women Entrepreneurs and the Global Environment for Growth*, Cheltenham, UK and Northampton, MA, USA: Edward Elgar, pp. 1–16.

Brush, C.G., A. de Bruin and F. Welter (2009), 'A gender-aware framework for women's entrepreneurship', *International Journal of Gender and Entrepreneurship*, 1 (1), 8–24.
Bushell, B. (2008), 'Women entrepreneurs in Nepal: what prevents them from leading the sector?', *Gender and Development*, 16 (3), 549–564.
Bygrave, W.D. (1992), 'Venture capital returns in the 1980s', in Sexton, D.L. and Kasarda, J. (eds), *The State of the Art Entrepreneurship*, Boston, MA: PWS Kent, pp. 438–462.
Carter, N.M. and Allen, K.R. (1997), 'Size determinants of women-owned business: choice or barriers to resources', *Entrepreneurship and Regional Development*, 9 (3), 211–220.
Chandler, G.N. and Hanks, S.H. (1994), 'Founder competence, the environment, and venture performance', *Entrepreneurship Theory and Practice*, 18 (3), 77–89.
Chea, A.C. (2008), 'Factors that influence the survival of women owned small business start-ups in the city of Tema, Ghana', *International Business Research*, 1 (3), 130–144.
Chirwa, E.W. (2008), 'Effects of gender on the performance of micro and small enterprises in Malawi', *Development Southern Africa*, 25 (3), 347–362.
Daniels, L. (2003), 'National private-sector survey of enterprises in Bangladesh, 2003', Dhaka, Bangladesh: International Consulting Group, and Micro Industries Development Assistance and Services.
Das, D.J. (2000), 'Problems faced by women entrepreneurs', in Sasikumar, K. (ed.), *Women Entrepreneurship*, New Delhi, India: Vikas Publishing House, p. xii.
Davidsson, P. (1991), 'Continued entrepreneurship: ability, need, and opportunity as determinants of small firm growth', *Journal of Business Venturing*, 6 (6), 405–429.
Davidsson, P. (2004), *Researching Entrepreneurship*, New York: Springer Verlag.
Davidsson, P., Achtenhagen, L. and Naldi, L. (2005), 'Research on small firm growth: a review', paper presented at the 35th European Institute of Small Business Conference, Barcelona, Spain.
De Bruin, A., Brush, C.G. and Welter, F. (2006), 'Introduction to the special issue: towards building cumulative knowledge on women's entrepreneurship', *Entrepreneurship Theory and Practice*, 30 (5), 585–593.
Flick, U. (1998), *An Introduction to Qualitative Research*, Thousand Oaks, CA: Sage.
Gatewood, E.J., Carter, N., Brush, C.G., Greene, P. and Hart, M. (2003), *Women Entrepreneurs, their Ventures, and the Venture Capital Industry: An Annotated Bibliography*, Stockholm, Sweden: ESBRI.
Halkias, D., Nwajiuba, C., Harkiolakis, N. and Caracatsanis, S.M. (2011), 'Challenges facing women entrepreneurs in Nigeria', *Management Research Review*, 34 (2), 221–235.
Holmquist, C. and Carter, S. (2009), 'The Diana project: pioneering women studying pioneering women', *Small Business Economics*, 32 (2), 121–128.
Huq, A. and Moyeen, A. (2011), 'Gender integration in enterprise development programmes', *Women's Studies International Forum*, 34 (4), 320–328.
Islam, N. and Sultana, N. (2006), 'The status of women in Bangladesh: is the situation really encouraging?', *Research Journal of Social Sciences*, 1(1), 56–65.
Kevane, M. and Wydick, B. (2001), 'Social norms and the time allocation of

women's labor in Burkina Faso', *Review of Development Economics*, 5 (1), 119–129.
Langowitz, N. and Minniti, M. (2007), 'The entrepreneurial propensity of women', *Entrepreneurship Theory and Practice*, 31 (3), 341–364.
Ljunggren, E. and Kolvereid, L. (1996), 'New business formation: does gender make a difference?', *Women in Management Review*, 1 (4), 3–12.
Mathew, V. (2010), 'Women entrepreneurship in the Middle East: understanding barriers and use of ICT for entrepreneurship development', *International Entrepreneurship and Management Journal*, 6 (2), 163–181.
McKelvie, A. and Wiklund, J. (2010), 'Advancing firm growth research: a focus on growth mode instead of growth rate', *Entrepreneurship Theory and Practice*, 34 (2), 261–288.
Mitra, R. (2002), 'The growth pattern of women-run enterprises: an empirical study in India', *Journal of Developmental Entrepreneurship*, 7 (2), 217–237.
Osmani, S.R. (2010), 'Realising the right to development in Bangladesh: progress and challenges', *Bangladesh Development Studies*, 33 (1–2), 25–90.
Parvin, L., Jinrong, J. and Rahman, M.W. (2012), 'Women entrepreneurship development in Bangladesh: what are the challenges ahead?' *African Journal of Business Management*, 6 (11), 3862–3871.
Peirce, C.S. (1855), 'The fixation of belief', http://bocc.ubi.pt/pag/peirce-charles-fixation-belief.html, accessed 28 February 2011.
Penrose, E. (1959), *The Theory of Growth of the Firm*, Oxford: Basil Blackwell.
Robinson, J., Blockson, L. and Robinson, S. (2007), 'Exploring stratification and entrepreneurship: African American women entrepreneurs redefine success in growth ventures', *Annals of the American Academy of Political and Social Science*, 613 (1), 131–154.
Roomi, M.A. (2009), 'Entrepreneurial capital, social values and Islamic traditions: growth of women owned enterprises in Pakistan', http://www.nwbc.gov/idc/groups/public/documents/nwbc/2009icsbpaper.pdf, accessed 17 May 2011.
Schwab, K. (ed.) (2011), *The Global Competitiveness Report 2011–2012*, Geneva: World Economic Forum, http://www.weforum.org/reports/global-competitiveness-report-2011–2012, accessed 27 February 2013.
Širec, K., Tominc, P. and Rebernik, M. (2010), 'Gender differences in the growth aspirations and technology orientation of Slovenian entrepreneurs', in Brush, C.G., de Bruin, A. and Gatewood, E.J. (eds), *Women Entrepreneurs and the Global Environment for Growth*, Cheltenham, UK and Northampton, MA, USA: Edward Elgar, pp. 323–342.
Taleb, N.N. (2008), *The Black Swan: The Impact of the Highly Improbable*, London: Penguin.
Tambunan, T. (2007), 'Development of SME and women entrepreneurs in a developing country: the Indonesian story', *Small Enterprise Research*, 15 (2), 31–51.
Tambunan, T. (2009), 'Women entrepreneurship in Asian developing countries: their development and main constraints', *Journal of Development and Agricultural Economics*, 1 (2), 27–40.
Tashakkori, A. and Teddlie, C. (1998), *Mixed Methodology: Combining Qualitative and Quantitative Approaches*, London: Sage.
Treanor, L. and Henry, C. (2010), 'Influences on women's entrepreneurship in Ireland and the Czech Republic', in Brush, C.G., de Bruin, A. and Gatewood, E.J. (eds), *Women Entrepreneurs and the Global Environment for Growth*, Cheltenham, UK and Northampton, MA, USA: Edward Elgar, pp. 73–95.

Welter, F. and Smallbone, D. (2008), 'Women's entrepreneurship from an institutional perspective: the case of Uzbekistan', *International Entrepreneurship and Management Journal*, 4 (4), 505–520.

Woldie, A. and Adersua, A. (2004), 'Female entrepreneurs in a transitional economy: businesswomen in Nigeria', *International Journal of Social Economics*, 31 (1–2), 78–93.

Yefimov, V. (2003), 'On pragmatic institutional economics', paper presented at the Information Society: Understanding its Institutions Interdisciplinary Conference of the European Association for Evolutionary Political Economy, Maastricht, Netherlands.

Zohir, S.C. and Greene, P.G. (2012), 'Women-owned SMEs in Bangladesh: challenges in institutional financing', in Hughes, K.D. and Jennings, J.E. (eds), *Global Women's Entrepreneurship Research: Diverse Settings, Questions and Approaches*, Cheltenham, UK and Northampton, MA, USA: Edward Elgar.

PART III

Micro: individuals and dynamics

10. Women entrepreneurs' networking behaviors: perspectives from entrepreneurs and network managers

Claire M. Leitch and Richard T. Harrison

INTRODUCTION

Networks are considered an essential element in entrepreneurial social processes and have generated an extensive literature (Slotte-Kock and Coviello, 2010). However, less attention has been paid to the process of networking. This is important because the nature of the networks in which entrepreneurs, whether male or female, are embedded, the positions they occupy and the patterns of their relationships in them, will influence their access to significant others and the resources they can yield. How individuals go about developing relationships with others in building networks, how they extend these over time and how they behave in them are critical to determining entrepreneurs' access to such resources.

In the entrepreneurship literature, the discourse on gender, networks and networking in particular has been relatively limited (Watson, 2012; Ibarra, 1993), and only recently has this been explored more fully (Foss, 2010). Specifically, this research has mainly been predicated on the analysis of men and women as distinct, homogeneous groups. In this chapter, therefore, we focus on understanding women's networking behavior in its own right. We do so by concentrating on the process of networking as it emerges in the context of formal networks. In line with recent research (Lockett et al., 2013), networking from the perspective of both entrepreneurs and network managers is examined. This research addresses four questions: What are women's motivations for participating in formal business networks and what are their expectations of such participation? What networking behaviors do they engage in, especially regarding the initiation, development and maintenance of contacts and relationships? What are the potential and actual benefits that they perceive to accrue from networking? To what extent can the establishment of a formal network encourage networking behavior, which in turn leads to the development of informal networks?

The chapter is structured as follows. First, we review a number of key issues in contemporary entrepreneurship research on networks and networking structure and process. Second, we summarize recent literature on gender, networks and networking and highlight a number of theoretical and methodological limitations. Third, we describe the research design and process for this study, focusing on the process of participant selection and the procedures for data collection and analysis. Fourth, we present our findings, and illustrate women's networking (focusing on their motivations and expectations, networking behaviors, potential and actual benefits from networking and their learning through networking) using the insights of the entrepreneurs themselves and the managers of the networks in which they participated. Finally, we conclude the chapter by identifying some implications for research and entrepreneurial practice.

NETWORKS AND NETWORKING: STRUCTURE AND PROCESS

Research on networks and networking is challenging, due to lack of clarity about the terms used (networks and networking), the units of analysis employed (individual, group or organization) and the focus of research (structure or process). Specifically, 'networks' and 'networking' are different constructs: the former being the outcome of the latter. A network exists through the actions of individuals, and the process of networking operates either at the individual and personal level or at a more formal, interorganizational one (O'Donnell et al., 2001). Networks are either formal or informal (Ibarra, 1992). Informal networks primarily comprise business contacts, family and personal relationships. Formal networks, by contrast, include professional relationships such as accountants, banks, lawyers and trade associations. These can be more beneficial to their members than informal ones because they are more likely to include more weak ties and structural holes (Watson, 2012). Central to our analysis is an investigation of formal networks established by an economic development agency, to stimulate networking activity. Using these as a framework, the focus is on the process and outcomes of networking itself, which is 'concerned with the actual behaviour of people developing, entering, maintaining, altering and leaving social networks' (Benschop, 2009, p. 221).

Entrepreneurial networks research is dominated by a concentration on their structural attributes rather than on social interaction within them

(Benschop, 2009: Neergaard et al., 2005). This includes their transactional content (what is exchanged by actors), the nature of links (the strength and qualitative characteristics of the relationship between two actors) and structural features (the overall pattern of relationships). This provides a limited understanding of networking processes for two reasons.

First, assuming that such structures are static leads to a cross-sectional approach; accordingly, any modifications in an entrepreneur's network over time in line with changes in their business resource needs has received insufficient attention. The evolution of firms will be reflected in changes in entrepreneurs' networks over time, from identity-based to more calculative ones. The former are 'egocentric networks that have a high proportion of ties where some type of personal or social identification with the other actor motivates or influences economic actions' (Hite and Hesterly, 2001, p. 278). Calculative networks are those in which an actor's ties are mainly based on expected economic benefits (Williamson, 1993).

Second, viewing networks as being *in situ* (Jack, 2005) ignores the fact that they are created, not exogenous, and that human agency impacts on their generation and development (Stevenson and Greenberg, 2000). Thus, understanding of networking, including 'how individuals generate networks in the first place' (Nebus, 2006, p. 615), remains restricted (Jack, 2010). The ability to network may be viewed as a key entrepreneurial competency (Szilagy and Schweiger, 1984), yet little attention has been paid to this skill (O'Donnell et al., 2001). To increase knowledge of entrepreneurial networking a deeper appreciation of individuals' motivations, expectations and outcomes of network participation is required.

Gender, Networks and Networking

Our knowledge of women entrepreneurs' networking behaviors remains incomplete (Foss, 2010). In particular, Neergaard et al. (2005) and Ahl (2004, 2006) have identified a number of issues in the entrepreneurship literature which restrict current discourse: first, a scarcity of empirical evidence, both on the types of networks in which women entrepreneurs are embedded and on their networking, that is, how they establish, maintain and use networks for business purposes; second, the dominance of an androcentric perspective and the pervasiveness of the normative male model which has, and continues to influence, how research is conducted and findings are explained; third, the tendency to treat men and women as homogeneous groups which can be compared with each other; and finally, a preponderance of research designs employing quantitative methods.

Gender differentiates biological sex from socially constructed sex, that is, practices and representations associated with femininity and masculinity, which can be ascribed to women and men (Ahl, 2006; Acker, 1992; Bruni et al., 2004). It is 'articulated through a binary division which presents a number of stereotypical behaviors associated with the masculine and feminine where the former is privileged over the latter' (Marlow and Patton, 2005, p. 719). In the social sciences generally, and in entrepreneurship particularly, the dominance of androcentrisim, where 'the elevation of the masculine to the level of the universal is the ideal . . . creates a belief in male superiority and a value system in which female values, experiences and behaviors are viewed as inferior' (Shakeshaft and Newell, 1984, pp. 187–188; Ahl, 2007). Consequently, as women's experiences have predominantly been defined in relation to those of men, knowledge about entrepreneurs' networks has been shaped by perceptions and experiences of male business owners (Neergaard et al., 2005).

In practice, researchers have tended to compare the networks of female and male entrepreneurs to determine sex- and gender-based disparities, and the effects of any variations on entrepreneurial success. They have focused on identifying differences between men and women at the expense of similarities (Ahl, 2004): 'the differences between individuals within the same sex are invariably much larger than the average differences, if any, between the sexes' (Ahl, 2006, p. 597). In other words, in women's entrepreneurship a lack of attention has been paid to within-sex differences, due to a preoccupation with between-sex ones based on a supposition of gender polarity (Harrison and Mason, 2007; Riger, 1992).

Foss (2010) has developed this position specifically in the context of entrepreneurial networks research. She used discourse analysis to examine the research problems, hypotheses, theoretical perspectives and findings in a sample of articles, published from 1980 to 2008, which had the common aim of exploring or testing the effects of gender on the personal networks of entrepreneurs. The hypotheses of these studies included: women networked less than men as their networks were smaller with fewer weak ties; the only criterion on which women were expected to score highly was on contact with friends and kin, identified in the literature as an ineffective means of securing resources for a business; and women do not benefit from the inclusion of other women in their networks. Essentially, all of this research used the networks of men as the standard against which to measure and assess women. However, adopting a 'gender-as-variable' approach can be problematic, as researchers are more inclined to document differences between men and women's networks instead of determining the cause of patterns that have emerged.

Although the empirical findings of the studies reviewed by Foss (2010) did not consistently identify differences between male and female entrepreneurs, she observed that 'hegemonic voices' remain in the literature.

These underpin the association of particular network characteristics with men and women: entrepreneurs use social networks strategically; women are disadvantaged compared to men and therefore cannot network effectively; weak ties are the source of men's success; strong ties are women's drawback; and women are inherently relational (Foss, 2010, p. 97). Inevitably, this perspective becomes normative and perpetuates the existence of unchallenged assumptions, including that the masculine approach to networking is best. Such hegemonic statements are influential because they shape the discourse of a phenomenon, which as it is never neutral 'has power implications for the object of which it speaks in that it forms what is held as knowledge or truth' (Ahl, 2006, p. 597). It is, therefore, vital to identify and question such suppositions to reveal the limits of particular discourses. Moreover, Foucault (1972) suggests that it is especially important to challenge the assumptions underlying the practices that shape the research process, as these 'influence the research questions asked, the methods chosen and the answers received' (Ahl, 2006, p. 598). In so doing, the production of rich, in-depth knowledge requires researchers to adopt diverse ontological and epistemological positions and draw on a range of theoretical and practice traditions from both the social sciences and the humanities (Leitch et al., 2010). While existing research, though dominated by cross-sectional surveys (Foss, 2010), has provided significant understanding of networks, methodological variety would provide additional insights (Neergaard et al., 2005). This would help to overcome the fact that we do not need more of the same stories (Haraway, 1988), in essence, 'studies conducted in the same manner and reporting more or less the same findings' (Foss, 2010, p. 88). We respond to this by undertaking research that deliberately seeks to give 'voice' to women's experiences as intrinsically interesting in their own right.

RESEARCH DESIGN AND PROCESS

Participant Selection

This study was undertaken in Northern Ireland where entrepreneurship, and especially female entrepreneurship, rates are low (Hill et al., 2011). When this research was conducted, Northern Ireland was ranked bottom of the 12 UK regions in terms of the rate of early-stage entrepreneurial activity among women (Hart, 2008). Over the last decade, to increase the numbers of women engaging in entrepreneurship, the regional economic development agency, Invest NI, has introduced a number of initiatives aimed at improving the low levels of entrepreneurial activity as well as the quality of start-ups by women. These included the cultivation of role models and the development of formal, women-only business networks, in addition to the existing trade associations and open-membership business networks, to promote networking and to offer support and encouragement to those starting their own ventures (Invest NI, 2010).

Given that the focus of this research is to examine networking as a process within the context of formal networks, women who were members of such networks were targeted and their networking behaviors explored. In other words, a purposive approach to participant selection was adopted to access women's perceptions and experiences of networking. Participants were drawn from five networks, three of which were Invest NI established women-only networks; the other two had unrestricted membership. All were formally constituted, with a board or committee structure. The women-only networks are relatively small, administered by part-time coordinators who are also entrepreneurs, while the mixed-gender ones have full-time staff. Each network provides a range of facilities and services for members.

Data were collected from two categories of participant: inexperienced, early-stage entrepreneurs whose businesses were aged less than three years (n = 8), and more experienced individuals with businesses aged three years or more (n = 10). In the absence of an opportunity to conduct a real-time longitudinal study (Benschop, 2009) a comparison between these groups can provide a surrogate insight into the temporal dynamics of the networking process (Jack, 2005). Network coordinators were asked to email explanatory letters to their members asking for volunteers. In addition, they were interviewed to provide both more detail on the history, structure and purpose of their network as well as their reflections on the networking processes of the women members.

Data Collection and Analysis

Network processes are too subtle to capture and understand using questionnaires (Neergaard et al., 2005). Given that the unit of analysis was the individual and the focus was on their self-understandings (Shapiro and Wendt, 2005) an interpretivist perspective, using qualitative, semi-structured interviews, was employed (Leitch et al., 2010, p.69). These were conducted as group interviews rather than on a one-to-one basis: the involvement of two or more participants in an interview permits a range of perspectives to emerge and for these to be challenged. All individuals have the opportunity of engaging with the issues under consideration, leading to a broad and in-depth participatory discussion (Boddy, 2005). Further, the resultant group interaction can produce meanings and insights that would be less accessible otherwise (Morgan, 1997). In this study five group interviews (one group of six participants, two groups of three and two dyadic interviews) were conducted. Two participants were unable to participate in the group interviews and were interviewed individually. In other words, we interviewed 16 entrepreneurs and five network managers. All interviews took place at the network venue, lasted between 60 and 90 minutes and were audio-taped with the permission of all the participants, who were also provided with background information about the project, offered the opportunity to opt out at any time and given a guarantee of confidentiality and anonymity.

Analyzing qualitative data is a difficult, intuitive, creative and dynamic process, the outcome of which is to understand the assumptions, categories and relationships that constitute the experiences of the participants (Leitch et al., 2010; Kempster and Cope, 2010; Braun and Clarke, 2006; King, 2004). We undertook thematic analysis (Guest et al., 2012) to identify, examine and record patterns or themes within the data relevant to the description of a phenomenon. It involves 'working with data, organizing it, breaking it into manageable units, synthesizing it, searching for patterns, discovering what is important and what is to be learned, and deciding what you will tell others' (Bogdan and Biklen, 1982, p.145).

FINDINGS

The findings are structured around four themes, which have been identified from the thematic analysis of the interview transcripts.

Motivations and Expectations

The motivations for joining formal business networks may be divided into two categories (Table 10.1): first, instrumental motivations, concerning the early-stage and subsequent development of a business; and second, social motivations, those primarily related to relationships with others. The differences between the motivations of the early-stage and more established entrepreneurs were less than anticipated. The instrumental motivations of early-stage entrepreneurs concerned making contacts and keeping up to date with the business environment (A1). The more established entrepreneurs mentioned gaining credibility in the business community through association with a respected network, finding out 'who's who and for people to find out who I am and what I do' and conveying legitimacy when seeking government funding.

Table 10.1 Motivations for and expectations of joining formal business networks

A: Motivations	B: Expectations
A1: I want to see who's doing what and how successful they are and what the success rate is and what the feedback is . . . And also I'm looking for contacts (Early-stage entrepreneur).	B1: I think that XXXX (a women-only network) needs . . . more visits with women's enterprise organizations internationally, women's enterprise organizations specifically focused on women's development and women's business development, women's business skills, personal development – all of that is required (Early stage entrepreneur).
A2: Basically the main reason I joined was I wanted to be with like-minded people and entrepreneurs etcetera so it was more inquisitive but I also wanted to be part of a women's group so to speak because the industry I am in is completely male dominated (More established entrepreneur).	B2: So it's just conversation for me and it's nearly a bonus if business comes out of it, I'm not there to sell, I'm there to meet like-minded people who may or may not then do business with me further down the line (More established entrepreneur).
A3: For business women to meet others in the same boat. Good to feel connected either face-to-face or by email. The idea of belonging, to be inspired, to overcome feelings of isolation (Network manager – women-only network).	B2: I think it's access to other women . . . the whole idea of somebody staring or somebody's being through this before me and give some pointers as to what to expect . . . help them build their confidence in terms of their approach to their business. They may not get sales out of it but there may also be developing support through existing businesses, almost like mentoring (Network manager – women-only network).
A4: I would say primarily, that their hope is that they will get business . . . they want to build relationships with other business people, they want to be around like-minded people and they give each other support and encouragement . . . I think that until people fully understand what networking is their primary goal is to make sales and then you kind of see it, dawning with them as time goes on that that's not going to happen. However, 'I'm getting this' or 'I'm getting that from it'. But, it's to build their business, without a shadow of a doubt (Network manager – mixed network).	B3: I think it's about profile. I think the support aspect of it cannot be underestimated . . . the business hopefully would follow out of that, increased sales or whatever . . . it's a very friendly environment . . . so there is a social aspect to it which is very important (Network manager – mixed network).

For some early-stage and more established entrepreneurs formal network participation was identified as a social outlet and an opportunity to interact with other women, especially when operating in a male-dominated sector (A2), while one of the more established entrepreneurs suggested that the relaxed environment of a women-only network was conducive to the personal and professional development of women. In addition to the instrumental aspect this suggests a relational aspect to women's networking (Foss, 2010). Network managers suggested that women-only networks are much more likely to emphasize the relational motives for network membership (A3), while managers of mixed networks believed that entrepreneurs' primary motivation for joining is to get business (A4).

Regarding participants' expectations of membership of a formal business network, the early-stage entrepreneurs believed that the services provided by such bodies should facilitate women in developing both business and networking skills (B1). More established entrepreneurs had more specific expectations of the services, including speed networking, introductions and the promotion of the network and participant businesses within it. As most of the networks in this research, especially the women-only ones, tend to have small budgets, such expectations could be unrealistic but, if not met, may have implications for members' continued participation in the networks and the development of their networking skills. Both early-stage and more established entrepreneurs stated that they had no expectation of making sales (B2). Nevertheless, it is clear from network managers that they see the support aspect of network participation, in terms of mentoring, learning from the experience of others and confidence-building as critical (B2–B3), all of which can lead to business development. In other words, for the managers the relational benefits of network participation are a necessary precursor to the realization of instrumental returns.

Networking Behaviors

Entrepreneurs' motivations and expectations are potentially significant influences on their networking behaviors and how they go about building their personal networks (Box 10.1). Given that many participants had instrumental motivations for joining a formal business network, it is perhaps not surprising that both early-stage and more established entrepreneurs were proactive about networking (C1). Further, a number of participants were tactical in the development of contacts (C2–C3) and there was a political awareness among some of the more established entrepreneurs regarding with whom they should interact (C4). For network

BOX 10.1   NETWORKING BEHAVIORS

C: Networking Behaviors

C1: You attend events . . . and once you go into that event then there's the opportunity to move around those people that are there, exchange cards, really get to know what their business is and what they are looking for and hoping that it will grow your own business. (Early-stage entrepreneur)

C2: I try not to run in there just to make a sale. I'd sooner get to know people, see how the land lies, find out what's happening and then, months down the line, I'll know how I fit into this and how I'm getting benefit from it. (Early-stage entrepreneur)

C3: Some people definitely go in there with a plan. They get out the list and they know whom they want to approach and so on. There's no one best way but it probably is a good idea to do that. (More established entrepreneur)

C4: When you join these organizations, make sure you know who's the head, who's the committee, who's the proactive people so you make yourself aware of them, you introduce yourself to them and then you are building a relationship with these people. (More established entrepreneur)

C5: I think it is useful to quickly get a contact with somebody but you are not establishing a relationship with that person you are talking to . . . you quickly make contact with somebody and understand what they do and say a quick 'hello'. You then have to follow it up. (More established entrepreneur)

C6: I feel quite strong about building business friends. That's where you go along and you've got your network of friends there in the business context and that's the way it should be, to build those relationships. (More established entrepreneur)

C7: You need to invest the time to get the return on networking . . . if they were prepared to give it more time they would get a greater return . . . rather than leaving things to the last minute and then not deciding. Again, it is a different approach, you know, because men would just simply decide and do it (Network manager – women-only network).

> C8: I think it depends on the women. I have met some who don't [capitalize on their network membership] and would be very reluctant to go to events. . . we need to make that an easier transition for women who join . . . sometimes they have to go to events on their own and some are more comfortable doing that than others (Network manager – mixed network).

managers active participation was identified as an area of concern and a number of them observed that some of their members, by not attending events, did not capitalize on their network membership (C7–C8).

This suggests an instrumental and tactical approach to networking, which belies one of the hegemonic statements identified by Foss (2010), namely that women cannot network effectively. While some participants made a clear distinction between an initial contact and the subsequent development of a relationship (C5–C6), most participants seemed to focus on building up a 'bank of contacts', one early-stage entrepreneur stating: 'I suppose it's like keeping a mental Roladex so you always know who to go to when you've a particular need.' A more established entrepreneur did observe that to be useful, contacts and relationships need to be reciprocal: 'It's up to you what you put into it. If you don't put something into it you are not going to get anything back out again.' Accompanying this, though, is the risk of exploitation: 'but I find I've given a phenomenal amount of business and contacts to a lot of other people and I've got very little back'. This assertion was made in the context of a women-only network. Although some authors have suggested that reciprocity is a universal norm or principle, Cropanzano and Mitchell (2005) observe that not everyone values reciprocity to the same degree and those with a strong exchange orientation are more likely to reciprocate than those with a weaker one. On the other hand, Molm (2003) argues that the risk and uncertainty inherent in reciprocal interdependence not only requires trust but also promotes it, therefore the risk of exploitation is relatively low and so members of social groups should not fear entering into exchange relations with unfamiliar others.

These findings are contrary to what the entrepreneurship literature on networks suggests, namely that women have a preference for strong ties, which can be disadvantageous (Foss, 2010; Granovetter, 1973). Indeed, few women mentioned the development of close dyadic relationships, even those whose articulated motivations for participating in a formal business network were social in nature. Consequently, they did not appear to expect to be involved in direct social exchanges. Instead, they seemed to focus on building a collective body of contacts perceived to be potentially helpful, either in the short or longer term. Where the majority of women in the networks are engaging in these behaviors, it suggests a tacit understanding of interdependence and the need for collective indirect exchange. Further, it is likely that, although some contacts may remain latent and dormant (Jack, 2005) and may never be activated, those that are will be activated at different times, suggesting that the pattern of each entrepreneur's personal network is not static but fluid, changing over time according to their needs.

Potential and Actual Benefits Perceived to Accrue from Networking

Potential benefits of participation in entrepreneurial networks include: enhancing one's image; gaining acceptance and credibility; accessing diverse and useful information; support; and locating a range of resources (Díaz García and Carter, 2009) (Box 10.2). From the thematic analysis, tangible and intangible benefits are perceived to accrue from networking. For early-stage entrepreneurs, intangible benefits included sharing experiences, companionship, emotional support and mentoring; information and advice; learning; motivation; and confidence (D1). For more established entrepreneurs, these benefits comprised companionship and solidarity; overcoming isolation and establishing links; problem-sharing; knowledge, information, ideas and advice; credibility; business development; and confidence: 'working together or just things that help my business grow'. This suggests that for early-stage entrepreneurs, intangible benefits tend to relate to personal development, while for more established entrepreneurs these are to do with both personal and business development, indicating some change in focus over time.

Concerning tangible benefits, early-stage entrepreneurs identified the value of services, such as the website, database of members, training events, referrals, contacts and leads. 'I have got leads, you know . . . and business contacts.' In addition to referrals, contacts and signposts, more established entrepreneurs also mentioned the importance of 'three-minute pitches' and talks. As we have seen above, neither category of entrepreneur identified sales as a particularly important benefit, though for some, this appeared in line with their expectations: 'If sales come out of it then well and good but that is not the overriding factor.' However, others clearly found this disappointing: 'but in terms of business, absolutely nothing'. By contrast with the entrepreneurs, network managers articulated the benefits from networking primarily in tangible terms, either represented in the expertise and experience available in the network (D6) or through building business relationships with other women (D5). There do appear

BOX 10.2 POTENTIAL AND ACTUAL BENEFITS PERCEIVED TO ACCRUE FROM NETWORKING

D: Benefits

D1: Motivational and confidence. When you ... go out, even if you've nothing specific to your business, it does sort of lift you again and give you another boost till the next time (Early-stage entrepreneur).

D2. . . there is confidence in being with other like-minded women where there is no pressure and your opinion is as valid as the person sitting beside you and you are kind of all in on it together (More established entrepreneur).

D3: Well I think the advantages . . . are that they can . . . look particularly at women's development, women's education, women's opportunities and women's place on corporate boards, women's role in society, and women's participation in politics (More established entrepreneur).

D4: [A]nd the advantage of the mixed (gender) thing is you are dealing with a mixed bag in your business anyway ... and you have to think and learn how to think like men and play the game and that's the way they operate (Early-stage entrepreneur).

D5: A number of them would join, specifically for the business opportunities . . . I think it is about building business relationships with other women, but I think women's and men's approach is very different. Men are very focused joining a network, on getting business and touting for business: women haven't got that same push . . . what we try and get across is that the business relationship will happen, if they invest the time in developing it and developing their networks (Network manager – women-only network).

D6: The network's the most important thing. The ability to lift the phone and to connect with at least four other people who are relevant to them, who are in the same boat or who have done something that they are thinking of doing and have done it well (Network manager – mixed network).

to be differences between mixed and women-only networks: the former are much more calculative in identifying benefits, while a number of the women-only network coordinators see their role as facilitating the development of a more instrumental approach by their members (D5).

While all of the women, whether in women-only networks, mixed-gender networks or in both, perceived benefits to accrue from networking, some only felt comfortable networking with other women (D2). One participant observed that women-only networks are not just concerned with business matters, but with a broad range of women's issues (D3). In other words, they gravitated towards such networks mainly to interact with other like-minded women, for support and because they felt comfortable in such an environment. Although one woman accepted this, she did perceive it to be a limitation of women-only networks (D4). After all, operating in a homophilous environment, whether male or female, may not be commercially advantageous. While less relevant to participants who belonged to both women-only and mixed-gender networks, this observation does resonate with Nebus's (2006, p. 615) note of caution that while existing relationships provide 'a convenient pool of advice contacts ... they also act as a constraint limiting the scope of the advice search by substituting for experts who would provide better advice'. This is similar to Burt's (1998, p. 8) observation that cohesive contacts of individuals strongly connected to each other are likely to share similar information and therefore provide redundant rather than additive information benefits. In Northern Ireland, homophily (McPherson et al., 2001) and cultural propinquity (Kogut and Singh, 1998) can be problematic, particularly in relatively small rural areas, where some of the networks were purposely located by Invest NI, since members of these communities tend to interact with each other regularly, whether or not they belong to the same formal networks.

Learning

Networking, especially with those who have greater experience and/or are prepared to act as mentors, can be an important source of learning (Harrison and Leitch, 2008), and participation in formal networks does appear to provide entrepreneurs with the opportunity to share learning experiences (Box 10.3). Similarly, events organized by network organizers, such as training and visiting speakers, can also facilitate learning (E10). Learning opportunities also included: observation of the behaviors of others; the identification of common problems and gaining advice from others; collective problem-solving; drawing on the experiences of others; knowledge acquisition; sharing ideas; and 'learning to play the game'. This

> **BOX 10.3 LEARNING AND NETWORKING**
>
> E10: Training is very important; I believe that you learn something every day from everybody ... Training benefits me because I learn something but also I get to network and make work and I have fun (Early-stage entrepreneur).
>
> E11: It's just learning from the experiences of people who are more experienced than you, that's really all it is because, as you can imagine, running a business on your own is quite an isolating experience and the difference for me is, I exist in a male-dominated industry (Early-stage entrepreneur).
>
> E12: It's access to information that probably wouldn't be that readily available to them on their own. They also acknowledge the program activity that we organize for them as well (Network manager – women-only network).
>
> E13: The aim is to get individuals to network in a context in which there is some learning ... social learning/networking doesn't always occur – sometimes it is hard to achieve ... due to shyness, modesty, the idea of the 'wee women with a wee business'. They don't recognize themselves as entrepreneurs or even business owners (Network manager – women-only network).
>
> E14: The way it's going is to be informal learning. People get easier with themselves ... there's trust issues to be overcome and group dynamics are important (Network manager – mixed network).

is consistent with Jack et al.'s (2010, p. 331) observation that 'the development of a personalized exchange network with peers has been shown to help overcome ... the liability of newness and help diminish feelings of isolation and loneliness' (E11).

Network managers consistently highlighted the opportunity for learning in their networks. For some, this was reflected in the network providing access to information and program activity that otherwise would not be available to their members (E12), while for others learning was viewed as being the purpose of the network. It provides a context within which trust and confidence can be built as the basis for informal learning through the sharing of experience (E14). In some cases the aim of the network was articulated as the encouragement of social learning through networking, which was often attenuated due to self-deprecation by the women entrepreneurs who did not recognize themselves as entrepreneurs or business owners (E13).

However, whether or not entrepreneurs perceive networking as a vehicle for learning is likely to relate to two factors. First, individual learning orientation, which in some cases was quite strong: 'and we all learn and I think that's what we were put on the earth to do – learn, evolve and grow' (more established entrepreneur). Second, women's motivations for engaging in networking: if these are instrumental, then the probability that learning is viewed as an outcome will be raised; if they are more social, this is less likely to be so.

SUMMARY

Our analysis suggests that the relational benefits of networking do not necessarily require the formation of close dyadic ties. Rather, in generalized exchange (one-to-many and many-to-one relationships) benefits flow unilaterally and reciprocity is indirect, and a member of a social grouping who provides a benefit to another will almost certainly receive one in return, though not necessarily from that same individual. In other words, the development of a wide range of contacts and relationships with which one is prepared to exchange reciprocally as necessary is the equivalent of 'saving for a rainy day'. Indirect reciprocity in generalized exchange seems to enhance solidarity and commitment to a network, which can lead to the development of 'positively connected relations' in which benefits flow both within and across relationships (Molm et al., 2007). In such circumstances there is no perception of competition or concern with power, both of which can impede relational networking. This is reflected in the apparently high level of trust among the network members, a consequential lack of concern for potential exploitation and little evidence of competition among them. However, since some of the women were members of networks specifically established by the local economic development agency to assist them in developing their networking capabilities, this is not unexpected.

Given the focus on the exchange relationship it is clear that all of the women perceived they had gained a range of benefits from networking. All participants had clear motivations for joining and participating in formal networks and also had specific expectations about the benefits of such membership. This was reflected in the tactical and instrumental behaviors in which they engaged. Only one woman expressed a desire to develop close dyadic relations with other network members; the remainder wished to build up a bank of contacts that might or might not lead to sales and/or grow into stronger relationships over time. In terms of learning, a network characterized by positively connected relations, a perceived lack of competition and risk is likely to facilitate such learning.

CONCLUSION

Within the entrepreneurship literature there are two contradictory assumptions: first, that entrepreneurial networks are already formed and static (Jack, 2005); and second, that they change over time, from identity-based to calculative ones (Hite and Hesterly, 2001). With regard to the former, the primary concern of research has been with structure, which ignores the fact that networks have to be initiated and developed through the process of networking. This research has shown that when the focus is on individuals' networking behaviors, personal networks are not static but fluid and dynamic, changing in shape and size according to need. With regard to the latter, there is some evidence to suggest that longer-established entrepreneurs are more calculative (that is, tactical and instrumental) in their networks.

In relation to the gendered nature of the entrepreneurial literature and the assumption of men and women belonging to homogeneous groups, when women or men are studied on their own rather than in relation to each other, this research has demonstrated that there are differences within the group of women entrepreneurs. On the basis of this, the hegemonic statements that dominate research into entrepreneurial networks (which focus on the assumed normality and supremacy of male behaviors) can be challenged. This research suggests that some women, like some men, use social networks strategically; some women are effective networkers; some women do not necessarily favor the development of strong ties as opposed to weak ones; and some women are concerned with developing relationships rather than contacts.

A key responsibility of researchers is to continually challenge the limitations of particular discourses to avoid recycling existing knowledge via research design replication, rather than creating new knowledge. In particular, gender research in entrepreneurship, and indeed research in entrepreneurship more generally, has traditionally been quite uninterested in ontology and epistemology (Ahl, 2004; Foss, 2010, Leitch et al., 2010; Harrison and Leitch, 2014). In this chapter we have responded to these calls by making an empirical contribution, which focuses on networking instead of networks, and on women entrepreneurs on their own terms. Although exploratory, the study suggests that if researchers have the courage 'to break the mold' by adopting new perspectives, the boundaries of existing discourses can be extended. Adopting greater theoretical and methodological heterogeneity would facilitate the capture of diversity, the exploration of complexity, including different lived experiences and meanings, and ultimately, the generation of a rich body of new knowledge.

On the basis of this study a number of directions for future research on gender and networking can be identified. First, this research was cross-sectional in nature and so has not addressed the evolution of networking behavior over time and there is, therefore, scope for the development of longitudinal studies to address this. Second, as there is increased importance being given to the establishment of membership-based formal networks, not least as an instrument of local and regional economic development policy, there is a need for more extended studies on the process of networking within such formal networks. Third, although only a small part of the present study, there appear to be some differences between women-only and mixed-membership networks. This represents an opportunity to examine the extent to which these differences are systemic and to assess the consequences for women entrepreneurs' networking behaviors and for the subsequent development of their businesses. Finally, while the focus here has been on women's networking, and in view of the arguments that competition and hence women's participation and performance varies across single- and mixed-sex environments, future research could explore the networking behaviors of men as well as women to capture both inter-group and intra-group diversity.

ACKNOWLEDGEMENT

This work was supported by the British Academy [Grant No: SG 47047].

REFERENCES

Acker, J. (1992), Gendering organizational theory, in Mills, A. and Tancred, P. (eds), *Gendering Organizational Analysis*, London: Sage, pp. 248–260.
Ahl, H. (2004), *The Scientific Reproduction of Gender Inequality*, Copenhagen: Copenhagen Business School.
Ahl, H. (2006), Why research on women entrepreneurs needs new directions, *Entrepreneurship Theory and Practice*, September, 595–621.
Ahl, H. (2007), A Foucauldian framework for discourse analysis, in Neergaard, H. and Ulhøi, J. (eds), *Handbook of Qualitative Research Methods in Entrepreneurship*, Cheltenham, UK and Northampton, MA, USA: Edward Elgar, pp. 216–252.

Benschop, Y. (2009), The micro-politics of gendering in networking, *Gender, Work and Organization*, 16 (2), 217–237.
Boddy, C. (2005), A rose by any other name may smell as sweet but 'group discussion' is not another name for a 'focus group' nor should it be, *Qualitative Market Research: An International Journal*, 8 (3), 248–255.
Bogdan, R.C. and Biklen, S.K. (1982), *Qualitative Research for Education: An Introduction to Theory and Methods*, Boston, MA: Allyn & Bacon.
Braun, V. and Clarke, V. (2006), Using thematic analysis in psychology, *Qualitative Research in Psychology*, 3, 77–101.
Bruni, A., Gheradi, S. and Poggio, B. (2004), Entrepreneur-mentality, gender and the study of women entrepreneurs, *Journal of Organizational Change Management*, 17 (3), 256–268.
Burt, R.S. (1998), The gender of social capital, *Rationality and Society*, 10 (1), 5–46.
Cropanzano, R. and Mitchell, M. (2005), Social exchange theory: an interdisciplinary review, *Journal of Management*, 31 (6), 874–900.
Díaz García, C. and Carter, S. (2009), Resource mobilization through business owners' networks: is gender an issue? *International Journal of Gender and Entrepreneurship*, 1 (3), 226–252.
Foss, L. (2010), Research on entrepreneur networks: the case for a constructionist feminist theory perspective, *International Journal of Gender and Entrepreneurship*, 2 (1), 83–102.
Foucault, M. (1972), The discourse on language (L'ordre du discourse), in Foucault, M., *The Archaeology of Knowledge*, New York: Pantheon Books, pp. 215–237.
Granovetter, M. (1973), The strength of weak ties, *American Journal of Sociology*, 78 (6), 1360–1380.
Guest, G., MacQueen, K.M. and Namey, E.E. (2012), *Applied Thematic Analysis*, Thousand Oaks, CA: Sage.
Haraway, D.J. (1988), Situated knowledges – the science question in feminism and the privilege of particle perspective, *Feminist Studies*, 14 (3), 575–599.
Harrison, R.T. and Leitch, C.M. (eds) (2008), *Entrepreneurial Learning: Conceptual Frameworks and Applications*, London: Routledge Publishing.
Harrison, R.T. and Leitch, C.M. (2014), Fighting a rearguard action? Reflections on the philosophy and practice of qualitative research in entrepreneurship, in Carsrud, A.L. and Brannback, M. (eds), *Handbook of Research Methods and Applications in Entrepreneurship and Small Business*, Cheltenham, UK and Northampton, MA, USA: Edward Elgar Publishing, pp. 177–200.
Harrison, R.T. and Mason, C. (2007), Does gender matter? Women business angels and the supply of entrepreneurial finance, *Entrepreneurship Theory and Practice*, 31 (3), 445–472.
Hart, M. (2008), *Global Entrepreneurship Monitor, Northern Ireland Summary*, Belfast: Invest Northern Ireland.
Hill, F.M., Leitch, C.M. and Harrison, R.T. (2011), Growing a high-tech business: gender, perceptions and experiences in Northern Ireland, in Brush, C.G., Gatewood, E.J., de Bruin, A.M. and Henry, C. (eds), *Women Entrepreneurs and the Global Environment for Growth*, Cheltenham, UK and Northampton, MA, USA: Edward Elgar Publishing, pp. 206–224.
Hite, J.M. and Hesterly, W.S. (2001), The evolution of firm networks: from emergence to early growth of the firm, *Strategic Management Journal*, 22 (3), 275–286.

Ibarra, H. (1992), Homophilly and differential returns: sex difference in network structure and access in an advertising firm, *Administrative Science Quarterly*, 37, 422–447.

Ibarra, H. (1993), Personal networks of women and minorities in management: a conceptual framework, *Academy of Management Review*, 18 (1), 56–88.

Invest NI (2010), Boost for women in business, http://www.investni.gov.uk, accessed 20 September 2010.

Jack, S.L. (2005), The role, use and activation of strong and weak ties: a qualitative analysis, *Journal of Management Studies*, 42 (6), 1233–1260.

Jack, S.L. (2010), Approaches to studying networks: implications and outcomes, *Journal of Business Venturing*, 25 (1), 120–137.

Jack, S.L., Moult, S., Anderson, A.R. and Dodd, S. (2010), An entrepreneurial network evolving: patterns of change, *International Small Business Journal*, 28 (4), 315–337.

Kempster, S. and Cope, J. (2010), Learning to lead in the entrepreneurial context, *International Journal of Entrepreneurial Behaviour and Research*, 16 (1), 6–35.

King, N. (2004), Using templates in the thematic analysis of text, in Cassell, C. and Symon, G. (eds), *Essential Guide to Qualitative Methods in Organizational Research*, London: Sage, pp. 256–270.

Kogut, B. and Singh, H. (1998), The effect of national culture on the choice of entry mode, *Journal of International Business Studies*, 19, 411–432.

Leitch, C.M., Hill, F.M. and Harrison, R.T. (2010), The philosophy and practice of interpretivist research in entrepreneurship: quality, validation and trust, *Organizational Research Methods*, 13 (1), 67–84.

Lockett, N., Jack, S.L. and Larty, J. (2013), Motivations and challenges of network formation: entrepreneur and intermediary perspectives, *International Small Business Journal*, 31, 866–889.

Marlow, S. and Patton, D. (2005), All credit to men, entrepreneurship, finance and gender, *Entrepreneurship, Theory and Practice*, 29 (6), 699–716.

McPherson, M., Smith-Lovin, L. and Cook, J.M. (2001), Birds of a feather: homophily in social networks, *Annual Review of Sociology*, 27, 415–444.

Molm, L.D. (2003), Theoretical comparison of forms of exchange, *Sociological Theory*, 21, 1–17.

Molm, L.D., Collett, J.L. and Schaefer, D.R. (2007), Building solidarity through generalized exchange: a theory of reciprocity, *American Journal of Sociology*, 113 (1), 205–242.

Morgan, D. (1997), *Focus Groups in Qualitative Research*, 2nd edn, Qualitative Research Methods, Vol. 16, London: Sage Publications.

Nebus, J. (2006), Building collegial information networks: a theory of advice network generation, *Academy of Management Review*, 31 (3), 615–637.

Neergaard, H., Shaw, E. and Carter, S. (2005), The impact of gender, social capital and networks on business ownership – a research agenda, *International Journal of Entrepreneurial Behaviour and Research*, 11 (5), 338–357.

O'Donnell, A., Gilmore, A., Cummins, D. and Carson, D. (2001), The network construct in entrepreneurship research: a review and critique, *Management Decision*, 39 (9), 749–760.

Riger, S. (1992), Epistemological debates, feminist voices: science, social values, and the study of women, *American Psychologist*, 47, 730–740.

Shakeshaft, C. and Newell, I. (1984), Research on themes, concepts and models

of organization behavior: the influence of gender, *Issues in Education*, 2 (3), 186–203.
Shapiro, I. and Wendt, A. (2005), The difference that realism makes: social science and the politics of consent, in Shapiro, I. (ed.), *The Flight from Reality in the Human Sciences*, Princeton, NJ: Princeton University Press, pp. 19–50.
Slotte-Kock, S. and Coviello, N. (2010), Entrepreneurship research on network processes: a review and ways forward, *Entrepreneurship Theory and Practice*, 34 (1), 31–57.
Stevenson, W.B. and Greenberg, D. (2000), Agency and social networks: strategies of action in a social structure of position, opposition and opportunity, *Administrative Science Quarterly*, 45, 651–678.
Szilagy, A.D. and Schweiger, D.M. (1984), Matching managers to strategies: a review and suggested framework, *Academy of Management Review*, 9 (4), 626–639.
Watson, J. (2012), Networking: gender differences and the association with firm performance, *International Small Business Journal*, 30 (5), 536–558.
Williamson, O.E. (1993), Calculativeness, trust, and economic organization, *Journal of Law and Economics*, 36, 453–586.

11. Heterogeneity of spousal support for French women entrepreneurs

Stephanie Chasserio, Typhaine Lebègue and Corinne Poroli

INTRODUCTION

Research today recognizes that, in order to understand the entrepreneurial process, the entrepreneur must be considered from a situated and dynamic perspective that takes into account the interactions between the various dimensions and multiple roles of their life (Brush et al., 2009; Danes et al., 2009; Dimov, 2007; Oughton and Wheelock, 2003). Family context plays a key role in the creation and development of an enterprise (Aldrich and Cliff, 2003; Eddleston and Powell, 2012; Jennings and McDougald, 2007; Jennings et al., 2013; Kirrane and Buckley, 2004; Powell and Eddleston, 2013). The broader approach to entrepreneurship, presented in the work on family businesses (Aldrich and Cliff, 2003), is also found in the research work devoted to women entrepreneurs which highlights the limits of traditional theoretical models of entrepreneurship (Ahl, 2006; Brush et al., 2009; Jennings and McDougald, 2007; Jennings and Brush, 2013). Hence, Jennings and Brush (2013, p. 689) ask, 'To what extent are consultations with family members, more generally, factored into opportunity evaluation and exploitation decisions?'

Support from a spouse or companion is clearly identified in research as a key factor for success (Sexton and Kent, 1981; Hisrich and Brush, 1983; Nelson, 1989). However, the issue of the gender dynamic within the couple is rarely mentioned, if at all. Moreover, male spousal/companion-based support (SCS) of women entrepreneurs (WE) remains a relatively unexplored field (Van Auken and Werbel, 2006).

This chapter, therefore, examines SCS for French WE. We will explore: (1) the different forms of SCS (instrumental and emotional) for WE and the evolution of these forms throughout the entrepreneurial process (from start-up, but also in the development phase of the company); and (2) the ways in which the entrepreneurial activities of WE interfere in the couples' relationships, and vice versa. In our literature review, we present the different forms of social SCS. Then we focus on SCS as a key factor in the entrepreneurial process. We detail the question of SCS for women and examine the specific place that women hold in French society. In our methodological framework, we describe our approach and our samples. Our findings highlight various forms of SCS for WE and its changes throughout the project development, the interference of entrepreneurial activities in the couple's relationship (and vice versa). We conclude with our suggestions for future research and practice.

LITERATURE REVIEW

Different Forms of Social Support Provided by a Spouse/Companion

Individuals receive social support from people who they meet in informal networks, from family members, and/or from people they know professionally. The spouse is identified in the literature as one of the possible sources of support that reduces tensions in the work–family balance (Carlson and Perrewé, 1999; Thomas and Ganster, 1995) and/or that improves quality of life (Md-Sidin et al., 2010). Two broad categories of support can initially be identified: instrumental and emotional support (Granrose et al., 1992; Parasuraman et al., 1996). Instrumental support takes the form of tangible help (that is, practical and technical assistance) (Etzion, 1984). Emotional support takes the form of moral support, empathy, an attentive ear and demonstrated interest in the spouse's work (Kim and Ling, 2001; Van Auken and Werbel, 2006).

Some studies conducted on employees and managers show that instrumental SCS has the greatest impact on well-being (Israel et al., 2002), while others emphasize emotional support as being a key factor (Ben-Ari and Pines, 2002). Still other studies show that both types of support are equally beneficial (Rao et al., 2003). Furthermore, it seems important to note the gap that may exist between the intention behind the support that the spouse/companion provides, and the ways in which the receiver perceives this support (Kirrane and Buckley, 2004).

Spousal/Companion-Based Support (SCS) as a Key Factor in the Entrepreneurial Process

Some researchers (e.g., Danes et al., 2010; Powell and Eddleston, 2013; Rogers, 2005; Ozcan, 2011) have explored factors relating to the family domain of the entrepreneur in order to ascertain whether certain characteristics of these arenas could explain the failures and successes observed. The role of spousal support emerges as a determinant because supportive spouses may apply their knowledge, skills and technical expertise to the entrepreneurial projects of their spouses. They can also provide access to professional networks that may be useful to the career development of their entrepreneurial spouses and may contribute to the building of their spouses' social capital (Ozcan, 2011). The effects of spousal support manifest at all stages of the entrepreneurial process, from the pinpointing of business opportunities, to the creation of the business, and throughout the subsequent development of activity (Baines and Wheelock, 1998; Kirkwood, 2011).

According to Danes et al. (2010), this support can play an actively positive role, but it can also become a limitation and a source of conflict and, therefore, be detrimental to the entrepreneurial project. The support lent to a project can evolve and change over time, reflecting as much the dynamic dimension of the couple's relationship as that of the entrepreneurial project. Unfortunately, however, these authors did not refine the results of their exploration by conducting a gender-based analysis.

In the research on family businesses, spousal support is equally highlighted as playing a crucial role in the ways in which a family business is conducted (Aldrich and Cliff, 2003). However, even if these researchers do recognize that men and women do not face the same social expectations in terms of societal roles, they have a tendency to treat spousal relationships from a neutral perspective, without gender differentiation. Yet expectations in regards to SCS are different depending on the gender of the supportive spouse/companion.

Instrumental and Emotional Support in the Context of Entrepreneurship

Instrumental support refers to behavior that provides tangible assistance to the entrepreneur. This support may be related to entrepreneurial activity and take the form of professional skills placed at the service of the entrepreneur (creating professional documents, for example). It may also take place in the private and domestic arena, with the supporting spouse/companion assuming responsibility for the children and/or household chores. Additionally, instrumental support may take the form of financial aid. The research underscores that these forms of instrumental support are important factors in the success of the entrepreneurial activity (Van Auken and Werbel, 2006).

By giving emotional support – by listening to the entrepreneur and taking an interest – the spouse/companion plays a key role in the entrepreneur's self-confidence and in their confidence in the project's value (Van

Auken and Werbel, 2006). Similarly, these authors emphasize the great value of 'pillow talk', where the entrepreneur is able to informally and privately discuss difficulties and worries with their spouse/companion, as well as potential business opportunities that may arise.

If the support received from a spouse/companion appears to be essential to the entrepreneur's project, it is important now to focus more particularly on the underexplored case of the woman as entrepreneur, as well as on the support she can expect from her spouse/companion.

The Question of SCS for Women Entrepreneurs

Spousal/companion-based support influences the ways in which entrepreneurial projects are carried out (Aldrich and Cliff, 2003; Rogoff and Heck, 2003). However, a surprising element appears when reading about SCS, which is that, most often, studies do not take into account the gender of their respondents. The focus is placed on the 'couple' as an entity – the relationship between the spouses – without introducing into the relationship the differences related to gender. However, the social roles assigned to women and men are far from being either identical or neutral but are instead definitively marked by gender. Thus, several leading authors have questioned this so-called neutrality, calling for an integration of the dimension of gender into entrepreneurial studies (Ahl, 2006; Bird and Brush, 2002; Bruni et al., 2004; Calás et al., 2009; de Bruin et al., 2007; Mirchandani, 1999).

Brush (1992) suggests that women do not perceive their entrepreneurship to be separate from their private lives; they perceive their businesses through a system of relationships that includes family, community and business, and they seek, instead, to create bridges between the domains. This drives women particularly to assess the impact that their entrepreneurial projects have on their spouses and children (Kirkwood, 2011).

Studies of the female spouses of male entrepreneurs show that these women play major roles in the development of their partners' enterprises (Baines and Wheelock, 1998; Van Auken and Werbel, 2006). They are particularly responsible for heavy administrative duties, but do not always achieve corresponding status within the enterprises, which can contribute to rendering them invisible (Baines and Wheelock, 1998; Richomme, 2000; Philbrick and Fitzgerald, 2007).

Studies of the spouses/companions of WE, however, are much more rare. SCS is a key element for WE (Buttner and Moore, 1997; Kim and Ling, 2001); however, WE do not always find the support they expect from those who share their lives (Stevenson, 1986; Fielden and Dawe, 2004; Kirkwood, 2009). Eddleston and Powell (2012) show that WE receive less instrumental support at home than do male entrepreneurs. Other authors show the impact that the support has on projects and on the launch of companies (Kim and Ling, 2001; Ozcan, 2011). Kim and Ling (2001) indicate that the 'spouse['s] emotional support reduces job–spouse conflict'. Additionally, 'instrumental support can reduce time pressure and parental demand that causes work–family conflict' (King et al., 1995).

We also have to consider the effects of the entrepreneurial context on couples. Several studies distinctly highlight the point at which the entrepreneurial venture tests the ways in which the couples function (Al-Dajani and Marlow, 2010; Amarapurkar and Danes, 2005; Danes and Morgan, 2004; Lewis and Massey, 2011; Winn, 2004). Financial issues, long work hours, the intensity with which one must be involved in the life of the company (especially at the start-up) – all these are areas of tension and possible points of friction for a couple (Winn, 2004) and can affect SCS. To understand interactions between different dimensions of the lives of French WE from an integrative perspective, we must also consider the French cultural context within which they are embedded.

The Context of Gender Roles in France and their Effects on the Distribution of Roles within the Couple

The distribution of social roles in Western societies is highly gendered (Crompton et al., 2007), and in France the traditional concept of role division between men and women remains predominant. Men are expected to partake in the public and professional arena more than women are, and men are still mainly represented as being the breadwinners of their families. Women remain predominantly the custodians of the private, familial and domestic domains. The couple is, therefore, a social construction and functions as a place where gender relations can be found.

If we focus on the age group ranging between 25 and 54 years, we see that 83.6 percent of French women work (DARES, 2012). French women are also distinguished in Europe by their fertility rate: a rate of 2.01 children per woman, when the average across the whole of the European Union was 1.59 in 2009 (DARES, 2012). French women continue to work even with one or two children, and of those who have children who are three years of age or older, 80 percent work. Thus, they adapt and modify their professional activities upon the arrival of children, but the fathers do not (Moschion, 2009). In France, the working woman is highly valued (Cocandeau-Bellanger, 2011, p. 93). But at the same time, in order to be considered a woman in the full sense of the word, she must become a mother. For a long time, this focus on motherhood found its expression through natalist family politics that were centered exclusively around the mother.

Crompton et al. (2007) show that French women are particularly dissatisfied because they are experiencing profound tension in trying to reconcile their professional lives with their private lives. For them, the explanation is to be found in the French gender roles, which are exceedingly traditional. French women, although fully present in the labor market, continue to take on virtually all of the tasks in the domestic and parental domains. Furthermore, stepping outside of this traditional framework can generate a great deal of tension and misunderstanding. Therefore, we can consider that French women who choose to be entrepreneurs exit the conventional paths for which they are traditionally destined. In 2010, 36 percent of new ventures in France were created by women (Hagège and Masson, 2011). These figures show that some progress has occurred over the last 30 years; in 1986, WE represented only 9 percent of French entrepreneurs. The Global Entrepreneurship Monitor (GEM) 2012 Women's Report (Kelley et al., 2013) indicates, through the TEA (total entrepreneurial activity for female adults ranging between the ages of 18 to 64), that in France, for every six male entrepreneurs, there are four female entrepreneurs. For comparison's sake, the same percentage is true for the United States, where for every 15 male entrepreneurs there are ten female entrepreneurs. The Kauffmann Report (Mitchell, 2011) mentions that women represent 35 percent of start-up business owners in the United States. However, the French rate remains within the average for the European Union (Kelley et al., 2013).

Considering these different theoretical elements, our purpose is to explore the different forms and evolution of SCS for WE throughout the entrepreneurial process and the ways in which the entrepreneurial activities of WE interfere in the couples' relationships, and vice versa. In the following section we discuss the methods that we used.

METHODOLOGY

In order to address the research question we conducted two separate qualitative studies in France. In the first, we conducted a four-year longitudinal study of ten WE. The establishment of a longitudinal study is a promising avenue of exploration for research on women's entrepreneurship (Stevenson, 1986; de Bruin et al., 2007; Patterson and Mavin, 2009). We asked the WE about their perceptions of the attitudes that their spouses/companions had at the time their companies were conceived. Then we questioned them about spousal/companion-based support. Finally, we addressed the subject of roles within the couples. We conducted semi-structured interviews that provided abundant room for the unexpected, for novelty and for discovery (Strauss and Corbin, 1990). Thirty-six interviews were conducted, recorded and fully transcribed. Six WE were interviewed at three different times. Two other WE were interviewed at four different times and two other WE were interviewed at five different times. A single researcher codified each interview.

The second study draws on 41 semi-structured interviews with WE who operate in very diverse economic sectors. Half of our respondents were recruited through a network of WE. The other half of the sample was constituted in a more random fashion, according to the recommendations we received and following the logic of a sample snowball. We interviewed the WE to the point of empirical saturation (Bertaux, 1981, p. 37). In the interviews, several questions caused the respondents to address their relationships with their spouses/companions. Two researchers shared the codification of these interviews. The empirical material of the two studies was subject to thematic analysis with the helpful software NVivo (Strauss and Corbin, 1990).

The goal of this chapter is to gather the data from these two studies, which are different in their methodological approaches but complementary in their objectives and in the quality of their samples. Furthermore, the studies are part of a similar abductive approach (Strauss and Corbin, 1990); consequently, not all of the themes were explored with each respondent.

Sample Description

Table 11.1 summarizes the characteristics of our two samples. In the first study, among the ten interviewed WE, four lived alone and six lived with a partner at the time they created their businesses. In the second study, among the 41 interviewed WE, five lived alone and 36 lived with a partner at the time they created their businesses. At the time of the interview, eight lived alone and 33 lived with a partner.

FINDINGS

Below we explore the dynamic of SCS through two main elements: the variety in both the form and evolution of SCS for WE, and the interference of entrepreneurial activities in the couples' relationships – and vice versa.

There is a great variety in the form and evolution of SCS for WE. From our transcripts, we identify different types of instrumental support provided by the spouse/companion in the professional sphere. The spouses would use their technical and professional expertise to perform tasks in order to help their wives/companions in their enterprises. This help could take the form

Table 11.1 Sample characteristics

	Survey 1	Survey 2
Sample size	10 WE	41 WE
Age (average)	40	42
Age (range)	26–48	27–59
Age at becoming entrepreneur	39	35
Divorced/separated	20%	17.07% (n = 7)
Widowed	0%	2.44% (n = 1)
Single	20%	4.88% (n = 2)
Percentage of WE who are mothers	60%	85.3%
Number of children per mother (on average)	2.5	2
Business activities of the company	Mostly service and commerce sectors	Retail trade; services to customers; services to businesses, such as communications, advertising, human resources, training; and manufacturing industry, such as textile, thermal compression and molding
Origin: started/founded company	100%	85.4% (35/41)
Origin: takeovers/inheritance	0%	14.6% (6/41)
Age of the company	Between 0 and 1 year at the beginning of study	Average: 16 years 26/41: under 5 years Youngest: 7 months Oldest: 179 years
Turnover	10/10: less than €40 000 at the beginning of the study and less than €80 000 at the end of the study	22/41: less than €250 000 per year
Number of employees	10/10: 0 at the beginning of the study 9/10: 0 at the end of the study 1/10: 1 at the end of the study	6/41: 0 22/41: 1 to 10 7/41: 11 to 49 4/41: 50 to 99 2/41: more than 200

of working on administrative documents and management dashboards, or the development of facilities, as suggested by the quote below:

Elaine: *My husband is a great engineer. He has really helped us with document creation.*

In our sample, 20 of the 39 WE (with partners) clearly mention that they receive instrumental support from their partners. Among them, six work with their partners in their companies.

SCS may also occur in the construction of the social capital of the WE. For example, the spouse/companion may be present, playing the role of spouse/companion alongside the entrepreneur at public events. This support is interesting because it marks the spouses'/companions' public acceptance of a real reversal of traditional social roles, whereby the man usually occupies the public center stage. But it is relatively uncommon: only seven of the 51 WE mention it explicitly.

Instrumental support may take place in both the private domain and family life, wherein spousal/companion-based participation involves domestic tasks (childcare, household activities such as cleaning or cooking). Nineteen of the 39 WE (with partners) mention instrumental support in their private lives. Valérie told us:

Valérie: *He didn't help me in my actual business, but he helped me by saying, 'if you need time, I can take care of the kids tonight. Go to your meetings, go do internet research, take care of your clients'.*

However, entry into entrepreneurship for these WE did not result in an automatic redistribution of tasks. Some of them found themselves with an increased number of tasks and roles. One of them notably mentions business trips that take her away from home, preceding which she has to take care of logistical domestic arrangements. In cases such as these, the unequal distribution of domestic and familial tasks has a direct impact on the time that the WE can focus on their businesses. But:

France: *In order to start, we know we need a lot of time.*

Sylvia: *It's not the same when it's me. He won't take over at home to give me time to create. I have to find a way to make my own time. But it's assumed that I will take over at home when he needs time.*

In certain cases these WE will condemn and complain about the lack of involvement on the parts of their spouses/companions in the domestic domain. But others are more ambiguous. Indeed, for some women it seems very important that, despite occupying a position socially qualified as being masculine (boss or entrepreneur), they can continue to be women 'like the others' and assume what they consider to be 'normal' roles – the traditional roles of mother and spouse – as illustrated in the following excerpt:

Nathalie: *It's true that it's a huge challenge for a woman, i.e., even though I'm a boss – you know, I have my factory and my employees – I have two children at home and my husband, and I take care of them as well. I do all the cooking. Sure, it's true that I have two jobs, in fact. I admit it; it's two workdays in one.*

For some women, their attachments to traditional roles are essential and serve as anchoring identities defining what it means to be a woman.

For many of the WE, SCS appears to be a key factor that helped them to leap into the entrepreneurial venture. A large number of our WE highlighted the ways in which the encouragement of their spouses/companions influenced the confidence they had in their plans to launch businesses, as illustrated in this testimony:

Annie: *For me he was, he was a trigger, because he supported me. When he saw that I was bringing in revenue to the firm, he told me, 'You should think about starting your own business' . . . finally he said, 'Why don't you be your own boss? What have you got to lose?' It's true that my husband was my first coach, my first fan.*

Thirty-six of the 42 WE (with partners) in our sample mention that they had received emotional support at the time that their companies were being set up, and six said that they had not received any emotional support. Nevertheless, any encouragement and confidence imparted by their spouses/companions helped the WE to acquire greater confidence and persevere more. Many WE also expressed the idea that they would not have pursued their entrepreneurial careers if their spouses/companions had not shown them significant emotional support:

Suzanne: *He boosts me – a bit too much sometimes. He supports me in my endeavors. At times I've thought about closing my business because it wasn't doing well, especially when I was going through a period of doubt; he would always tell me 'Don't close! You can do it'.*

Emotional support from a spouse/companion may contribute significantly to the self-confidence of the entrepreneur (Kirkwood, 2009). Indeed, if the future female entrepreneur sees that the people who are important to her believe in her idea, she in turn starts to believe more strongly in herself (Greenberger and Sexton, 1988). Furthermore, through emotional support, the spouse/companion participates in the construction of the woman's self-made identity as entrepreneur. According to De Singly (1996), in order to become themself, the modern individual needs feedback from those most important to them. Following this thinking, the budding female entrepreneur constructs a more positive self-image if she thinks that her spouse/companion believes in her.

As identified in the literature, WE think very positively about discussing and sharing aspects of their business lives with their spouses/companions, and they do so in order to obtain advice, opinions and an outside point of view. Our respondents (26 of 51 WE) regularly referred to these moments of exchange as being very important. They are moments that allow the WE to focus on aspects ranging from daily management to strategic issues. These moments provide time during which the WE can share their entrepreneurial experiences and, to some extent, help their spouses/companions to understand their lives, thus including them in their entrepreneurial domains. These moments, also known as 'pillow talk', contribute to a better understanding between the spouses/companions in regards to the obligations held by each partner, thus reducing potential tensions.

Conversely, a lack of discussion between the spouses/companions is very difficult for some WE:

Flore: *The thing that's missing is the support of my spouse. There is no support more precious then his, and it's the thing I miss the most . . . because that would have carried me. And, as a result, I would have recognized this feeling as something profound, encouraging, enduring, and reassuring in difficult moments.*

Some WE who do not always receive the expected support from their partners tend, nevertheless, to subtly implicate them in the lives of their businesses. This strategy of inclusion, explicitly mentioned by five women, is firmly based on the wishes of the WE to maintain links between the personal and the professional domains, which confirms the overlap of these spheres (Brush et al., 2009).

The Changing Nature of Support

While the spouse/companion may by enthusiastic about the entrepreneurial project when it launches, the test of time, as well as difficulties that may arise, can start to diminish the amount of instrumental and emotional support provided through the duration of the project's development.

Possible tensions generated by the demands that an entrepreneurial life makes on both the family life and the couple's relationship can lead to diminished support, or even a negative attitude, on the part of the spouse/companion in regards to his partner's project. The following example is very telling in this respect:

Diane: *[At the beginning] my husband was amazing, really amazing. He really supported me and helped ... Now, much less. It bothers him. He's tired of my work stories. But at the beginning he was amazing, really amazing .... he's fed up, he can't do it any more.*

Moreover, it seems that as certain WE see their firms developing over time, they tend to 'protect' their spouses/companions and their relationships with them, seeking less and less support. In that light, the quotes below speak for themselves:

Sandra: *At the beginning – speaking of support – it was with him [my husband] that I shared everything. He was there to help with any loss of morale, or anything. But as the years pass I talk less and less about my work because maybe I need less; I've found other ways of dealing with things.*

Sophie: *I also protect [the relationship] a little. I sometimes say, 'I had some great news today,' but I don't recount everything that's happened because, already, when I get home in the evening, I have a lot to manage, so you protect [things] a little bit.*

These two testimonials highlight how these two WEs have succeeded in their businesses, but nevertheless maintain rather traditional attitudes by adopting strategies of compartmentalization between the two domains.

Certain WE manage, in turn, to obtain the support of their spouses/companions as and when their businesses develop. Certain spouses/companions show little interest at the beginning of the entrepreneurial ventures, but begin to be supportive and become more involved as the projects take shape and evolve, as shown in the following quote:

Sofia: *At the beginning he was indifferent. It was pretty amazing, a real indifference, like 'Don't talk to me.' Then, when it started to go well, it happened – we started to have exchanges when the business started to develop ... Support happened.*

From the interviews, it is clear that SCS for the woman entrepreneur is not a fixed thing. On the contrary, it is dynamic and can evolve in one way or another throughout the entire entrepreneurial process. We have seen that, in some cases, if the spouse is initially enthusiastic, over time his enthusiasm may wane (as in four out of the 36 cases wherein the WE had moral support at the early stages of the businesses). The opposite can also be true, but in rare cases: in six cases, there was no support initially and two of these WE received support later on. It should be noted that for one of the women interviewed, the support came from the fact that the spouse became co-manager of the company. The issue of unsupportive spouses at the time of creation must be the subject of extensive research.

However, SCS is essential; it contributes to an increase in the self-confidence of these WE and to their feelings of legitimacy. It also increases their 'self-efficacy' (Bandura, 1977, 1982) and participates in the entrepreneurs' self-construction and their recognition of themselves as being entrepreneurs. Consequently, in a certain manner, support contributes to the development of their entrepreneurial processes.

When Entrepreneurial Activities Interfere in the Couple's Relationship, and Vice Versa

Some WE do not receive SCS; however, they try to minimize the effects of this lack of support. One striking example unfolded through interviews that occurred at different stages of one woman's entrepreneurial process. At the time of her enterprise's creation, Flore recounted the difficulty she was having with her husband, who did not seem to want to help her:

Flore: *He doesn't realize the extent of the work and the energy that it monopolizes. That said, I think it's pretty extreme, the level of absenteeism he shows in regards to me and my work.*

After a few months, Flore observed, during the second interview, that her spouse was displaying a sort of 'benign neglect'.

If the spouse/companion offers no real support, the woman entrepreneur can glean a sort of support in the sense that the complete absence of support leaves her to fend for herself and to learn independently, as indicated by this entrepreneur:

Céline: *I used to ask him, to say, 'I don't know how to do this, you're going to help me,' and he would say no. He would say, 'You put yourself in this position.' That would piss me off because I had thought he was going to help me. But it helped me in some way because I had to dive in; so, in his own way, he did help me.*

This quote is based on the entrepreneur's *a posteriori* rationalization. It's interesting to place this in the context of French culture, a culture in which many WE already feel very lucky that their spouses/companions allow them to start their own businesses. Such an attitude could not, however, conceal the tensions that can hinder the entrepreneurial process.

Sources and Consequences of Frictions

As emphasized by Aldrich and Cliff (2003), ignorance of what is involved in an entrepreneurial venture can result in significant friction and misunderstandings between WE and their spouses/companions when expectations do not coincide. In our sample, 15 women talked about friction with their current or past husbands. Support provided by spouses/companions can be undermined, and even called into question, as a result of the fears and questions, particularly related to finances. These doubts are not inconsequential for the WE, and can generate stress, as clearly illustrated by the excerpt below:

Elise: *He asks me 'Is everything ok? Have you had a good month? Did you get any new clients this week?' He's always interrogating me; he needs to be reassured even though he's not part of the company . . . You can't stay cool when someone's asking these types of questions. Yes, the fact that he worries sometimes bothers me.*

Another recurring source of friction is when work time encroaches on family time. This disrupts the established family routine and generates tension between the couple:

Domitille: *['What does your partner think of your business activity?' He thinks it excessive; he thinks that it's too large an investment.*

Similarly, business events can disrupt family life, causing the spouse/companion to resent the business:

Monique: *I was having problems getting my payroll done yesterday, I don't know why but something in the fund-transfer process was blocked. Computers! So I had to work it out and get the wages paid instead of going to the Open House at my children's school. So my husband went alone with the children. The kids were a little disappointed, and my husband was very much so.*

These situations can lead to the spouse/companion withdrawing support from the entrepreneur. Indeed, he may feel that the business is having too heavy an impact on the family life, either in terms of time stolen away from the family, or in terms of finances, in that the business does not make enough revenue to justify the time that it takes up. He can then express his disapproval by way of decreased support.

These tensions seem more intense when the couple's life is based on traditional norms in regards to division of labor. In a case such as this, a woman's entrepreneurial activity challenges classic gender roles within the couple.

The choice to become an entrepreneur is not a trivial one; it is a first step on a path that reaches beyond that which is traditionally reserved for women (even for those who choose industries that are considered to be feminine). We saw earlier that entrepreneurship remains strongly infused with masculine norms. Sylvia's spouse supported her, but she brings up an interesting point concerning the desire for independence in the couple:

Sylvia: *He was fine with it because he felt it was good for me to leave the hospital . . . but he was very worried that my new professional independence was about me looking for independence within our relationship and therefore was a signal that I would leave him. He experienced it a little bit like that.*

The conclusion reached by this entrepreneur is not an isolated one; it is found repeatedly in regards to WE. A woman's choice of an entrepreneurial career can be perceived by her spouse/companion as a desire for change and perhaps as a threat to the couple's future. The entrepreneurial project will thus come to modify the daily life of the couple, which will have to retrieve its equilibrium with more or less difficulty, in accordance with the developing stages of the business. This transformation, whilst more or less acceptable to the spouse/companion, can sometimes lead to the couple's separation when changes in the roles and expectations of each person are stretched too far. But this transformation can also be positive for the couple, as evidenced by the following quote:

Sylvia: *Relationally, in our marriage, it's true that I always referred to him in regards to the decisions that were mine to make . . . It's true that his opinion is very important . . . But I was working on my business with someone else. Finally, I no longer turn to him, and it's good because it has rebalanced many things in our relationship.*

This example illustrates how entrepreneurship has enabled women to take a more egalitarian position within the couple. The WE in our sample particularly discussed the impact that their new professional roles had on their confidence building, a process that allowed them to assert themselves within the domestic structure.

It seems, therefore, that while the structure of a couple's relationship can impact the entrepreneurial process, the entrepreneurial process can help to re-establish a certain equilibrium within the couple. Therefore, the professional and private spheres are strongly interdependent. The entrepreneurship of these WE could not be fully analyzed without taking into account this complex dynamic.

DISCUSSION

The entrepreneurial career is littered with obstacles, and a supportive spouse/companion can be a real ally to the woman entrepreneur. However, the spouse/partner can also create additional intense trials for the woman and her business. SCS is complex in nature and does not always manifest in all spheres. Our results reflect the great variability in both the amount and the form of SCS. Certain spouses/companions may provide significant emotional support, but at the same time assist very little with the daily operational lives of the businesses or the households. Furthermore, if the spouse/companion is supportive, he can nevertheless express fear in regards to the professional and personal independence of the entrepreneur, or have doubts in regards to the financial situation. Thus, the WE are confronted with situations that are also at times sources of tension for them.

Such support appears to be essential all throughout the entrepreneurial process: from start-up through development of the business. It is also a practical necessity that may enable WE to successfully juggle all of their obligations. Additionally, our respondents clearly indicated that SCS is a key factor in the building of their self-confidence as they took on the roles of entrepreneurs.

SCS for WE also calls into question the traditional definition of gender roles within heterosexual couples. In this respect, our results indicate a wide variety of stances happening within couples. In some cases, gender roles alter very little, if at all; the woman entrepreneur takes on the traditional roles of mother and wife while simultaneously inhabiting the role of entrepreneur. But in other cases, we observed roles being shared in ways that differ from traditional configurations. It should be noted, however, that the women in these non-traditional couples described their relationships as having been egalitarian from the beginning. For these WE, entering into entrepreneurship was easier; domestic chores, for example, were already being shared within the couples, allowing the women more time to devote to their entrepreneurial projects.

It is important to put our results into perspective within the French cultural context. Through our analysis, we showed that the entry of these WE into entrepreneurship does not always challenge or alter the traditional roles that they take on within the domestic domain. Some will persist in shouldering all of the roles that are socially expected of them even though they are sometimes difficult to reconcile: being both a successful entrepreneur and a perfect mother and wife, as ascribed by social norms. Other women, with support from their spouses/companions, further redefine the contours and content of the different roles. These WE, by way of their arrangements within their couples, challenge the traditional depictions of marital gender roles and, thereby, call into question the traditional social norms accepted in our societies.

IMPLICATIONS

Our research contributes by adding new theoretical elements regarding the ways in which interactions between SCS and the entrepreneurial process challenge the larger social structure by calling into question the traditional dynamics of the male–female relationship. We also put forth elements regarding whether these interactions do or do not lead the WE to question their gender roles. In that regard, future research could explore deeply the impact of SCS on the entrepreneurial process of WE but also on that of men entrepreneurs. Moreover, we show that SCS support is a key condition for the existence of entrepreneurial activity of WE. It could be interesting to question further the links between SCS and economic performance of women led-companies. Powell and Eddleston (2013) find that family-to-business support is more positively related to entrepreneurial success for female entrepreneurs than it is for male entrepreneurs. Our findings additionally suggest that this support may also be an opportunity to call into question the traditionally held ideas of men and women, and that SCS may be a factor of social change.

This research can additionally be used on more practical levels by the actors who accompany women into the entrepreneurial world. Indeed, it seems that the role the spouse/companion plays in the entrepreneurial project must be clearly considered in order to determine if he will be a facilitator or a restraint for the woman entrepreneur. Therefore, the family dimension, particularly the role of SCS, needs to be considered in the content of the entrepreneurship training programs. Furthermore, women's growing awareness of gender roles seems to be an equally important prerequisite in order for WE to conduct their business ventures with more confidence.

Entry into entrepreneurship (a largely male-dominated field) leads these women to encounter confrontation between social roles that dictate that which is expected of an entrepreneur and that which is traditionally expected of a woman. Through their experiences, these WE also begin to question the traditional gender roles that exist within the couple. Indeed, the long work hours that are necessary for the creation and development of an enterprise interfere with the time traditionally devoted to 'women's' domestic tasks, causing the WE to call into question the couple's division of domestic labor. Education in regards to the gendered structure of our society can contribute to a deepening of these women's understanding of the daily tensions that they experience, and may thus diminish these tension- or guilt-causing situations.

LIMITATIONS AND FUTURE RESEARCH

In regards to this still relatively underexplored subject of SCS for WE, we are aware that our studies contain limitations. First, we did not interview the spouses/companions themselves; it would undoubtedly have been interesting to compare their perceptions with those of their partners. This would certainly be important to include in the design of future research projects regarding this subject.

Furthermore, in our studies, we included only heterosexual couples (with one exception in each survey). We are not seeking to defend a heteronormative definition of a couple. In further studies it would be interesting to observe the different postures of support in same-sex couples, that is, to see the ways in which gender roles are reproduced or modified in this configuration.

Additionally, although it includes a sizable number of respondents, this research is not intended to provide generalizations. It serves mainly to show that there is a diverse range of WE – and the support provided by their spouses/companions varies from one entrepreneur to another – and it questions the traditional representation of the couple and the relationships between spouses/partners. Furthermore, as Jennings et al. (2013) suggest, it would be also extremely relevant to explore the perceptions of other family members; children were referred to extremely frequently during our interviews, and appeared as essential components of the entrepreneurial lives of the WE. Lastly, it would be interesting to undertake international comparisons in order to see how the social structure of gender roles differently impacts the support provided by the spouses/companions of WE worldwide.

Our study can serve as food for thought in regards to work aimed at further analyzing the effects that SCS has on women's entrepreneurial processes. In addition, our work can help to encourage women's entrepreneurship while reconsidering the gender roles within couples, but also, more broadly, the roles traditionally reserved for men and women in our societies. It clearly appears that family and professional dimensions are unwaveringly linked in the lives of WE. Therefore, through entrepreneurship, women challenge traditional links between spheres. In this way, entrepreneurship could be a vehicle for social change in the roles of and relationships between women and men in our societies.

REFERENCES

Ahl, H. (2006), Why research on women entrepreneurs needs new directions. *Entrepreneurship Theory and Practice*. 30 (5), 595–621.

Al-Dajani, H. and Marlow, S. (2010), Impact of women's home-based enterprise on family dynamics: evidence from Jordan. *International Small Business Journal*. 28 (5), 470–486.

Aldrich, H.E. and Cliff, J.E. (2003), The pervasive effects of family on entrepreneurship: toward a family embeddedness perspective. *Journal of Business Venturing*. 18 (5), 573–596.

Amarapurkar, S.S. and Danes, S.M. (2005), Farm business-owning couples: inter-relationships among business tensions, relationship conflict quality, and spousal satisfaction. *Journal of Family and Economic Issues*. 26 (3), 419–441.

Baines, S. and Wheelock, J. (1998), Working for each other: gender, the household and micro-business survival and growth. *International Small Business Journal*. 17 (1), 16–35.

Bandura, A. (1977), Self-efficacy toward a unifying theory of behavioral change. *Psychological Review*. 84 (2), 191–215.

Bandura, A. (1982), Self-efficacy mechanism in human agency. *American Psychologist*. 37 (2), 122–147.

Ben-Ari, A. and Pines, A.M. (2002), The changing role of family in utilization of social support: views from Israeli Jewish and Arab students. *Families in Society – The Journal of Contemporary Social Services*. 83 (1), 93–101.

Bertaux, D. (1981), *Biography and Society, The Life History Approach in the Social Sciences*. Beverly Hills, CA: Sage.

Bird, B. and Brush, C. (2002), A gendered perspective on organizational creation. *Entrepreneurship Theory and Practice*. 26 (3), 41–65.

De Bruin, A., Brush, C.G. and Welter, F. (2007), Advancing a framework for coherent research on women's entrepreneurship. *Entrepreneurship Theory and Practice*. 31 (3), 323–339.

Bruni A., Gherardi, S. and Poggio, B. (2004), Entrepreneur-mentality, gender and the study of women entrepreneurs. *Journal of Organizational Change Management*. 17(3), 256–268.

Brush, C. (1992), Research on women business owners: past trends, a new perspective and future directions. *Entrepreneurship Theory and Practice*. 16 (4), 5–30.

Brush, C.G., Bruin, A. de and Welter, F. (2009), A gender-aware framework for

women's entrepreneurship. *International Journal of Gender and Entrepreneurship.* 1 (1), 8–24.
Buttner, E.H. and Moore, D.P. (1997), Women's organizational exodus to entrepreneurship: self-reported motivations and correlates with success. *Journal of Small Business Management.* 35 (1), 34–46.
Calás, M.B., Smircich, L. and Bourne, K. (2009), Extending the boundaries: reframing 'entrepreneurship as social change' through feminist perspectives. *Academy of Management Review.* 34 (3), 552–569.
Carlson, D.S. and Perrewé, P.L. (1999), The role of social support in the stressor-strain relationship: an examination of work–family conflict. *Journal of Management.* 25 (4), 513–540.
Cocandeau-Bellanger, L. (2011), *Femmes au travail. Comment concilier vie professionnelle et vie familiale.* Paris: Armand Colin.
Crompton, R., Lewis, S. and Lyonette, C. (2007), *Women, Men, Work and Family in Europe.* New York: Palgrave Macmillan.
Danes, S.M., Matzek, A.E. and Werbel, J.D. (2010), Spousal context during the venture creation. In Stewart, A., Lumpkin, G.T. and Katz, J.A. (eds), *Entrepreneurship and Family Business.* Advances in Entrepreneurship, Firm Emergence and Growth. Bingley: Emerald Group Publishing, pp. 113–161.
Danes, S.M. and Morgan, E.A. (2004), Family business-owning couples: an EFT view into their unique conflict culture. *Contemporary Family Therapy.* 26 (3), 241–260.
Danes, S.M., Stafford, K., Haynes, G. and Amarapurkar, S.S. (2009), Family capital of family firms: bridging human, social, and financial capital. *Family Business Review.* 22 (3), 199–215.
DARES (2012), Les disparités sur le marché du travail entre les hommes et les femmes. Une analyse sur une longue période. DARES Analyses (015).
De Singly, F. (1996), *Le soi, le couple et la famille: la famille, un lieu essentiel de reconnaissance et de valorisation de l'identité personnelle,* Paris: Nathan.
Dimov, D. (2007), Beyond the single-person, single-insight attribution in understanding entrepreneurial opportunities. *Entrepreneurship Theory and Practice.* 31 (5), 713–731.
Eddleston, K.A. and Powell, G.N. (2012), Nurturing entrepreneurs' work–family balance: a gendered perspective. *Entrepreneurship Theory and Practice.* 36 (3), 513–541.
Etzion, D. (1984), Moderating effect of social support on the stress–burnout relationship. *Journal of Applied Psychology.* 69 (4), 615–622.
Fielden, S.L. and Dawe, A. (2004), Entrepreneurship and social inclusion. *Women in Management Review.* 19 (3), 139–142.
Granrose, C.S., Parasuraman, S. and Greenhaus, J.H. (1992), A proposed model of support provided by two-career couples. *Human Relations.* 45 (12), 1367–1393.
Greenberger, D.B. and Sexton, D.L. (1988), An interactive model of new venture initiation. *Journal of Small Business Management.* 26 (3), 1–7.
Hagège, C. and Masson, C. (2011), En 2010, hausse des créations d'auto-entreprises mais aussi des sociétés. INSEE Premières 1334.
Hisrich, R.D. and Brush, C. (1983), The woman entrepreneur: implications of family, educational, and occupational experience, in Hornaday, J.A., Timmons, J.A. and Vesper, K.H. (eds), *Frontiers of Entrepreneurship Research, Frontiers in Entrepreneurship Research.* Wellesley, MA: Babson College, pp. 255–270.
Israel, B.A., Farquhar, S.A., Schulz, A.J., James, S.A. and Parker, E.A. (2002),

The relationship between social support, stress, and health among women on Detroit's East Side. *Health Education and Behavior.* 29 (3), 342–360.

Jennings, J.E., Breitkreuz, R.S. and James, A.E. (2013), When family members are also business owners: is entrepreneurship good for families? *Family Relations.* 62, 472–489.

Jennings, J.E. and Brush, C.G. (2013), Research on women entrepreneurs: challenges to (and from) the broader entrepreneurship literature. *Academy of Management Annals.* 7 (1), 663–715.

Jennings, J.E. and McDougald, M.C. (2007), Work–family interface experiences and coping strategies: implications for entrepreneurship research and practice. *Academy of Management Review.* 32 (3), 747–760.

Kelley, D.J., Brush, C.G., Greene, P.G. and Litovsky, Y. (2013), *Global Entrepreneurship Monitor. Women's Report 2012.* http://www.babson.edu/Academics/centers/blank-center/global-research/gem/Documents/GEM%20201 2%20Womens%20Report.pdf, p. 58.

Kim, J.L.S. and Ling, C.S. (2001), Work–family conflict of women entrepreneurs in Singapore. *Women in Management Review.* 16 (5), 204–221.

King, L.A., Mattimore, L.K., King, D.W. and Adams, G.A. (1995), Family support inventory for workers: a new measure of perceived social support from family members. *Journal of Organizational Behavior.* 16, 235–258.

Kirkwood, J. (2009), Is a lack of self-confidence hindering women entrepreneurs? *International Journal of Gender and Entrepreneurship.* 1 (2), 118–133.

Kirkwood, J. (2011), Spouse roles on motivations for entrepreneurship: a qualitative study in New Zealand. *Journal of Family and Economic Issues.* 30 (4), 372–385.

Kirrane, M. and Buckley, F. (2004), The influence of support relationship on work–family conflict: differentiating emotional from instrumental support. *Equal Opportunities International.* 23 (1–2), 78–96.

Lewis, K. and Massey, C. (2011), Critical yet invisible: the 'good wife' in the New Zealand small firm. *International Journal of Gender and Entrepreneurship.* 3 (2), 105–122.

Md-Sidin, S., Sambasivan, M. and Ismail, I. (2010), Relationship between work–family conflict and quality of life. An investigation into role of social support. *Journal of Managerial Psychology.* 25 (1), 58–81.

Mirchandani, K. (1999), Feminist insight on gendered work: new directions in research on women and entrepreneurship. *Gender, Work and Organization.* 6 (4), 224–235.

Mitchell, L. (2011), Overcoming the gender gap: women entrepreneurs as economic drivers. http://www.kauffman.org/uploadedFiles/Growing_the_Econ omy_Women_Entrepreneurs.pdf, p.15.

Moschion, J. (2009), Offre de travail des mères en France: l'effet causal du passage de deux à trois enfants. *Economie et statistique.* 422 (1), 51–78.

Nelson, G. (1989), Factors of friendship: relevance of significant others to female business owners. *Entrepreneurship Theory and Practice.* 13 (4), 7–18.

Oughton, E. and Wheelock, J. (2003), A capabilities approach to sustainable household livelihoods. *Review of Social Economy.* 61 (1), 1–22.

Ozcan, B. (2011), Only the lonely? The influence of the spouse in the transition to self-employment. *Small Business Economics.* 37 (4), 465–492.

Parasuraman, S., Purohit, Y.S., Godshalk, V.M. and Beutell, N.L. (1996), Work and family variables, entrepreneurial career success and psychological well-being. *Journal of Vocational Behavior.* 48, 275–300.

Patterson, N. and Mavin, S. (2009), Women entrepreneurs: jumping the corporate ship and gaining new wings. *International Small Business Journal.* 27 (2), 173–192.

Philbrick, C.A. and Fitzgerald, M.A. (2007), Women in business-owning families: a comparison of roles, responsibilities and predictors of family functionality. *Journal of Family and Economic Issues.* 28, 618–634.

Powell, G.N. and Eddleston, K.A. (2013), Linking family-to-business enrichment and support to entrepreneurial success: Do female and male entrepreneurs experience different outcomes. *Journal of Business Venturing.* 28, 261–280.

Rao, K., Apte, M. and Subbakrishna, D.K. (2003), Coping and subjective wellbeing in women with multiple roles. *International Journal of Social Psychiatry.* 49 (3), 175–184.

Richomme, K. (2000), Contribution à la compréhension des systèmes de gestion des entreprises artisanales, Thèse de doctorat en gestion. Université de Montpellier 1.

Rogers, N. (2005), The impact of family support on the success of women business owners, in Fielden, S.L. and Davidson, M.J. (eds), *International Handbook of Women and Small Business Entrepreneurship.* Cheltenham, UK and Northampton, MA, USA: Edward Elgar, pp. 91–102.

Rogoff, E.G. and Heck, R.K.Z. (2003), Evolving research in entrepreneurship and family business: recognizing family as oxygen that feeds the fire of entrepreneurship. *Journal of Business Venturing.* 18 (5), 559–566.

Sexton, D.L. and Kent, C.A. (1981), Female executives and entrepreneurs: a preliminary comparison, in Vesper, K. (ed.), *Frontiers of Entrepreneurship Research, Frontiers in Entrepreneurship Research.* Babson College. Wellesley, MA, pp. 40–55.

Stevenson, L. (1986), Against all odds: the entrepreneurship of women. *Journal of Small Business Management.* 24 (4), 30–36.

Strauss, A. and Corbin, J. (1990), *Basics of Qualitative Research: Grounded Theory Procedures and Techniques.* London: Sage Publications.

Thomas, L.T. and Ganster, D.C. (1995), Impact of family–supportive work variables on work-family conflict and strain: a control perspective, *Journal of Applied Psychology.* 80, 6–15.

VanAuken, H. and Werbel, J.D. (2006), Family dynamic and family business financial performance: spousal commitment. *Family Business Review.* 19 (1), 49–62.

Winn, J. (2004), Entrepreneurship: not an easy path to top management for women. *Women in Management Review.* 19 (3), 143–153.

12. The divisions of labour and responsibilities in business and home among women and men copreneurs in the Czech Republic

Alena Křížková, Nancy Jurik and Marie Dlouhá

INTRODUCTION

This chapter examines the divisions of labour and responsibilities in the business and family lives of copreneurs in the Czech Republic (CR). Copreneurs are romantic and business partners who own and operate businesses together (Barnett and Barnett, 1988). Copreneurs are an under-researched but important group because they provide an excellent point for unpacking the interplay among business, family life, and gender (Blenkinsopp and Owens, 2010). Since the 1989 Velvet Revolution catalysed the renewal of small businesses in the CR, these enterprises constitute an important yet unexplored component of Czech economic and social life. In this chapter, we address this gap. We examine the constructions of the divisions of labour in business and home and strategies to balance these two spheres, and locate both within the socio-historical context of the CR.

Entrepreneurs have historically been portrayed as disembodied males without household responsibilities, and living in Western market economies (Bruni et al., 2005; Brush, 1992). Growth in the numbers of women-owned businesses worldwide has brought attention to their achievements and to the gendered nature of entrepreneurial experiences (Hughes and Jennings, 2012). The study of women business owners highlights how family responsibilities inspire and impinge on entrepreneurship (De Bruin et al., 2007; Jurik, 1998). Research on family-owned businesses has stressed the gendered links between business and family dynamics (Lee et al., 2006). Family-owned businesses constitute a significant component of many nations' economies, but it is now recognized that family dynamics are important, although in different ways, to all entrepreneurial ventures (Aldrich and Cliff, 2003).

The CR is a unique research site. Under socialism, entrepreneurship was suspended between the 1950s and early 1990s. However, like other Central and Eastern European (CEE) nations, the CR underwent extensive economic and social transformation beginning in the early 1990s, and joined the European Union in 2004. The transition to a market economy fuelled new entrepreneurial ventures. Small businesses have been important in this transition, yet with some exceptions (Křížková, 2007; Lituchy and Reavley, 2004), social scientific study of CR entrepreneurship, particularly small businesses and the gender issues surrounding them, has been rare.

Our study responds to this gap in the literature on gender in entrepreneurship, especially in transitional economies with gender regimes that differ from Western nations that are the typical site for entrepreneurial research. For our analysis, we interview copreneur partners separately, an approach that better facilitates the examination of male and female partner views about divisions of labour than when men and women copreneurs are interviewed together.

Intellectually, we are informed by perspectives that consider gender and entrepreneurship to be dynamic and emergent social constructions, that is, 'doing gender' (Jurik, 1998; West and Zimmerman, 1987) and 'doing entrepreneurship' (Bruni et al., 2005). Also consistent with feminist narrative approaches (Presser, 2005; Hertz, 1997), our reflexive approach treats the interview context as data to reflect on in analysis.

We contribute to the literature on gender and entrepreneurship by revealing the diversity of women's and men's contributions to business and by illustrating how both partners describe tasks and credit in gendered ways. We suggest ways that gendered identities reinforce the diminished recognition of women's labour in business and at home.

In the next section, we explain our conceptual framework. Then we describe the historical and contemporary context of gender and entrepreneurship in the CR. Next, we describe our methodology and findings. We will argue that our analysis offers insights into the variations, fluidity, and contradictions of Czech copreneurs' constructions of gender, family, and entrepreneurship across ventures, stages of business and family life stages. We link these findings to the CR socio-economic context, and draw conclusions.

CONCEPTUAL FRAMEWORK

The gender and entrepreneurship literature has often assumed a male-centred model of entrepreneurship (see criticisms by Bruni et al., 2005; Mulholland, 2003; Connell, 2002). Regardless of whether they conform to male-centric definitions or challenge them, women entrepreneurs seem to be exceptions to the rule as they either overcome or are limited by barriers posed by gender inequalities in business (Ahl, 2006).

Increasingly, researchers recognize the importance of studying family businesses and copreneur couples as a starting point for understanding the degree to which all businesses (whether family-operated or not) are shaped by both business and family concerns (Blenkinsopp and Owens, 2010; Sharma, 2004). Copreneur research makes visible the often invisible recursive link between paid work and family life for men and women.

However, much research on family businesses – even studies of copreneurs – emphasizes the role of patriarchal employment and family regimes in the exploitation and underestimation of women's contribution to the ventures (e.g., Shelton, 2006; Lee et al., 2006). In these analyses, the business becomes little more than the outcome of gender inequality in the home.

In contrast, some research suggests that through the use of qualitative interpretive methodologies and narrative analysis, it is possible to uncover greater contradictions and nuances in the role of women in these businesses, and to identify how patriarchal relations are simultaneously replicated and challenged in copreneurial ventures (e.g., Kirkwood, 2009; Nordqvist et al., 2009; Křížková, 2007; Hamilton, 2006; Bruni et al., 2005). These interpretive and feminist-informed analyses critically assess rather than simply reinforce patriarchal discourses about entrepreneurship generally, and family businesses in particular. In this vein, our research draws on perspectives that view gender and entrepreneurial identities as ongoing social constructions emergent in social interactions and located within larger cultural contexts (see Bruni et al., 2005; Jurik, 1998; West and Zimmerman, 1987). We examine ways in which gender, family and entrepreneurship are ongoing productions within CR copreneur ventures. By including narratives of both men and women partners interviewed separately, we are able to examine and compare the presentation of the business–family partnership by each copreneur.

Our research design and analysis adopt a reflexive approach to consider how the interview context framed the data collected (Presser, 2005). We view research interviews as providing a site for respondents to tell stories about themselves, their partners, businesses and home-life. Yet, the interview also sets certain parameters for telling (for example, interview questions, time concerns) and provides a particular type of public audience for stories (for example, interviewer and readers of research products). Thus, our analysis focuses on the interview presentations of copreneurs and businesses rather than attempting to discern the so-called 'objective facts' about business activities and personalities that might appear to a third-party 'independent, scientific' observer.

Consistent with Bruni et al.'s (2005) 'doing gender, doing entrepreneurship' approach, our analysis of respondent narratives is sensitive to the interwoven, varied and fluid constructions of gender, family and entrepreneurship across ventures, and business or family life stages. Our sample was purposely selected to capture likely variations in the perceptions of these phenomena. And not surprisingly, our data reveal gender, entrepreneurship and family constructions not only as changing but also often as contradictory identities. The data also reveal the importance of the cultural context, as we discuss in the next section.

CONTEXT OF THE CR: GENDER, LABOUR MARKET AND ENTREPRENEURSHIP

Research on gender and entrepreneurship in the context of the socio-economic development in the CEE region since 1989 (Welter et al., 2006; Manolova and Yan, 2002; Smallbone and Welter, 2001) establishes that the CR is important for several reasons. First, business ownership was not permitted during the CR socialist era. Second, the former Czechoslovakia and the CR represent examples of gender regimes that differ from other Western European nations. Thus, the growth of entrepreneurship in the CR (and to a large extent in other post-socialist countries) and in Western European countries is different because, in most Western European nations, the opportunity to run a business was uninterrupted. Moreover, the CR remains a European nation with some of the most gender-stereotypical attitudes about the divisions of labour in the family and views regarding the impact of mothers' work on children and the family (Hašková, 2007).

The opportunity for running an independent business was reintroduced in 1990 when a long history of full employment was ending, and unemployment was becoming an increasing problem. Most Czech women and men entrepreneurs were dealing with the experience of having lived part of their lives under the state socialist regime, when participation in the labour market was compulsory for men and women. Even so, during the era of state socialism extensive gender labour market inequalities (for example, gender stereotyping and occupational sex segregation) were permitted

(Křížková et al., 2010; Treanor and Henry, 2010), and a double workday in the home was the norm (Křížková, 1999). The undervaluation of women's work relegated them to the 'secondary' workforce (Čermáková, 1997). Men's participation and equality at home was never a matter for public discussion. After 1989, women faced similar undervaluing and inequality in the labour market. Further, values of domesticity were re-emerging and many viewed this as an ideal time for women to return to their 'rightful place' in the home. Strong re-familization policies included a severe decrease in childcare facilities (Saxonberg and Sirovátka, 2006). Parental leave was extended until the child was three. Instead of protecting women's jobs these trends increased discrimination (Křížková et al., 2011). Czech women also lack part-time and flexible employment opportunities (Vohlídalová and Formánková, 2012).

Despite calls for increased domesticity, most Czech women did not leave the labour market to become housewives because the economic realities for many families prohibited reliance on a male breadwinner alone. However, the opportunity to start a business was attractive to families that were dependent on two incomes but wanted more time for childrearing. Research on small and home-based businesses suggests that women and families see them as promoting flexibility to combine work and family duties (Jurik, 2005). Women play an important role in CR entrepreneurial trends both as sole owners and as partners, including partnership in family-owned ventures. In the CR 12.2 per cent of all employed women and 22 per cent of all employed men operate businesses (Czech Statistical Office, 2011). However, compared to many nations (for example, Western European, US) in the CR, entrepreneurship is still a new phenomenon, and women are still under-represented in entrepreneurial ventures.

Women's entrepreneurship, particularly among women in precarious employment positions, likely reflects post-socialist policies that ignore gender inequalities in the home and family. Women's business ownership may offer the opportunity to combine work and family, but at the same time reinforces stereotypical gender divisions of household labour (Křížková, 2007).

METHODOLOGY

Our research aimed to examine the construction of gender, family and entrepreneurship in copreneur businesses. Because of our 'doing gender, doing entrepreneurship' framework (Bruni et al., 2005; Jurik, 1998; West and Zimmerman, 1987), we sought to examine how copreneurs mutually construct their roles in businesses and households. Consistent with this framework, we used a qualitative approach with semi-structured interviews. Copreneurs were interviewed separately with an interview schedule that included these topics: work history; business type, history and future plans; positive and negative aspects of entrepreneurship; respondent/partner roles in the business and household; work–life balance strategies. Our interview asked each member of the copreneurial couple (whether married or not) to describe their work in the business and household as well as any conflicts or complementarity they experienced between the two spheres.

In 2012, we completed 24 interviews with 12 heterosexual copreneur couples (see Table 12.1). Interviews ranged from 35 to 70 minutes. Respondents were of Czech origin and mostly from Prague. Respondents' ages ranged from 36 to 46 years for men, and 20 to 47 years for women. Just over half the copreneurs had university degrees; the rest had a high school education. One couple had no children; four couples had adult children, several of whom were raised while operating the business; and seven couples had children living with them at the time of the interview. Four couples had incorporated their children into the firm. Businesses fell under the internet and retail sales, creative product and sales, and professional and non-professional service categories. Specific examples include organic produce delivery, real estate, sports event management, jewellery, language school, and toy imports. Copreneurs' years in business together ranged from three to 23 years.

Contacts were obtained from the internet, acquaintances and referrals. We included only firms that involved both romantic partners regardless of their position in the firm. We focused on small and medium-sized businesses with from 1 to 20 employees.[1] Two couples operated multiple businesses; and in two other couples, the female partners had side businesses in addition to the business operated by the couple. In two couples, one partner (one man and one woman) was employed full-time in order to provide financial stability while building the copreneur business. Several couples had been employed around the time of their business start-up for similar reasons. Small business owners commonly rely on the 'packaging' of multiple ventures including full- and part-time employment to enhance income (Jurik, 1998).

We coded our interview data according to the predefined topics described earlier, and later for emergent analytic themes (described below). The two interviewers wrote research memos after each interview about interviewer–respondent dynamics. All interviews were conducted by women. We discuss the dynamics of these interactions and their significance in our analysis sections.

Table 12.1 List of interview respondents (pseudonyms only)

	Couple	Age	Business type	Years in business together	Children at home	Number of employees
#1	Eda and Ester	18–34	Service	Less than 5	None	Over 5
#2	Kristýna and Karel	Over 45	Sales	More than 5	One	1–4
#3	Adam and Alice	Over 45	Sales	Less than 5	None	1–4
#4	Prokop and Patricie	35–44	Creative product/sales	More than 5	Three	Over 5
#5	Ota and Olga	Over 45	Service	More than 5	None	1–4
#6	Dora and David	Over 45	Sales	More than 5	None	1–4
#7	Vanda and Viktor	Over 45	Service	More than 5	Two	Over 5
#8	Marta and Michal	35–44	Service	Less than 5	One	1–4
#9	Johana and Jakub	18–34	Creative product/Sales	More than 5	One	1–4
#10	Zina and Zdenek	35–45	Creative product/Sales	Less than 5	Three	1–4
#11	Lada and Libor	Over 45	Sales	More than 5	None	1–4
#12	Borek and Bohdana	Over 45	Service	More than 5	One	Over 5

Note: Because of the small size of our sample and in order to protect the confidentiality of individual responses, we have coded business type, years in business together, number of children and employees into very broad categories. In developing this coding scheme, we were guided by distinguishing classifications that have been stressed in the business literature (for example, in business together less than five years or five years or more).

ANALYSIS AND FINDINGS

With only two exceptions, copreneurs were uniformly positive about their partner's contribution to the business. One woman was somewhat negative about her male partner's role in their business, describing him as 'smart but too slow' (#8F[2]), and one man failed to mention much about his female partner's role in their business (#3). The rest of the respondents were largely positive despite occasional criticism, a tendency that may be an artefact of the interview situation in which respondents want to appear socially acceptable (Hertz, 1997). Although interviews were conducted separately and respondents were assured confidentiality, respondents sometimes referenced what their partner might think about their own comments. Accordingly, we recognize that although separate, respondent narratives were often constructed with partners' possible responses in mind.

Below, we examine couples' narratives about their divisions of labour in business and domestic spheres. Descriptions revealed the varied and significant roles played by both women and men in copreneur ventures.

Divisions of Labour in Business

Our data suggest that the divisions of labour in businesses varied considerably across couples, and that divisions were often more complex and nuanced than strict sex or gender role perspectives would suggest. In some businesses, women handled finances, met with customers and clients, ran the office; in other cases, men performed these duties. Narratives did not restrict women to traditionally feminine business chores. In two couples, both partners stressed that they shared decision-making responsibilities. In five couples, each partner had separate components or enterprises in which they were the central decision-maker. Women copreneurs included a jeweller, a sports event manager and a lawyer. Women handled public relations and designed websites. Women sometimes resisted efforts to lock them into domestic roles within the business. For example, one woman found herself doing the cleaning for her husband and employees around their store, but tired of this and told her male partner and other employees that they must clean up after themselves. Across couples, the business tasks reported for men and women were variable and changing in ways that often challenged notions of gender as fixed dichotomies. These findings are consistent with notions of gender as fluid and dynamic social constructions (West and Zimmerman, 1987). However, interestingly, the interview characterizations of even similar tasks took on different tones and terminology depending on the gender of the person performing the task. Consistent with a 'doing gender, doing entrepreneurship' approach (Bruni et al., 2005; West and Zimmerman, 1987), regardless of the variety of their actions or patterns of task allocation, men and women still connect actions to views about socially appropriate ways of doing gender. For example, men were described by both male and female partners as 'handling the financial side of the business'. Women 'kept the books' (for more examples see Table 12.2).

With regard to credit for starting the business, both partners in three couples indicated that they had started the business together (#1, #5, #7). Both partners in five couples indicated that the business was either inherited or started by the woman (#3, #4, #8, #11, #12). Four couples agreed that the business had been started by the male partner (#2, #6, #9, #10). However, the stories of business progression frequently constructed men as one or more of the following: the public face of the business, the dominant partner, or the key business decision-maker. This was the case even in businesses started by women and where the woman's particular skill was the basis of the business. In one of these couples, a female partner whose creative force was the centre of a business that she started reported: 'My husband tells me he is my boss and I don't disagree' (#4F). In another business, the female partner said that the couple did every aspect of the business together, but her male counterpart emphasized that he 'made the final decisions' (#1M). Some couples stressed their collaborative decision-making. However, even in some of these couples, men and women described him as having the more visible public presence. In one of these couples, the man described himself as the 'face of the business', because he recruited clients. He described his wife, who ran the day-to-day business operations, as 'protecting his back' (#7).

In only one couple did the female partner describe herself as the primary partner of the business, but she also predicted that her partner would disagree with her assessment because 'men always want to be managers or in charge' (#5F). And indeed, he did not name her as the primary partner of their business. These narratives again indicate a tendency to gender contributions to the business in a manner that constructs men as more visible and primary. Yet, neither men nor women's narratives indicated that female partners always acquiesced to their copreneur partners. Two men acknowledged that they and their female partners had lots of disagreements about the business. Another woman stressed that although her husband was very involved and had lots of vision in one of their businesses, he knows little about their other business that she inherited and runs without him (#10F). Several women located themselves in spheres of the business in which they had a degree of control and independence from their male partners, either through separate, co-owned businesses,

Table 12.2 Illustrative quotations re copreneurs' division of labour (DOL)

Couple ID#	He says . . .	She says . . .
DOL, business:		
3	She's not so creative in business; She's holding back my flight.	He's a pioneer . . . [but] he is trying to expand too quickly.
1	She has good intuition . . . I make the final decisions.	We make every decision in the business together.
DOL, home:		
7	Sometimes I cook.	I married well. My man cooks and he likes to cook.
5	There it [dinner] is cooked somehow twice a week. Cleaning is somehow managed continuously. There is no mess, so I don't know. I don't cook, I am not good at it. But I won't starve. My wife cooks very economically.	I clean in the morning very quickly . . . and my husband is not able to do it. He simply washes two plates for two hours.
6	So we are lucky, the washing machine washes, but my wife does it more than me.	I have a lady for ironing and cleaning. I wouldn't manage it alone.
Balancing:		
10	Sometimes there is no time and we cook completely simple things.	We don't have ironing. I have quite reduced ironing. I just iron shirts.
12	I must say that I am lucky that I manage to switch off at 7 in the evening. As a baby sitter, we had always the granny and . . . we had a neighbour working part time.	[I]t interferes a bit, that I work home, so some things are simply adapted . . . so I kind of cannot go to movies, or . . . bike on Saturday, because I work. Do I have some charwoman? No, I don't . . . I am rather the person who thinks that I do everything best.

their own side businesses, or a branch of their joint ventures (online versus retail shop).

Couple narratives often included language that naturalized divisions of labour. Divisions of labour in the business were often described by men and women alike as naturally evolving patterns consistent with each partner's personality. These descriptions were often gendered in predictable ways: 'He is very outgoing'; 'he has a good business sense'; 'she does not care so much about the business side of things'. These characterizations were made by partners about themselves and each other. As noted above, however, the characterizations in some cases adopted a tone of gender stereotyping that when taken together tended to limit the recognition of women's contribution to their businesses.

Consistent with findings of Bruni et al. (2005), the business narratives of female partners blurred family and business concerns to a greater extent than did the narratives of male partners. Men discussed interactions and relationship dynamics between them and their female partners, referenced involvement with children, and sometimes spoke about wanting better work–life balance. Yet no men discussed the ways in which having children affected their work in the business. Women were far more likely to discuss the ways that they structured work in the business around caring for children: 'The advantage was that when we then had children, I didn't want to work fulltime. This wasn't possible in my previous job' (#2F). Even women whose children were adults reflected on the ways that they managed business and childcare when their kids were younger. We will discuss these strategies later in the chapter, but first we discuss the division of household labour and childcare. These discussions will further reveal the ways in which business and domestic labour are not only interwoven but also recursive dynamics.

Divisions of Labour in Domestic Sphere

In contrast to the tendency to credit men as primary in the business, women were the ones almost uniformly credited by both partners as being in charge of the household and children. Several men exhibited discomfort or confusion when asked about the division of labour in the home or about what they did in the home. Men might have been more comfortable or spoken more frankly if they had been speaking to another man. Their discomfort may have occurred because asking what they did in the home made them feel that they should be doing more in the home. Only three couples indicated that they shared housework and childcare; in the remaining nine couples, women indicated that they did all or most of the housework and childcare, and their male partners concurred. In several cases, the men tried to avoid discussion of housework by changing the topic back to the business. Indeed, to the extent that the men participated in domestic responsibilities, they picked up or played with the children, stopped for groceries, and did work in the garden. Only one man was described as cooking regularly. Even when couples both described sharing household work, the narratives did not suggest an equitable sharing.

As in narratives about business labour, descriptions of household work that men and women performed were gendered. Both partners used adjectives to describe the tasks that men did as 'heavy,' 'technical' or 'manly' jobs at home. One man said that he washes the upper windows because they were hard to reach, but he cannot wash the lower windows because he is not good enough to clean them properly (#11). In some narratives, women were described as 'naturally' more capable in the home and men were described as 'naturally' not aware or knowledgeable about the home. Several men said that they could not cook as an obvious indicator of their lack of skill in the household. Interview responses often took on a 'taken-for-granted' tone about men's neglect or inability regarding housework and women's caring for family and home. One woman described herself as doing cleaning more effectively: 'I clean in the morning, very quickly . . . and my husband is not able to do it. He simply washes two plates for two hours' (#5F).

Although respondents may have been trying to appear socially acceptable when being interviewed by female academics, few overtly suggested that women should perform all the housework and childcare. Men and women more frequently referenced female partners' desire to structure work time around being with children. Two women (#2F, #10F) viewed their performance of more home and family work as legitimate. One said: 'So I cook, I care about the kitchen, simply what a woman should do' (#10F). However, she also indicated some doubts about this legitimacy when she added, 'I don't say that a woman *belongs* to a cooking range' (#10F).

Other women did not describe the unequal division of household labour as legitimate but exhibited a sense of resignation to the situation. They described their husbands as unwilling or incapable of doing housework. One woman said that, beginning with her maternity leave, she did everything around the house and he became spoiled, and that it was too much trouble to try to change it now (#2F). Another woman said, 'He doesn't do it [housework] and he won't ever do it, I guess' (#6F).

Some respondents, men more often than women, minimized the importance and amount of housework. One of the men professed an almost magical assessment about household chores. He said: 'There it [dinner] is cooked somehow twice a week. Cleaning is somehow managed continuously. There is no mess, so I don't know' (#5M). This quotation illustrates how men sometimes minimized housework to the point of invisibility. Yet, the female partner of this man described herself as 'overwhelmed by the housework'. Two women minimized concerns about the division of household labour (#1F, #12F). One said: 'So you simply have some common life, some cohabitation in which something is formed and it is not about some management, each simply does something somehow in the household' (#12F).

These narratives revealed some key linguistic processes whereby household work is gendered, made invisible and unrecognized. In the next section, we discuss strategies to balance business and domestic duties and the ways in which the two spheres are blurred and mutually reinforcing.

Balancing Strategies

There were a variety of strategies that couples identified for balancing business and family life. Couples identified numerous strategies to reduce housework (see Table 12.2). One man described how he lowered his standards of cleanliness because they are both too busy with the business (#1M). Especially in businesses where the couple had no children living at home, the importance and extent of housework tended to be minimized most often by the men but sometimes by women as well. Dining on takeaway food and hiring house cleaners and gardeners, and daily cleaning were strategies that such couples emphasized for minimizing housework. Yet no matter how successful, the narratives ultimately revealed that such plans failed to completely eliminate housework.

For most, the pressure for juggling business and family responsibilities ultimately fell on the woman, but her acceptance of disproportionate responsibility for housework and childcare may have also reduced her time and/or visibility in the business. Moreover, the narratives suggest how women's management of the home may have reduced their male partner's attention to home life and allowed him to focus more on business and personal time. One man said that he does not want to do even the 'heavy work' around the house because he wants to concentrate as much as possible on the business (#9M).

Women often described histories of conscientious time management, including curtailing work in the business, scheduling business around childcare and other household chores, and finding paid and unpaid helpers. Unlike men, women describe housework as a job: one woman said that it is her second business (#4F). Regardless of the success of these strategies, women reported feeling stressed and missing out on personal time. Women with small children often moulded their involvement in the business to make it more compatible with bearing and raising children. Two women started their businesses while on maternity leave because their bosses in their paid employment were not supportive of childcare demands (#2F). These 'flexibility' strategies entailed some women cutting down on their hours or locating some of their business work in the home (for example, managing online components) when their children were small or ill. Several women described working late at night or early in the morning while their children and mates slept. Women perceived these strategies as effective, but they may have diminished their recognition in the business. For example, one female partner who worked at home regularly reported that neighbours and family thought she did not work because she was at home (#3F).

Often men were supportive and even instigators of hiring paid helpers, but some women were resistant to hiring childcare even if it was available (#6F, #11F). Help was typically restricted to cleaning the house. In the four couples that hired household help, some women were embarrassed about it and drew boundaries around what they would and would not allow a paid helper to do. One woman talked about doing the ironing for her family: 'I myself want to iron my husband's shirts' (#4F). Another woman said she refused to ever hire anyone; in contrast, her male partner reported that they had hired a neighbour in the past (#12). Men often believed that once help was hired, the household labour problem was solved and again housework became more invisible: 'We have a lady who comes to us once a week, more or less, above all to iron, yes. Other things are not such a problem' (#8M).

Help from family – parents or children – was another balancing mechanism. Even women opposed to hiring help often relied on the unpaid support of parents or grandparents. Children also helped out. Three women trained their children (sons and daughters) to help with household chores. The male partner in one of these couples said: 'I am embarrassed. I do nothing, but my son vacuums' (#12M). One couple trained their children together and cleaned the house as a family. These examples suggest that gendered divisions of household labour might be more blurred in future generations.

Female partners with children described myriad ways (past and present) that they had either curtailed work time in the business or structured the nature and scheduling of their business work around their children's needs. Not one male partner described such strategies. This blurring between business and household responsibilities for women was taken for granted to the point that no respondent questioned whether childcare should be disproportionately performed by female partners. Women's dual responsibilities facilitated men's less distracted commitment to businesses and some men's access to personal time after work. Although some men's narratives indicated that most or all of their waking hours were spent on the business, more men than women spoke about having time for hobbies and personal interests. Women discussed personal time as something available to them only after their children were grown up and after their business had matured: 'So I have more time for myself when the girl is out of home [daughter grew up] and I play golf' (#6F).

Our respondent narratives reveal the interwoven and recursive nature of doing entrepreneurship, doing family and doing gender. In the overwhelming majority of copreneur businesses, women bore the brunt of balancing business and reproductive labour. Paid and unpaid help offered relief for couples who could afford it and, over time, the growing up of children reduced women's pressure. Women were rarely happy with this burden but to varying degrees accepted this double work-day, and structured their business labour around it. Women working at home, after hours, and in online rather than in-shop capacities may have inadvertently contributed to men's increased visibility and view of themselves as in charge of the copreneurial ventures.

CONCLUSION

Our interviews with Czech copreneur couples suggest varied divisions of business labour. Notwithstanding the short timespan within which business ownership has been legal in the CR, we were able to interview 12 thriving businesses, four that involve children to varying degrees. Most of these partners, males and females, described themselves as happy to be their own boss and hoping to avoid becoming an employee in the future. Copreneurs drew on former employment under socialism as well as family and social networks to build successful businesses, and women played significant and often non-traditional roles in these ventures. Consistent with Hamilton's (2006) findings, these narratives revealed that women provided leadership roles in establishing the businesses whether or not they were defined as owner-managers. They also identified areas of Czech law and economy that need further development (for example, increased work flexibility and childcare services). Women's narratives also detailed employment experiences of discrimination and inflexible working arrangements for mothers. Interview responses reflected men and women's acceptance of situations wherein mothers more than fathers are responsible for children's care.

Despite the non-traditional divisions of labour in several businesses, our analysis revealed a tendency for respondents to gender the tasks and responsibilities performed in the business according to the partner's sex category. Usually, women labelled men and men labelled themselves as the more visible or the manager in the business. Women were never recognized by men as in charge, and only one woman recognized herself in this way. The rationales are reflective of traditional stereotypes about divisions of labour that are common in the CR. Kirkwood (2009, p. 382) also concludes that culture is an important barrier for female spouses especially in locations like the CR with little exposure to entrepreneurship. These findings may be a result of a path-dependency associated with Czech family and gender regimes. For many years, both partners' incomes have been necessary for family survival. Yet, the man has exclusively been viewed as the one having the 'career', being the primary breadwinner. For decades, discrimination against women and the underestimation of women's work has been part of the CR labour market structure and family policy (Křížková et al., 2011; Čermáková, 1997). Our study suggests that a consequence of this situation is the strong construction of women copreneurs as secondary in the business even when they began or played a central role in the business. Our findings that divisions of business responsibilities are variable, yet descriptions and justifications of it are repeatedly gendered, are consistent with cultural views in the CR. Czech attitudes are very gender-traditional, although actual practice may be changing due to the ongoing imperative for women and men to engage in paid work. Women must still perform both paid and unpaid work. The paradox is that more than half of the Czech population agrees that women should take care of the children and household, and men should be the breadwinners (Hašková, 2007).

In contrast to work in the business, narratives about the division of housework and childcare reflected a traditionally gendered division. With few exceptions, women performed most or all of the family household labour. They structured business activities around childcare in several ways, leaving men to concentrate on the business. Most women assumed their disproportionate share of the household work resentfully, but also with resignation. Men sought to avoid discussion of what they did around the home, but both men and women described men's housework contributions in traditionally gendered ways: men did the 'heavy' work around the home, 'the man's work'. This is probably also a consequence of the path-dependency of the Czech gender regime where no debate about the need to involve men in housework and childcare occurred either before or after 1989. Housework and childcare is still largely constructed as women's domain.

Importantly, our narrative analysis revealed linguistic mechanisms whereby gender, family and entrepreneurship were interwoven and simultaneously reproduced. Women's work – often made invisible in the narratives – blurred but maintained both business and home functioning. As Lewis and Massey (2011) note, women who have subordinated their role in the business to that of their male partner offered narratives about working full-time in the business and taking care of the household, even if the business work was done after everyone in the house was asleep. Through women's work, men were able to better separate from and focus on the business. Women's work made possible the disembodied male entrepreneur. Consistent with earlier research (Lewis and Massey, 2011; Kirkwood, 2009), stressing the need to incorporate both copreneurs' viewpoints into the research design, we find both complementary and contradictory views about the division of labour and unpack the process whereby gender inequalities and the invisibility of women's work are reproduced.

Despite the long tradition of CR women's labour force participation, our research reveals continued ideologies and practices of gender inequalities among copreneur couples. Yet, it is important not to overstate the differences between the CR and other Western industrialized nations because women entrepreneurs and workers in those nations also experience the burdens of the double work-day and the underestimation or devaluation of women's contributions to both work and family domains. While our future research will offer more systematic comparisons of CR copreneur couple narratives with those of respondents from other nations, the findings we have presented from this study at least begin to address the lack of research on Czech copreneurs.

ACKNOWLEDGEMENT

This chapter was written as part of the research project 'Changes in partnership and family forms and arrangements from the life course perspective' (grant no. P404/10/0021), funded by the Czech Science Foundation and with the support of long-term strategic development of research organization RVO: 68378025 at the Institute of Sociology, Czech Academy of Sciences. We also wish to thank several organizations at Arizona State University, USA that provided funds in support of this research: the Institute for Social Science Research (ISSR), the Global Engagement Fund and the School of Social Transformation.

NOTES

1. The size exception was one firm with approximately 300 employees. We included it in our sample because the 300 employees were scattered over several regional offices owned by the copreneur couple. The central office out of which the firm was run offered an environment similar to that of the smaller firms in our sample. Also this firm began as a small firm, and the owners sought to replicate their original office management strategy for all of their regional offices. Inclusion of this larger firm in our study offers an opportunity to examine a copreneur business that has grown to a large size and to compare it with the mostly smaller businesses that comprise the majority of our sample.
2. Number signifies number of couple interviewed (see Table 12.1), F represents female and M represents male.

REFERENCES

Ahl, H. (2006), 'Why research on women entrepreneurs needs new directions', *Entrepreneurship, Theory and Practice*, 30 (5), 595–621.

Aldrich, H. and Cliff, J. (2003), 'The pervasive effects of family on entrepreneurship: Toward a family embeddedness perspective', *Journal of Business Venturing*, 18 (5), 573–596.

Barnett, F. and Barnett, S. (1988), *Working Together: Entrepreneurial Couples*, Berkeley, CA: Ten Speed Press.

Blenkinsopp, J. and Owens, G. (2010), 'At the heart of things: the role of the "married" couple in entrepreneurship and family business', *International Journal of Entrepreneurial Behaviour and Research*, 16 (5), 357–369.

Bruni, A., Gherardi, S. and Poggio, B. (2005), *Gender and Entrepreneurship*, London: Routledge.

Brush, C. (1992), 'Research on women business owners: past trends, a new perspective and future directions', *Entrepreneurship Theory and Practice*, 16 (4), 5–30.

Čermáková, M. (1997), 'Postavení žen na trhu práce' (Position of women in the labour market), *Sociologický časopis/Czech Sociological Review*, 33 (4), 389–404.

Connell, R.W. (2002), *Gender*, Malden: Blackwell Publishers.

Czech Statistical Office (CZSO) (2011), *Ženy a muži v datech (Women and men in data) 2011*, available at http://www.czso.cz/csu/2011edicniplan.nsf/publ/1417-11-n_2011 (accessed 10 March 2013).

De Bruin, A., Brush, C. and Welter, F. (2007), 'Advancing a framework for coherent research on women's entrepreneurship', *Entrepreneurial Theory and Policy*, 31 (3), 323–339.

Hamilton, E. (2006), 'Whose story is it anyway? Narrative accounts of the role of women in founding and establishing family businesses', *International Small Business Journal*, 24 (3), 253–271.

Hašková, H. (2007), 'Fertility decline, the postponement of childbearing and the increase in childlessness in Central and Eastern Europe: a gender equity approach', in Crompton, R., Lewis, S. and Lyonette, C. (eds), *Women, Men, Work and Family in Europe*, Houndmills: Palgrave Macmillan, pp. 76–85.

Hertz, R. (1997), *Reflexivity and Voice*, Thousand Oaks, CA: Sage.

Hughes, K. and Jennings, J. (2012), *Global Women's Entrepreneurship Research: Diverse Settings, Questions and Approaches*, Cheltenham, UK and Northampton, MA, USA: Edward Elgar Publishing.

Jurik, N. (1998), 'Getting away and getting by: the experiences of self-employed homeworkers', *Work and Occupations*, 25 (1), 7–35.

Jurik, N. (2005), *Bootstrap Dream: US Microenterprise Development in an Era of Welfare Reform*, New York: Cornell University Press.

Kirkwood, J. (2009), 'Spousal roles on motivations for entrepreneurship: a qualitative study in New Zealand', *Journal of Family and Economic Issues*, 30 (4), 372–385.

Křížková, A. (1999), 'The division of labour in Czech households in the 1990s', *Sociologický časopis/Czech Sociological Review*, 7 (2), 205–214.

Křížková, A. (2007), *Životní strategie žen a mužů v řízení (a) podnikání* (Life strategies of women and men in management of/and entrepreneurship), Prague: Institute of Sociology, Academy of Sciences of the Czech Republic.

Křížková, A., Maříková, H., Hašková, H. and Formánková, L. (2011), *Pracovní dráhy žen v České republice* (Working paths of women in the Czech Republic), Prague: SLON.

Křížková, A., Penner, A.M. and Petersen, T. (2010), 'The legacy of equality and the weakness of law: within-job gender wage inequality in the Czech Republic', *European Sociological Review*, 26 (1), 83–95.

Lee, Y., Hong, G. and Rowe, B. (2006), 'Third shift women in business-owning families', *Journal of Family and Economic Issues*, 27 (1), 72–91.

Lewis, K. and Massey, C. (2011), 'Critical yet invisible: the "good wife" in the New Zealand small firm', *International Journal of Gender and Entrepreneurship*, 3 (2), 105–122.

Lituchy, T. and Reavley, M. (2004), 'Women entrepreneurs: a comparison of international small business owners in Poland and the Czech Republic', *Journal of International Entrepreneurship*, 2 (1), 61–87.

Manolova, T.S. and Yan, A. (2002), 'Institutional constraints and entrepreneurial responses in a transforming economy, the case of Bulgaria', *International Small Business Journal*, 20 (2), 163–184.

Mulholland, K. (2003), *Class, Gender and the Family Business*, New York: Palgrave Macmillan Press.

Nordqvist, M., Hall, A. and Melin, L. (2009), 'Qualitative research on family businesses: the relevance and usefulness of the interpretive approach', *Journal of Management and Organization*, 15 (3), 294–308.

Presser, L. (2005), 'Negotiating power and narrative in research: implications for feminist methodology', *Signs: Journal of Women in Culture and Society*, 30 (4), 2067–2090.

Saxonberg, S. and Sirovátka, T. (2006), 'Failing family policy in post-communist Central Europe', *Journal of Comparative Policy Analysis*, 8 (2), 185–202.

Sharma, P. (2004), 'An overview of the field of family business studies: current status and directions for the future', *Family Business Review*, 17 (1), 1–36.

Shelton, L.M. (2006), 'Female entrepreneurs, work–family conflict, and venture performance: new insights into the work–family interface', *Journal of Small Business Management*, 44 (2), 285–297.

Smallbone, D. and Welter, F. (2001), 'The distinctiveness of entrepreneurship in transition economies', *Small Business Economics*, 16 (4), 249–262.

Treanor, L. and Henry, C. (2010), 'Influences on women's entrepreneurship in

Ireland and the Czech Republic', in Brush, C.G., Bruin, A., Gatewood, E.J. and Henry, C. (eds), *Women Entrepreneurs and the Global Environment for Growth. A Research Perspective*, Cheltenham, UK and Northampton, MA, USA: Edward Elgar, pp. 73–95.

Vohlídalová, M. and Formánková, L. (2012), 'Částečné úvazky v České republice: šance nebo riziko?' *Fórum sociální politiky*, 6 (5), 17–21.

Welter, F., Smallbone, D. and Isakova, N.B. (2006), *Enterprising Women in Transition Economies*, Aldershot: Ashgate Publishing.

West, C. and Zimmerman, D. (1987), 'Doing gender', *Gender and Society*, 1 (2), 125–151.

13. Centering Caribbean women's gendered experiences and identities: a comparative analysis of female entrepreneurs in St Lucia and Trinidad and Tobago

Talia Esnard

INTRODUCTION

Changes in the global economy continue to change the face of entrepreneurship throughout the world. One critical development is the increasing access to and participation of women in entrepreneurial activities (Kelley et al., 2010). However, while this growing development translates into encouraging labor market trends, the persistence of gender inequality in access to entrepreneurial opportunities and the peripheral positioning of their experiences remain burning issues for policymakers, feminist advocates, researchers and, most importantly, women in the economy.

In that regard, many studies have substantiated the centrality of gender and related normative assumptions underpinning the masculine nature of entrepreneurship to the experiences of female entrepreneurs (Ahl, 2006; Marlow et al., 2009). Such analyses have indeed made a significant contribution to the increasing visibility of female entrepreneurs in developed societies and to the broader ideologies and corresponding structural and cultural frameworks that underlie their experiences. However, what remains is the indiscernibility of Caribbean research that seeks to widen our understanding of the ways in which female entrepreneurs experience and negotiate gendered discourses and conflicts in the formation of their identities.

As a response to this research gap, and paucity of qualitative research that seeks to deepen our understanding of the relationship between gendered self-employment and work–family conflict (Reynolds and Renzulli, 2005), this chapter attempts to: (1) problematize the meanings and experiences of gendered discourses and conflicts and its effects on negotiations of entrepreneurial identities among female entrepreneurs; and (2) advance discussions on the potential theoretical relevance of feminist social constructivist-rationalist choice frameworks for understanding the complex nature of their identities. In order to do this, the chapter explores the comparative perceptions, experiences and challenges of female entrepreneurs in two Caribbean countries, namely, St Lucia (SLU) and Trinidad and Tobago (T&T). Using a phenomenological research design, the chapter examines the narratives obtained through in-depth interviewing of 15 female entrepreneurs in various industries across the two countries. It is hoped that this centering of Caribbean women's gendered experiences will spark greater examinations and theorizations of female entrepreneurship in the Caribbean and, by extension, encourage further considerations of these experiences in understanding female entrepreneurship across the globe.

CONTEXTUALIZING CARIBBEAN WOMEN'S ENTREPRENEURSHIP

The Caribbean region represents a diversified, fragmented population with small dependent economies (McElroy and Sanborn, 2005) and a shared history of European colonialism (Mintz and Price, 1985) that points to the troubling vulnerability of Caribbean peoples. In the contemporary era, such unfortified political economies have intensified, albeit with varying degrees and magnitude, with the penetration of neoliberal reforms (Klak, 1998) and the related unwavering impact of globalization. In this context of fragility, policymakers have promoted and substantively increased women's participation in their overall entrepreneurial development agenda. It is with this in mind, not disregarding the significance of the collective picture of Caribbean women, that St Lucia and Trinidad and Tobago represent two countries of particular interest.

In the case of Trinidad and Tobago, its lucrative oil and gas sectors, high level of market innovation and contribution to wider regional economic activity have drawn attention to its increasing entrepreneurial activities and potential role as the financial hub of the Caribbean. St Lucia, on the other hand, is characterized by a slow yet growing focus on the diversification of the service industry where women are increasingly concentrated (Government of St Lucia, 2011). Its comparatively greater vulnerability to natural disasters (such as hurricanes) and external economic developments also present an interesting context for assessing women's labor force experiences. Table 13.1 presents a comparative description of the outlooks for the two countries.

Table 13.1 Social and economic profiles of St Lucia and Trinidad and Tobago

Country	Size (square miles)	Population	Racial mix	Sex distribution	Human development rank	Gender ranking for women's participation	Gender gap in established businesses	Gender gap in labor force	Classification by income	Economic mainstay
Trinidad and Tobago	1980	1.3 million	34.2% African 35.4% Indian 22.8% Mixed	50.2% males 49.8% females	62/187	47/135	6%	19–24%	High	Oil and gas
St Lucia	238	166 526	81% African 11.9% Mixed 2.41% East Indian 1% White 3.7% Other	51% females 49% males	82/187	Not available	36%	6%	Middle	Tourism and offshore banking

Sources: Compiled by the author using the following sources: Government of Trinidad & Tobago (2001, 2011, 2012), Government of St Lucia (2001, 2011), Harriott et al. (2012), Murdock et al. (2010).

While both countries have witnessed varying advances in labor force participation and human development, persistent gender gaps in entrepreneurial activities (particularly in St Lucia), gender discrimination, and an absence of a gender-sensitive entrepreneurial policy continue to remain major areas of concern (Reddock and Bobb-Smith, 2008; Association of Caribbean States, 2012). In the case of Trinidad and Tobago, what is evident is that while women appear to be penetrating the established business sector, gender-based differences within the labor force still remain sizable. The reverse appears in St Lucia where the gender differences in the patterns of labor force participation are considerably lower than that which exists for the comparisons within the established business sector. This persistence of gender inequality raises renewed questions on potential dilemmas related to gender vulnerability (Bailey and Ricketts, 2003) and, by extension, the underexplored nexus between gender, work and family and negotiations of these in both countries. However, despite calls for further questioning of socio-historical ideologies, structures and practices that continue to shape female entrepreneurship in the Caribbean (Hart, 1996; Mohammed and Perkins, 1999), 'women's entrepreneurial activities are significantly absent from the literature on women in the Anglophone Caribbean' (Barriteau, 2002, p. 222).

THEORETICAL FRAMEWORK

Feminist-Social Constructivist-Rational Choice Approach

Postmodernist feminist theory has long been used to challenge cultural narratives of gender. Butler's pioneering interrogation and theorization of gender as performative remains central to the broader postmodernist feminist goal of dismantling Cartesian logic that sustains false dichotomies which govern our understandings of gender identities (Leavy, 2007). However, despite research findings that point to the centrality of gender to work and family experiences (Halford and Leonard, 2006; Marlow et al., 2009), few studies in the Caribbean attempt to advance theoretical explorations that question the discursive and situated configurations of gender and entrepreneurship.

In order to fill in this gap, I embrace the explanatory value of the gendered identity construct in the understanding of working selves (Butler, 1990; Salih, 2002). In *Gender Trouble*, Butler (1990, p. 25) espoused that 'identity is performatively constituted by the very expressions that are said to be its results'. In this sense, we all do gender (Marlow and Patton, 2005) as part of our everyday social performance. For Salih (2002, p. 10):

rather than assuming that identities are self-evident and fixed as essentialists do, Butler's (1990) work traces the processes by which identity is constructed within language and discourse; a conjecture that promotes understandings of gender as 'becoming' [or as a process] and performance as 'doing' rather than the ontological state of 'being' [or as an essence].

However, Butler (2004, p. 1) also speaks to the bi-directional nature of 'becoming undone' insofar as 'normative conceptions of gender can undo one's personhood . . . [but can also generate] normative restriction [where] becoming undone can also . . . [serve] to inaugurate a newer one that has greater livability as its aim'.

Halford and Leonard (2006, p. 10) also captured the shifting and complex nature of contexts in their argument that 'as individuals negotiate their identities, they do so in the context of their everyday lives: as they move between the spaces . . . [and] places of their work and home'. In this understanding, 'both women and men use competing discourses, from within and beyond organization life, to take up distinctive positions along an axis from acceptance, via modification, to resistance' (ibid., p. 6). Here, I also take up this non-essentialist notion of 'space' as a physical epitomization of discursive constructions, 'place' as performative, and as 'becoming' with ongoing (re)articulation of macro-social, cultural and economic processes and discourses at multiple levels in particular locales, that define spatial and temporal relations (at the micro level) and the negotiation of identities.

Other researchers declare this process as both constraining and facilitating (Kikooma, 2011) and point to the importance of exploring the role of choice and agency in the negotiations of gender norms and entrepreneurial identities for female entrepreneurs (Evetts, 2000; Kikooma, 2011; Esnard, 2012). In taking this eclectic approach forward and using the analytical lens of gender to center the experiences of Caribbean women, this chapter draws on emerging theoretical issues related to: (1) the nature of the situated contexts; and (2) the negotiations of these in the formation of their entrepreneurial identities. It is hoped that such theorizing will: (1) offer alternative means for addressing important questions of structure, culture and action as it relates to female entrepreneurship; and (2) support further considerations of gendered landscapes and entrepreneurial identities in the Caribbean.

Work–Family Conflict

With the changing nature of economic and social life in the global era and the related increasing penetration of women into the labor force over the last two decades, 'policy discussions and public discourse about the challenges and the importance of integrating work and family life have expanded and attained a degree of visibility that is hard to ignore' (Whitehead et al., 2008, p. 3). Within this dialogue, one of the major points of contention remains that of the incompatibility between work and family roles for female entrepreneurs (Clark, 2000; Reynolds and Renzulli, 2005). In this regard, empirical research embedded within resource scarcity theory points to a dominant understanding of these tensions as one that emerges from clashing demands for scarce time, energy and resources; and psychological flexibility in the performance of the various responsibilities attached to work–family domains (Greenhaus and Beutell, 1985; Voydanoff, 2005). More specifically, researchers point to the empirical relevance of gender norms, psycho-social and cognitive factors to the inherent dynamics of work–family conflict (Clark, 2000; Desrochers and Sargent, 2004).

In the literature on female entrepreneurship, the gendered nature of entrepreneurship remains a major focal point. More specifically, overwhelmingly scholarship suggests that socially constructed ideals of gender and entrepreneurship affect the perception and experiences of female entrepreneurs (Gupta et al., 2009; Eddleston and Powell, 2012). Within this area of research, several scholars have pointed to the primacy of patriarchal structures in relation to assumed normative gender roles, role identity, gender-specific motives and the differentiated responses that these evoke between men and women as they navigate and make decisions surrounding their work and family roles (Porter and Nagarajan, 2005; Ergeneli et al., 2010). Within this vein, research has confirmed that some female entrepreneurs internalize these expectations and make conscious attempts to respond in terms of negotiations of their entrepreneurial activities and identities (Salmenniemi et al., 2011; Eddleston and Powell, 2012). Thus, in balancing of family responsibility with entrepreneurship, women face a growing challenge of negotiating dominant, yet challenging, gender-based discourses of mothering as child-centered (Mohammed and Perkins, 1999) and entrepreneurship as masculine (Mirchandani, 1999; Ahl, 2006). This need to balance the demands of these often conflicting domains inadvertently opens the need for ongoing discussions that go beyond work–family conflict to those that uncover the need for and ways in which women integrate the two (Speakman and Marchington, 2004; Damaske and Gerson, 2008). Such theorizing, however, necessitates an appreciation of the dynamic roles of structural and cultural landscapes in negotiations between the two domains.

Thus, although partially holding on to role balance theory, Grzywacs and Carlson (2010, p. 113) presented a more socially embedded definition of work–family balance as 'accomplishment of role-related expectations that are negotiated and shared between an individual and his or her role-related partners in the work and family domains'. However, while this social conceptualization takes the overriding meaning of balance away from the individual to the interactional aspects of situated contexts, it falls short of embracing more fluid conceptualizations of 'integration' that take into account the atypical ways in which contextual and cognitive factors shape choices and practices of female entrepreneurs. Thus, incomplete understanding of work–family dynamics lingers (Shelton, 2006). What remains is a need for greater research that seeks to unveil the contexts by which they understand and negotiate roles within their work and family life (Emslie et al., 2004).

METHODOLOGY

Phenomenological research designs explore the common meanings in the lived experiences for individuals or 'descriptions of the universal essence' (Creswell, 2013, p. 76). In this study, I aim to provide deeper insights into the dialectical cultural and social walls within which female entrepreneurs engage and cognitively negotiate their identities. In order to achieve this, I engaged in the combined use of purposive and snowball sampling. In the first instance, female entrepreneurs were identified through various government ministries responsible for small enterprise development in the respective countries. These female entrepreneurs then recommended others in similar or varied sectors. In all, 15 Afro-Caribbean women were interviewed about their perceptions and experiences of negotiating their identities. In so doing, questions focused on the what, when, why and how of the meanings, practices and routines of their daily lives that are recreated in their narratives (Halford and Leonard, 2006), while situating them within social and economic contexts. Using pseudonyms, Table 13.2 captures the socio-economic profiles of these interviewees.

Interviews were transcribed, manually coded, inductively and thematically reduced and analyzed (Reissman, 1993; Marshall and Rossman, 1999) with specific statements or quotes as textural descriptions of what was experienced and structural descriptions of how they experienced (Creswell, 2013). In this case, the use of this phenomenological research design underscores the underlying situated contexts and experiences that shape negotiations of embedded work–family conflicts and identities for female entrepreneurs in St Lucia and Trinidad and Tobago. However, two main limitations of this approach are that it negates comparative analysis of male entrepreneurs in both countries and ethnic differences between

Table 13.2 Socio-economic profiles of participants

Interviewees	Country	Industry	Number of employees	Years of establishment	Age	Number of children
Petal	SLU	Floral	5	8	33	1
Lisa	T&T	Marketing	2	5	54	2
Jane	SLU	Media	15	16	51	1
Jessica	SLU	Beauty	10	8	35	1
Samantha	T&T	Food	3	3	28	0
Joan	SLU	Art and craft	2	28	63	2
Chrystal	T&T	Fashion	2	4	32	1
Myrtle	T&T	Entertainment	15	9	26	2
Anna	T&T	Food	3	5	31	2
Virginia	SLU	Textile and garments	23	7	34	2
Georgia	SLU	Textile and garments	18	13	48	3
Natasha	T&T	Body fitness	2	3	28	0
Alicia	T&T	Cosmetics	3	9	36	3
Marcia	SLU	Textile and garments	10	17	55	2
Jewel	SLU	Health	2	4	26	2

female entrepreneurs. Despite these limitations, such exploratory research stimulates needed theorizing and discussions on the complex nature of negotiating identities for female entrepreneurs in the Caribbean.

FINDINGS

The study scrutinized the extent to which gender shaped the entrepreneurial perceptions, experiences, challenges and identities of female entrepreneurs in St Lucia and Trinidad and Tobago. With this focus, the themes were analytical and theoretically grounded around critical experiences that attempt to deepen existing understanding of structural and cultural complexities of female entrepreneurship. By so doing, themes emerged as expressions of the significance or meaning structures of their lived experience and choices as female entrepreneurs. Thus in looking at the data, four key themes emerged: (1) the push and pull factors of female entrepreneurship; (2) entrepreneurship as a gendered space; (3) 'splace' as troubling; and (4) identities as fluid and shifting.

Push and Pull Factors of Female Entrepreneurship

In more recent times, 'the woman becomes an entrepreneur because of the lack of opportunity in the labor market and the need for increasing the family's income' (ACS, 2012, p.18). In the case of this study, most narratives pointed to a salience of socio-economic factors including those of economic necessity and opportunity, the need for autonomy and to translate their passion into economic activity. However, one distinguishing reason that separates the cases of St Lucia and Trinidad and Tobago is the economic outlook of the respective countries. Thus, while many female entrepreneurs in St Lucia cited the 'downturn in the economy', 'growing poverty', 'restricted opportunities in the formal labor market' and the 'need for supplemental income' as push factors, female entrepreneurs in Trinidad and Tobago referred to the 'buoyancy of the local economy', 'noticeable growth of small and medium sized enterprises' (SMEs), and 'the opportunities created' for them therein as critical pull factors. Such comparative differences in the economic rationales for self-employment entry mirror that of the variability in the economic profiles of the two countries and its link to the structural characteristics of female entrepreneurship therein.

Gendered Entrepreneurial Contexts

The social contexts, or what Halford and Leonard (2006) referred to as the 'place' as enacted through performance, also provides compelling insights into the nature of their conflicts and the complex identities which they adopt. More specifically, unlike the touted successful and daring male (Orser et al., 2011), the female entrepreneur is perceived as lacking these qualities and generally inferior (Grandey et al., 2005; Gupta et al., 2009). Mirchandani (1999) also suggested that the masculine norm of entrepreneurship is often used as a yardstick to judge female entrepreneurship. Within such theorizing, women's entrepreneurial activities are relegated to their stereotypical feminine nature, thereby labeling them as substandard to that of men. Findings provide compelling evidence for this assertion.

In that regard, female entrepreneurs in both countries were conscious of these gendered contexts and the effects of such processes on inherent conflicts, the perception of and the broader nature of their entrepreneurial activity. In St Lucia, Joan commented that 'to get respect you have to first be successful or referred to as a prominent business woman with lots of money, companies and employees and, second, take on the challenge of succeeding in a male dominated field'. In Trinidad and Tobago, Samantha suggested that 'there is this perception that a catering operation as small as mine wasn't really seen as a business because you provide a little [small scale] service'. Similarly, Chrystal complained that 'there is a bias in this society that men are more successful than women in business . . . [as] there is no maternal instinct to get in the way'. Here, Chrystal drew on the gendering of women in business where they are personified as feminine insofar as they are associated with traditional gender roles that introduce perceived shortcomings and orientations in the business world. As a case in point, Myrtle stated that 'men still have the advantage . . . they are free to pursue their career while women have to consider their family'. In a similar vein, Anna suggested that this primacy of family relations for women in the Caribbean often overshadows that of their entrepreneurial pursuits. She stated that 'people [in T&T] ignore the reality that you might be successful in what you do, they always look at the social cost of your business . . . they think that you are sacrificing your family and your relationships with them'. Thus, despite the attempt to explore more independent economic 'places', these female entrepreneurs remain constrained by the very constructions that socially define their femininity, and particularly those related to the centrality of the family.

Narratives also provided support for a growing line of research that suggests that the internalization of gender norms shape definitive perceptions of entrepreneurial selves and choices (Evetts, 2000; Esnard, 2012). Jane (SLU) stated that 'my experience as a banker has shown me that men are the ones who take big loans . . . the women tell you that they prefer to squeeze with their personal finance'. In this case, Jane's narrative goes beyond that of awareness to an argument that the internalization of their feminized nature and roles (as expressed in their preferences) predisposes them to avoid taking risks. Jessica reasoned that 'in St Lucia . . . women in business tend to be constrained because they think about their families so they take baby steps . . . but the men . . . they take bolder steps'. This also extends to the cases of female entrepreneurs in Trinidad and Tobago, where four interviewees disclosed a strong fear of failure as indicative of their concerns for risking the asset base of their family. Given such modes of reasoning and assessments of risks as linked to the potential impact on the family, female entrepreneurs who imbibe these perceived orientations and gender-based limitations in both countries accentuated the need for caution, skepticism and conservatism in their entrepreneurial pursuits.

In accounting for the impact of such gendered contexts, many interviewees referred to the patriarchal nature of Caribbean societies. In the case of St Lucia, Virginia expressed that 'I don't like bringing this up but historically a woman would be in a house cooking, cleaning and a man was always seen to go out and work'. In such cases, the cultural perception of women as household managers in the Caribbean creates social hindrances to potential economic success (ACS, 2012). For Virginia, the persistence of such ideology and its clash with more economic or self-reliant attitudes are due to the conservative nature of her St Lucian people and lack of economic opportunities and exposure to more liberated ways of life. She called for some degree of social equality and transformation where women can draw on their own strength and 'to come to the realization that they can do anything'. Momsen (1991) reminded us Caribbean women continue to participate in the labor market despite clear pressures to conform to a Victorian ideology of 'housewifization'. In the case of this study, the narratives suggest that their notion of their entrepreneurial and personal selves both remained constrained by these discursive contexts. This reinforced the persistence of their invisibility, their taken-for-granted attempts to be more resilient and the unique contributions that they make within their entrepreneurial practices.

Drawing on the historicity of Caribbean societies, female entrepreneurs in both countries pondered on the legacies of colonialization. Jessica described how:

> we are still affected by the colonial experience; the notion that its men more than women, tie and coat versus dressing casual in business, being Caucasian or Indian rather than being black, having a foreign accent rather than a local one. What I found in my experience in starting the business is that when I state my name one of the first things I get is, 'I thought you were white when I heard your name'. Next question I get is, 'Are you married to a white man?'

Jessica's reflection points to a complex interplay between broader stratifying notions of race, gender, class and ethnocentrism in relation to the perceptions and experiences of female entrepreneurs in Trinidad and Tobago. Though beyond the objectives of this chapter such findings direct attention to needed theorizing of female entrepreneurship that takes into consideration the ways in which post-coloniality intersects with other stratifying factors to shape female entrepreneurs' social and occupational mobility. Drawing a cultural parallel, Joan (SLU) claimed that while her culture has predisposed her to being self-reliant, the St Lucian culture promotes the very opposite. She stated that 'since I am American I have a very independent attitude . . . but I find it hard to employ people . . . if you treat those like you have a stick and you are "massa" [master] then they perform'. While at a comparative level, the peculiarities of the colonial experience that define the social structure of these two countries introduce some qualitative differences in their explanations, these narratives bring to bear the perceived relevance of an enslaved colonial history and mindset to gendered contexts (Brereton, 1992) and its marginalizing effects on female entrepreneurs (Browne, 2001). Such historicized realities and its stratifying effects within entrepreneurial spaces and places remains insubstantial in Caribbean literature.

'Splace' as Troubling

Using gender as an analytical lens, Halford and Leonard (2006) advanced notions of 'space' as physical epitomizations of discursive constructions and 'place' as performative. In attempting to move between the spaces of home and work, these female entrepreneurs face ongoing dialectical confrontations related to dominant yet conflicting gender discourses embedded within specific situated 'performative places'. In navigating what I call 'splace', these female entrepreneurs drew attention to the incompatible and troubling nature of their experiences. While interviewees located the dominant discourses of femininity within the home, they expressed growing concern for contradictions that emerged once these feminine values were transferred into masculine spaces of entrepreneurship. Such contradictions forced these entrepreneurs to rethink the gendered nature of their expressions and actions based on the perceived incompatibility between work and family spaces and places.

In St Lucia, Alicia stated that:

> during the busy periods I found myself going home late . . . my ex . . . started to tell me that I did not have enough time for him . . . and that he will not support this business once he has to make up for me being absent from home . . . and I felt really bad.

Jessica also stated that her business ventures affected family relations. In providing a critical instance in which this occurred, Jessica revealed that 'one day . . . [my] daughter told me that I don't spend time with [her] . . . it is always a rush-rush . . . she doesn't see me at nights anymore – that touched me!'

In Trinidad, Lisa revealed that 'I try to balance the two but to be honest one or the other suffers especially my marriage'. Myrtle reported that 'at one time I used to think that my husband was jealous . . . [and although he denied it] . . . the comments after I do an event tell me otherwise'. In all instances, while these women attempted to defy and integrate the expected norms related to practicing their femininity with those of their self-reliant endeavors, they remain continuously burdened by discursive separation of the two spheres. These experiences provide undeniable support for Momsen's (1991, p. 1) argument that 'Caribbean gender relations are a double paradox: of patriarchy within a system of . . . matrifocal families; and of domestic ideology co-existing with the economic independence of women'.

In accounting for these conflicts, Jane stated that 'some men believe that regardless of race and even some measure of level headedness, women have inherited a subservient nature . . . but they have also failed to realise that a lot of influence come from the male dominance in terms of where they put us'. Likewise, Samantha stressed that 'even though a lot of women are educated, they seem to fall back into motherhood and, as such, struggle for time when they are also in business'. These interviewees underscored that while they continue to pursue economic autonomy, they were also curtailed by prevailing norms surrounding mothering, gender identity, and relations within work and family domains.

As a way of coping with these dilemmas, the women also made conscious decisions based on their assessments of these challenges. For example, they drew on the need for strategic planning. Georgia suggested that 'you have to plan ... so if you know you want to have kids then you need to draw up a financial plan for having a nanny ... or have good friends and family members cause you are going to need the help'. Marcia attempted to decentralize her family and work responsibilities: 'I try to balance by using my sales reps and I delegate so that I can spend time with my children'. Jewel plans her activities around the demands of husband and children. She stated: 'seek alternative care for children and work with your femininity and embody that type of business that complements it'.

It is important to recognize that within such situations these women exercised agency in both their compliance and their resistance to gender norms (Martin, 2006) and as an indication of their political capacity or resistive potential (Leavy, 2007). This provides an avenue for both doing and undoing gender (Butler, 1990; Jeanes, 2007) and has significant implications for theory and policy. Foremost is the need for greater research that makes a focal point of the effect of patriarchal ideals and gender norms on the entrepreneurial experiences, particularly in Caribbean contexts.

Identities as Fluid and Shifting

Gendered discourses and contexts serve as both constraining and facilitating factors. In 'doing gender', narratives revealed that interviewees moved along a continuum from performing femininity to masculinity dependent on the salience of these values and the contexts in which they were evoked. More specifically, most interviewees saw their femininity as an advantage insofar as it allowed them to solicit greater responses from their male counterparts and to tap into feminine industries that serve the interests of those who they can relate to at a personal and business level. Jessica declared that 'I do business in a woman's world [image enhancement] and more than eighty [percent] of my clients are women'. Beyond that, other interviewees saw the sexualized nature of their femininity as a powerful political tool in negotiating entry and acceptance into this male dominated space. Natasha reported that 'I think being a woman it's a plus, because in this [sporting] industry ... if you think as an entrepreneur and use your womanhood to make money, men are more willing to help you and they don't see you as a threat. So I'm using that to my advantage'. In Trinidad and Tobago, Chrystal suggested that 'our culture is one where men sexualize their encounters with women and if a young attractive woman comes in for a loan they read the documents but it is very likely that his attraction to her will influence his decision'. Thus, in giving meaning to her experience and by extension understanding of female entrepreneurship, Chrystal and Natasha stressed the perceived relevance of feminized sexuality to entrepreneurial engagement.

In contrast, some interviewees also pointed to the ways in which sexualized notions of femininity introduced sources of conflict within their business ventures. Jewel (SLU) complained that men see massages as a sexual experience and, thus, they 'have no respect for the business or me ... and [demand] that I provide sensual massages and that is not what my business is about'. Similarly, Angel stated that 'sometimes when my male clients come in ... they make ... sexual advances before they can decide whether or not to buy ... [this] always bothers me'. In both cases, these female entrepreneurs remain troubled by the sexualized expressions and expectations of femininity in their work 'space'. Thus, performing or 'doing gender' (Powell et al., 2009) as constituted through the saying, doing and relating (Martin, 2006) embedded in their narratives, these female entrepreneurs not only accepted the sexualization of their entrepreneurial identities but performed it based on the situation. In this sense, these normative restrictions indirectly define understanding of their entrepreneurial selves.

As a way of coping with such gendered contexts, some female entrepreneurs also attempted to undo gender, that is, they rejected expected feminine values and replaced them strategically with masculine ones. More specifically, in responding to the stereotypes of women, they consciously internalized the masculine discourses of entrepreneurship and transferred that to their entrepreneurial behavior. In adopting masculine entrepreneurial identity traits Natasha commented that 'when women are in business they tend to replace the soft side with a tough one. This is purely for survival'. In St Lucia, Jane commented that 'women must demand respect by being assertive and less emotional if they need to be recognized as serious businesspersons'. In both cases, the need for social alignment to what Wenger (1998, cited by Warren, 2004) referred to as the community of practice or perceived masculine nature of entrepreneurship resulted in the strategic rejection of these feminized notions of women; in this sense, to think entrepreneurship is indeed to think male (Marlow et al., 2009). Here, 'doing gender involves a complex of socially guided perceptual, interactional and micro political activities that cast particular pursuits as expressions of masculine and feminine natures' (West and Zimmerman, 1987 cited by Powell et al., 2009, p. 414).

DISCUSSION

The relevance of gender to entrepreneurial identities remains a growing yet underdeveloped area of research. By examining the effects of situated gender contexts and discourses on female entrepreneurship in the Caribbean, this chapter adds to and empirically widens discussions of entrepreneurship as a gendered profession (Lewis, 2006; Gupta et al., 2009; Orser et al., 2011). The findings illustrate that in both countries these women are not only conscious of the normative historicized and gendered contexts and its implications of their experiences, but also respond to the weight of these norms in the formation or negotiating of a gendered entrepreneurial identity (either through acceptance or rejection of gender as enacted through performance). The findings of this study also show that they shift between these gender identities based on the place that they occupy at any one point in time (that being, entrepreneurial and familial) and the peculiarities of space (that is, in St Lucia and Trinidad and Tobago). Thus, 'while women are becoming undone in a good way and breaking barriers about womanhood by entering male dominated arenas, they are simultaneously becoming undone in a bad way, when their gender is disqualified as a condition for their success in that area' (Powell et al., 2009, p. 413). Thus, future research could further explore the complex processes within which female entrepreneurs continuously and dialectically (de)shift and (re)negotiate their identities as they navigate between entrepreneurial and familial spaces.

Theoretically, this chapter shows how situated contexts serve as macro social structures in which female entrepreneurs act as what Porter (1995) calls interpretive agents in the negotiations of their complex identities. Such rationalized responses provide growing evidence in support of the relevance and validity of the social constructivist feminist-rational choice perspective in the understanding of gender and entrepreneurship. Future research could therefore further problematize situated gendered contexts, its effects on female entrepreneurs throughout the Caribbean region, and the varied ways in which they respond. It is also important to support special policies and programs that encourage female entrepreneurs to employ their unique practices (Gupta et al., 2009) en route to promoting empowerment of female entrepreneurs in both St Lucia and Trinidad and Tobago.

CONCLUSION

Multiple contradictions and ambiguities make 'doing gender' difficult to deconstruct (Powell et al., 2009). In the case of this chapter, the central contribution is that as these female entrepreneurs move between the cultural and economic walls of entrepreneurship and family, they increasingly face troubling dilemmas related to socially and historically embedded dominant discourses of gender that vary depending on the splace and the salience of this combination for women and those who assess them. As a way of negotiating these conflicts, female entrepreneurs in both countries consciously and actively worked along a continuum of gendered entrepreneurial identities based on the situation or space; the primacy of socially appropriate gender values and roles; and broader structural, socio-political and economic realities of post-colonial societies like the Caribbean. Such findings point to taken-for-granted paradoxes of female entrepreneurship and the theoretical importance of questioning contexts, cognitive processes and responses, and coping strategies in the formation of gender-based policies focused on reducing social and economic inequalities. Moving forward it must also be acknowledged that the complexities and ambiguities of female entrepreneurship require further questioning of the roles of historicity, temporality and the intersectionality of race, class, gender and choice. Future research could attempt to unpack these intricacies and the outcomes of such processes and structures for understanding experiences, meaning and action located therein. Such research could reveal the coping strategies, unique entrepreneurial practices and necessary support systems required for effective engagement and integration of entrepreneurial activities. Such examinations and deeper understanding may present useful insights and greater appreciation of the contextual and dynamic nature of female entrepreneurship across the globe.

REFERENCES

Ahl, H. 2006. 'Why research on women entrepreneurs needs new directions', *Entrepreneurship Theory and Practice*, 30 (5), 595–622.

Association of Caribbean States (ACS). 2012. Report on women's entrepreneurial participation in the Greater Caribbean countries. 27th Meeting of the Special Committee on Trade Development and External Economic Relations. Port of Spain, Trinidad and Tobago, 11–12 July, http://www.acs-aec.org/sites/default/files/women_entrepreneurs_inf.009_eng.pdf, accessed 17 January 2013.

Bailey, B. and Ricketts, H. 2003. 'Gender vulnerabilities in Caribbean labour markets and decent work provisions', *Social and Economic Studies*, 52 (4), 49–81.

Barriteau, E. 2002. 'Women entrepreneurs and economic marginality: rethinking

Caribbean economic relations', in P. Mohammed (ed.), *Gendered Realities: Essays in Caribbean Feminist Thought*, University of the West Indies Press, Kingston, Jamaica, pp. 212–248.

Brereton, B. 1992. 'Searching for the Invisible Woman', *Slavery and Abolition*, 13 (2), 86–96.

Browne, K. 2001. 'Female entrepreneurship in the Caribbean: a multisite, pilot investigation of gender and work', *Human Organization*, 60 (4), 326–342.

Butler, J. 1990. *Gender Trouble: Feminism and the Subversion of Identity*, New York: Routledge.

Butler, J. 2004. *Undoing Gender*, Abingdon: Routledge.

Clark, S.C. 2000. 'Work/family border theory: A new theory of work/family balance', *Human Relations*, 53 (6), 747–770.

Creswell, W.J. 2013. *Qualitative Inquiry and Research Design: Choosing among Five Traditions*, 3rd edn, Los Angeles, CA: Sage.

Damaske, S. and Gerson, K. 2008. 'Viewing 21st century motherhood through a work–family lens', in Korabik, K., Lero, D.S. and Whitehead, D.L. (eds), *Handbook of Family Work Integration: Research, Theory and Best Practices*, London: Academic Press, pp. 233–248.

Desrochers, S. and Sargent, L.D. 2004. 'Boundary/border theory and work-life family integration', *Organizational Management Journal*, 1 (1), 40–48.

Eddleston, A.K. and Powell, G.N. 2012. 'Nurturing entrepreneurs' work–life balance: a gendered perspective', *Entrepreneurship Theory and Practice*, 36 (3), 513–541.

Emslie, C., Hunt, K. and Macintyre, S. 2004. 'Gender, work–home conflict, and morbidity amongst white-collar bank employees in the United Kingdom', *International Journal of Behavioral Medicine*, 11 (3), 127–134.

Ergeneli, A., Ilsev, A. and Karapinar, B.P. 2010. 'Work–family conflict and job satisfaction relationship: the roles of gender and interpretive habits', *Gender, Work and Organization*, 17 (6), 679–695.

Esnard, T. 2012. 'The personal plan is just as important as the business plan: a feminist social constructivist-rational approach to female entrepreneurship', *Journal of the Motherhood Initiative*, 3 (1), 168–181.

Evetts, J. 2000. 'Analyzing change in women's careers: culture, structure and action dimensions', *Gender, Work and Organization*, 7 (1), 57–67.

Government of St Lucia (GOSL) 2001. 'Labor force statistics', Department of Statistics, GOSL, Castries.

Government of St Lucia (GOSL) 2011. '2010 Population and Housing Census: preliminary report', Department of Statistics, Castries.

Government of Trinidad and Tobago (GOTT) 2001. 'Labour force report, 2001', Central Statistics Office, Port of Spain.

Government of Trinidad and Tobago (GOTT) 2011. 'Labour force report, 2011', Central Statistics Office, Port of Spain.

Government of Trinidad and Tobago (GOTT) 2012. 'Trinidad and Tobago 2011 Population and Housing Census: demographic report', Central Statistics Office, Port of Spain.

Grandey, A.A., Cordeiro, B.L. and Crouter, A.C. 2005. 'A longitudinal and multi-source test of work–family conflict and job satisfaction', *Journal of Occupational and Organizational Psychology*, 78 (3), 305–323.

Greenhaus, H.J. and Beutell, J.N. 1985. 'Sources of conflict between work and family roles', *Academy of Management Review*, 10 (1), 76–88.

Grzywacs, G.J. and Carlson, D.S. 2010. 'Conceptualizing work–family balance: implications for practice and research', *Advances in Developing Human Resource*, 9 (4), 455–471.

Gupta, K.V., Turban, B.D., Wasti, S.A. and Sikdar, A. 2009. 'The role of gender stereotypes in perceptions of entrepreneurs and intentions to become an entrepreneur', *Entrepreneurship Theory and Practice*, 33 (2), 397–417.

Halford, S. and Leonard, P. (eds) (2006). *Negotiating Gendered Identities at Work: Place, Space and Time*, New York: Palgrave Macmillan.

Harriott, A., Munoz, H., Justiano, F., Fabiancic, N. and Mercado, L. 2012. *Caribbean Human Development Report*, New York: United Nations Development Programme.

Hart, K. 1996. *Women and the Sexual Division of Labour in the Caribbean*, Kingston, Jamaica: Canoe Press.

Jeanes, E.L. 2007. 'The doing and undoing of gender: the importance of being a credible female victim', *Gender, Work and Organization*, 14 (6), 552–571.

Kelley, J.D, Brush, G.C., Greene, G.P. and Litovsky, Y. 2010. 'Global entrepreneurship monitor. 2010 women's report', Center for Women's Business Research and Center for Women's Leadership, Babson.

Kikooma, J. 2011. 'Negotiating enterprising identities: African woman entrepreneur stories of challenge, perseverance and triumph', *China–USA Bulletin Review*, 10 (7), 573–586.

Klak, T. (ed.). 1998. *Globalization and Neo-Liberalism: The Caribbean Context*, Lanham, MD: Littlefield Publishers.

Leavy, L.P. 2007. 'Feminist postmodernism and post structuralism', in Hesse-Biber, S.N. (ed.), *Feminist Research Practice*, Thousand Oaks, CA: Sage, pp. 83–108.

Lewis, P. 2006. 'The quest for invisibility: female entrepreneurs and the masculine norm of entrepreneurship', *Gender, Work and Organization*, 13 (5), 453–469.

Marlow, S., Henry, C. and Carter, S. 2009, 'Exploring the impact of gender upon women's business ownership: introduction', *International Small Business Journal*, 27 (2), 139–148.

Marlow, S. and Patton, D. 2005. 'All credit to men? Entrepreneurship, finance and gender', *Entrepreneurship Theory and Practice*, 29 (6), 717–735.

Marshall, C. and Rossman, G.B. (eds) 1999. *Designing Qualitative Research*, 3rd edn, Thousand Oaks, CA: Sage.

Martin, P.Y. 2006. 'Practising gender at work: further thoughts on reflexivity', *Gender, Work and Organization*, 13 (3), 254–276.

McElroy, L.J. and Sanborn, K. 2005. 'The propensity for dependence in small Caribbean and specific islands', *Bank of Valletta Review*, 31, 1–16.

Mintz, S. and Price, S. 1985. *Caribbean Contours*. Johns Hopkins Studies in Atlantic History and Culture, Johns Hopkins University Press, Michigan.

Mirchandani, K. 1999. 'Feminist insight on gendered work: new directions in research on women and entrepreneurship', *Gender, Work and Organization*, 64 (4), 224–235.

Mohammed, P. and Perkins, A. 1999. *Caribbean Women at the Crossroads: The Paradox of Motherhood among Women in Barbados, St Lucia and Dominica*, Kingston, Jamaica: Canoe Press.

Momsen, J. 1991. 'Introduction', *Women and Change in the Caribbean: A Pan-Caribbean Perspective*, Kingston, Jamaica: Ian Randle Publishers.

Murdock, A.K., McDonald, C., Joseph, J., Edwards, A. and Carillo, G.M. 2010.

'Global entrepreneurship monitor: Trinidad and Tobago Report', Port of Spain: European Union.

Orser, J.B., Elliott, C. and Leck, J. 2011. 'Feminist attributes and entrepreneurial identity', *Gender in Management: An International Journal*, 26 (8), 561–589.

Porter, D.J. 1995. 'Scenes from childhood: the homesickness of development discourses', in Crush, J. (ed.), *Power of Development*, London: Routledge, pp. 61–84.

Porter, G.E. and Nagarajan, K.V. 2005. 'Successful women entrepreneurs as pioneers: results from a study conducted in Karaikudi, Tamil Nadu, India', *Journal of Small Business and Entrepreneurship*, 18 (1), 39–52.

Powell, A., Bagilhole, B. and Dainty, A. 2009. 'How women engineers do and undo gender: consequences for gender equality', *Gender, Work and Organizations*, 16 (4), 11–428.

Reddock, E.R. and Bobb-Smith, Y. 2008. 'Reconciling work and family: issues and policies in Trinidad and Tobago, No. 18', Geneva: International Labour Organization.

Reissman, C.K. 1993. *Narrative Analysis*, Newbury Park, CA: Sage.

Reynolds, J. and Renzulli, L.A. 2005. 'Economic freedom or self-imposed strife: work–life conflict, gender and self-employment', in Keister, A.L. (ed.), *Entrepreneurship: Research in the Sociology of Work*, Vol. 15, Netherlands, Elsevier, pp. 33–62.

Salih, S. 2002. *Judith Butler*, London: Routledge.

Salmenniemi, S., Karhunen, P. and Kosonen, R. 2011. 'Between business and byt: experiences of women entrepreneurs in contemporary Russia', *Europe–Asia Studies*, 63 (1), 77–98.

Shelton, M.L. 2006. 'Female entrepreneurs – work–family conflict and venture performance: new insights into work–family interface,' *Journal of Small Business Management*, 44 (2), 285–297.

Speakman, S. and Marchington, M. 2004. 'The bounded workplace: defence, development and domestication strategies amongst male shift-workers', *Industrial Relations Journal*, 35 (2), 122–138.

Voyandoff, P. 2005. 'Towards a conceptualization of perceived work–family fit and balance: a demand and resource approach', *Journal of Marriage and Family*, 67 (4), 822–836.

Warren, L. 2004. 'Negotiating entrepreneurial identity: communities of practice and changing discourses', *International Journal of Entrepreneurship and Innovation*, 5 (2), 25–37.

Wenger, E. 1998. *Communities of Practice: Learning, Meaning and Identity*, New York: Cambridge University Press.

West, C. and Zimmerman, D. 1987. 'Doing gender', *Gender and Society*, 1 (2), 125–151.

Whitehead, L.D., Korabik, K. and Lero, S.D. 2008. 'Work–family integration: introduction and overview', in Whitehead, L.D., Korabik, K. and Lero, S.D. (eds), *Handbook of Work–Family Integration: Research, Theory and Best Practices*, London: Academic Press, pp. 3–12.

14. Self-employment and motherhood: the case of Poland
Ewa Lisowska

INTRODUCTION

With the rise in women's level of education and their increasing aspirations to achieve economic independence, owning a business is increasingly being perceived in Poland as an alternative to wage employment, attractive for its financial advantages (EC, 2010). It appears that for well-educated women, launching their own company may be easier than trying to break through the glass ceiling on the path to managerial positions (Buttner and Moore, 1997; Lisowska, 2004). This shift follows a similar move in Canada and the United States where women are increasingly resigning from paid employment in big corporations and starting their own businesses (Mattis, 2005). Reasons for this phenomenon include: receiving lower remuneration than their male counterparts, being passed over for promotion, having their needs and expectations ignored by employers, a lack of initiatives around achieving a work–life balance, and personal development (Mattis, 2005; Hewlett and Luce, 2005).

In Poland 78 per cent of women managers surveyed in 2010 described their place of work as gender-unequal: women got lower pay than men, women were overlooked for promotions, they needed to be much better than men in order to gain the same level of esteem, and employers did not care about creating a working environment that allowed women to combine work with family life (Bilińska and Rawłuszko, 2011). It would appear that the typical place of work in Poland conforms to male needs and is organized in such a way that it accommodates the capabilities and expectations of men (for example, hierarchy, control, power, high earnings) but not of women (for example, cooperation, flexibility, freedom from gender stereotypes).

According to research studies on women entrepreneurs in Poland, women decide to take up self-employment in order to more effectively use the knowledge, skills and experience they have gained; and to have the freedom to determine their tasks and hours of work (Lisowska, 1997). In people's perceptions, self-employment also provides the opportunity to more easily reconcile paid work and childcare.

This chapter discusses the phenomenon of women's entrepreneurship in Poland through a period of political and economic transition and (using data from surveys conducted in 2011) specifically focuses on the issue of balancing work and family responsibilities. The objective of this analysis is to answer the following questions: How do contemporary self-employed women in Poland cope with childcare? What are their expectations for combining economic activity with family responsibilities? And does having one's own business reduce this potential role conflict?

THE CONTEXT: ECONOMIC TRANSITION

The recent phenomenon of women's entrepreneurship in Poland can be traced back to the beginning of the 1990s. In 1989, a crucial systemic transformation took place as Poland entered the road leading to democracy and a market economy. On the one hand, the period of transformation threatened employed women with the possibility of losing their jobs and privileges, while on the other, it created opportunities for launching their own businesses.

The first companies to go bankrupt due to the economic transition were light industry enterprises that employed mainly low-educated female workers: seamstresses, weavers and dressmakers. Next were the foreign trade head offices that employed mainly well-educated women. The unemployed population grew dynamically (from about 56000 in January 1990 to over 2 million in December 1991); women constituted a majority of this population (51 per cent in 1990, and 55 per cent in 1991). The changes observed in the labour market in Poland in the first years of transformation have also been observed in other countries, and have been referred to as 'transitional' unemployment (Boeri, 1994; OECD, 1994). This period was marked by low mobility of workers, particularly in the case of women, and also by a strong territorial differentiation in terms of employment and unemployment (Kotowska, 1997).

As leaving unemployment and finding a job in the formal sector was much more difficult for women than for men, many women decided to take up self-employment (Lisowska, 2004). From 1990 to 1997, the rate of growth in the number of the companies set up by women was decidedly higher than the respective rate for men. In 1993, the number of self-employed persons, excluding private agriculture, was three times higher than in 1985, while in the case of women it was five times higher (Lisowska, 2004).

PRESENT CONTEXT

Self-employment as a form of occupational activity is viewed quite positively in Poland. In a 2007 survey of a representative sample of adult female Poles, over half declared that it was better to own a business than to work as an employee (Lisowska, 2008). According to the 2012 Global Entrepreneurship Monitor (GEM), entrepreneurial intentions to start a business are higher in Poland than in the United States, the United Kingdom or Sweden (GEM, 2012).

GEM 2012 results show that there is greater interest in starting and owning businesses in countries with a higher Power Distance Index (Hofstede and Hofstede, 2005). In countries with a high Power Distance Index, human relationships are based on a hierarchic order, subordination and the observance of particular rules regulating the functioning within organizations. In such environments entrepreneurial individuals feel stifled; they are not able to develop to their full potential, therefore they decide to set up their own businesses. Poland is among those countries with a high value on the Power Distance Index (GEM, 2012). According to the annual World Bank Doing Business survey, it is also a country where launching and growing a company is relatively difficult. Poland sits 55th among the 185 countries that were analysed on this dimension (Doing Business, 2013).

Poland is also one of the GEM countries with a high percentage of companies that have been established out of necessity, and it has the largest percentage of male entrepreneurs compared to female entrepreneurs. Over twice as many men as women are engaged in a new business in Poland (GEM, 2012).

SELF-EMPLOYMENT OF WOMEN IN POLAND: STATISTICAL DATA

According to the Labor Force Survey (first quarter of 2012), the population of self-employed in Poland comprises slightly over 3 million (non-agricultural sector and agriculture together), with women comprising slightly over 1 million (LFS, 2012). Thus, women constitute some 34 per cent of the total number of self-employed. Poland is one of the leading European countries with regard to the proportion of women entrepreneurs,

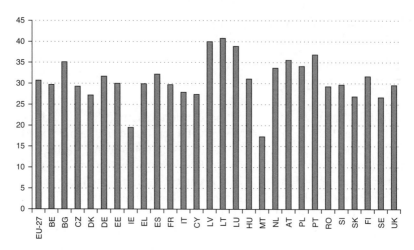

Note: BE – Belgium; BG – Bulgaria; CZ – Czech Republic; DK – Denmark; DE – Germany; EE – Estonia; IE – Ireland; EL – Greece; ES – Spain; FR – France; IT – Italy; CY – Cyprus; LV – Latvia; LT – Lithuania; LU – Luxembourg; HU – Hungary; MT – Malta; NL – Netherlands; AT – Austria; PL – Poland; PT – Portugal; RO – Romania; SI – Slovenia; SK – Slovakia; FI – Finland; SE – Sweden; UK – United Kingdom.

Source: Own calculation based on Eurostat (2012, p. 6).

Figure 14.1 Percentage of women aged 15 years and older among all self-employed persons in EU countries, 2011

alongside countries such as Lithuania, Latvia, Luxembourg, Austria, Bulgaria and Portugal (see Figure 14.1). Regarding the percentage of business women who hire employees, Poland is one of the highest in Europe (comprising 30 per cent), along with Latvia (34 per cent) and Bulgaria (31 per cent) (GEM, 2012). The population of employing business owners in Poland comprises 642 000 people, including 188 000 women (LFS, 2012).

From Figure 14.2 it can be seen that the self-employed in Poland are mainly persons aged 35–44 years (26 per cent of men and 30 per cent of women), and 45–54 years (29 per cent of men and 29 per cent of women). In Poland, it is relatively rare for either women or men to launch a business immediately after completing their education (PARP, 2011). In terms of the ratio of women entrepreneurs to employed women, Figure 14.3 illustrates that this ratio is lowest for women aged 29 and under, and highest for women aged 60 and over.

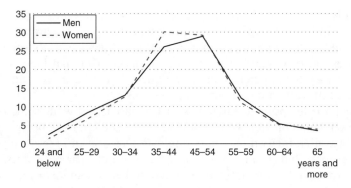

Source: Own calculation based on Eurostat (2012, p. 147).

Figure 14.2   Percentage of self-employed women and men, by age in Poland

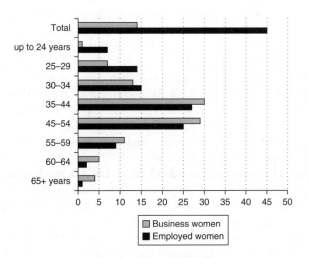

Source: Own calculation based on Eurostat (2012, p. 147).

Figure 14.3   Percentage of business women (entrepreneurs) and employed women, by age in Poland

PRIOR RESEARCH

Prior research has investigated the self-employment of women in Poland both because of a basic interest in the phenomenon and also to develop appropriate socio-economic policy. Entrepreneurship is perceived as a typically masculine activity and, therefore, it is of interest to discover why women decide to set up businesses. In particular, prior research has been interested in determining whether the actions of women establishing new ventures are precipitated by 'pull' or 'push' motivational factors; what barriers they encountered when they launched their businesses; and what hindered the further development of their businesses.

Much of this prior research was survey-based, and while some of the surveys focused only on women (and are rather descriptive), other survey-based research focused on comparing men and women in terms of: their demographic and social characteristics; the size of their businesses; their access to capital; their motivation to undertake self-employment; and the barriers they encountered, both at start-up and later in the firm's history.

Research on Women Entrepreneurs in Poland

The first two surveys on women's entrepreneurship in Poland were initiated in 1991 and 1993. Using quantitative surveys, these studies explored self-employed women in large cities, because this is where women business owners are more numerous. The 1991 survey covered 290 women business owners from Warsaw, while the 1993 survey dealt with 100 women business owners from the area of Gdansk, Lodz and Warsaw (Masłyk-Musiał and Lisowska, 1997). Subsequently, in 1994–1995, in-depth interviews were conducted with 40 company owners in Warsaw and Chicago (Ben-Yoseph et al., 1997). The main conclusion from this qualitative Polish-American cross-cultural research was that 'there are more similarities than differences between American and Polish women business owners' (Ben-Yoseph et al., 1997, p. 107). Similarities were found with respect to the goals and reasons for business start-ups, management styles and, in the case of women, the inseparable connection between their business and family and personal life. Differences were found in terms of educational backgrounds, work experiences and business skills.

Comparative-Based Research on Women and Men Entrepreneurs

A quantitative survey conducted by the Warsaw School of Economics in 1995 was the first to compare female and male entrepreneurs in Poland in terms of their motivations to start a business and the barriers they faced. The sample consisted of 1050 entrepreneurs, of which 305 (including 143 women) completed the survey (Lisowska, 1995, 1997). The results of this survey confirmed findings from the 1970s, 1980s and the beginning of the 1990s from Western developed countries (Buttner and Moore, 1997; Hisrich and Brush, 1986). The main factors motivating women to launch their own company were to: gain autonomy and independence; gain reasonable earnings; achieve flexibility in balancing work and family life; and to escape the glass ceiling. In particular, females over 40 years of age appeared to become self-employed to escape the glass ceiling; while women under 40 wanted to run their own business with the objective of creating personal wealth and having an influence on their business strategy (see also Still, 2005).

Women's motivations to launch their own businesses can be discussed in terms of 'pull' and 'push' factors (Hughes, 2003; Orhan, 2005). 'Pull' factors to set up one's own business include: a desire for independence, the opportunity to earn money, an innate spirit of enterprise and an inclination to take a risk. 'Push' factors towards self-employment include income maintenance, unemployment, redundancy and a lack of career and job prospects (glass ceiling). The desire for a work–family balance, family obligations (for example, inheriting a business from a husband or father) or to find a fit with domestic commitments may also be included as 'push' factors (Kariv, 2013). In Poland 'push' factors appear to apply more often to women, while 'pull' factors appear to apply more often to men. This was true in the 1990s (Lisowska, 1997) and still proves true in contemporary Polish surveys (PARP, 2011).

Barriers to entrepreneurship in Poland identified in earlier surveys (Lisowska, 1997; PARP, 2011) were mainly of an economic nature (for example, high taxes, high cost of labour, problems with obtaining new customers and a lack of access to capital), or as the result of administrative deterrents (for example, complicated formalities and procedures, and frequent changes in the legislation regulating economic activity). Other barriers noted include access to knowledge and training and, in the case of women, additional socio-cultural barriers (Hisrich and Brush, 1984; Lisowska, 2004; GEM, 2012).

Opinions of the entrepreneurs participating in a 2005 survey (500 women and 500 men) indicated that owning a business was connected with a feeling of success and satisfaction, but also with risk. Women entrepreneurs were more satisfied with their achievements in managing their companies than were men entrepreneurs. They were also more likely to choose the same career again than men: 91 per cent compared to 68 per cent (Raport 16, 2006).

In 2011, women and men in Poland had similar assessments of their chances for entrepreneurship, yet men perceived their capabilities as higher than women's, and women's fear of failure was clearly stronger (GEM, 2012). It should be noted, however, that cultural factors in Poland appear to have less of an impact on the decision to launch one's own business among the youngest generation of women, compared to older generations. It appears that young Polish women are not afraid of taking a risk; they have higher self-esteem than their mothers' generation and a stronger belief in themselves and their skills. Yet, as discussed earlier, younger women are not pursuing self-employment at the same rate as older women in Poland. Why young women are less likely to set up their own businesses is an interesting question. Could it possibly be connected with motherhood? In the following section past research related to this question is discussed prior to presenting an examination of the latest research results available in Poland.

SELF-EMPLOYMENT AND WORK–LIFE BALANCE

There have only been a few prior studies in Poland that have asked whether self-employment allows women greater flexibility in combining work and family responsibilities; in particular, whether it facilitates childcare and motherhood. One such study was a survey undertaken in 2004–2005 by Matysiak and Mynarska (2012, p. 1), which found that self-employment 'can become an attractive option for women after they have children because of the flexibility it offers'.

A subsequent survey conducted in 2005[1] reported that for a majority of business owners (68 per cent of men and 57 per cent of women), their family responsibilities did not hinder their work. Only 13 per cent of men and 15 per cent of women indicated that their family responsibilities represented an obstacle to maintaining their businesses. However, because of limited access to institutional childcare facilities, the women business owners indicated problems relating to combining work and family responsibilities (PARP, 2011). Further, almost 40 per cent of self-employed men and about 30 per cent of self-employed women indicated that, because of their business activities, they did not spend enough time with their children and family (Raport 16, 2006). Finally, about 12 per cent of women owners said they had postponed motherhood due to self-employment, while another 5 per cent indicated that they had decided not to have children. By way of contrast, postponing fatherhood and deciding not to have children affected only 4 per cent and 2 per cent of men owners, respectively (Raport 16, 2006).

Latest Research on Self-employment and Work–Life Balance

The following discussion is based on two surveys carried out in 2011. One covered women aged 25–44 and included 141 female entrepreneurs, 868 female employees, and 347 economically inactive or unemployed women.

The other covered both women and men entrepreneurs: 806 women aged 18–59 years, and 996 men aged 18–64 years (PARP, 2011).

The results from these surveys indicated that female entrepreneurs were more likely to be unmarried and/or without children than either female employees or economically inactive or unemployed women. Over half (53 per cent) of the surveyed female entrepreneurs did not have children, whereas in the case of female employees and economically inactive women the rate was 33 per cent and 30 per cent, respectively (PARP, 2011). Similarly, the percentage of divorcees was higher among the female entrepreneurs than it was for the female employees (PARP, 2011).

The opinions of the female respondents concerning the reconciliation of work and family responsibilities are interesting. Both the female employees and the economically inactive women felt that one advantage of self-employment was the fact that it facilitated combining these dual responsibilities. By way of contrast, however, the female entrepreneurs rarely, or never, viewed self-employment in this light. Indeed, the self-employed women who were still at the procreative age (25–44 years) appeared to struggle to combine the various spheres of their lives that were important to them. As noted in previous research from other countries (see Carrier et al., 2008), attaining an appropriate equilibrium between work and family is the key problem for female entrepreneurs who are mothers. The intensity of this problem depends on the kind of economic activity being undertaken, the support available from family members, and the availability of institutional forms of childcare. In Poland, unfortunately, the situation with respect to access to institutional forms of childcare is considered to be the worst in the European Union (Matysiak, 2011; Thévenon, 2011).

It is perhaps not surprising, therefore, that when asked about potential solutions that might allow a better reconciliation of their professional and family roles, the female business owners in Poland appeared to favour improving access to institutional forms of childcare (nurseries and kindergartens), rather than longer maternity or post-maternity leave (see Table 14.1).

In Poland, female employees are entitled to three years of childcare leave; however, this does not apply to self-employed women, who are entitled to only a half-year of paid maternity leave. However, a recent legislative change grants equal rights to all working women, irrespective of their status in the labour market (that is, employed or self-employed).[2] Unfortunately, this legislative change might not solve the work–life balance dilemma for women entrepreneurs as they may not be able to afford long periods of time away from their businesses.

It would appear that the lack of easily accessible institutional forms

Table 14.1 Potential solutions facilitating a reconciliation between work and family responsibilities, by occupational status

Solutions	% of persons indicating a particular solution by occupational status		
	Contract female employees N = 868	Female entrepreneurs N = 141	Unemployed and inactive females N = 347
Greater accessibility to nurseries	85.5	90.3	80.2
Greater accessibility to kindergartens	88.3	90.3	79.3
Longer maternity leave	79.4	56.3	75.1
Post-maternity leave for women entrepreneurs	84.7	56.3	77.6
Flexible forms and hours of work	92.3	90.3	88.9

Source: PARP (2011, p. 122).

of childcare is perceived by Polish women as the most significant reason for women entrepreneurs (and women employees) postponing procreative decisions. That is, for women entrepreneurs it would seem that the most favoured solution to the problem of combining economic activity and family responsibilities is easier access to nurseries and kindergartens. Entrepreneurs of small businesses find it difficult (if not impossible) to delegate their management responsibilities and, therefore, owners cannot afford to leave their businesses for long periods of time (in the same way as employed women are able to). For this reason, the self-employed women did not see an extension to the maternity leave provisions as a good solution for them in managing the balance between self-employment and family responsibilities.

CONCLUSION

Attempting to combine motherhood and paid work can cause significant role conflicts for women, irrespective of whether they work as employees or are self-employed. The responses from women business owners in Poland to a survey conducted in 2011 suggest that self-employment does not significantly reduce this conflict; at best it might ease it slightly. This is at odds with the broader perception (on the part of employed and unemployed Polish women) that self-employment offers more opportunities (than paid employment) for balancing work and childcare responsibilities.

Indeed, it would appear that being self-employed reduces the probability of becoming a mother.

For entrepreneurs who are mothers (and for female employees bringing up children) there is a continual struggle to balance the competing needs of work and family. It seems, therefore, that many young women postpone having a child because they are aware of this problem. They prioritize their professional development and achievement of material stability, and only after reaching these goals do they plan permanent relationships and fulfilment of their procreative plans. The initial development of a business requires a strong involvement on the part of the business owner and, therefore, it would appear that young women rarely make the decision to launch their own businesses, preferring to find work as employees as this provides better maternity benefits. More often a decision to open one's own business is made by women who are over 45 years old, when they no longer have dependent children.

According to the Polish female entrepreneurs surveyed in 2011, the development (and better availability) of institutional forms of childcare is the most desired solution to promoting a reconciliation of work and family responsibilities. The Polish institutional and cultural context is currently deemed to be unfavourable for combining work and family. While extending childcare leave rights to parents who are self-employed may provide an incentive for unemployed and economically inactive women to opt for self-employment, it does not however appear to provide the best solution for solving the work–family conflict for women with dependent children. It seems that what is needed is more nurseries and kindergartens.

It would be interesting to know whether the results on women business owners in Poland generalize to women business owners in other countries. For example, do women entrepreneurs aged 25–35 years old see motherhood as one of the most significant barriers to starting up and successfully growing a business? Comparative international surveys and studies on this subject would be of great value.

NOTES

1. The survey covered 500 women and 500 men who owned their own businesses. The survey was carried out as a direct interview with a questionnaire (Raport 16, 2006).
2. This law was introduced in September 2013.

REFERENCES

Ben-Yoseph, M., Gundry, L. and Masłyk-Musiał, E. (1997), Women business owners: American and Polish perspectives, in Masłyk-Musiał, E. and Lisowska, E. (eds), *Polish Women in the Business World*, Lublin: Marie Curie-Skłodowska University Press, pp. 101–108.

Bilińska, A. and Rawłuszko, M. (2011), Women managers for success 2011 – opportunities and obstacles to women's career path in Poland, *Women and Business*, 1 (4), 42–59.

Boeri, T. (1994), Transitional unemployment, *The Economics of Transition*, 2, 1–25.

Buttner, H.E. and Moore, D.P. (1997), Women's organizational exodus into entrepreneurship: self-reported motivations and correlates with success, *Journal of Small Business Management*, 35 (1), 34–46.

Carrier, C.P., Julien, A. and Menvielle, W. (2008), Gender in entrepreneurship research: a critical look at the literature, in Aaltio, I., Kyrö, P. and Sundin, E. (eds), *Women Entrepreneurship and Social Capital. A Dialogue and Construction*, Copenhagen: Copenhagen Business School Press, pp. 39–66.

Doing Business (2013), *Smarter Regulations for Small and Medium-Size Enterprises, Comparing Business Regulations for Domestic Firms in 185 Economies*, 10th edn, Washington, DC: World Bank.

EC (2010), Self-employment in Europe 2010, *European Employment Observatory Review*, September.

Eurostat (2012), European Union Labour Force Survey – annual results 2011, Eurostat Statistic in Focus No. 40.

GEM (2012), Global Entrepreneurship Monitor, Poland, Warszawa: Polish Agency of Entrepreneurship Development and University of Economics in Katowice.

Hewlett, S.A. and Luce, C.B. (2005), Off-ramps and on-ramps: keeping talented women on the road to success, *Harvard Business Review*, 83 (3), 43–54.

Hisrich, R.D. and Brush, C.G. (1984), The woman entrepreneur: management skills and business problems, *Journal of Small Business Management*, 22 (1), 30–37.

Hisrich, R.D. and Brush, C.G. (1986), *The Woman Entrepreneur: Starting, Financing, and Managing a Successful New Business*, Lexington, MA: Lexington Books.

Hofstede, G. and Hofstede, G.J. (2005), *Cultures and Organizations. Software of the Mind*, New York: McGraw-Hill.

Hughes, K.D. (2003), Pushed or pulled? Women's entry into self-employment and small business ownership, *Gender, Work and Organization*, 10 (4), 433–454.

Kariv, D. (2013), *Female Entrepreneurship and the New Venture Creation: An International Overview*, New York: Routledge.

Kotowska, I.E. (1997), Równość kobiet i mężczyzn na rynku pracy, in Siemieńska, R. (ed.), *Wokół zawodowego równouprawnienia kobiet i mężczyzn*, Warszawa: Scholar, pp. 85–106.

LFS (2012), Labor Force Survey in Poland in the first quarter 2012, Warsaw: Central Statistical Office.

Lisowska E. (1995), Women business proprietors in Poland, *Women and Business*, 2–3, 52–57.

Lisowska, E. (1997), Women's participation in SME sector development: motivations and barriers, in Masłyk-Musiał, E. and Lisowska, E. (eds), *Polish Women in the Business World*, Lublin: Marie Curie-Skłodowska University Press, pp. 108–116.

Lisowska, E. (2004), Business initiative of Polish women, *Gender and Economic: Opportunities in Poland: Has Transition Left Women Behind?* Warsaw: World Bank, pp. 45–70.

Lisowska, E. (2008), Analiza położenia kobiet na rynku pracy, in Lisowska, E. and Kasprzak, R. (eds), *Zarządzanie mikroprzedsiębiorstwem. Podręcznik dla przedsiębiorczej kobiety*, Warszawa: Warsaw School of Economics, pp. 159–193.

Masłyk-Musiał E. and Lisowska E. (1997), *Polish Women in the Business World*, Lublin: Marie Curie-Skłodowska University Press.

Mattis, M.C. (2005), 'I'm out of here': Women leaving companies in the USA to start their own businesses, in Fielden, S.L. and Davidson, M.J. (eds), *International Handbook of Women and Small Business Entrepreneurship*, Cheltenham, UK and Northampton, MA, USA: Edward Elgar Publishing, pp. 221–237.

Matysiak, A. (2011), *Interdependencies between Fertility and Women's Labour Supply*, 1st edn, European Studies of Population, Vol. 17, New York: Springer.

Matysiak, A. and Mynarska, M. (2012), Women's self-employment in Poland: a strategy for combining work and childcare? https://iweb.cerge-ei.cz/pdf/gdn/RRCXI_72_paper_01.pdf (accessed 2 March 2013).

OECD (1994). *Unemployment in Transition Countries: Transient or Persistent*, Paris: OECD.

Orhan, M. (2005), Why women enter into small business ownership, in Fielden, S.L. and Davidson, M.J. (eds), *International Handbook of Women and Small Business Entrepreneurship*, Cheltenham, UK and Northampton, MA, USA: Edward Elgar Publishing, pp. 3–16.

PARP (2011), Women entrepreneurship in Poland, Research Report, Warsaw: Polish Agency for Enterprise Development, http://badania.parp.gov.pl/files/74/75/76/479/13556.pdf.

Raport 16 (2006). Właściciele małych firm, *Krajowy system monitorowania równego traktowania kobiet i mężczyzn*, t. 2, Warszawa: Scholar, pp. 1061–1104.

Still, L.V. (2005), The constraints facing women entering small business ownership, in Fielden, S.L. and Davidson, M.J. (eds), *International Handbook of Women and Small Business Entrepreneurship*, Cheltenham, UK and Northampton, MA, USA: Edward Elgar Publishing, pp. 55–65.

Thévenon, O. (2011), Family policies in OECD countries: a comparative analysis, *Population and Development Review*, 37 (1), 57–87.

Index

academic entrepreneurship: multi-level factors associated with female-led incubator projects 32–49
  analysis 42–3
  data and methods 38–42
    incubator context and business support system in Sweden 39
    incubators and database 39–40
    sample (Innovationsbron) 38–9
    variables 40–42
  discussion 43–4
  hypotheses development 35–8
    female faculty in senior positions and hypothesis 2 (H2) 36–7, 43
    incubator leadership and hypothesis 3 (H3) 37–8
    proportion of female-led start-ups and hypothesis 1 (H1) 35–6
    technological sector of new incubator projects and hypothesis (H4) 38
  implications 44–5
  limitations and suggestions for future research 45–6
  theoretical foundations for 33–5
    academic entrepreneurship and gender 33–5
    incubators/incubator projects 34
advancing theory development in venture creation (and) 11–31
  application of the framework 19–24
    proposition 1: structural embeddedness 21
    proposition 2: degree of cultural embeddedness 23
    proposition 3: degree of family embeddedness 24
    see also embeddedness
  building the conceptual framework 16–18
    perceived desirability 16–17
    perceived feasibility 17–18
  embeddedness in entrepreneurship research 13–15
  embeddedness perspective 12–13
    see also embeddedness
  influence of gender 18–19
    see also venture creation
Ajzen's theory of planned behaviour 16
article on Chinese women entrepreneurs (Forbes) 101
Asia 3, 95, 97, 98
Aslanbeigui 194
Austria 300

Bangladesh 1, 5, 186–212
  Constitution of the People's Republic of 189
  Dhaka 186, 190, 196, 204
  Economic Census (2001–2003) 190
  female subordination in 189
  government's definition of SMEs (2008) 195
  National SME Women Entrepreneurship Award 196
  Outstanding Women of the Year in Business (2008–10) 196
  Women Chamber of Commerce and Industry-EBL Progressive Award 196
  women-owned SMEs in 189–90
  see also growth process of small and medium-sized manufacturing in developing countries
Bulgaria 300

Caribbean 1, 6
case studies
  China: women entrepreneurs and their environment – Xiuzhen Zhang Taiyuanli Investment Guarantee Co, Ltd 99–103

Japan: women entrepreneurs and their environment – Makiko Fukui Harmony Residence 103–9
summary – networks and mentoring 109
Catalyst Centre for Education of Women (University of Michigan) 119
centering Caribbean women's gendered experiences and identities (and) 278–96
  conclusion 293
  contextualizing Caribbean women's entreneurship 279–81
  discussion 292
  findings for 285–92
    gendered entrepreneurial contexts 286–8
    identities as fluid and shifting 290–92
    push and pull factors of female entrepreneurship 286
    'splace' (space/place) as troubling 289–90
  methodology for 284–5
  theoretical framework for 281–4
    feminist–social constructivist–rational choice approach 281–2
    work–family conflict 282–4
Central and Eastern European (CEE) nations/region 259, 261
childcare (in)
  the Czech Republic 262, 268–73
  female-dominated 60–62, 65
  France 140, 154, 244
  Japan 104–7, 110
  institutional forms of 6
  Poland 298, 304–7
China/Chinese 1, 3, 17, 95–101
  Confucian history of 96
  female entrepreneurial activity (2010) 96
  friends and family networks 103
  gender discrimination in 102
  gender equity in 101–2
  and one-child policy 102
  and Shenzhen 99, 100–101

Special Economic Zone Act to Promote Gender Equality 102
  Women's Federation 102
cultural embeddedness 13–14, 21–3, 26
Czech Republic (CR) 1, 6, 258–77
  see also divisions of labour/responsibilities in business/home in the CR

decision-making, exclusion of women from 161
definition(s) of
  innovation 134
  innovation in context of the firm 122, 125
  structural embeddedness 12
Diana Project/Diana International Project 1, 11, 98, 118, 187
discrimination 52, 54–60
  buyer 54
  and finance for women business owners 56–60
  perceived 3, 55, 60, 62
divisions of labour/responsibilities in business/home in the CR (and) 258–77
  analysis and findings 265–72
  balancing strategies 270–72
  divisions of labour in business 265–8
  divisions of labour in domestic sphere 268–70
  background for gender, labour market and entrepreneurship 261–2
  conceptual framework for 260–61
  conclusion 272–4
  methodology 262–4
Durbin–Watson (DW) statistic 178

embeddedness 2, 12–26
  cognitive 12–13
  contextual 25
  cultural 12–14, 15, 19, 21–3, 26
  in entrepreneurship research 13–15
  family 15, 19, 23–4, 25
  forms of 2
  institutional 13
  perspective 12–13

political 12, 13
social 12
spatial 25
structural 12, 15, 19, 20–21, 26
entrepreneurial networks 20–21,
 216–18, 226, 231
 research 216–17

family firm 21, 141, 143, 146, 147–8,
 153
 defining the 138–9
 see also gender perspective on family
  business succession
female entrepreneurs in St Lucia,
 Trinidad and Tobago *see* centering
 Caribbean women's gendered
 experiences and identities
female entrepreneurship in rural
 Vietnam (and) 74–94
 analysing *see* frameworks for
  analysing female
  entrepreneurship in a rural
  setting
 discussion and conclusion on 90–91
 livelihoods of rural women 79–80
 methodology: sample selection 83–5
 responses from rural female
  entrepreneurs on 85–8
  motivations 85
  raising capital 86–7
  relationships and networking 87
  societal expectations 87–8
  training 85–6
 responses from rural female
  non-entrepreneurs 88–90
 see also rural development; Vietnam
finance, women's access to 52–60
Finland 96
frameworks *see* Global
 Entrepreneurship Monitor (GEM)
frameworks for analysing female
 entrepreneurship in a rural setting
 80–82
 community context 82
 concept of 'necessity' vs
  'opportunity' entrepreneurship
  80–81
 GEM model of entrepreneurship
  80–82
 Hindle framework/model 82

France 1, 4
 female entrepreneurs and spousal
  support in 6
 see also spousal support
 see also a gender perspective on
  family business succession

gender
 and culture 22
 differences 25
 and perceptions of barriers to
  entrepreneurship 22
 stereotyping 22
 understanding *see* advancing theory
  development in venture creation
gender differences in innovation among
 US entrepreneurs 117–37
 data and characteristics for 120–22
 and gender differences in approaches
  to innovation 122–8
 multivariate analysis for 128–32
 prior research on 118–19
 summary and conclusions for 132–5
gender perspective on family business
 succession (and) 138–64
 discussion on 155–61
 findings: environmental factors
  152–5
  exclusion and separation 154–5
  family roles 153–4
  socialization: family business
   initiation and expectations
   152–3
 findings: individual factors 147–51
  ability 147–8, 149–51
  interest 147, 149–51
 method and sample 143–6
  data collection and analysis 146
  research objectives and context
   142–3
 theoretical grounding 138–42
  environmental explanations and
   socialization 140–42
  family business research –
   succession and gender 138–9
  individual explanations 139–40
gender role congruency theory (and)
 50–73
 discussion on 64–7
 findings of study for 63–4

study method for 60–63
women, business ownership and access to finance 20, 55–60
see also discrimination
gender role stereotypes/stereotyping 22, 23, 36–8, 44, 194, 261, 268, 297
gender and technology, connection between 45
gender-based differences in performance of Slovenian high-growth companies (and) 165–85
  control variables: industry, legal form, governance structure 174–5
  data 171–2
  dependent variable 173
  discussion and conclusion 179–80
  findings 176–9
    descriptive statistics 176
    regression results 176–9
    using Chow test 178
  'gazelles' 166–7
  independent variables: firm size, profitability, indebtedness, labour costs 173–4
  methodology 173
  models
    female 175–6
    male 175
  research hypotheses for 168–71
    1. firm size moderated by gender 169–70
    2. firm's profitability mediated by gender 170
    3. firm's gender-mediated indebtedness 170–71
    4. labour costs mediated by gender 171
  theoretical background and previous research for 166–8
Global Entrepreneurship Monitor (GEM) 11, 95
  5M framework 23
  data on perceptions of feasibility of opportunity 22
  Women's Report (2012) 241
Global Microcredit Summit (Canada, 2006) 74
Growth Oriented Women Entrepreneurs and Their Businesses: A Global Research Perspective xvi

growth process of small and medium-sized manufacturing in developing countries 186–212
  conceptual framework for 190–94
    1. individual factors and family context 190–91
    2. internal (firm) environment 192
    3. external environment 192
    4. venture concept 193
    5. growth resources and actions 193
    and operationalizing the framework 194
  concluding remarks for 208–9
  context of women-owned SMEs in Bangladesh 189–90
  discussion of 206–8
  and growth of women-owned small firms in developing countries 187–9
  methodology for 194–9
    data collection and analysis 196–9
    sample selection of award-winning women entrepreneurs 196
    semi-structured interview schedule (box) 197–8
    unit of analysis 195–6
  results for 199–206
    four medium-sized manufacturing firms 199–203
    and their common patterns 200–203
    four small manufacturing firms 203–6
    and their common patterns 204–6
Guanxi networks 102–3

Harmony Residence 103–9
  see also case studies
heterogeneity of spousal support for French women entrepreneurs *see* spousal support

Iceland 96
India 96
indirect reciprocity 5, 230
intellectual property (IP)/protection (for)
  copyrights 134

industrial design rights 133–4
licences 134
patents 133
International Fund for Agricultural Development (IFAD) 80
international multi-level research analysis 1–7
  macro: the entrepreneurship ecosystem 2–3
  meso: firm-level analysis 4–5
  micro: individuals and dynamics 5–7
Islam and Arab society, customs and traditions of 14
Islamic society 5, 189
  see also Bangladesh

Japan (and) 1, 3, 95–6, 97, 98, 99
  gender discrimination in 106–7
  Keidanren study on recruitment and hiring 107
  women entrepreneurs: Makiko Fukui/Harmony Residence 103–9
  see also case studies
Jordan, home-based embroiderers in 15

Keidanren 107
Korea 96

Latvia 300
legislation
  Equal Employment Opportunity Law (Japan, 1986) 104
  maternity laws 105
  Shenzhen: Special Economic Zone Act to Promote Gender Equality (2013) 102
Lithuania 300
Luxembourg 300

male spousal/companion-based support (SCS) of women entrepreneurs (WE) see spousal support
Mao Zedong 95, 101
Micro-Credit Summit (Washington, 1997) 74
Millennium Development Goals 74

National Association of Women Business Owners 120
National Population Census (2009) 79
networks and networking 216–19
  formal/informal 216
  and gender 217–19
  see also women entrepreneurs' networking behaviors
Nordic welfare model 14
North America 76
  see also United States (US)
Northern Ireland 1, 5, 58, 219–20
  see also women entrepreneurs' networking behaviors

OECD countries 107

planned behaviour theory (Ajzen) 16
Poland (and) 1, 6, 300
  childcare/childcare leave in 305–6
  difficulties of launching/growing companies in 299
  its high value on Power Distance Index (GEM 2012) 299
  see also self-employment and motherhood in Poland
Portugal 300
post-Soviet countries 15

references for
  academic entrepreneurship and female-led incubator projects 46–9
  advancing theory development in venture creation 26–31
  centering Caribbean women's gendered experiences and identities 293–6
  divisions of labour/responsibilities in business/home in the Czech Republic 275–7
  female entrepreneurship in rural Vietnam 92–4
  gender congruency theory, discrimination and access to finance 68–73
  gender differences in innovation among US entrepreneurs 135–7
  gender perspective on family business succession 161–4

gender-based differences in
  performance of Slovenian high-
  growth companies 181–5
heterogenity of spousal support for
  French women entrepreneurs
  254–7
international multi-level research
  analysis 7
self-employment and motherhood:
  the case of Poland 308–9
study of women-owned firms in
  Bangladesh 209–12
women entrenepreneurs' networking
  behaviors 232–5
women entrepreneurs in Asia 111–14
reports (on)
  percentage of women start-up
    business owners in US
    (Kauffmann Report, 2011) 241
research (on)
  amount of prior business experience
    as strongest predictor of
    entrepreneurial firm-level
    success (US) 110
  Asia and cultural differences 96
  beliefs people hold about the sexes
    142
  business in China and importance of
    guanxi networks 102–3
  entrepreneurship embedded in
    traditions, rules and values 14
  female entrepreneurs in developing
    countries 76
  fewer barriers to women's
    entrepreneurship in China 101
  finance for businesswomen (1980s) 58
  firm growth 168
  gender and entrepreneurship in CEE
    region 261
  impact of broader social norms on
    succession 141–2
  portfolio entrepreneurship in farm
    households context 23
  predictors of entrepreneurial firm-
    level success (US) 110
  socio-cognitive influences on
    entrepreneurial behaviour 18–19
rural development
  importance of entrepreneurship in
    75–6

importance of female
  entrepreneurship in 76
see also Vietnam
Russia 17

Schumpeterian 'creative destruction'
  process 97
segregation, entrepreneurial 51–2
self-employment and motherhood in
  Poland (and) 297–309
  barriers to entrepreneurship 303
  childcare/childcare leave 305–6
  conclusion 306–7
  economic transition 298–9
  present context 299
  prior research on 301–4
    women entrepreneurs in Poland
      302
    women and men entrepreneurs
      (comparative-based) 302–4
    see also surveys
  'push' and 'pull' factors in setting up
    own businesses 303
  self-employment and work–life
    balance 304–6
  statistical data for self-employment
    of women 299–301
  see also Poland
self-employment as potential easing
  mechanism 6
sex-as-a-variable approaches 3
Singapore 95, 96, 97
Slovenia 1, 5
  Dnevnik newspaper company in
    171
  and Slovenian 'gazelles' 166–7, 179
  see also gender-based differences in
    performance of Slovenian high-
    growth companies
social networking/networks 14, 15, 82,
  120, 188, 202, 216, 219, 231, 272
socialization 4, 19, 22, 140–42, 152–3,
  155, 160
South East Asia 75, 76
South Korea 97, 106, 168, 203
spousal support (and) 6, 236–57
  changing nature of 246–8
  discussion 251–2
  findings 242, 244–6
  implications 252–3

interference of entrepreneurial
  activities in couple's relationship
  and vice versa 248–9
limitations and future research
  253–4
methodology and sample description
  242–3
sources and consequences of
  frictions 249–51
see also spousal support, literature
  review for
spousal support, literature review for
  237–41
  context of gender roles in France/
    effects on role distribution
    within the couple 240–41
  forms of social support provided by
    spouse/companion 237
  instrumental and emotional support
    in context of entrepreneurship
    238–9
  question of SCS for women
    entrepreneurs 239–40
  spousal/companion-based support
    (SCS) as key in entrepreneurial
    process 237–8
STEM disciplines (science, technology,
  engineering and math) 118
studies (of/on)
  female entrepreneurship in Arab
    countries (2009) 76
  see also Weeks, J.R.
  increase in academic
    entrepreneurship 33–4
  innovation in women-owned firms
    (UNCTAD) 120
  loan decisions (Buttner and Rosen,
    1989) 58
  manufacturing industry relationship
    between growth and size
    168–9
  new venture strategies 21–2
  Northern Irish business owners
    (1997) 58
  outcomes in management practice,
    enterprise performance and
    firm characteristics via gender
    comparative approaches 4
  promotion of women's
    entrepreneurship (Malaya) 76

women entrepreneurs in China
  (2001) 102
women's academic entrepreneurship
  and gender as form of social
  structure 44
surveys (of/on)
  barriers to entrepreneurship in
    Poland 303
  discrimination (Survey of Small
    Business Finances, 1998) 57
  female-owned firms in Japan (2010)
    107–8
  gender discrimination encountered
    by women in China (Shenzhen
    Women's Federation 2011) 102
  launching and growing companies
    (World Bank Doing Business,
    2013) 299
  Polish female entrepreneurs re.
    childcare (2011) 307
  poverty in Vietnam (IFAD, 2010) 80
  poverty in Vietnam (World Bank,
    2011) 80
  self-employed in Poland (Labor
    Force Survey, 2012) 299
  self-employment and work–life
    balance in Poland 304–5
  social status of women in China
    2010 (Project Group 2011) 101
  women and men entrepreneurs in
    Poland (Warsaw School of
    Economics, 1995) 302
  women's entrepreneurship in Poland
    (1991, 1993) 302
Sweden (and) 1, 33, 38–42, 96
  Innovationsbron 38, 39
  Statistics Sweden 41
  Swedish Agency for Economic and
    Regional Growth 41
  Swedish National Agency for Higher
    Education 41
  VINNOVA 39

technology and gender, connection
  between 45
Thailand 95, 96–7
The Theory of Growth of the Firm 187
Tibet 99
Trans-Pacific Partnership trade
  agreement (2010) 76

United Kingdom (UK) 96, 108, 199, 219, 299
United States (US) 2, 3, 4, 60, 96, 96, 97, 98
   Census Bureau 50–51, 52
   Characteristics of Business Owners 54–5
   importance of entrepreneurship in 75
   Small Business Administration Dynamic Small Business Search listing 120

variance inflation factors (VIFs) 178
venture creation
   advancing theory development in 11–26
   influence of gender in 18–19
   see also embeddedness
Vietnam (and) 1, 3
   Chamber of Commerce and Industry (VCCI) 90
   economic context of 76–7
   Farmers' Union 86, 90
   Gender Economic Development Working Group 90
   livelihoods of rural women in 79–80
   micro-economic reforms in 77
   rural 77–9
   savings plans 86–87
   Small Traders Association 86
   Veterans Association 86
   Women Entrepreneurs Council (VWEC) 79, 90
   Women's Union 86, 90
   see also female entrepreneurship in rural Vietnam

Western Europe 76
women (and)
   business ownership and access to finance 20, 55–60
   confidence in capabilities and perceptions of risk 22
   defined by roles connected to family and household 22
   entrepreneurs in post-Soviet countries 15
   spousal support 6

women-owned firms in Western Europe and North America 76
   see also discrimination
women entrepreneurs in Asia (and) 95–114
   case studies of female 'opportunity' entrepreneurs 98–109
   study parameters and methods for 98–9
   see also case studies
   cultural vs statist approach 96–8
   the culture thesis 96–7
   the state intervention thesis 97–8
   networks and mentoring 109
   see also Asia; China; Japan
women entrepreneurs' networking behaviors (and) 215–35
   findings 221–30
     learning 228–30
     motivations and expectations 221–3
     networking behaviors 223–6
     potential and actual benefits perceived to accrue 226–8
   learning and networking (Box 10.3) 229
   networking behaviors (Box 10.1) 224–5
   potential and actual benefits perceived to accrue from networking (Box 10.2) 227
   research design and process 219–21
     data collection and analysis 220–21
     participant selection 219–20
   structure and process 216–19
   summary and conclusions on 230–32
   see also networks and networking
Women Presidents' Organization 120
Women's Business Enterprise National Council 120
working mothers 105–7
   see also Japan
World Bank (and)
   Doing Business Survey (2013) 299
   poverty in Vietnam (2011) 80
World Trade Organization (WTO) 76

Xconomy.com 120